The Obstruction of Peace

The United States, Israel, and the Palestinians

Naseer H. Aruri

Common Courage Press   Monroe, Maine

Library of Congress Cataloging-in-Publication Data
Aruri, Naseer Hasan, 1934-
The obstruction of peace: the United States, Israel,
and the Palestinians/Naseer H. Aruri.
p. cm.
Includes index.
ISBN 1-56751-055-8. -- ISBN 1-56751-054-X (pbk.)
1. United States--Foreign relations--Israel. 2. Israel--Foreign relations--
United States. 3. Jewish-Arab relations--1967-1973. 4.Jewish-Arab
relations--1973- 5. Palestinian Arabs--Politics and government. I. Title.
E183.8 I7A77 1995
327.7305694--dc20   95-7690
CIP

Common Courage Press
Box 702
Monroe, ME 04951

207-525-0900   fax: 207-525-3068

First Printing

Contents

Dedication and Acknowledgments   7
Prologue: Continuity in the Palestinian Bantustans   9

Introduction   19

Part I   A COLD WAR LEGACY

  1   The Arab East and American Policy During The   31
      Cold War
      The Evolution of the United States Global Strategy

  2   After the Cold War   61
      The Irrelevance of Containment

  3   The Obstruction of Peace   71
      United States Opposition to an International Peace Conference

  4   The Special Relationship and Strategic Alliance
      During and After the Cold War   85

Part II   MARGINALIZING THE PALESTINIANS

  5   The Marginalization of the Palestinian Question   111
      From Carter to Bush and Baker

  6   Further Marginalization   151
      The Impact of The Gulf War

  7   The Road to Madrid And Beyond   169
      Baker and the Palestinians

  8   The Clinton Administration and   191
      the Israeli-Palestinian Accords

  9   From Oslo To Cairo and Beyond   217
      Repackaging The Occupation

 10   Oslo And The Crises In Palestinian Politics   233

Part III UNITED STATES MIDDLE EAST POLICY
          AND AMERICAN POLITICS

 11   United States Policy and Electoral Politics   249

 12   The Campaign of De-legitimization in Congress   285

 13   Jerusalem and A Changing American Policy   311

Conclusion   345

Index   358

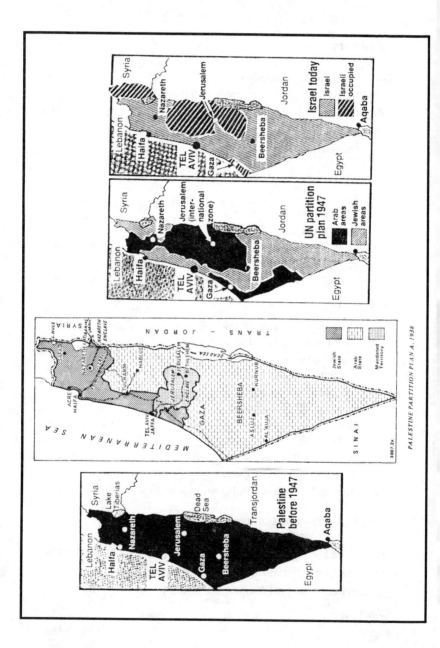

PALESTINE PARTITION PLAN A. 1938

Dedication and Acknowledgments

This book is dedicated to the Palestinian people whose ordeals it describes, the Palestinians who perished in the struggle for their national and human rights; also to Palestinians in prison, under the occupation, and in the camps; and to the Palestinians who belong nowhere as equal citizens, but for whom Palestine will always be home.

I am indebted to many people, whose various contributions helped bring this project to full fruition. My son, Jamal, read the entire manuscript and made numerous substantive comments and suggestions. Throughout the entire period of work on this book, his interest in it was no less than mine. A number of colleagues shared valuable insights with me and made many useful suggestions. Professor Samih Farsoun of American University commented on the chapters dealing with the earlier period, provided important source material, and has offered much encouragement over the many years of our friendship. Professor Elaine Hagopian of Simmons College read chapters two and three and made considerable suggestions and insightful comments. Professor Cheryl Rubenberg of Florida International University read parts of the manuscript and made valuable comments. Dr. Nancy Murray of the Massachusetts Civil Liberties Union shared with me essential source material from the files of the Middle East Justice Network. Together with her critique of chapters eleven and twelve, the material on Congress and the Clinton administration made a remarkable contribution, for which I am grateful. My colleague, John J. Carroll of the University of Massachusetts, read the chapter on Congress and made substantive comments. I am particularly thankful to him for allowing me to incorporate some of the concepts and ideas which he and I have developed in collaborative work published during the past ten years.

I am also grateful for editorial assistance rendered by Professor Khalil Barhoum of Stanford University and by Greg Bates of Common Courage Press. Cheryl Phillips typed the largest portion of the manuscript and met every deadline skillfully and with a great deal of patience. My assistant, Susan Sculley, rendered valuable service, from document preparation to making endless additions on the word processor. Margaret Thomas has supplied an uninterrupted flow of clippings during the past fifteen years, even when she was in a hospital bed recovering from major surgery. The University of Massachusetts Center for Policy Analysis provided much of the funds needed for typing the manuscript.

Throughout the many years of research, and at various stages of preparation and writing of the manuscript, my wife Joyce has been a constant source of inspiration and encouragement. Her marvelous sense of priorities has not only provided a perfect work environment, but has made the entire experience most pleasant. This book is also dedicated to her.

Prologue: Continuity in the Palestinian Bantustans

The suicide bombing on January 22, 1995 which killed 21 Israelis—"the children who will not return"—at a bus stop in Beit Lid is widely believed to be the catalyst for the stalemate in the peace process, dashing the hopes of the Declaration of Principles (DOP) signed between Arafat and Rabin in Washington. Israel, with great magnanimity, struggles to continue the process with Arafat despite the terrorism.

That, at least, is the official story as told in the U.S. All acts of terror against civilians are contemptible and deserve condemnation. But a closer look at the history and context of the bombing and the DOP provides a different understanding than what is available in the mainstream media. It has been widely assumed in the U.S. that the "peace process" can be taken at face value, with the U.S. playing the role of disinterested party valiantly searching for the resolution of conflict. But casting the U.S. as chief conciliator with implied impartiality is contradicted by the alliance with Israel. Further complicating efforts for peace is the hard political reality that 28 years of de facto annexation of the occupied West Bank by Israel will render peace, based on Israeli withdrawal from the occupied territories, virtually impossible. Nonetheless, the historic handshake between Rabin and Arafat at the White House in September of 1993 misled the public that this was the first real step towards genuine peace, and at last, an unyielding conflict has been miraculously unraveled.

Eighteen months later, however, a real standoff threatens to freeze the peace process in Gaza and Jericho and prevent its extension to the rest of the West Bank, as envisaged in the PLO-Israel agreement. This rapid turn of events is not unusual. Just as before the historic accords, so it is today: the Middle East is polarized between the "peace camp", today comprising Rabin, Mubarak, Hussein and Arafat; and the "enemies of peace," whose address is Islamic fundamentalism. Prior to the accords, Yasir Arafat was the quintessential terrorist, the devil incarnate. Three years ago, King Hussein was high on the roster of the bad guys, who refused to support the war against Iraq. Today, these men are in the company of the United States' most trusted allies: Israel and Egypt, who together account for 45% of the total U.S. foreign aid. Once, in the 1960s, political Islam had been the U.S. answer to radical Arab nationalism; it was Sadat and Mubarak's counterweight to Egyptian Nasserites in the 1970s and early 80s. It was also Rabin's counterweight to secular Palestinian nationalism in the 1980s. Hamas was in fact tolerated by Israel during the Palestinian *Intifada* in the late 1980s as part of Defense Minister Rabin's efforts to undermine and suppress the secular forces of the PLO .

The U.S. public, confused about this role reversal and the contrast between the Oslo euphoria of 1993 and the crippling impasse of today, is told that Islamic activists and regimes in Iran, Algeria, the Sudan, Egypt, Southern Lebanon and Gaza are part of a world-wide menace emerging as the central threat to the West. This menace has even begun to constitute a clear and present danger in the heart of the United States. The bombing of the World Trade Center in New York, the alleged plot to strike at Wall Street as a venerable symbol of American capitalism, and the publicized trial of Sheikh Abdul Rahman can only increase the sense of threat and make it appear more plausible. Clearly, some of these issues are for the law enforcement agencies to deal with. Making an issue of the religious affiliation of the perpetrators, however, is unacceptable in a society which prides itself on the sanctity of the First Amendment. Moreover, the confrontation between Islamic parties and regimes in the Middle East is an issue of political development which relates to the proper distribution of power. But the confrontation of Islamic parties and the Israeli government must be seen in the context of resistance to a military occupation. Lumping these issues together now will be just as confusing to the U.S. public as the deliberate lack of distinction between communist ideology, third world nationalism, and the Soviet state during the Cold War.

Islamic "terrorists" are thus perceived to threaten stability in the

Middle East and to constitute a potential danger to tranquillity in the U.S. In Palestine, they are already indicted as the stumbling block to further diplomatic progress. Secretary of State Warren Christopher told Yasir Arafat on December 6, 1994 that he must put a stop to Islamic attacks against Israel if he expects to spread Palestinian "self-rule" across the West Bank.

Justifying Israeli refusal to redeploy its forces in the West Bank and to permit Palestinian elections there, Christopher said, "It's clear that unless there is security the fundamental commitments cannot be met... without security they cannot properly go forward."[1] Giving Israel what amounted to a blank check, the Secretary of State added:

> No one who is familiar with Israel's history can reasonably expect Israel to move toward the objective without insuring that their security remains a constant companion of the peace and the efforts to succeed in peace efforts[sic]. [2]

These remarks, which reinforce Israel's longtime reliance on security to facilitate territorial aggrandizements, are hardly appropriate for someone whose government considers itself a catalyst for peace in the region. But both the media and the public tend to be more forgiving when the issue relates to Israel. A few suicide attacks against Israeli soldiers and civilians in the aftermath of Christopher's statement served to uphold the dichotomy of a peace camp and the enemies of peace. Images of Islamic suicide bombers creating a security nightmare for ordinary Israelis, displayed prominently in the U.S. media, reinforce official arguments in Israel and in Washington and confirm the stereotypic views which have developed in the U.S. about the Arab-Israeli conflict over several decades.

While the media focuses on the suicide bombing which killed 21 Israelis (18 of them soldiers, not merely "children"), what is absent from the consciousness of most consumers of the U.S. mass media is the other kind of terrorism—state terrorism—which involves constant bureaucratic harassment, assassinations by death squads, confinement of civilians to towns, villages, or districts, long curfews, administrative detention, torture, and systematic confiscation of land for building settlements and roads for the exclusive use of settlers. Not a single mainstream newspaper in the U.S. has ever dared, during 28 years of occupation, to refer to the separate legal standards and physical facilities applied to and available for settlers and indigenous people in the West Bank and Gaza as a form of apartheid. Rabin's call for "separation" on the day following the Beit Lid attack, as the "solution" to the problem of "terrorist attacks which have become a strategic threat to Israel" was covered widely in the U.S. media, but without the slightest reference to the ominous implications of that term. By contrast, the Israeli media devoted considerable space and attention to the proposed 300 kilometer "Maginot Line" with a fence, electronic sensors, watch towers, video monitors, and even watchdogs. The daily newspaper *Ha'aretz* (January 25, 1995), for example, quoted the right-wing former Defense Minister Moshe Arens, who was raising questions concerning the violation of basic human values that the implementation of the apartheid-like "separation" plan would necessarily entail.[3]

The drastically increased scale of settlement activity since the signing of the Declaration of Principles (DOP) in September of 1993 makes a mockery of the peace process. Not only does the Clinton administration look the other way as the settlements threaten to foreclose on the option of the DOP, it continues to ease restrictions on U.S. tax dollars going for building settlements, and it takes no position on the flow of private funds enjoying tax-exemptions.

The Beit Lid incident has provided Israel with the justification to not only halt any serious negotiations with the PLO, but also to build more settlements in the occupied territories. Motti Basuk described the fate of negotiations and the issue of settlements in an article in the Israeli daily *Davar* (January, 27, 1995). On the first issue he wrote:

Perhaps ceremonial meetings will be held next week or the week after, but not on matters of principle. And when talks are held on matters of principle the Israeli representatives will come with an unequivocal directive from Jerusalem: let off some steam but constantly remain in neutral, constantly be idle ... the Israeli army will not withdraw from even one West Bank city or village in the near future.

On the question of settlements, Basuk wrote:

Israeli reaction to the murder at Beit Lid was not only on the level of talks with the PLO. Rabin has decided with the government's approval to approve massive construction of housing units in several areas in the territories. What the government prohibited in November 1992 Rabin permitted this week. What was done covertly in the past 18 months was officially permitted this week by the Labor-Meretz government ... Israel is limiting the PLO options even before the beginning of serious talks, certainly before the talks began on permanent settlement ... Palestinian terrorism and violence will enable the government to carry out its settling program with relative calm in world public opinion, certainly in U.S. public opinion.

The green light to build and expand settlements openly was also verified by numerous Israeli journalists in January and February 1995. Hanna Kim, for example, wrote a detailed article about the Israeli government's "Comprehensive Plan" for 1995 in *Ha'aretz* (January 13, 1995) in which he said:

Despite the government decision from November 1992 to freeze all construction in the territories, the Housing Ministry has allowed Jews to construct private buildings there, and did not include "Greater Jerusalem" in the area in which construction was frozen. Any Jew wishing to do so can hire an entrepreneur to build a home in the territories, and the Housing Ministry is obliged to supply the infrastructure.

The Israeli "Peace Now" movement, which opposes the settlements, has released a report saying that Rabin's government is currently "implementing a policy of cutting up the West Bank into Jewish and Arab areas with the intention of creating Palestinian cantons encircled by territories held by Israel." This is the plan which was proposed by the religious settler leader, Rabbi Yoel Ben-Nun, which seems to be acceptable to the "leftist" Environment Minister Yossi Sarid, and his Meretz colleagues in Rabin's cabinet, and apparently to President Clinton and Secretary of State Warren Christopher, who seem to consider "terrorism" as a valid reason for the U.S. to acquiesce in the ultimate Israeli solution to the conflict.

Meanwhile, President Clinton himself took the unusual step of announcing, in his 1995 State of the Union message, a series of measures which criminalize fund-raising by Islamic and Arab-American groups in the United States, arguing "We cannot permit the future to be marred by terror and fear and paralysis." The phrase was subsequently used as a title for a *New York Times* political advertisement by major Zionist organizations in the U.S. seeking to justify Israel's refusal to move forward on the diplomatic front.[4]

The double standard should be clear for all to see. Acts of resistance and violence are uniformly labeled terrorism. Meanwhile, the much more systematic state terrorism remains hidden at best or excused at worst. In the absence of public debate about the Middle East in the U.S. political arena (including Congress, the media, the theater, the universities and even the business community), and given the lack of an objective analysis of the DOP, the realities of the conflict remain misunderstood.

The reasons are clear as to why such a double standard is possible. Israel is the publicly-identified ally of the U.S., and as such it serves the "national interest" of mainstream U.S. society. In the U.S., Israel is perceived as a victim itself, and thereby enjoys a certain immunity against criticism, at the same time that its Palestinian victims in the diaspora and under military occupation do not qualify for that status. It is ironic that despite military censorship in Israel, the Israeli press is far more open on the question of the Israeli-Palestinian issue, and does not apply the double standard as rigidly as the U.S. press, which is not subject to formal censorship.

The U.S. public, fed a steady diet of the communist threat during the Cold War, is now being conditioned to fear an Islamic threat. Islam has already replaced communism as "the principal opponent of Western liberal democracy and the values it enshrines," according to Mortimer Zuckerman, Editor-In-Chief of the *U.S. News and World Report*. This view, which was also expressed by the Secretary General of NATO, is shared by a broad assortment of influential U.S. publications, including *Foreign Affairs*, the *Reader's Digest*, and the *New York Times*.[5] "Terrorism experts" such as Steven Emerson, produce "documentaries" on the role of Islamic groups in the U.S. His program aired on PBS with previews the preceding week on CBS' "Sixty Minutes." All of this expertise is with no knowledge of the history of the Middle East or the Arabic language.

Nahum Bernea, an Israeli journalist, outlined the success of this U.S.-Israel campaign against political Islam:

> Its most important advantage is that it lets Israel please the American public. Even in the U.S. Congress some dare to say that Israel lost its former value as a major American strategic asset. To that, the anti-Islamic campaign provides an answer... Israel will become the Western vanguard in the war against the Islamic enemy. The second benefit Israel derives from its anti-Islamic campaign is that it justifies the peace process.[6]

This forthright analysis, appearing in an Israeli mainstream newspaper, is not likely to be counted as what the *New York Times* considers "fit to print." Although the U.S. media occasionally supply pertinent and useful facts about the Middle East conflict, it is the spectacular acts of suicide bombings which make the headlines, cover stories and television briefs. Sound bites and dramatic reports have become a substitute for real news or insightful analysis in the prevailing culture in the U.S. Meanwhile, state terrorism, much of which is conducted under the rubric of government business, carries on with little notice in the media.

Indeed the "peace process" has been so bankrupted by state terrorism that the campaign against Islam has been stepped up in order to exempt both Israel and the U.S. from any responsibility for the paralysis while focusing blame on the Palestinians.

The July 1994 DOP deadlines for Israeli redeployment in the West Bank in order to permit Palestinian elections have long gone. The Palestinians are faced with the prospect of a unilaterally-redefined agreement. Elections could now take place only for an administrative rather than a purely legislative assembly, under Israeli bayonets, in clear violation of the agreement. They would have to concede an indefinite Israeli military presence in the West Bank, and they would have to be satisfied with a collection of bantustans rather than the "single territorial unit" made up of the West Bank and Gaza, whose "territorial integrity will be preserved during the interim period," in accordance with Article 4 of the DOP.

Acknowledging this, Israeli Cabinet Minister Ephraim Sneh, a former West Bank military governor—who is regarded as a liberal—told Israel Radio that elections would have to be held without prior Israeli redeployment. The contempt for Palestinians, which characterizes the language of many Israeli officials, was rather obvious in his remarks: "We've proposed elections to them. If they are prepared...[these elections] must be held while we are in the towns."[7]

When challenged that this violated the DOP, he responded: "Correct. The Oslo Agreement said to implement it on 15 July 1994, but for us security is sacred and not the dates of Oslo, with all due respect... We will not take steps that are, from our point of view, a danger to security."[8]

The same Israeli attitude prevails regarding the impact of settlements on the Oslo agreement. Since the suicide bombing at Beit Lid, there is an open admission that Rabin's commitment to freeze construction in order to facilitate a joint Palestinian-Israeli decision on the future of settlements in mid 1996 no longer stands. The current prevailing view in government and in the society at large is that the "peace process" and the anti-Islamic campaign provide an effective cover for the existing plan to retain control over the West Bank, irrespective of the final status talks. This is plainly admitted by Jacques Neria, a former advisor to Rabin. "The intention all along," he says, "was for the interim agreement to be very near the final settlement."[9] The same sentiment was echoed by Moshe Shahal, the Israeli police minister: "You are not going to invest a lot of money in redeploying the army for a period of two years... Any arrangement for the interim phase will be in contact with the final status of the settlements and borders [sic]."[10]

Shahal's and Neria's meaning is clear: what is being taken now under the cover of the "peace process" will stay Israeli. Even the presumed voices of Foreign Minister Shimon Peres and his deputy Yossi Beilin are on record concurring with this view. The former told a Labor Party meeting in December 1994 that: "There will be no evacuation from Judea/Samaria...the Oslo Agreement began and ends in Gaza."[11]

Referring to the Israeli threat to "separate" Israel from the West Bank in the wake of the Beit Lid suicide bombing, Beilin explained: "The idea of separation relates much more to the permanent solution than to the interim one."[12] The distinction between interim and final phase has become superfluous. By its own admission, Israel does not intend to relinquish control of the West Bank, either now or during the final status talks. Arafat's Palestinian Authority (PA) is too weak and corrupt to make an effective challenge to Israel's admitted intent to "reconsider" the Oslo Agreement. The Clinton administration is much too committed to Israel and much too obsessed with "terrorism" to remind Israel that agreements held under its own auspices must be honored. The Europeans have no leverage with Israel, and could only answer Arafat's successive appeals for pressure on Israel with some donations to keep his faltering regime afloat. Peace, therefore, remains elusive, as indeed, it has been during the past twenty-eight years of diplomatic pretense. As we will see, the earlier period of U.S. diplomatic involvement did not succeed significantly better than the present effort.

Naseer Aruri
March 1995

1. *Boston Globe.*, December 7, 1994.
2. Elaine Sciolino, "Arafat Tells Christopher He'll Act Against Terrorism," The *New York Times*, December 8, 1994.
3. Quoted in *The News From Within*, Vol. XI No. 2 (February 1995), Jerusalem: the Alternative Information Center, p. 22.
4. The *New York Times*, January 31, 1995. On February 10, 1995, the Clinton administration sent Congress a bill it drafted with Jewish organizations, known as the "Omnibus Counter-Terrorism Act of 1995." It prohibits fund-raising in the U.S. by "terrorist" groups, creates special deportation courts, and expands surveillance. See Jane Hunter, "Act Against Terror", *Middle East International*, February 17, 1995, p.12.
5. *Foreign Affairs*, Agenda 1994;
   Reader's Digest, January 1995;
   many articles by A.M. Rosenthal, William Safire and Leslie Gelb in the *New York Times*.
6. Yediot Ahoronot, December 16, 1994

7. The *Boston Globe*, February 12, 1995.

8. *Ibid.*

9. Ethan Bronner, "Israel Starts to Shape Future of the West Bank," *Boston Globe,* January 30, 1995.

10. *Ibid*

11. *Ha'aretz,* January 6, 1995.

12. Bronner, *op cit.*

Introduction
Conciliation or Collaboration?

A striking feature of United States policy towards the Arab-Israeli conflict since the 1967 occupation was the insistence by the U.S. on playing the role of chief arbiter, if not sole peacemaker, when in fact it has been co-belligerent. The steady growth of the U.S.-Israeli special relationship, transformed into a full-fledged strategic alliance, during and after the Cold War, was paralleled by a corresponding ascendancy of the U.S. diplomatic role. That role has now dwarfed and eclipsed all the conventional methods of conflict resolution, which were attempted since 1967, including mediation, multilateral initiatives, regional endeavors and UN-sponsored peace-making.

Since 1969, when Secretary of State William Rogers enunciated his plan, based on the exchange of territory for peace, Arabs and Palestinians have had to contend with a dangerous illusion; that the United States was capable of delivering a fair, just and durable peace in the region. But the duality of the U.S. diplomatic posture was a constant barrier to the kind of peace which should not have to be built on the bones of the vanquished and the banners of the victor. Assuming the role of referee and principal conciliator, however, simultaneously with the role of Israel's chief diplomatic backer, bank-roller and military supplier, the United States had placed itself at odds with the global consensus, which called for a political settlement with an international framework and sponsorship.[1] As ally and protector of Israel, the U.S. was simply unable to credibly discharge its self-assigned mission as the catalyst for peace. This pattern is rooted in the twenty-eight year history of U.S.-Israeli relations, which constitutes the scope of this book.

The diplomatic history of the Middle East during that period reveals that half-a-dozen U.S. administrations stood consistently in opposition to a settlement supported by an international consensus, one that would provide for an end to the Israeli occupation and the establishment of a Palestinian state, existing side by side with Israel. Such opposition had occurred, despite the fact that the Palestine Liberation Organization began to align its position with that of the Arab states in the early 1970s.[2] It had given up the revolutionary option and began to move towards a two-state solution. Accordingly, the PLO was declared by the Rabat Arab Summit Conference of 1974 as the "sole legitimate representative" of the Palestinian people in return for its renunciation of the armed struggle in pursuit of the goal of a democratic secular state in all of Palestine, providing equal protection for Muslims, Christians and Jews. Palestinian adherence to the much scaled-back objective of a mini-state in the West Bank and Gaza alongside Israel, however, failed to impress Washington, despite the fact that the new position was consonant with the global consensus on the requirements for a just and durable peace in the Middle East. Although Washington tried to reconcile its strategic requirements with those of the global consensus, the outcome for the Palestinians continued to mean national deprivation and the denial of basic human rights, including self-determination.

At the same time, Israel had managed to reject every U.S. initiative involving a territorial settlement, even when such initiatives excluded Palestinian sovereignty. Israel still adheres to the position that Security Council Resolution 242 of 1967 did not obligate it to withdraw from all the occupied Arab territories, despite a universal interpretation of that resolution to the contrary. That position received implicit yet consistent support from the United States, which became more and more effective with each presidency, beginning with Lyndon B. Johnson. A minimal peace with justice in the entire region was, therefore, obstructed.

The Palestinians have been confronted with two protagonists intent on denying them a national existence and a sovereign order. This is not to imply that U.S. and Israeli policies have been consistently in tandem. U.S. policy throughout the post-Second War period was preoccupied with regional stability in order to assure hegemony and facilitate unimpeded access to and control of petroleum resources.

Also, at the heart of this policy was the containment of a host of domestic oppositional forces as well as the containment of external challengers of that hegemony whose convenient address was "communism" or "Soviet aggression." That endeavor, which was classified in the category of "vital national interests," converged with the Israeli interest of reducing the influence of Arab and Palestinian nationalists to manageable proportions. The two interests also coincided to the extent that succeeding U.S. administrations viewed the disaffected Palestinians as a volatile anti-establishment group whose irredentist goals precluded any stakes in the existing regional order; hence the convergence of U.S. strategic designs and Israeli territorial ambitions.

Harvest Time

The U.S. endeavor to impose its hegemony on the Middle East, which predates the Arab-Israeli war of 1967, has finally succeeded. The new additions to the Middle East diplomatic vocabulary—Madrid, Washington, Oslo and Cairo—symbolize harvest time. A four decade U.S. investment of military hardware, economic aid, and diplomatic capital has finally paid off. The signing ceremonies at the White House (September 13, 1993) and at Wadi Araba (October 27, 1994) sponsored and witnessed by President Clinton, underscore a proclaimed domination based on a U.S.-Israeli alliance, which is beginning to generate deep concern among ordinary Arabs.

The outcome was clearly the result of a coherent and consistent policy, which aimed to realize clearly-defined, though euphemistically proclaimed, objectives: a region in which advocates of a variety of ideas or programs, including Arab unity, self-sufficiency, independent foreign policy, democratic governance, Palestinian self-determination and Arab-Israeli parity and mutuality, would be removed to the sidelines or held at bay. Instead, the region is being recolonized in the age of decolonization, and its post-World War II status is being settled on the basis of pax-Americana, pax-Israelica.[3] And yet, the endeavor is widely known as the "peace process," as if peace has some other meaning.

These objectives have been pursued relentlessly by U.S. politicians representing the right, "left" and center. It did not matter that Truman, Kennedy, and Johnson, who represented the liberal trend, had pursued policies similar to those of John Foster Dulles and Richard Nixon, the conservatives. Nor was it strange that Jimmy Carter and Ronald Reagan adhered to the same Middle East policy consensus, irrespective of the fact that the former's name is synonymous with human rights and international conciliation, while the latter was the advocate of rollback, vowing to exorcize some of the demons of Vietnam which had haunted a whole generation of Americans. Now Clinton, whose mission is to expand and promote the new and strange concept of "market democracies" throughout the world, is collecting the "pay-off," which represents the fruit of the combined energies and resources mobilized by his liberal and conservative predecessors. This is a remarkable testimony to the ability of the U.S. politico-strategic establishment to forge a stable foreign policy consensus.

American policy objectives have remained fixed, while the means may have had to undergo periodic adjustments. Such durability has prevailed, not only despite changing administrations and political parties, but also despite shifting regional and global circumstances, and despite U.S. domestic changes influencing the media and public opinion.

The tools of U.S. policy were constantly in place but they were not fully understood by those who were the object of that policy. Arabs and Palestinians in top-level positions have often misconstrued policy aberrations as policy changes, ignoring the permanence of U.S. long-term policy objectives. Short-term signals and seductions emanating from Washington, which invariably included widely-advertised threatened reassessments of U.S.-Israeli relations by disgruntled presidents, were mistakenly read as movements at last in the direction of fairness. Exceptional deviations, such as Gerald Ford's call for a reassessment, Carter's confrontation with Menachem Begin in 1977, Baker's ordeal with Yitzhak Shamir in 1990, the dialogue between the U.S. and the PLO, and the conflict over loan guarantees, among other episodes, were not seen by Palestinian and other Arab leaders as manifestations of normal disagreements in need of tactical adjustments, but as signs of a fundamental change. Such naiveté or wishful thinking stems from a political culture in which policy changes derive from pronouncements of autocratic rulers decreed not by structural changes, but by short-term imperatives or the leaders' own preferences. Hence the simplistic comparisons between U.S. presidents, ignoring the role of strategic considerations and objective factors, both domestic and international.

Thus, Arafat's appearance at the White House Rose Garden on September 13, 1993, was seen by him and by many around him as the crowning achievement of his career and the sure sign of a new American policy, when in fact Clinton, Rabin, and the informed public regarded it as a form of his surrender. His reference to the "fact" that the Palestinians have a new friend in the White House was not only unrealistic, but it made him seem like a person who derives pleasure from being dominated. It would have made more sense had President Clinton been the one to thank Arafat three times on September 13, 1993, rather than the other way around; Arafat, after all, had enabled Clinton to proclaim the realization of objectives detrimental to fundamental Palestinian rights, which U.S. policy-makers have been struggling to achieve since before Clinton reached the voting age. The Oslo accord was, therefore, not only the product of fundamental changes in the global and regional environments, but it was also a culmination of U.S. persistence and tenacity, coupled with a proclivity for ad hoc methods of decision-making by Arab leaders.

The Arab States as Instruments of U.S. Policy

Among the tools of U.S. foreign policy in the Middle East were the Arab regimes themselves. The Jordanian military onslaught against the Palestinian movement in September 1970 had inflicted structural damage, the effect of which continued to retard the Palestinian struggle for years to come. Not only had King Hussein terminated the Palestinian-enforced de facto dual authority in Jordan between 1967 and 1970, but he also helped accomplish policy objectives for the U.S. and Israel. Similarly, when Palestinian fighters regrouped in Lebanon after the "Black September" debacle of 1970 and began to threaten the delicate balance inside Lebanon and in the region, Syria was tacitly accepted by the U.S. and Israel as the logical candidate for policing Lebanon in 1976. The Palestinian national movement once again had to be reduced to manageable proportions; this time, however, not by a conservative pro-western monarchy, but by a "revolutionary" Arab nationalist regime. The modus operandi, in which Israel and Syria came to share suzerainty over Lebanon, with U.S. blessings until this day, was the product of that mission. Egypt was subsequently drafted to deliver the coup de grace, peacefully this time, against the Palestinians. Camp David had inflicted more damage on Palestinian nationalism by non-military means in 1978 than did the two previous armed onslaughts combined. Thus, the first Arab state to assume responsibility for strategic balance vis-à-vis Israel, from the mid-1950s until 1970, was transformed in the late 1970s to an enforcer of U.S. policy and a facilitator for Israel. Not only had Camp David secured the removal of Egypt from the Arab strategic arena, but it also allowed Israel to dodge its legal responsibilities to the Palestinian people, and to shrug off its obligation to withdraw from Palestinian, Syrian and Lebanese territories, under Security Council resolutions.

Even Iraq, the third and most recent contender for strategic balance vis-à-vis Israel (after Egypt and Syria), had allowed itself to become an instrument of U.S. foreign policy during the Iran-Iraq war in the 1980s. U.S. policy makers were gratified to see Iraq inflict damage on the Islamic Republic in Iran without cost to the U.S., and also to weaken itself in the process, together with its opportunity to play the role of pace-setter in the Gulf. Moreover, Iraq's war against America's enemy in the Gulf had refocused Arab attention away from the Israeli threat and towards an imaginary new "Shiite Iranian threat." The Palestinian cause, already battered by Camp David, was further bruised by the new priorities of Saddam Hussein. And when the latter began to exaggerate his own importance for the U.S. strategy in the Gulf, he was reduced to size, not only with the acquiescence of Arab regimes, but also with the active participation of many of them.

A "Window of Opportunity" for the U.S.

With the destruction of Iraq, followed by the dissolution of the Soviet Union, a settlement based on U.S. designs had suddenly become possible and operational; Madrid was the venue. Although James Baker III was the architect of the Madrid Conference in 1991, much of the construction work on the road to Madrid had already begun under Baker's predecessors. In fact, the Madrid framework represents a synthesis of previous U.S. diplomatic initiatives. The two-track approach, the self-rule concept, and transitional arrangements are derived from the Camp David accords negotiated under Carter's auspices in 1978. The Jordanian dimension of a Palestinian-Israeli settlement is grounded in the Reagan Plan of 1982.[4] The linguistic bait designed to attract the Palestinians were largely inherited from the Shultz Plan of 1988, which itself incorporated the salient features of Camp David and the Reagan Plan.[5]

Two characteristics are shared in common by all of these initiatives. First, they were all occasioned by structural changes in either the regional or the global environment. The de-Nasserization of Egypt, and the subsequent collapse of Soviet influence there in 1972, created a strategic imperative for U.S. diplomatic action, and the outcome was the meeting at Camp David. The Israeli invasion of Lebanon in 1982 had so weakened the Palestinian national movement that President Reagan declared the outcome an "opportunity" for peace, which effectively removed Palestinian national rights from the active global agenda.

Having just embarked on a new cold war with the Soviet Union and on revolutionary nationalism, Reagan welcomed the opportunity to rearrange the strategic landscape of the Middle East. His plan, however, was thwarted by a junior ally with strategic designs of its own. The prompt and categorical rejection of the Reagan Plan by the Israeli cabinet, only a few hours after it was announced on prime television time, had simply sealed its fate. The plan's denial of sovereignty in the West Bank and Gaza to both Israel and the Palestinians in favor of Jordan guaranteed Israel's quick rejection. The stillborn plan was thus shelved, but aspects of it were resurrected six years later in the Shultz Plan, which deferred the issue of sovereignty for final status negotiations. The Shultz Plan itself, also failed to impress Israel, whose prime minister Shamir declared it "unwelcome" in 1988, causing it to be shelved until the following year, when Baker began to revive it. Baker's "opportunity" in 1991, however, proved to be more auspicious than Reagan's opportunity in 1982. The U.S. defeat of Iraq in 1991 was more decisive than the Israeli storming of Lebanon in 1982, and more damaging to the Palestinians, hence Baker's "opportunity," which produced Madrid. Although the Madrid formula was based on the principle of the exchange of territory for peace, in accordance with a speech by

President Bush to the U.S. Congress on March 6, 1991, it was not made clear whether that exchange included the West Bank and Gaza and not only the Golan Heights of Syria. In fact, the Madrid formula, through the separate negotiating tracks for Israel and the Arab states, as well as the interim arrangements for the West Bank and Gaza, had effectively enabled Israel to defer West Bank and Gaza sovereignty while it derived Arab state recognition and obtained a measure of normalization with the Arab world. In that sense, it was utilized by Israel as a cosmetic ploy to do no more than reorganize its occupation.

The second important common denominator of the four plans by the United States is that in all of these plans the roles of the protagonists in the "peace process" were always overshadowed by the strategic dimension of that process. Interest on the part of these protagonists has often lagged far behind that of the United States, thus creating a corresponding disparity between the pursuit of comprehensive peace and the search for comprehensive security. The parties to the conflict did not share Washington's diagnosis that the circumstances were propitious for peaceful relations. And while Israel said "no" to the Reagan and the Shultz Plans, and later renounced its own election plans in 1989 in order to avoid a territorial settlement, most of the Arab parties opted for negotiations, despite the adverse conditions, in order not to displease Washington.

Given all of that, it was not a coincidence that most of the previous U.S. proposals for peace had ended in failure. Camp David may have terminated the belligerency on the Israeli-Egyptian front, but it has fallen short of establishing genuine peaceful relations between the two countries, let alone the comprehensive regional peace it promised to build.

The U.S., however, pursued its objectives relentlessly, despite its rather isolated position in the world community, hedging its bets on favorable global or regional circumstances in the not-too-distant future. Help was extended by the unintended acts of two tragic figures; Mikhail Gorbachev and Saddam Hussein. The former initiated the process which led to the demise of the Soviet Union. The fateful decision of Saddam Hussein to invade Kuwait gave George Bush the green light to reshape the strategic landscape of the Middle East, terminate the existing Arab political order, and resolve the impasse in favor of

Washington's Palestinian and Arab agenda.[6] It was a windfall for the U.S., a superpower facing relative economic decline and sagging credibility, yet anxious to remain "number one."

The same decision had spelled disaster for the Palestinian people, whose leadership decided in 1993 to acquiesce in the U.S. and Israeli agendas, which constitute a reformulation of old plans that exclude Palestinian self-determination and circumvent the national rights upheld by the international community. These rights are enshrined in numerous international declarations and UN resolutions. Even the "full autonomy" promised by Camp David is effectively excluded from the active peace agenda. The Palestinian people are now at a crossroad with limited options: either they insist on total Israeli withdrawal, as the only path to a Palestinian state in the West Bank and Gaza, with an arrangement for sharing sovereignty in Jerusalem; or they accept a neo-apartheid system with Palestinian "autonomous zones," i.e., reservations and enclaves within a greater Israel. The first option is now unacceptable to Israel and to the United States. An alternative might be a Jordanian solution, in which King Hussein rather than Arafat would be charged with the administrative chores while Israel enjoys sovereignty. Either way, a Jordan option or neo-apartheid, the Palestinians would be faced with having to surrender the basic rights recognized by the United Nations; the right of the refugees to return to their homes and property, the right of self-determination, the right to struggle against the occupation, and their rights as civilians under occupation under the 1949 Geneva Convention, which implies the nullification of all the unilateral and illegal measures undertaken by Israel in the course of the occupation.

While these denials constitute the real Israeli agenda, under the Clinton administration they became effectively the U.S. agenda. For the Palestinians, however, there is no credible alternative to self-determination.

Notes

1   According to Democratic Senator Robert Byrd of West Virginia and for-

mer Senate Majority Leader, total U.S. aid to Israel between 1949 and 1991 amounted to $53 billion, equal to 13% of all U.S. aid for that period. Since the Camp David treaty in 1979 the amount totals $40.1 billion equal to 21.5% of all U.S. aid. see Donald Neff. "Israeli Dependence on the U.S.: The Full Extent of the Special Relationship" *Middle East International* No. 424 (1 May 1992) pp. 16–17.

2   For a discussion of Palestinian relations with the Arab states after the 1967 war, see Naseer Aruri, "Palestinian Impasse: Constraints and Opportunities." Hisham Sharabi (ed.) *The Next Arab Decade* (Boulder: Westview Press), 1988.

3   Naseer H. Aruri "The Recolonization of the Arab World" *Arab Studies Quarterly.* Vol XI Nos 2&3 (Spring/Summer 1989), pp. 273–286.

4   For an analysis of the Reagan Plan, see Naseer H. Aruri and Fouad Moughrabi, "The Reagan Middle East Initiative", *Journal of Palestine Studies* Vol. XII No 2 (Winter 1983), pp. 10–30.

5   see State Department, Bureau of *Public Affairs,* "U.S. Policy In The Middle East," No 27 (June 1988). Appendix I

6   See the following articles on the regional and global significance of the Gulf War: Tom Naylor. "American Aims In The Persian Gulf." *Canadian Dimensions* (March 1991), pp. 34–37; James Petras. "The Meaning of The New World Order: A Critique." *America* (May 11, 1991), pp. 512–514; Noam Chomsky. "U.S. Gulf Policy" *Open Magazine* (Jan. 18, 1991) pp. 1–17; Noam Chomsky. "What We Say Goes: The Middle East In The New World Order." *Z Magazine* (May 1991) pp. 50–64.

Part I

A Cold War Legacy

1

The Arab East and American Policy During the Cold War

The Evolution of the United States Global Strategy
An Impressive Continuity

The United States military intervention in the Gulf in the wake of the end of the Cold War is a natural extension of the policy it has pursued for four decades. Since the end of the Second World War the Middle East has been viewed by the U.S. establishment through the prism of the Cold War and East-West relations. The U.S. strategic doctrine underlying the course of the Cold War has been based on a distorted assessment of Soviet intentions. The Carter Doctrine as well as the Reagan Codicil has remained consistent with the substantive assumptions of the Truman Doctrine, which had set a pattern of direct or indirect intervention in the Middle East to keep the balance overwhelmingly in the U.S. favor.

The policy was based on the proposition that there existed a legitimate world order, for which the U.S. assumes the major responsibility, and that the Soviet Union, together with disaffected Third World nations, including Arab nationalist forces, were intent on challenging that order. A succession of U.S. doctrines and strategies which expressed a resolve to contain that challenge included the Truman Doctrine (1948), the Eisenhower Doctrine (1957), Kennedy's flexible response, the corollaries of limited nuclear war, counterinsurgency, the Johnson Doctrine (1965), the Nixon-Kissinger Doctrine (1969), and finally the Carter Doctrine (1980) and Reagan's Codicil (1981). These doctrines were predicated on the assumption that the United States has a title to the Arab world's petroleum resources, a privileged access to its markets and waterways, and an undisputed right to define, contain and roll back the region's enemies, be they internal dissidents, revolutionaries or external aggressors.

These doctrines were consistent with the fundamental objectives of the U.S. global policies since the end of World War II; to ensure, through the threat of force, that the status quo remained irrevocably and unalterably in the U.S. favor. The proliferation of American power on behalf of the status quo, deemed as unjust by more than two-thirds of the world's population, was always rationalized by America's leadership as a necessary component of the containment of communism. Prior to 1970, this leadership was able to unite disparate groups behind a consensus which perpetuated the fear of communism and advocated the necessity of suppressing social revolution. But the consensus which had sustained a policy of direct military intervention began to exhibit the stresses and strains of a world policeman's role under the devastating impact of Vietnam. The general disillusionment and failure resulted in a reassessment of the policy.

Nixon and Kissinger began a new phase by placing emphasis on indirect U.S. intervention through well-armed surrogates, while pursuing accommodation with the U.S.S.R. in pursuit of Kissinger's "stable world order." Detente was intended to arrest the steady erosion of U.S. credibility and viability as world policeman. The moral and material costs of empire were more than the American people could afford. No longer was the U.S. able to fulfill the responsibilities of central banker, chief arms supplier and world policeman. No longer was it able to maintain its control of the economic superstructure; the ability to produce, exploit, and distribute, to coerce both within and across international boundaries. No longer was it able to act as the guardian of Western interests and the judge of proper behavior in the context of the East-West struggle, imposing discipline on allies and clients by using the threat of withholding arms, credits and industrial commodities. America no longer had the fastest rate of economic growth, and the dollar was no longer the international medium of exchange. The dollar was devalued in 1971, when the first deficit in the balance of payments was also registered, and both coincided with an impending defeat in Vietnam. At that very juncture, the pursuit of detente was in full swing as a curative measure.

While the U.S. seemed to be operating from a position of relative weakness vis-à-vis the Soviet Union in Southeast Asia and in Angola during the early seventies, it enjoyed a decisive edge over the U.S.S.R. in the Middle East. It presented the U.S.S.R. with several threats in the region forcing the erosion of Soviet influence and a corresponding ascendancy of American power. In his State of the World message in February 1970, President Nixon declared, "The U.S. would view any effort by the Soviet Union to seek predominance in the Middle East as a matter of grave concern." Henry Kissinger called for and secured the expulsion of Soviet personnel from Egypt in 1972. The Soviet Union, on the other hand, applied a strategy in the Middle East similar to its own in Indochina—to provide its allies with the military hardware and the training necessary to secure the overthrow of foreign intruders. But the Middle East was different from Indochina. Many of the Arab states were tied to U.S. interests, which rendered their opposition to the Israeli occupation ineffective. Here, unlike in Vietnam, there was an absence of a cohesive national liberation movement with clearly defined objectives and a coherent ideology. From the very start, the Arabs limited their struggle to the restoration of occupied territories through diplomacy. In Vietnam, on the other hand, the diplomatic struggle proceeded simultaneously with the military struggle. The Geneva Conference of 1956 and the Paris agreement of 1973 had simply ratified the military realities in Southeast Asia and provided face-saving formulae for declining empires.

The second difference from the situation with Vietnam concerns the economic linkage between the U.S. and the Middle East. The status quo in the Gulf, which succeeding doctrines pledged to uphold, has provided the United States with an exceedingly favorable economic climate, one in which the levels of economic penetration are maintained and enhanced. Here, much more than in Vietnam and Central America, the economic stakes are very high, and the U.S. was bound to project its military power. Hence, when President Bush claimed in 1991 that his goal was to protect our jobs and our way of life, he really meant, first and foremost, corporate interest defined as a matter of national security. Such interests frequently condition military and political decisions.

Middle East trade had more than doubled its share of total U.S. trade between 1960 and 1980, almost tripled its share of Japanese trade, and increased by 50% its share of European Community (EC) trade. By 1980, Middle East oil provided 20% of U.S. supplies, 70% of EC supplies and over 75% of Japanese supplies. The region has the largest concentration of oil and natural gas reserves in the world. The countries of Saudi Arabia, Kuwait, Iraq, Iran, and Abu Dhabi each contain greater oil reserves than those found in the United States. In fact, Saudi Arabia alone has reserves six times greater than the U.S possesses. Middle East oil is not only plentiful, but cheap as well. The cost of producing a barrel of oil in the Gulf has been estimated at $2, compared to between $15 and $18 in Alaska.

U.S. economic gains are further enhanced by the exceedingly high rate of return on investments in the oil industry. While Middle East oil accounts for less than 2% of U.S. investments, its share of total U.S. foreign earnings is about 33%. Moreover, U.S. and British financial institutions claim the lion's share of Middle East oil surplus, which they recycle as loans to impoverished Third World nations. Throughout the post-World War II period a lucrative arms trade has claimed a sizeable portion of the Middle East market, by far the largest arms-importing region in the world, with the highest military expenditure on a per-capita basis and in terms of the Gross National Product. Seven of the largest ten arms importers during the past decade were Middle Eastern countries, and the West, particularly the United States, is their largest supplier. Annual per-capita military expenditure in the Gulf region ranges between $1,060 for Oman to $2,400 for Saudi Arabia.

The post-World War II period has witnessed increases in arms sales to the region at astronomical levels; from $2.36 billion for the fifteen-year period between 1955-1969 to $3.2 billion per year between 1970 and 1975 to $8.9 billion per year between 1975 and 1979. The Middle East accounted for $40 billion of the world military spending of $500 billion in 1980, with Saudi Arabia leading at the level of $20.7 billion.

Given these interests—the oil companies, major financial institutions and the defense industry—together with the political and social forces which supported them, they projected their power into the policy-making arena and shaped the perimeters of U.S. interventionist policies in the Middle East. During the 1950s the defense of these economic interests was predicated on a network of alliances pulling together conservative pro-Western regimes in the area and on the readiness of the U.S. to intervene directly.

The history of the U.S. involvement with this region reveals a great deal behind George Bush's claim that the 1990-91 military conflict in the Gulf was about moral principles and jobs. It also explains the discovery of Saddam Hussein as the most dangerous man in the world, the latest incarnation of Hitler. The sudden transformation of Saddam's Iraq from a virtual U.S. proxy in the Iran-Iraq war (1980-1988) and protector of the pro-American dynastic regimes, including the Houses of Saud, Sabah, Khalifa, Qabus and Thani, to a radical perpetrator of instability and the most menacing threat to U.S. vital interests in the Third World since Korea and Vietnam, is connected to this history.

The virtual occupation of the Gulf by the U.S. is the logical product of the transfer of imperial control (or responsibility, as Bush sees it) from Britain to the United States. That transfer was completed in the mid-1980s, when the U.S. Navy began its reflagging operation on behalf of Kuwaiti commercial shipping. The term "responsibility," transferred from Britain to the U.S., means safeguarding the region for the conservative rich dynasties which rule in the Gulf and who are in a virtual partnership with the U.S. U.S. policy has endeavored to contain and defeat the enemies of that status quo and so the containment policy, whose strategic doctrine was based on the assumption that there existed a legitimate world order for which the U.S. assumed major responsibility, was extended to the Middle East in the early days of the Cold War. The stated enemy was, of course, Soviet communism. But the unstated enemy of the 1950s and 1960s was Arab nationalism, which vowed to unify the Arab world, nationalize its wealth and resources, and declare itself non-aligned in the East-West conflict. The methods of containment ranged from military alliances facilitating direct U.S. intervention to informal arrangements providing for constellations and networks capable of acting as proxies.

America's global posture has been characterized by an impressive consistency in terms of policy objectives since George Kennan's Mr. X article.[1] The pursuit of these objectives in the Middle East region revealed two general patterns which entailed alternating between direct intervention and reliance on surrogates or regional influentials: (1) containment through military alliances, followed by an interlude of attempted containment through nationalism, and (2) the politics of informal alliances and what Zbigniew Brzezinski called "regional influentials." The first phase, during the period 1948-1960, was dominated by vigorous and consistent attempts to build a network of military alliances that would link up NATO with SEATO, thus forming a wall of encirclement around the Sino-Soviet periphery. The potential members of the alliance were Arab and Islamic states, but not Israel. The interlude between 1960 and 1966 saw the U.S. seek a rapprochement with radical Arab nationalism in an attempt to "contain" the Soviet Union. The latter phase, during 1967 to the end of the 1980s, had its principal emphasis on the promotion of an anti-communist constellation of forces including Arab and Islamic states as well as Israel. The de facto alliance of regimes which shared U.S. strategic perspectives was counted on to hold the region within the U.S. sphere of influence. Crisis in the projected alliance, however, contributed to zigzags in U.S. policy between a direct U.S. presence in the aftermath of the downfall of the Shah's regime in Iran to a reliance upon surrogates. Actually, the second phase of U.S. policy is divided into subphases showing these policy swings.

Regardless of the means employed to accomplish America's policy objectives, these objectives remained constant; to ensure, through the threat of force, either directly or via certain regional influentials, that the region remained unalterably and irrevocably in the U.S.'s favor. That implied a fairly high level of U.S. strategic and economic penetration through control of the area's strategic waterways, its most precious resources, oil, derivative financial surpluses and vast markets, all of which were defined as a matter of national security. The status quo which U.S. policy has attempted to uphold during the past four decades was a region free of Soviet intrusion and free of nationalist forces committed to social transformation, Arab unity, and liberation from foreign domination and occupation.

Palestinian nationalism remained the single most important impediment to the maintenance of that status quo for a quarter of a century, since the 1967 Arab-Israeli war. Keeping it at bay was perhaps the major concern of United States Middle East policy during that period.

A. Containment Through Military Alliances

During the 1950s the defense of the vast economic and strategic interests of the United States was predicated on a network of alliances pulling together conservative pro-Western regimes in the Middle East and on the readiness of the U.S. to intervene directly. These interests developed during World War II, with Middle East oil serving U.S. strategic supplies in the Far East. The lend-lease supply line to Russia had to be maintained with the aid of U.S. troops in Iran. A network of U.S. air bases in Saudi Arabia, Libya and Egypt served as a link between North Africa and the Far East.

The growing weakness of the British Empire convinced the United States that its wartime presence in the Middle East would have to be extended. Gradually, the U.S. perceived itself as the replacement for Britain and France and the sustainer of Western interests in a future bipolar world.

A.1 The Truman Doctrine and Its Derivatives

The emerging view of the Middle East as a strategic prize which must be denied to the Soviet Union found an early expression in President Truman's Army Day address in 1946:

> The Near and Middle East...contains vast natural resources...lies across the most convenient route of land, air and water communication...might become an arena of intense rivalry among outside powers....[2]

President Truman underscored U.S. determination to prevail in such rivalry by committing military and economic aid to support Greece and Turkey on March 12, 1947, shortly after Britain declared discontinuation of its own aid program. The Truman Doctrine, which embodied that commitment, ushered in an era of U.S. intervention to contain a presumed Soviet threat. This military pact was the principal instrument of an interventionist policy. In his message to Congress on May 24, 1951, President Truman urged the establishment of a mutual security program:

> In the free nations of the Middle East lie half of the oil reserve of the world. No part of the world is more directly exposed to Soviet pressure. There is no simple formula for increasing stability and security in the Middle East. The program I am now proposing is a balanced program for strengthening the security of the Middle East.[3]

The "balanced program" included two stillborn regional military alliances—the Middle East Command, a British idea, and the Middle East Defense Organization—both of which were rejected by Egypt in 1951. Britain and the U.S., however, continued to search for a formula which would fulfill the objectives of Western policy in the Middle East. They found it in the ill-fated Baghdad Pact, when Royalist Iraq broke ranks with the Arab League and announced its decision to conclude an alliance with Turkey, a country which already had a treaty with Pakistan. Iran became the fourth regional member of the Baghdad Pact in 1955. Britain was a full-fledged member of the pact. The U.S. refrained from formal membership, but participated in some of its military committees and provided military aid. The pact corresponded to the concept of then northern tier put forth by Secretary of State John Foster Dulles in 1953. At that time, he had concluded that the Arab states were "more fearful of Zionism than of the communists."[4] And yet the Baghdad Pact did not bypass the Palestine problem. In fact, it polarized the Arab world along the lines of neutralism versus pro-West. That polarization was exacerbated by the Israeli raid on Gaza on February 28, 1955, killing thirty-eight persons and exposing Egypt's military weakness. The arms which President Nasser of Egypt required to bolster his defenses were not to be found in the West, where the price was adherence to Western-sponsored military alliances. In fact, he found them in the communist bloc after his attendance at the conference of Afro-Asian states at Bandung in April 1955. It was reported that Chinese Premier Chou En-Lai had suggested to Nasser that the Soviets might be responsive to a request for arms.[5] The Egyptian-

Czech arms deal, which ended Egypt's dependence on the West for weapons, was announced on September 27, 1955.

A.2 The Suez War

By the end of 1955 America's allies were upset by the unfolding events in the Middle East. Britain's failure to replace its 1936 treaty with Egypt with a region-wide alliance, such as the Middle East Command, that would permit the continuation of the British military presence in the Suez Canal area and other parts of the region, came as a great disappointment. Instead, the new Nasser government had successfully negotiated British evacuation in 1954, thus making the Egyptian army, rather than British forces, the ultimate repository of power for the first time since the 1882 British occupation. Moreover, the Egyptian army was now equipped with Soviet weapons, a fact which symbolized the entry of the Soviet Union as a major power to the Mediterranean Sea area, hitherto considered a Western lake.

The U.S.'s other ally, France, was unhappy with Egypt's material and diplomatic support for the Algerian struggle for independence and held Nasser responsible for the escalation of the resistance in the mid-1950s. Also, Nasser was the kind of leader whom Israel did not want to see emerge on the scene, as the following comment by Prime Minister David Ben-Gurion testifies:

I always feared that a personality might rise such as arose among the Arab rulers in the seventh century or like him [Kemal Ataturk] who arose in Turkey after its defeat in the First World War. He raised their spirits, changed their character, and turned them into a fighting nation. There was and still is a danger that Nasser is this man.[6]

As the combined interests of Britain, France and Israel converged on the need to deal Nasser a crushing blow, the United States was eager to avoid conflict. Given the imminent decline of Anglo-French influence in the region, the U.S. was ready to fill a power "vacuum." It did not matter that the Eisenhower administration was in the midst of an election campaign; U.S. corporate interests, defined as national interest, required a firm stand against aggression. Less than two weeks before the Suez invasion, Dulles articulated these interests at a high-level policy meeting in candid terms:

> We are in the present jam because the past administration had always dealt with the Middle East from a [domestic] political standpoint and had tried to meet the wishes of the Zionists in this country. That had created a basic antagonism with the Arabs. That was what the Russians were capitalizing on. It is of the utmost importance for the welfare of the United States that we get away from a [domestic] political basis and try to develop a national non-partisan policy. Otherwise, we may be apt to lose the whole area and possibly Africa. This would be a major disaster for Western Europe as well as the United States.[7]

President Eisenhower dispatched two letters, on October 27 and 29, 1956, to Ben-Gurion, warning that a hostile initiative by Israel could endanger the emerging close relationship between the two countries.[8] And when the invasion took place on October 29, the U.S. issued an equivocal condemnation and worked through the United Nations to secure withdrawal of all foreign forces. President Eisenhower made it clear in a national address where the U.S. stood:

> The actions taken can scarcely be reconciled with the principles and purposes of the United Nations to which we have all subscribed...there can be no peace without law. And there can be no law if we were to invoke one code of international conduct for those who oppose us and another for our friends.[9]

Such pursuit of balance had also been seen earlier when the United States temporarily suspended aid to Israel on September 18, 1953 for refusing to comply with a UN request to suspend work on its hydroelectric project in the demilitarized zone near the Syrian border.[10] It also condemned the Israeli raid on the village of Qibya in the West Bank the following month and decreased aid in 1954.

The Suez war would have been a catalyst for the improvement of U.S.-Arab relations with the United States, which in turn was conscious of Egypt's importance for the realization of its policy objectives. Egypt was pivotal in U.S. efforts to cultivate close relationships with Saudi Arabia in order to ensure steady oil supplies to Europe and to facilitate U.S. economic penetration in the Middle East. Hence the U.S. reluctance to accept Israeli overtures for a formal alliance and a guarantee of security, particularly as Israel refrained from defining its boundaries. Dulles was reported as telling Israel's ambassador Abba Eban that America could not "guarantee temporary armistice lines."[11] He and Eisenhower were fearful of alienating the Arab world and driving it towards the Soviet Union. But the withdrawal of U.S. funds promised earlier for the Aswan Dam project, as well as the enunciation of the Eisenhower Doctrine, nevertheless derailed the attempted rapprochement.

A.3 The Eisenhower Doctrine

The Eisenhower Doctrine was proclaimed by the president before a joint session of Congress on January 5, 1957, to which he appealed for discretionary power to spend up to $200 million in aid money for the region. He sought and obtained authorization to employ U.S. military forces against "overt armed aggression from any nation controlled by international communism."[12] It was made clear that Egypt, as the primary advocate of revolutionary Arab nationalism and Arab unity and the spoiler of America's alliance policy, was the doctrine's principal target. Like the Baghdad Pact, the Eisenhower Doctrine served to polarize the region, drawing the lines sharply between conservative pro-Western regimes (Saudi Arabia, Jordan, Lebanon, Iraq) and nonaligned nationalists (Egypt, Syria, Yemen). Moreover, it ensured that the Middle East's regional and local conflicts were now integrally tied to the Cold War. And just as the Baghdad Pact had provoked Syria to sign a military alliance with Egypt and seek Soviet arms, the Eisenhower Doctrine paved the way for the first civil war in Lebanon and a military coup in Iraq in 1958, and led to the first U.S. military intervention in the area.

The Eisenhower Doctrine was also applied in Jordan during the spring of 1957, when the country's first government to emerge from a free parliamentary election was abruptly dismissed by King Hussein. The ensuing street demonstrations protesting the dismissal were declared by the monarch to be the work of international communism aimed at overthrowing him. Secretary Dulles agreed:

> We have great confidence and regard for King Hussein because we really believe that he is striving to maintain the independence of his country in the face of very great difficulties.... It is our desire to hold up the hand of King Hussein in these matters to the extent that he thinks that we can be helpful.[13]

A few days later King Hussein was awarded $10 million, but he denied that it was part of the $200 million allotted to the Eisenhower Doctrine. King Saud had also received $50 million three months earlier as payment for renewal of the lease of the Dahran base for five years. In Lebanon, President Camille Chamoun, seeking an unprecedented second term in 1958, faced internal opposition. Claiming that his opponents were armed and financed by Syria, which was already labelled communist-influenced, he called for U.S. intervention in accordance with the doctrine. The U.S. obliged, sending the Marines in July 1958.

The Eisenhower Doctrine, which became law on March 9, 1957, was described as having marked "a watershed in U.S. policy towards the Middle East because it specified the area as a vital national interest."[14] But this was really a continuation in which "the Truman administration had treated the area as though it were vital." From that point on, threats to the vital American national interests would be construed so broadly that they would include actions by nationalist forces challenging conservative regimes, Israeli transgression or U.S. hegemony. That was probably the beginning of the evolution of the U.S.-Israeli special relationship, which reached the stage of maturity in the aftermath of the June 1967 war and developed into a strategic alliance during Reagan's presidency.

President Eisenhower was interested in a strong Egypt, and to that end he put forward a proposal for respecting Arab neutrality in a major address to the UN General Assembly on August 13, 1958.[15] The domestic American environment, however, proved unreceptive to a major reorientation affecting traditional allies and friends (Britain,

France and Israel) and traditionally perceived enemies like Egypt and Syria. A major opportunity for an international settlement of the Middle East crisis was therefore missed, and the Israeli invasion of Arab land in 1956 was to be repeated by new generations in 1967, 1978 and 1982. But unlike 1956, the invasions of 1967 and 1982 were supported by the United States, as it supported Israel in the October war of 1973.

B. Containment Through Regional Influentials

By the end of Eisenhower's presidency, American policy, which encouraged formal alliances to contain Soviet influence and Arab nationalism, had suffered a serious failure. The region was polarized between conservative pro-Western monarchies and "radical" non-aligned military republics. The decade of the 1950s was marked by an erosion of monarchical power and a corresponding ascendancy of nationalism. Western interventions in Egypt, Lebanon, and Jordan were not sufficient to stem the tide of militant nationalism. That tide, which ushered in successful uprisings in Iraq and Yemen in 1958 and 1962, and which generated challenges to the political order in Jordan and Lebanon in 1957 and 1958, was seen as a viable threat to American strategic and economic interests. It was postulated that the defeat of the United Arab Republic (Egypt and Syria) would remove the potential threat to the stability of the conservative regimes, preserve U.S. strategic interests, and thus assure the continued exploitation of the region's resources by American business. This conclusion was reached during Johnson's presidency by prominent men in congress and in the military.

B.1 Israel and the Nixon Doctrine

A tendency to identify United States security interests with a militarily strong Israel was beginning to take hold in Pentagon circles in the 1960s. A congressional sub-committee on Middle East peace concluded in April 1967 that the United Arab Republic constituted the principal obstacle to peace, thus legitimizing the future offensive which came to be known as the Six Day War. Israel, which prior to 1967 was receiving the highest per capita aid from the U.S. of any country—a fact which remains true today—had indeed anticipated a proxy role for itself prior to the 1967 war and prior to the Nixon Doctrine. A spokesman for the Israeli foreign office expressed that readiness on June 11, 1966:

> The United States has come to the conclusion that it can no longer respond to every incident around the world, that it must rely on a local power, the deterrent of a friendly power as a first line to stave off America's direct involvement. Israel feels that it fits this definition.[16]

Indeed, Israel had emerged as the principal U.S. surrogate, entrusted with blunting the nationalist tide in the West's favor. The defeat of Egypt and Syria in June 1967 and the subsequent rise to prominence in inter-Arab affairs of such conservative Arab states as Saudi Arabia was cited as a vindication of this assumption. Although the offensive against Egypt and its brand of Arab socialism was not to involve the deployment of American troops, the 1967 war brought about consequences desirable not only to Israel, but to the U.S as well, namely, the defeat of Nasserism as a potent force in Middle Eastern politics. This fact was emphasized by the former prime minister of Israel, Levi Eshkol, in 1968:

> The value of Israel to the West in this part of the world will, I predict, be out of all proportion to its size. We will be a real bridge between the three continents and the free world will be very thankful not only if we survive, but if we continue to thrive in secure and guaranteed frontiers.[17]

The June 1967 war, in which the American "hose and water" were placed in the hands of Israeli "firemen," anticipated the Nixon-Kissinger Doctrine. The Nixon-Kissinger Doctrine was premised on the ability and willingness of certain countries in key regions of the world to play the role of local policeman under the direction of the United States. The doctrine was articulated in several presidential speeches and policy statements, beginning with the Guam speech of November 3rd, 1969, and the State of the Union message of 1970.[18] The new guiding principle postulated that unilateral intervention was expensive at home and unpopular abroad. Thus Israel, guaranteed by the U.S. a "margin of technical superiority"[19] over its Arab neighbors, was thrust into a position of dominance, enabling it to bring about conditions suitable to United States' as well as Israeli interests. Nixon's State of the World message explained this concept of partnership thus: "Others now have the ability and responsibility to deal with local disputes which once may have required our intervention." The *New York Times* reported that the Nixon administration remained "firmly committed to Israel's security and to her military superiority in the Middle East, for *only Israel's strength can deter attack and prevent a call for direct American intervention.*"[20]

The first test of this partnership concept came in 1970, when during the confrontation between the Palestinian nationalist movement and the Jordan army, the U.S. alerted airborne units from its Sixth Fleet, which began to steam toward the East Mediterranean, and Israel expressed readiness for intervention in the event of a Palestinian triumph over King Hussein. Since the battle of al-Karameh between the Palestinian resistance forces and Israel in March 1968, which galvanized Palestinian and Arab masses into action, the Palestinian guerilla movement was beginning to be viewed as a serious challenge not only to Israel but to America's ambitions in the area as well as to the conservative Arab states. The Rogers Plan of December 1969, which was based on the exchange of land for peace in accordance with UN Resolution 242, was in fact intended to effect a Jordanian settlement that would bypass the Palestinian resistance. It was followed by a determined Jordanian attempt to suppress the Palestinians, who had already begun to rival King Hussein for sovereignty in Jordan. The unfolding of events in Jordan which led to an all-out Jordanian attack against the Palestinians in the autumn of 1970 suggested a close coordination of policies between Jordan, the U.S. and Israel, whose interests converged on the need to contain the Palestinian national movement. For the next twenty years, succeeding U.S. governments attempted to reduce the Palestinian movement to manageable proportions and render it peripheral to any Middle East settlement.

The October 1973 Arab-Israeli war and the ensuing oil embargo enabled Secretary of State Kissinger to embark on a post-Vietnam strategy in the Middle East. Gradually, the Big Four talks on the Middle East, which began shortly after the 1967 war, had dwindled to talks between the two superpowers. By the end of the October 1973 war, the United States was beginning to act as if there was only one superpower in the Middle East. Kissinger's shuttle diplomacy as well as the American decision to ensure the failure of the Geneva Conference at the end of 1973 marked the start of a new era in Middle East diplomacy. The phrase "peace process" became synonymous with U.S. diplomatic efforts conducted in a solo fashion. One of the salient features of U.S. diplomacy was its consistent opposition to the internationalization of the Palestine question and the Arab-Israeli conflict. The U.S. was to emerge as chief arbiter despite a steadily growing special relationship with Israel, which compromised its credibility as mediator.

Kissinger's post-October 1973 mediation revealed three objectives. The first was to bring about a general eclipse of Soviet influence in the region. The departure of some 20,000 Soviet personnel from Egypt, a standing U.S. objective, as well as Sadat's de-Nasserization program, began the process of reorienting Egypt away from non-alignment and a pro-Soviet tilt towards the United States.

The second objective was to obtain a political settlement capable of creating a transformation of the very nature of the Arab-Israeli conflict, a settlement which would remove the conflict from its ideological context and transform it into an ordinary territorial conflict. Such an approach was inherently detrimental to the Palestinians and Arab nationalists, who viewed the struggle as one against settler colonialism and imperialist penetration. Kissinger devised a settlement which would highlight the global concerns of American policymakers and address the economic and strategic imperatives of American foreign policy, i.e., the steady flow of oil to the West, the security of American investments and trade with the Arab world, the stability of the region, the security of pro-Western conservative regimes, and the maintainance of a strategic military presence.

The third objective was to provide Egypt with such a vested interest in stability (through economic aid and territorial adjustments) as to insure its neutralization and effective removal from the Arab front against Israel.

The overall aim was to give the United States the necessary leverage not only to neutralize Egypt but also to pressure Syria and the PLO

into making significant concessions to Israel. The Sinai accord negotiated by Egypt and Israel under U.S. auspices in 1975 was calculated
to achieve that end. It granted Israel time to consolidate the occupation and build up its offensive capability vis-à-vis the Arab states on
the eastern front. Moreover, it granted Israel, for the first time, what
amounted to an American security guarantee. According to the
September 1975 "U.S.-Israel Memorandum of Agreement," the United
States was to hold "consultations" with Israel in case a third party—
meaning the Soviet Union—intervened militarily. Furthermore, the
U.S. agreed to be "fully responsive…on an on-going and long-term
basis" to Israel's military requirements. Translated into figures, the
New York Times (October 31, 1975) put that commitment at $2.24 bil-
lion annually, the bulk of which was used to acquire the latest equipment in the American arsenal, including the 450-mile Lance Pershing
missile, the F-15 and F-16A fighters, and the laser-guided "smart
bombs." The introduction of this massive equipment into the Middle
East signified a special version of the Nixon Doctrine—a special brand
of Vietnamization. The United States restricted its role to supplying
the military muscle which enabled surrogates or regional influentials
to maintain the balance in its favor.

Furthermore, the United States committed itself, in the U.S-Israel
Memorandum of Agreement, to continue refusing to recognize or
negotiate with the PLO until the latter recognized Israel's right to exist
and agreed to abide by UN Security Council Resolution 242. No such
reciprocal demands recognizing Palestinian national rights were made
on Israel, which still refuses to recognize the PLO and the peoplehood
of the Palestinians. Israel, of course, contests the operative paragraph
of Resolution 242, which calls for Israeli withdrawal from occupied
Arab territories. The practical implication of Kissinger's 1975
Memorandum, which decreed a diplomatic blockade against the PLO,
was thus twofold: first, the final settlement of the Palestine question
would not be based on any form of Palestinian sovereignty in the West
Bank and Gaza; secondly, Israel, as the principal surrogate and cornerstone of U.S. policy in the region, would be guaranteed access to
military technology and the latest equipment in the U.S. arsenal. The
implied marginalization of Palestinian national rights inherent in the

Sinai accord was to be confirmed and developed further in later American plans.

B.2 The Carter Doctrine and the Regional Influentials

By the end of the Ford administration, the list of regional influentials was headed by Israel, Iran and Saudi Arabia. The first acquired a global mission in addition to the regional role, already discussed. The global role included arming and training U.S. clients in Central and South America and maintaining a special relationship with South Africa.[21] The Shah's regime in Iran, which was making a serious bid for the role of policeman of the Gulf, suppressed a leftist insurgency in Dhofar against pro-Western Oman. Saudi Arabia emerged as the banker and "moderating" influence in the Arab region, while Israel kept Syria, the Palestinians and their Lebanese allies in line.

Carter's contribution to the unfolding strategy was the incorporation of Egypt into the constellation of regional powers that would relieve the burden of U.S. intervention. The Camp David formula, which created a separate peace with Israel, would free Egypt to join the ranks of the regional influentials and make its contribution to regional stability.

That strategy, however, was dealt a severe blow when the new recruits were upset by internal unrest. The Shah's regime was overthrown by the Islamic revolution in 1979, and two years later Sadat was assassinated by Islamic fundamentalists. Not only was Iran a principal linchpin of American interests in the Gulf, it was also a test case for the Nixon Doctrine. Iran was to determine whether U.S.-trained forces would be effective in arresting social revolution in a crucial region of the Third World. The Islamic revolution created an irreparable breech in the informal security arrangements of Henry Kissinger. Former Undersecretary of State George Ball underscored the failure of the Nixon Doctrine in an article entitled "The Lessons from Iran" (*Boston Globe*, April 2, 1979):

> With Iran eliminated as the "protector" of the Gulf area, a mindless reflex is leading many to search for another surrogate country, such as Egypt or Saudi Arabia, to assume the Shah's role as "policeman." This is, it seems to

me, a temptation we should sturdily avoid. If the debacle of Iran proves anything, it is that we cannot assure—as the Nixon Doctrine assumed—the security of a strategic region by stuffing a backward state with massive quantities of arms.[22]

Ball's prescription for remedy was a U.S. military buildup in the region coupled with improving the ability of the U.S. to deliver force quickly from American bases:

We should substantially beef up our presence in the Indian Ocean, assist the Saudis with surveillance [hence the AWACs, two years later] and give constant reminders of our improving ability to deliver quickly, even from American bases.[23]

The military buildup which began at that time and which was promoted by "dovish" members of the Democratic establishment such as George Ball and Cyrus Vance developed into the military machine which the hawks in the Republican administration of George Bush utilized in the destruction of Iraq in 1991. That buildup was justified on the pretext of defending the area from Soviet expansionism. But the centrality of U.S. economic interests was spelled out by key figures in the foreign policy establishment. Secretary of State Vance said in a speech before the Los Angeles World Affairs Council:

We must maintain a defense establishment modern and strong enough to protect ourselves and our allies. We must protect American investments overseas and insure continuing access to vital raw materials.

In the Iranian aftermath, a strategic adaptation by the U.S. combined a return to the principle of direct intervention with reliance on partners. A Rapid Deployment Force (RDF), conceived by presidential advisor Zbigniew Brzezinski in 1977, would enable the United States to become the principal guarantor of its enormous economic and strategic interests in the region. Besides strengthening the Diego Garcia base in the Indian Ocean on the edge of the Arabian Sea, arrangements for access to strategic bases were made by the Carter administration with Egypt (Ras Banas and Cairo West), Somalia (Berbera), Kenya

(Mombasa), Oman (El-Messira and Se'eb), and Israel. Joint U.S. military exercises were undertaken with Egypt, Oman, and Somalia. Operation "Bright Star," conducted in November 1981, was a test of RDF ability to defend American interests in coordination with local forces. The Iran-Iraq conflict provided another opportunity to bolster the U.S. presence. Four U.S. manned radar war planes (AWACs) were sent to Saudi Arabia in addition to a guided missile cruiser and two tanker planes. Six hundred U.S. military personnel were involved in the AWACs projects. Moreover, the U.S. used the Gulf War to pressure Western Europe to join the Fifth Fleet. Britain and France agreed to do so as part of the informal security arrangements.

Carter's "security framework" for Southwest Asia (as U.S. policymakers began to refer to the region) was given concrete meaning by the enunciation of the Carter Doctrine on January 23, 1980:

> Let our position be absolutely clear: Any attempt by any outside force to gain control of the Persian Gulf region will be regarded as an assault on the vital interests of the United States of America, and such an assault will be repelled by any means necessary, *including military force.*[24]

This new commitment was to receive added impetus with Reagan's pledge to defend Saudi Arabia against *internal* threats as well: "We will not permit Saudi Arabia to be an Iran.... No way we will stand by and see it taken over."[25] That became known as the Reagan Codicil, which together with the Carter Doctrine was to mark yet a new approach to the Middle East and the Arab-Israeli conflict.

C. The Reagan Period: A New Cold War or Continuity?

After fewer than four months in office, Ronald Reagan appeared as the most ardently anti-communist president since Harry Truman. In this short period, he committed the United States to suppress a social revolution in El Salvador; lifted a ban imposed by Carter on export-import loans to Chile's fascist dictatorship; received the South Korean dictator as his first guest in the White House; invited Argentina, which had been denied U.S. military aid for the disappearance of 6,000 persons after arrest, to send a delegation to Washington; referred to South

Africa on March 3, 1981 as "a friendly nation" that "has stood beside us in every war" and "whose minerals are strategically essential to the free world"; reduced appropriations for economic help for poor Third World countries; and stepped up arms shipments to Southwest Asia—the name used then for the Middle East—all the way from the Bosporus to the Arabian/Persian Gulf and the Indian Ocean and up to the Khyber Pass.

Those moves included significant departures from the Carter approach, which was embellished with human rights slogans and calls for disarmament, and from Kissinger's attempts at accommodations with the U.S.S.R. Journalistic comparisons between the two presidents revealed an exaggerated dichotomy which dismissed important continuities. Gone was the angel of human rights, the advocate of North-South dialogue, the proponent of SALT II, black majority rule in Africa, and the champion of autonomy for the Palestinian people. With Reagan in the White House and General Haig in the State Department, Americans were told that the U.S. was about to "return to a geomilitary or strategic concept for its Middle East policy,"[26] that "the wheel may be turning full circle, that we are about to resume the...containment policies of an earlier era...."[27] And that while Kissinger viewed the U.S.S.R. as a rival power with whom he sought detente, Reagan and Haig preferred to lecture Soviet leaders on their need for a "code of conduct." In a January 29th 1981 press conference, Reagan accused Soviet leaders of "willingness to commit any crime, to lie, to cheat..." in order to attain world revolution. Secretary Haig accused them, in his first press conference, of "training, funding and equipping" international terrorism. By the time Reagan established himself on the political scene, all the ingredients of a highly militarized interventionary policy were set in place—the bases, the arms sales, the armada, the European allies, and a U.S. public opinion actuated by Walter Cronkite's daily count of the number of days Americans had to endure Iranian captivity.

Ronald Reagan did not resume the containment policy of an earlier era, nor did he deal a crippling blow to detente. These were already in process. He did not return the U.S. to a geomilitary or strategic concept for its Middle East policy; he was simply building up on that policy. His proposed budget for military credits and economic support for the Middle East represented an increase of a half a billion over Carter's proposals. Israel was expected to receive $2.2 billion plus $600 million to "compensate" for the Saudi F-15 and AWACs deals; Egypt's share was $1.685 billion plus $106.4 million to beef up the military base at Ras Banas. Israel and Egypt alone accounted for $4.3 billion out of $6.9 billion for military assistance in the 1982 budget—more than 80%.

Moreover, Reagan spent $75 million in Oman for improvement of the El Messira base and Se'eb airfield, which commands the Strait of Hormuz. He spent $24 million on improvement of the port of Berbera in Somalia and $40 million as a grant in lieu of using Mogadishu and Berbera. Sudan received $100 million, Tunisia $95 million, Turkey $700 million and Pakistan $500 million. U.S. forces controlled and operated a substantial part of the Saudi air force, its air defense, and the training and arming of its ground forces. This massive presence gave Washington total leverage in integrating and subordinating Saudi foreign policy to U.S. needs in reshaping a new regional alliance.

These arrangements resulted in the breaking of regional solidarity, subordinating and tying Arab wealth to a U.S.-led alliance. America's huge presence in the region enabled it to shape all aspects of its clients' policies. Their weakness, which resulted from the fragmentation of the Arab world, prevented them from effectively exercising any pressure on the U.S. to dislodge the Israeli occupation. In fact, Washington was in a better position to discourage local conflicts in which local interests took precedence over global U.S. concerns. It was also in a better position to discourage political initiatives on the Palestine question by the Europeans, whose economic advantage was being offset by the U.S. military presence. While Washington was "protecting" the supply line for Europe and Japan, it was hardly possible for the latter to pursue an independent policy on the Palestine question. The buildup of the U.S. military presence was a compensation for the lack of economic competitiveness. A new colonial presence was emerging in the Middle East. It was discussed openly by officials in the Reagan administration. Both defense secretary Weinberger and Reagan himself stressed the need to supplement the U.S. naval presence with a ground presence. In fact, a U.S. ground force was stationed in the Sinai in April 1982 in accordance with the Egyptian-Israeli treaty. This so-called peacekeeping force constituted the first step toward a permanent U.S. ground presence in the Arab world. It became a principal link in the strategic framework under construction since Carter's presidency. General Haig described this framework, in testimony before the Senate Foreign Relations Committee on March 19, 1981, as a "consensus of strategic concerns" that would stretch from Turkey to Pakistan.[28] He told the House Foreign Affairs Committee on the day before:

It is fundamentally important to begin to develop a consensus of strategic concerns throughout the region among Arab and Jew and to be sure that the *overriding* danger of Soviet inroads is not overlooked.

Haig considered it a sophisticated strategy which shunned formal military alliances and recruited both Arabs and Israelis towards a common cause. He told the Senate Foreign Relations Committee on September 17, 1981:

Although we are building up U.S. military capabilities...the use of U.S. military force can only be considered as a last resort. And to deter major Soviet threats, for which the U.S. role is indispensable, we also need the help of our friends, both in the region and outside it...that is the reason why we are pursuing intensified strategic cooperation with Israel, Egypt, Saudi Arabia, and many other concerned countries...we are not seeking to construct formal alliances or a massive structure of U.S. bases. We are pursuing a sophisticated strategy, one guided as well by a sense of urgency.[29]

The thrust of this consensus was the containment of Soviet "expansion," which received administration priority over all other matters, including the Arab-Israeli conflict. The former was global and strategic, while the latter was considered to be regional and peripheral. As a result, the U.S. strategy in the Middle East was undergoing some revisions calculated to broaden its base. But in fact, global strategy was inseparable from regional considerations and, to the extent that the strategic consensus implied a convergence of Arab and Israeli interests, the United States faced the challenge of reconciling the irreconcilable.

But Washington insisted that the Arab-Israeli conflict must not stand in the way of the strategic consensus. Both Reagan and Haig stressed publicly the importance of Israel in the larger global arena. According to General Haig, the security of Saudi Arabia was intertwined with that of Israel:

> We are wholeheartedly and permanently committed to the security of Israel. Without a strong Israel, our hope to improve the prospects for peace and security in the region cannot be fulfilled. A secure Saudi Arabia and a strong U.S.-Saudi relationship are central to these same tasks.[30]

Accordingly, the central assumption of the strategic consensus was the need to subordinate the Arab-Israeli conflict and its requirement of comprehensive settlement to the Soviet "threat" and the requirement of "comprehensive security." The Palestine question, which came to be regarded by the Reagan administration as secondary, would cease to enjoy its usual priority as the region's principal concern. Its divisive effect on the regional powers would thus be contained, and the collective energies would be marshalled to meet the challenges to individual country and regional stability.

The project was hampered, however, by the U.S. special relationship with Israel, which proved to be incompatible with strategic consensus. The U.S. had failed to offer the Arabs and Israel a viable formula for cooperation. The issues which divided them at the time, in 1981, included the proposed U.S. sale of AWACs to Saudi Arabia, the Israeli raid on Iraq's nuclear research facility, the Golan annexation, the proposed Jordanian strike force, the Israeli invasion of Lebanon in 1982, and the Palestine question.

The attempt to reconcile the two endeavors foundered when the Reagan administration failed to satisfy the minimalist position of the Arab component of the strategic consensus. Neither the 1981 Fahd Plan nor the 1982 Fez Plan[31] evoked even a slight measure of enthusiasm from Washington, despite strong indications of Arab willingness to recognize Israel as part of a peaceful settlement. Even the Reagan

Plan of September 1, 1982[32] was allowed to drift into oblivion after it was promptly and categorically rejected by Israel. The administration had also failed to determine whether the Israeli use of American-supplied aircraft in the bombing of the Iraqi nuclear facility had violated the amended Arms Control Act of 1976. That act restricts the use of American-supplied arms to acts of "self-defense" and requires the president to report any violations to Congress. More blatant was the Israeli invasion of Lebanon in the summer of 1982 and U.S. complicity in that invasion,[33] as well as its association with Israel's war aims; the quest for a new political map of Lebanon, the attempt to obliterate Palestinian nationalism and to reduce Syria to manageable proportions. President Reagan spoke of an "opportunity" which the war of 1982 had afforded. He placed the Israeli "achievements" within the context of America's broader goal of promoting stability in the region. But the prospects for building a strategic consensus, which required even-handedness, were hardly improved by a virtual U.S. partnership in an Israeli war followed by the attempted imposition of humiliating terms as the price of Israeli withdrawal.

The strategic consensus had also suffered from the inability of the Reagan administration to obtain congressional approval of money and arms for Jordan and Israeli cooperation in the creation of a climate for negotiations. The endeavor to set up a Jordanian Logistics Force (JLF) as a rapid-deployment force for the Gulf was seen by Reagan as an assured instrument for keeping the Strait of Hormuz "open." It was also intended to make the transition to the Reagan Codicil from the Carter Doctrine by facilitating intervention in internal crises in the Gulf states. But despite a clear intent to deny Jordan an autonomous decision over its use and the administration's conveyance of its "determination to see that Israel's qualitative technological edge is maintained,"[34] congressional opposition remained unabated. It was rather ironic that the Reagan administration had planned to ask Israeli Defense Minister Moshe Arens to intercede with congressional opponents of the Jordanian force.[35] But Israel remained publicly opposed to one of Reagan's principal ingredients of strategic consensus, and it was its opposition to the Jordan missile deal which dealt that project a deadly blow. Reacting to all of this, King Hussein made a rare suspension of his diplomatic poise. His *New York Times* interview of March 16, 1984 was the harshest public criticism to date of U.S. policy by any Jordanian official. It seemed as though Jordan had finally declared independence in foreign affairs. The king said that "Israel is on our land...by virtue of American military assistance and economic aid." He continued:

> It is there by virtue of American moral and political support to the point where the United States is succumbing to Israeli dictates.... This being the case, there is no way by which anyone should imagine it would be possible for Arabs to sit and talk with Israel as long as things are as they are.... You obviously have made your choice, and your choice is Israel. Therefore there is no hope of achieving anything.[36]

The stipulation that arms shipments be linked to Jordanian acceptance of Camp David, among other conditions, led the king to raise a concern about the "U.S. and its double standard everywhere" and to accuse the U.S. of having "succumbed to Israeli dictates," as well as to those of "AIPAC and Zionism." On January 5, 1985 the Jordanian army commander Lt. General Zayd Ibn Shaker announced that Jordan had purchased a Soviet air defense system. The cancellation of the Stinger missile deal in March 1984 thus resulted in arms purchases by two pro-Western Arab countries (Jordan and Kuwait) from the Soviet Union.[37]

Such were the constraints on the administration's ability to ease Jordan's "security problem," deemed essential to the success of the strategic consensus. As for the second requirement—helping Jordan solve its "negotiating problem"—it fell victim to Israel's rejection of the Reagan Plan and its refusal to consider putting a freeze on the building of new settlements in the West Bank. The most that the administration was willing to try in that regard was a promise to urge Israel to freeze further settlements, and the argument that once King Hussein came to the table, pressures would develop in Israel for compromise. Neither Jordan's "security problem" nor its "negotiating problem" was within Washington's capabilities. The "strategic consensus," in fact, suffered from a lack of consensus. While Israel and the so-called moderate Arab states shared Reagan's concern about the

Soviet "threat," they nevertheless disagreed on the order of priorities. The Arabs argued that regional stability as a safeguard against revolution and Soviet influence required a durable and just solution to the Palestine problem. Israel dismissed the Palestine question as a secondary matter that must not become an issue between a superpower and an important partner. Israel, moreover, wanted to remain the *sole* power in the Middle East.

In summation, for many years during the Cold War, the United States had vainly striven to become simultaneously the major power and the pre-eminent honest broker in the Middle East. Although Haig's endeavor to forge a consensus among unwilling parties failed, it nevertheless served as a catalyst for what Washington's strategists called the pursuit of "comprehensive security," that is, containment of communism, through Israel. No longer would Israel be seen as defending only its own security, even within the 1967 borders, but the hegemony of its major ally as well. Its expanded role, which required an upgrading of the special relationship, however, had caused Washington's Arab clients to refrain from direct cooperation. Such cooperation had to wait until the end of the Cold War, when the containment of Saddam Hussein would resonate far louder than the containment of communism.

Notes

1. "The Sources of Soviet Conduct," *Foreign Affairs,*(July 1947).
2. *Department of State Bulletin,* April 21, 1946, p. 622.
3. *Department of State Bulletin,* June 4, 1951, p. 887.
4. *Department of State Bulletin,* June 15, 1953, p. 831.
5. Charles Cremeans, *The Arabs and the World* (New York: Praeger, 1963), p. 146.
6. Quoted in Donald Neff, *Warriors at Suez: Eisenhower Takes America into the Middle East* (New York: Linden Press/Simon & Schuster, 1981), pp. 439–440.
7. Ibid., p. 107.
8. Moshe Dayan, *Diary of the Sinai Campaign* (Jerusalem: Steinatzky Agency Ltd., 1966), pp. 71–73.

9. *Department of State Bulletin*, November 12, 1956, pp. 745–746.

10. Cheryl Rubenberg, *Israel and the American National Interest*, (Urbana: University of Illinois Press, 1986), p. 64.

11. Neff, op. cit., p. 104.

12 . See an analysis of the doctrine in Fred Halliday, *Arabia Without Sultans* (London: Penguin Books, 1974), p. 54.

13. From a news conference on April 23, 1957, *Department of State Bulletin*, May 13, 1957, p. 768.

14. Melvin Gurtov, *The United States Against the Third World: Anti-Nationalism and Intervention* (New York: Praeger, 1974), p. 14.

15. Malcolm Kerr, "Coming to Terms with Nasser," *International Affairs* (January 1967), pp. 73–76.

16. *New York Times*, June 12, 1966.

17. *Newsweek*, February 17, 1968.

18. *New York Times*, November 4, 1969.

19. Nixon's campaign promise.

20. *New York Times*, December 24, 1969; emphasis added.

21. For a discussion of Israel's counter-revolutionary role, see Israel Shahak, *Israel's Global Role: Weapons for Repression* (Belmont, Mass.: AAUG Press, 1982); also Milton Jamail and Margo Gutierrez, *It's No Secret: Israel's Military Involvement in Central America* (Belmont, Mass.: AAUG Press, 1986).

22. *Boston Globe*, April 2, 1979.

23. Ibid.

24. *New York Times*, January 24, 1980.

25. *New York Times*, October 2, 1981.

26 . Wm. R. Brown, "Middle East: The Flaws of Military Strategy," *Christian Science Monitor*, February 19, 1981.

27. Charles Yost, "The Risks of Resuming Containment," *Christian Science Monitor*, February 20, 1981.

28. *New York Times*, March 20, 1981.

29. "Secretary Haig: U.S. Strategy in the Middle East," U.S. Department of State, Bureau of Public Affairs, Current Policy No. 312.

30. See Haig's testimony before the Senate Foreign Relations Committee and the House Foreign Affairs Committee on March 19 and 20, 1981 in the *New York Times*, March 20, 1981. See also "Secretary Haig: U.S. Strategy in

the Middle East," U.S. Department of State, Bureau of Public Affairs, Current Policy No. 312.

31. Text of the Fez Plan in N. Aruri, *et al.*

32. Text in Ibid., pp. 79-84; see also *New York Times*, September 2, 1982.

33. Ze-ev Shiff, "The Green Light," *Foreign Policy*, Vol. 50 (Spring 1983).

34. *Boston Globe*, February 17, 1982.

35. *Washington Post*, October 15, 1983.

36. David Newsome, "Hope or Delusion," *Christian Science Monitor*, December 27, 1983.

37. *New York Times*, March 8, 1984.

2

After the Cold War
The Irrelevance of Containment

The massive United States military deployment in the Arabian peninsula, which began in August 1990 and culminated in the Gulf War, completed the process of recolonization of the region which has been ongoing for more than two decades. It was preceded by the United States naval buildup of the 1980s and the reflagging of the Kuwaiti oil tankers during the Iraq-Iran War.

The transfer of imperial control—euphemistically described as "responsibility"—from Britain to the United States has been accomplished under the auspices of a long string of strategic doctrines, beginning with the Truman Doctrine of 1948. The declarations and actions of President Bush in the Gulf reconfirmed, complemented, and supplemented the Carter Doctrine (1980) and the Reagan Doctrine (1981), which pledged to defend the region from external aggression, and Saudi Arabia, in particular, from internal uprisings. They reversed the Nixon Doctrine, which had assigned the protection of the status-quo to local gendarmes equipped with United States weapons and training. In 1990-1991, it was the G.I.'s who had to perform the fireman's role, the role of mercenary, while a substantial portion of the cost for the "hose and the water" was borne by local emirs and kings and partly raised in the industrial North, which relies on Gulf oil resources.

The crisis in the Gulf was the first important indication of the way the United States was going to respond to the much touted "New World Order". Military intervention in that region was an ominous sign that the United States perceived its international role as unchanged from the Cold War period. As it did throughout the Cold War, the U.S. continued to invest extraordinary resources in support of its military power, and the Gulf response was yet another demonstration of a foreign policy oriented to the use of that power. This remained so even while America's relative economic status continued to decline and a domestic debate raged over whether the U.S. should divert substantial resources from the military "peace dividend" to rebuilding an economy plagued with massive debt, bank failures, and a crumbling infrastructure.

What President Bush believed to be at stake in the Gulf was American hegemony within its sphere of influence, the preservation of which has been a primary goal of U.S. foreign policy since the Truman administration, as noted above. The official name of that policy was, of course, containment of communism, under which the U.S. sphere of influence had been given the widest possible definition, and the United States stood ready to intervene in every corner of the World. Every social revolution, left wing government and challenge to its allies, clients and dependencies were inspected carefully for communist influences and such suspicions used as the pretext for actual or threatened American sanctions.

In the "New World Order", containment has lost its original rationale as a response to the Soviet challenge. Regional interventions can no longer be explained in terms of Soviet aggression or Soviet sponsored insurrections. The Soviet bloc has disintegrated following the democratic revolution throughout Eastern Europe; while the Soviet Union itself, which was in the grip of social, economic and ideological crisis, ceased to exist by the end of 1991. In such a context, the idea of global containment as a tool for maintaining the geopolitical balance of power has lost its force and indeed its raison d'etre. The anti-communist rhetoric of containment, however, masked the identity of another real enemy of American hegemonic designs: Third World nationalism and social revolution.

This can be seen in the Gulf where, following the invasion and annexation of Kuwait by Iraq, the focus of U.S. policy was not on the presumed—and never really existent—communist threat in the region. Rather, this was containment pursued in an ideological vacuum, and President Bush had strained to provide credible rationales for U.S. intervention. At various points, he had summoned up the old rhetoric calling for a defense of the U.S. "way of life", but without the old anti-communist theme it had not played well at home. He found it hard to defend an intervention on behalf of cheap energy when the price of gasoline at the pump had risen by 50 percent and the potential cost in lives was so extreme. It was not easy to convince a cautious public that cheap gasoline was the cornerstone of the "American way". While President Bush's appeal to rid the world of noxious dictators has played better on the congressional campaign trail, it was clear that Saddam Hussein was hoping to lead a regional power in what was once a regional conflict, and the geopolitical stakes were much lower than the U.S. would have been able to credibly claim if the Cold War had been still at its height.

Up until the Iraqi invasion of Kuwait on August 2, 1990, the real threat to the Gulf status-quo was presumed to emanate from the Islamic Republic of Iran and local dissidents and oppositional Arab socio-political forces tied in one way or another to Islamist revival or to Arab nationalism. These forces questioned the special relationship between the United States and the local family regimes, which anchor their stability in American protection rather than democratic legitimacy. With the invasion, annexation and reconquest of Kuwait, the focus was on a regional power, Iraq, which was determined to challenge the rules of the Arab state system and American hegemony in the region.

The Rationale For Post-Cold War Intervention

As the U.S. was emerging in the post-Cold War as the uncontested superpower in a militarily unipolar world, it seemed more determined than ever to prevent any and all regional socio-political forces, either now or in the future, from questioning any aspect of the state system. That included the control of petroleum reserves, levels of production, and pricing, as well as the political or military balance.

The states and dynasties of the Gulf, which succeeding doctrines pledged to uphold, have continued to provide the United States with an exceedingly favorable economic climate, one in which the levels of economic penetration are maintained and enhanced. Here, much more than in Vietnam and Central America, the economic stakes were very high, and the U.S. was bound to project its military power. Hence, when President Bush claimed that his goal was to protect "our jobs" and "our way of life" he really meant, first and foremost, corporate interests, defined as a matter of national security.

The military posture in the Gulf, rather than protecting the interests of ordinary American citizens or their way of life, was designed to insure the profits of oil corporations, major financial institutions, and military contractors, who together with the political and social forces that support them, shape the parameters of Washington's policy in the region. In addition the extravagance of the action succeeded in diverting the attention of Americans away from the profound economic problems gripping the nation. The military buildup had instantly dwarfed the savings and loan crisis and rendered the trade and budget deficits secondary for a while.

Saddam Hussein was an unlikely candidate to incur the wrath of the United States. His career was built on dealing ruthlessly with Iraqi communists, Shiite and Kurdish dissenters; his reputation was never that of a proponent of Arab unity, socialism or non-alignment. He has not been an Arab nationalist, a champion of the Palestinian cause, or even a democrat. He was favored by the United States with $4.5 billion of agricultural credits between 1983 and 1990 to free up his resources for his continued war against Iran. Washington had encouraged the French to sell him missiles and the Saudis to finance him. He was provided with military intelligence from U.S. satellite systems. A few months before Hussein invaded Kuwait, the Bush administration vetoed legislation that would have punished him for using agricultural credits for the purchase of weapons and ammunition.

There had been a sudden transformation of Hussein's image in the United States from shield against Iranian extremism and custodian of the regional Arab order to the "most dangerous man in the world."[1] This had resulted from his challenge to the established order in the Gulf and to the legitimacy of the local regimes which have anchored their stability in American protection and through which American corporate interests are in turn protected. His sin was the attempt to play the role of pace setter in an environment of decreasing oil revenues caused by the oil glut. His ensuing clash with local overproducers, Kuwait and the United Arab Emirates, was transformed into a global conflict. Hence, the issues of the territorial integrity of Kuwait and the restoration of its own dynasty were elevated to the status of a vital U.S. interest worthy of the most massive deployment since the Vietnam war. To be sure, Hussein acted illegally by occupying and annexing Kuwait to Iraq. But the Bush strategy was designed to preempt a real test of the effectiveness of the international embargo. Moreover, the crisis and the subsequent war were not over legal moral principles, or over Saddam Hussein's dismal human rights record. Many of Washington's Third World clients are among the worst violators of human rights. This was a conflict over resources, first and foremost— the first major conflict between the North and South in the post-Cold War period.

Thus, the appeal to principles enunciated by President George Bush was hardly credible in view of many invasions of sovereign territory recorded in recent history which received little or no reaction from the American government. It is even less credible when the provocative military actions taken by the United States against Nicaragua, Panama, Grenada, and Libya are considered. Nor was the Iraqi occupation of Kuwait less susceptible to diplomatic resolution than the Vietnamese occupation of Cambodia or the Soviet occupation of Afghanistan. Washington's decision to go to war was thus dictated by what the Bush administration perceived as regional and global imperatives of the post-Cold War period. The unstated objectives of that strategy emanated from American power decline and decreased ability to compete effectively against the new economic giants—Japan and Germany. They include the rearrangement of the existing structure of international relations in such a way that America's structural economic weakness would not diminish its strategic overextension and imperial stretch. Thus America, which had effectively lost its post-World War II power position, would retain its imperialist aspirations as if it were the world's only superpower, when a multipolar system was in fact emerging. In that setting of a highly competitive economic environment, America's enormous military establishment may prove a liability. The dollars which support military research, standing forces and the purchase of armaments, are dollars which are not invested in infrastructure, debt retirement and industrial development.

Desert Storm As A U.S. Domestic Policy

Since the United States is the only nation that can project power overseas, the situation in the Gulf afforded an opportunity to abort a major foreign policy debate in the U.S., and vindicate the assumption that a dominant role in world politics does not need a flourishing economy. Thus victory in the Gulf war would reconfirm American global primacy without incurring the cost of that primacy. Not only would the German and Japanese economic challenges be contained but Japan and Germany, along with a constellation of so-called allies, would finance America's first post-cold war adventure. America's prestige and power could be enhanced through the military buildup and the use of precision military tools and a decisive victory at no real cost to the economy. After all, the United States can no longer afford to finance the military forces which the containment doctrine required. George Bush was facing a rapidly deteriorating political situation at home; he inherited one of the longest periods of economic growth in the nation's history, low inflation and high unemployment. The illusion of the Reagan years was that America could spend freely and did not have to pay for it. Tax rates could be lowered but tax revenues would magically increase. The legacy of the Reagan years was beginning to catch up with Mr. Bush midway through his term, for the prosperity was built on cheap energy , massive public debt, and a disregard for the niceties of social equality. The poor became poorer during the Reagan years: low cost housing became increasingly scarce forcing some to live on the streets, while the electorate had come slowly to the realization that the rich profited during this period at the expense of everyone else. The social equity issue has been clearly examined by the extended debate in 1990 over the budget, during which the president and his party campaigned openly for tax breaks for the wealthy; a reduction in the capital gains tax and maintenance of the tax cap at the upper income levels.

War in the Gulf, which would marshal a traditional rallying towards the president's policy and the troops, was capable of rendering these endemic problems to the sidelines. Moreover, the debate over the military budget in the aftermath of the cold war was bound to be settled in favor of the Pentagon and its industrial-military backers against advocates of the long-awaited peace dividend. The use of advanced weaponry with great efficiency, against a Third World army was also intended to insure public support for the maintenance of military appropriations for new systems. The military establishment would not only gain a new lease on life, when the USSR was not deemed a threat, but would re-emerge as a symbol of a new national pride which had been bruised by Vietnam. American obsession with being "number one" simplified that task and the war solidified the alliance of the industrialists and the military, who strained to react to the German and Japanese challenges.

A New World Order?

The war option was seen as the best means to substitute the military muscle for economic power and thus compensate for real American weakness. This is what American politicians mean by the phrase "New World Order." American intervention did not follow the models which were constructed as part of the containment policy during four decades following World War II. Neither the Baghdad Pact nor Alexander Haig's consensus of strategic concerns or the Nixon Doctrine served as a model. American troops in the hundreds of thousands, deployed under the banner of a New World Order, were joined by those of twenty-eight other nations, ostensibly united and actuated by a common impulse to uphold international legitimacy. Most of them came to reap the benefits of the unstated goals of America's policy. For example, Britain, the most important junior partner in that endeavor, underwent a transformation in its role as the sponsor of the Sabah dynasty in Southwest Asia to being an instrument for U.S. domination of Arab petroleum resources. Moreover, British financial institutions contain nearly $250 billion in Kuwaiti assets. Egyptian participation was rewarded with a significant debt forgiveness—nearly $7 billion—in addition to the fact that Egypt had aspired without success to become chief regional mercenary in charge of protecting Gulf thrones. As for Syria, it was provided with a green light to subdue dissidents on all sides of the Lebanese conflict and promote the fledgling central government in Beirut under its own sovereignty. Having been denied strategic parity with Israel as a result of Soviet diminished influence, the war coalition against its arch enemy, Iraq, was seen as the alternate route that would yield money and political power.

Others like the USSR, China, Turkey, and Ethiopia were rewarded with loans, protection from human rights scrutiny, and intercession with the European community. The single ally, however, who received a price for *non-participation* was Israel. In addition to U.S. aid at the level of $13 million per day, it was promised the following: debt cancellation, a compensation for destruction supposedly due to Iraqi scud missile attacks in the amount of $650 million; emergency military aid in the amount of $700 million; ten F-15 Jets worth $65 million; and the pre-positioning of $300 worth of weapons which Israel could use in the event of war. The biggest item, however, was Israel's request for a $10 billion loan to provide housing for Soviet Jews settling in Palestine, which the Bush administration had initially held up for better diplomatic terms but finally released during the heat of presidential elections, which George Bush had lost anyway.

The New World Order is the sum total of all these deals, rearrangements, commitments and transactions which the U.S. manages under the rubric of international legitimacy, in accordance with a newly-interpreted international law. Saddam Hussein's first problem was an inability and unwillingness to comprehend the new rules of the game and to appreciate the consequences of challenging the precepts of this New World Order. The imperial borders of the late 19th and 20th century are regarded as sacrosanct; hence, a Kuwaiti district in a newly-defined Iraq was simply unacceptable. Hussein's second problem was his ambition to become the third Arab leader to assume responsibility for strategic parity vis-à-vis Israel. An independent and advanced Arab arsenal in the aftermath of the Soviet eclipse was simply taboo, particularly if it was going to involve production, adaptation and importation of parts for the local manufacture of weapons of destruction. It is one thing for a country like Iraq to import weapons from the capitalist West and help repair deficits in their balance of trade; it is quite another thing for Iraq, or any other ambitious Third World power for that matter, to aspire for independence in military technology and strategic planning. Thus, as long as Saddam Hussein was engaged in battling the Shah's successors in Iran, who were bent on challenging American primacy in the Gulf, the U.S. aided him economically and diplomatically and certified him as worthy of acquiring Western weapons and technology. The altered reality, however, was the emergence of Iraq from its war with Iran as an ambitious power with the capacity to develop weapons of mass destruction and the potential to appeal to Arab masses left without anchor for the restoration of the military balance with Israel, since the death of Jamal Abdul Nasser. Iraq was seen by the U.S. and the Zionist movement as a particularly more dangerous foe than Egypt of the 1960's and 70's or Syria of the 1980's. Hence the decision to go to war and to preempt every possible diplomatic means to settle the crisis short of all-out war.

That decision, in turn, has turned out to be the single most important factor, if not the real catalyst leading to the Madrid process and eventually to the Oslo-Cairo solutions which have yet to deliver the promised durable peace in the Middle East. The reluctance of the Arab states to participate in American military and diplomatic projects in the region, prevalent throughout the Cold War, had been diminished in the "New World Order" of Bush and Clinton.

Notes

1. "Public Enemy Number One" was the headline of a *Newsweek* story April 9, 1990 pp. 26-28. *U.S. News and World Report* (June 4, 1990) featured a cover story with a drawing of Saddam Hussein looking stern and devious. The caption read, "The Most Dangerous Man in the World." Another headline in the *New York Times* (April 3, 1990) read: "Iraq Can Deliver, U.S. Arms Chemical Experts Say." The *Washington Post* headlined "Iraq's Arsenal of Horror." *The Wall Street Journal* (April 23, 1990) headlined "Iraq's Buying Spree on Arms Bodes Ill for its Neighbors".

3

The Obstruction of Peace

United States Opposition to an International Peace Conference

Direct Negotiation versus International Settlement

During the past quarter of a century two approaches emerged for set-tling the Palestinian-Arab-Israeli conflict; a comprehensive settlement under international auspices and a "peace process" conducted under United States supervision. The two approaches remained dichotomous throughout the post-1967 war, in terms of both substance and proce-dure; and the unbridgeable gap continued to sustain an impasse until the end of the Gulf War. U.S. and allied victory in that war signaled the effective demise of the idea of an international conference called for in Resolution 338, after the October 1973 War and the consecration of U.S. diplomacy as the sole agent of an Arab-Israeli settlement. Not only had Secretary of State James Baker succeeded in replacing the inter-national conference with a "regional" parley, whose sole function was to legitimize the bilateral talks between Israel and the Arab states, but he also secured Soviet and Syrian acquiescence, which became possible as a result of the end of the Cold War and of the Gulf War, thereby eliminating any effective obstacle to the plan. This chapter will trace the rise and fall of the international approach to peacemaking in the region culminating in the apparent triumph of American unilateral-ism as the de facto approach for solving the Palestine question.

The mere fact that numerous international conferences have been held in the modern period to tackle global conflicts testifies to the util-ity of this concept as a viable means of conflict resolution.[1]

The Palestine question and its derivative, commonly referred to as the Arab-Israeli conflict, is one which is particularly suited to this method of conflict resolution. First, the problem itself was created by the imperialist powers during the inter-war period. It was later perpetuated and expanded to dangerous dimensions by the same powers of the post-World War II. The world community called for the creation of two states in Palestine, one of which (Israel) was realized in 1948, while the Palestinian Arab state was not. Thus the exercise of the right to self-determination by a primarily settler community, in a country whose indigenous people are still denied that right, is a problem whose resolution is necessarily an international responsibility. Secondly, this is a conflict in a highly strategic area of the world, in which two superpowers claimed vital interests throughout the Cold War period. Thus the people of the region, the Third World, and the big powers shared a common objective: the avoidance of an all-out world war in the nuclear age.

More specifically, numerous United Nations resolutions have called for a settlement. Even Resolution 242, which relegated Palestinian national rights to the sidelines, recognized a focal role for the world community by requesting the secretary general to designate a special representative who would report to the Security Council on his efforts towards promoting a settlement. Resolution 338 of October 22, 1973 called for negotiations "between the parties concerned under appropriate auspices aimed at establishing a just and durable peace in the Middle East." The result was the ill-fated largely ceremonious Geneva Conference, which met briefly in December 1973 and was never convened again. Eighteen years later, the Madrid Conference was convened under the auspices of the U.S. and the dying USSR. Its principal mission was to provide a semblance of an international character to a meeting which would launch bilateral negotiations on separate tracks between Israel and the Arab parties under U.S. auspices. It was clearly a vindication of the U.S.-Israeli approach, a victory for the obstruction of an international settlement.

The international approach to a Middle East settlement had been championed by the Soviet Union and the Arab States and supported by the great majority of Third World nations during the 1970s and 80s. Western Europe maintained a relatively independent position and largely distanced itself from its American ally, ie. Israel, by accepting the legitimacy of the Palestinian national movement and its leadership, the PLO, and by affirming the illegality of the 1967 occupation of Arab territories as well as continued Israeli colonization of these territories. This position was proclaimed by the Western European nations in the Venice Declaration of June 1980 and reaffirmed in subsequent statements and resolutions of various EC and later European Union (EU) forums. This approach envisioned an international framework with authority to shape a settlement in accord with recognized legal principles and accepted practices. These would include the inadmissibility of territorial acquisition by force, hence UN Security Council Resolutions 242 and 338; and equal rights for the Palestinian people in accordance with General Assembly Resolution 3236 of November 22, 1974, which established the rights of the Palestinian people to self-determination, national independence and sovereignty. That resolution also requested the UN secretary-general to establish contacts with the PLO on all matters concerning Palestine.

The international consensus, associated with this approach, embodied an historic compromise, based on the exchange of territory for peace. The Arab states and the Palestinians, through the PLO, would recognize the permanence of Israel within the 1967 borders, in return for the recognition of the right of the Palestinians to self-determination. Resolutions 242 and 338 were universally considered as the cornerstone of a proper settlement. This position was broadly accepted in the Arab world and gained endorsement of Arab summit conferences from Algiers and Rabat in 1973 and 1974, to Fez and Amman in 1982 and 1987. It received an implicit sanction from the 1977 Palestine National Council (PNC) session in Cairo, and an explicit acknowledgment from the 1988 PNC session in Algiers, which was made even more specific by PLO chairman Yasir Arafat's statements to the UN General Assembly session in Geneva, his subsequent press conference and the "Stockholm Document," all in December 1988.

The second approach also claimed UN Security Council Resolutions 242 and 338 as a foundation for a reasonable settlement, but endorsed the concept of direct bilateral negotiations between states in a step-by-step process, leading towards a comprehensive settlement. The exchange of territory for peace aspect of this approach remained unclear and seemed to allow a degree of territorial acquisition through negotiated agreement, inasmuch as Israel assumed the position that the resolution calls for withdrawal "from occupied Arab territories," and not from *the* occupied territories. The concept of direct negotiations was of course designed to allow Israel to avoid the international framework, which embodies UN resolutions calling on Israel to accommodate Palestinian rights. Those included the right of the Palestinian refugees to return to their homes and property, or to be compensated, as well as their right to establish an independent state under the General Assembly Partition Resolution 194 of November 29, 1947.

United States Opposition to an International Peace Conference

The diplomatic history of the Middle East for the past two decades reveals that five United States administrations adhered consistently to the second approach, thereby thwarting an international settlement. And yet, that undertaking, which shielded Israel from international scrutiny, succeeded only in permitting Israel to consolidate its occupation of Palestinian and other Arab territories. Israel was also able to escape accountability to the American body politic; it rejected every single U.S. initiative for a settlement, which involved territorial withdrawal from any part of Palestine, starting with the plan of Secretary of State William Rogers in 1969 and ending with that of George Shultz in 1988 and James Baker in 1990. And in between, it scuttled President Carter's 1977 initiatives, whose fate was sealed by Camp David, and the 1982 Reagan Plan, which emerged stillborn. The Baker initiative prior to the Gulf War was also rebuffed by Israel, causing the secretary of state to express his anger in public.

Throughout, the United States failed to sell Israel its own "peace process." Between 1967 and 1973, U.S. diplomacy succeeded in tipping the balance against the international consensus. While great international pressure was exerted to effect Israeli withdrawal from Arab land, the U.S. was engaged in a vast attempt to persuade Egypt to conclude a separate peace with Israel. The *quid pro quo* was Israeli withdrawal and Egyptian termination of belligerency. That endeavor, which remained at the heart of U.S. policy, was temporarily suspended when the pressure for a comprehensive solution began to mount in July 1969.

Between March 1969 and October 1973 various attempts were made to strengthen the United Nations and restore it as the framework for a settlement. The UN mediator, Ambassador Gunnar Jarring, was charged with preparing the grounds for implementation of Resolution 242. The "Big Four" talks, which were proposed by France in January 1969, were conceived as an added pillar for the Jarring mission. Israel's reaction to the involvement by the "Big Four" was swift and unambiguously hostile. It cautioned Washington about the spectre of an "imposed settlement," which would deny Israel the ability, as the victor, to impose a peace on the vanquished.[2] And while the U.S. went along with the "Big Four" talks in 1969, it insured that these talks remained perfunctory and would not evolve into an international peace conference. In fact the United States used the "Big Four" forum to advocate the Rhodes Formula, a form of direct negotiations favored by Israel.[3] That advocacy was invigorated in the aftermath of Israel's rejection of the Rogers Plan of December 1969, which called for a settlement based on the exchange of territory for peace in accordance with Resolution 242. Thus whatever ingredients of a comprehensive settlement the Rogers Plan might have contained were sacrificed at the altar of the U.S.-Israel special relationship. And whatever potential the "Big Four" talks had as a peace conference was rendered barren by a manipulative U.S. diplomacy.

While French president Charles de Gaulle envisioned the "Big Four" talks as the proper forum for a political settlement which would be guaranteed by a subsequent big power conference, President Richard Nixon and Henry Kissinger were determined not to allow these talks to succeed.[4] Nixon's memoirs reveal that he wanted the U.S., not the UN, to get credit for a Middle East settlement, and Seymour Hersh's account of Kissinger's tenure in Nixon's White House shows that Nixon and Kissinger's opposition to an Israeli withdrawal ordered by the UN or the "Big Four" stemmed from a real concern that such a withdrawal would appear as a victory for the U.S.S.R. or Arab leftists.[5] Both Moshe Dayan and Yitzhak Rabin's memoirs corroborate Hersh's conclusions that Nixon and Kissinger encouraged Israel to escalate the war of attrition in the Suez Canal area and to attack the Soviet anti-aircraft missiles deployed there in the aftermath of Israel's penetration bombing in 1970.[6] These efforts to thwart a comprehensive settlement and to frustrate an international solution were continued by Nixon and Kissinger until the October 1973 war.

The period between the October 1973 war and Carter's assumption of the presidency in 1977 witnessed a triumph of U.S. diplomacy in its endeavor to promote separate agreements away from the Palestine question and outside the UN framework. The Geneva Conference, which was held in December 1973 pursuant to Resolution 338, produced no substantive results, and none had been expected. Absent from the conference, which was convened by the UN secretary-general and chaired jointly by the U.S. and the U.S.S.R., were the other three permanent members of the Security Council and two principal parties to the conflict: Syria and the PLO. Syria's absence was dictated by policy disagreements, while the PLO was simply not invited.

Not unlike the previous "Big Four" talks, Geneva was not meant for any culmination of a comprehensive peace. Kissinger's manipulative diplomacy subordinated that goal to Washington's own objectives in the region. Kissinger's swift attempts to put together a meeting without any form of commitment from Israel on substantive issues and Sadat's proclivity to separate solutions, as well as his haste to move the tent from the Kilometer 101 (in Egypt) to Geneva, deprived the conference of its assigned mission and international character. Geneva, in effect, served as a smokescreen for Kissinger's "shuttle diplomacy." Kissinger used it as a cover for negotiating two troop disengagement accords between Egypt and Israel in January 1974 and September 1975. In his opening statement to the Conference on December 21, 1973, he said:

> I believe that the work of this conference should be to achieve early agreement on the separation of military forces.... [S]erious discussions have already taken place between the military representatives of Israel and Egypt at Kilometer 101.[7]

It is significant to note that the process of military discussions at Kilometer 101 culminated in an Israeli-Egyptian agreement, which was signed in Geneva by the Egyptian prime minister rather than the chief of staff.[8] His pledge to terminate the state of belligerency while Israel occupied most of Sinai, the Golan Heights, the West Bank and Gaza gave it the character of a separate peace, notwithstanding Kissinger's announcement that it was a step in the direction of a comprehensive solution.

Far from being a step towards a comprehensive peace, the September 1975 Sinai Accord was particularly harmful to the cause of peace. First, it came as a result of the resumption of Kissinger's step-by-step diplomacy, which was temporarily interrupted by President Gerald Ford's threatened reassessment in April 1975.[9] When Israel and its domestic U.S. lobby countered the president by mobilizing 76 U.S. senators against the policy recommendations to pursue a comprehensive settlement in Geneva, the administration was forced back in line, and a new momentum was created for exacting concessions from the White House. In return for withdrawing from a small portion of Egyptian territory, Israel obtained from the United States important concessions, three of which proved detrimental to a comprehensive settlement under international auspices. (1) The U.S. pledge against dealing with the PLO meant that the Palestine question can be treated, at best, as a territorial and security-related matter rather than as a national question which involves self-determination. (2) The pledge to coordinate with Israel in any Geneva talks gave Israel a virtual veto over U.S. policy in the Middle East. (3) The U.S. agreement that Arab-Israeli negotiations would be conducted on a bilateral basis was a formal endorsement of Israel's policy aiming to divide the Arab states and to maximize its goals at the expense of Palestinian rights.

U.S. efforts to deter the concept of an international peace conference were interrupted somewhat during President Carter's first nine months in office, but after the interlude it was business as usual. Initially, Carter attempted to revive the Geneva Conference in order to achieve a comprehensive settlement. Some of the Carter administration top policy advisors had been involved in drafting the Brookings Report of 1975, which called for a comprehensive solution based on Israeli withdrawal and Palestinian self-determination. The salient features of the Brookings Report were incorporated into Carter's approach from January until November 1977, when Anwar Sadat made his trip to Jerusalem, and derailed the Geneva train to Camp David. In a September news conference, President Jimmy Carter said that there could be no Middle East settlement unless there was "adequate Palestinian representation" at Geneva, and he expressed the view that the PLO represented a "substantial part" of the Palestinian people.[10]

President Carter's 1977 offensive was climaxed in the October 1, 1977 joint U.S.-U.S.S.R statement calling for a comprehensive political settlement in Geneva:

> The United States and the Soviet Union believe that the only right and effective way for achieving a fundamental solution to all aspects of the Middle East Problem in its entirety is negotiations within the framework of the Geneva Peace Conference, specially convened for those purposes, with participation in its work of the representatives of all the parties involved in the conflict including those of the Palestinian people....[11]

The reference to "legitimate rights" of the Palestinian people and its implication of a reactivated Soviet role provoked opposition from the U.S.-Israel lobby, right-wing political forces, and the governments of Menachem Begin and Anwar Sadat.[12] It took only four days to bring about the virtual nullification of the October 1 statement. Protracted negotiations between Israel's foreign minister, Moshe Dayan, and President Carter in New York produced a paper on October 5, 1977, which effectively accomplished that task. It drilled a crucial nail in the coffin of the Geneva Conference, while the Sadat visit to Jerusalem issued its death certificate. The Carter interlude was over, and since then Camp David remained at center stage of Middle East diplomacy. It signified the effective abandoning of the idea of an international peace conference and a corresponding ascendancy of the pursuit of separate deals under U.S. auspices. This phase was also characterized by the consolidation of the U.S.-Israel strategic alliance, which provided a green light for the Israeli invasion of Lebanon.

Neither the Arab proposal of August 1981, known as the Fahd Plan, nor the Brezhnev Plan of October 1981, swayed the U.S. towards an international approach.[13] The Fahd Plan envisaged a role for the UN Security Council and was supported by Britain and France. The Brezhnev Plan called for an expanded international peace conference that would include Western Europe, North Africa, and South Asia. A year later (on September 1, 1982), the United States proposed the Reagan Plan, again bypassing the United Nations, the Soviet Union, and Syria. Both the Arab Fez Plan and the Brezhnev Plan of

September 6 and 15, 1982, respectively, referred to a peace among all states in the region, including the independent Palestinian state that will be guaranteed by the Security Council or the big powers. But neither of these plans was put into effect. The United States prevented the international community from acting in accordance with the well-established global consensus, and was at the same time unable to implement its own separatist solutions, thus perpetuating the diplomatic paralysis, which it had caused in the first place.

United States obstruction of an international settlement persisted throughout the Reagan period and continued beyond it until the world finally accepted the Madrid Conference of 1991, which served as Washington's alternative to the universal notion of an international settlement. U.S. opposition continued even after Jordan and the PLO reached an accord on February 11, 1985 to accommodate the Reagan Plan which called for a settlement based on Jordanian sovereignty in the West Bank and Gaza.[14] Secretary of State Shultz's first reaction to the accord was couched in the form of questions: Will it lead to direct talks between Israel and a Jordanian-Palestinian delegation? Will the Arabs insist on a broad international conference?[15]

Let us examine the status of an international conference in the Amman framework. Title I of that framework agreement stipulates that:

> ...peace negotiations will take place under the umbrella of an international conference with the participation of the five permanent members of the UN Security Council, and all other parties to the conflict, including the PLO, the sole legitimate representative of the Palestinian people....

Surely Jordan and the PLO were not expecting a sudden change of heart in Washington and Tel Aviv, where opposition to an international solution remained vehement and was unlikely to vanish. Indeed, the available evidence shows that the commitment of Jordan and Egypt to an international conference was never serious, it was a cover for direct negotiations. Neither King Hussein nor President Hosni Mubarak, however, wanted to be accused of "pulling a Sadat." Reiterating their public commitment was part of the ritual, which continued until the Gulf War. King Hussein had already watered down the real meaning of an international conference when he addressed the 17th Palestine National Council in October 1984. His foreign minister also expressed the view that although his government supported that concept, it had no objection to a revival of the Reagan Plan.[16] At the same time, Egypt's foreign minister revealed that his government did not regard the international conference method as the only forum for pursuing peace, nor did it regard such an international conference as incompatible with Camp David.[17] President Mubarak stated in his initiative of February 24, 1985 that "The international conference could be the last stage...as a blessing of the solution."[18] And later King Hussein echoed: "We need the international umbrella to offer us the opportunity to negotiate."[19]

It was small wonder then that Washington seemed to be paying special attention to finding a face-saving formula which would permit some sort of international ratification of whatever might have been agreed in *direct* negotiations between Israel and Jordan, with Palestinian participation.

Far from being the "framework" for negotiations envisaged in the joint communiqué of October 1, 1977, this conference was to be limited to endorsing the direct talks which Israel had relentlessly demanded in the face of consistent international and Arab opposition. United States distortion of the concept of a Geneva Conference was best expressed in the search for what Secretary of State George Shultz described as a "supportive international context."[20] That would translate to a United Nations-sponsored meeting at the request of Israel and Jordan for the explicit purpose of implementing UN Resolutions 242 and 338 in direct negotiations. Had the secretary-general refused to allow the world organization to be used as an instrument of U.S. diplomacy, the United States and Egypt would have been willing to host such a meeting.[21]

Despite all that, Israeli compliance was not even assured. Speaking in Washington on June 3, 1985 Defense Minister Yitzhak Rabin expressed anxiety about the use of the term "international umbrella" by officials in the Reagan administration, which he said was "contradictory to our common experience, of Israel, the United States, and I also think Egypt in the last 12 years."[22]

As for the possible inclusion of the Soviet Union in Secretary Shultz's "supportive international context," the State Department placed conditions, which the Soviets found impossible to meet. These were:

1. Resumption of full diplomatic relations with Israel.
2. Ending "anti-Semitic" propaganda.
3. Improved treatment of and more emigration visas for Soviet Jews.
4. Soviet pressure on its "clients" to reduce arms supplies to Iran.
5. "Desisting from efforts to obstruct positive moves toward expanding the peace process in the region."[23]

Rejecting this concept of "one side setting preconditions for the other to meet," the Soviet government renewed its commitment to establishing working contacts with the United States to prepare for a Geneva-style conference.[24] Foreign Minister Andrei Gromyko made it clear to King Hussein that his government wanted to "co-sponsor" an international conference with the United States rather than simply participate as a member of the UN Security Council.[25]

Setting impossible conditions which the Soviet Union could not meet and remain a superpower was part of the obstruction of a diplomatic settlement on terms acceptable to the world community.

The Price of Strategic Alliance

The formalization of the strategic relationship between the United States and Israel (discussed in the next chapter) constituted an important restraint on the former's ability to view the Middle East in terms other than strategic terms. The frequently mentioned phrase "peace process" has been nothing more than a reference to Washington's search for comprehensive security in the geo-strategic sense of the term. Whatever the degree of merit the Palestinian cause had in the eyes of the U.S. establishment, it was always peripheral to the strategic considerations of U.S. policy, defined in Cold War terms.

Israel was, therefore, allowed to make a mockery of the global consensus, to escape the international scrutiny and to eventually substitute its own framework of bilateral agreement for the multilateral approach. International legality, defined in terms of United Nations resolutions, had been vigorously and steadily undermined during the 1970s and 80s until it was finally rendered ineffectual.

The two decades since the October 1973 war witnessed the emergence of the United States as the defacto superpower of the region, its principal custodian and sole arbiter of peace. Unlike other regions of the world, the Middle East was deprived of the natural and inevitable competition between the two superpowers, and Israel took the credit for the strategic coup and expected to reap the benefits. The suspension of real peace in the Middle East was the price of unilateralism.

That was the crux of U.S. opposition to the concept of an international peace conference, which would have had to include not only opponents of the U.S. global strategy, but its principal target as well, the Soviet Union. The more the United States continued to promote itself as the sole legitimate conciliator in the Middle East, and as long as a growing number of Arab interests acquiesced in that role, the more the U.S.S.R., Syria and other indigenous forces coalesced behind an international settlement. The plans which the United States offered as substitutes for an international conference created a facade of diplomacy, which provided Israel with time and a cover to divide, conquer, and flaunt the global consensus. The resultant diplomatic perversion, described as a "peace process," rendered the concept of an international peace conference to the periphery, while the United States posed as collaborator, judge, and prosecutor.

United States opposition to an international conference on the Middle East remained persistent, vigorous, and unambiguous since the 1967 war. It differed from Israel's opposition only in style, but not in substance. America's diplomatic enterprises, starting with the Rogers Plan, and including Kissinger's "shuttle diplomacy," Camp David, the Reagan Plan and its derivatives, succeeded in keeping an international solution a distance away; yet they have not brought the Palestine-Israel conflict closer to a settlement. Only when the PLO decided that it ran out of options, after the Gulf War and the collapse of communism in the Soviet Union and Eastern Europe, did a settlement emerge. It was not, however, the kind of settlement that guaranteed Palestinian self-determination and insured co-existence in mutuality, equality and reciprocity. The peace process was reduced, in effect, to an exclusive American undertaking, and eventually the correlation of forces resulted in the triumph of American unilateralism, and the consequent marginalization of Palestinian rights. That was Israel's price for strategic alliance.

Notes

1. The cities of Geneva, Vienna, and Paris, among other major world centers were the scenes of international peace conferences which followed major world conflicts. The Congress of Vienna followed the great Napoleonic wars; the Versailles peace conference followed the First World War; Yalta, Potsdam, and San Francisco were among the many conferences on Korea, Indochina, the "Big Four" Spirit of Geneva summit, and the Berlin question before the convening of the first peace conference on the Middle East, in 1973.

2. Israeli Foreign Minister Abba Eban expressed that concern in Washington during a March 1969 visit and tried to persuade President Nixon and Secretary of State William Rogers to abandon the talks. See Leila S. Kadi, *The Arab-Israeli Conflict: The Peaceful Proposals 1948–1972* (Beirut: NEE-BIL, 1973), p. 68.

3. The Israeli Cabinet's statement declared:
   Israel entirely opposes the plan to convene the representatives of states which lie outside the Middle East in order to prepare recommendations concerning the region. Such a procedure undermines the responsibility devolving on the States of the region to attain peace among themselves. Kadi, p. 68.

4. For an analysis of French policy towards the Middle East after the 1967 war, see Naseer Aruri and Natalie Hevener, "France And the Middle East, 1967–1968," *The Middle East Journal* (Autumn 1969) pp. 484–502.

5. Seymour Hersh. *The Price of Power: Kissinger in the Nixon White House* (New York: Summit Books, 1983), pp. 216–217; also see *The Memoirs of Richard Nixon* (New York: Grosset & Dunlop, 1978) and the two volumes of Kissinger's memoirs, *The White House Years* (Boston: Little Brown, 1979) and *Years of Upheaval* (Boston: Little Brown, 1982).

6. *The Rabin Memoirs* (Boston: Little Brown, 1979).

7. Department of State, *U.S. Policy in the Middle East, Dec. 1973–Nov. 1974.* Special Report No. 12 (Washington: Bureau of Public Affairs, 1975), p. 12.

8. The September 1975 Sinai Accord (second disengagement agreement) was signed by Mamduh Salem at Sadat's request. See Ismail Fahmy, *Negotiating for Peace in the Middle East* (Baltimore: The Johns Hopkins University Press, 1983), pp. 163–166.

9. President Ford's "reassessment" was based on recommendations by Averill Harriman, Cyrus Vance, Dean Rusk, George Ball, and William Scranton. Most of them recommended a U.S. policy based on the pursuit of a comprehensive settlement at an international Geneva Conference.

    See also Cyrus Vance, *Hard Choices: Critical Years in America's Foreign Policy* (New York: Simon & Schuster, 1983); Ismail Fahmy's memoirs cited above, and Mahmoud Riad, *The Struggle for Peace in the Middle East* (London: Quartet Books, 1981).

10. *Department of State Bulletin,* October 31, 1977, p. 585.

    See Cyrus Vance, cited above; Ismail Fahmy's memoirs cited above, and Mahmoud Riad, cited above.

11. *Ibid.,* November 7, 1977, pp. 639–640.

12. *New York Times,* October 2, 1977.

13. *Washington Post,* August 9, 1981; *New York Times,* October 28, 1981.

14. See Naseer Aruri, "The PLO And The Jordan Option," *Third World Quarterly,* Vol. 7, No. 4 (October 1985), pp. 882–906.

15. *New York Times,* February 15, 1985.

16. *New York Times,* December 2, 1984.

17. *Ibid.,* December 7, 1985.

18. *Ibid,* February 25, 1985.

19. *Christian Science Monitor,* May 30, 1985.

20. *Boston Globe,* May 31, 1985.

21. See William Beecher, "Three Forums Reported Considered for Mideast Talks," *Boston Globe,* October 4, 1985.

22. David Ottoway, "Israeli Opposes 'Umbrella Parley,'" *Washington Post,* June 4, 1985.

23. *Boston Globe,* May 31, 1985.

24. *Washington Post,* June 8, 1985.

25. *Ibid.*

4

The Special Relationship and Strategic Alliance During and After the Cold War

The preceding chapters have shown that U.S.-Israeli relations are an important part of U.S. policy in the Middle East. Both the executive and legislative branches of the U.S. government have placed considerable emphasis on the maintenance of an amicable and supportive relationship. The principal instrument for expressing support for Israeli policies, much of which has been at variance with the global consensus, has been U.S. foreign aid. Israel has not been economically self-sufficient, and has relied upon U.S. aid, German reparation payments and Arab resources, plundered through military conquests (land, water and labor) to maintain its economy.

U.S. aid to Israel since 1949 has totaled about $79 billion. This figure does not included an invisible amount of "side benefits", which accrues to Israel annually from various projects and sources in the United States. According to a congressional research report, "it is estimated that Israel receives about $1 billion annually through philanthropy [United Jewish Appeal and other tax-deductible funds], an equal amount through short-and long-term commercial loans, and about $500 million or more in Israel Bonds proceeds."[1]

Since 1976, Israel has been the largest annual recipient of U.S. foreign assistance and it is the largest recipient on cumulative basis. From 1949 through 1965, U.S. aid to Israel averaged about $63 million per year.[2] It increased to an average of $102 million annually between 1966 and 1970, and then jumped to about $1 billion annually during the next five years. From 1976 to 1984, it averaged about $2.5 billion, then with the upgrading of the special relationship to a strategic alliance during the Reagan period, U.S. aid began to escalate reaching to more that $5 billion annually at present, over one-third of the total U.S. foreign aid.

Economic aid to Israel was changed to "forgiven loans," i.e., all grant

Table 1. U.S. Assistance to Israel,
FY1949 - FY1989 (millions of dollars)

Year Grant	Total	Military		Economic		Food for Peace	
		Loan	Grant	Loan	Grant	Loan	Grant
1949	100	-	-	-	-	-	
1950	-	-	-	-	-	-	
1951	35.1	-	-	-	0.1	-	-
1952	86.4	-	-	-	63.7	-	22.7
1953	73.6	-	-	-	73.6	-	*
1954	74.7	-	-	-	54.0	-	20.7
1955	52.7	-	-	20.0	21.5	10.8	0.4
1956	50.8	-	-	10.0	14.0	25.2	1.6
1957	40.9	-	-	10.0	16.8	11.8	2.3
1958	85.4	-	-	15.0	9.0	34.9	2.3
1959	53.3	0.4	-	10.0	9.2	29.0	1.7
1960	56.2	0.5	-	15.0	8.9	26.8	4.5
1961	77.9	*	-	16.0	8.5	13.8	9.8
1962	93.4	13.2	-	45.0	0.4	18.5	6.8
1963	87.9	13.3	-	45.0	-	12.4	6.0
1964	37.0	-	-	20.0	-	12.2	4.8
1965	65.1	12.9	-	20.0	-	23.9	4.9
1966	126.8	90.0	-	10.0	-	25.9	0.9
1967	23.7	7.0	-	5.5	-	-	0.6
1968	106.5	25.0	-	-	-	51.3	0.5
1969	160.3	85.0	-	-	-	36.1	0.6
1970	93.6	30.0	-	-	--	40.7	0.4
1971	634.3	545.0	-	-	-	55.5	0.3
1972	480.9	300.0	-	-	50.0	53.8	0.4
1973	492.8	307.5	-	-	50.0	59.4	0.4
1974	2,646.3	982.7	1,500.0	-	50.0	-	1.5
1975	803.0	200.0	100.0	-	344.5	8.6	-
1976	2,362.7	750.0	750.0	225.0	475.0	14.4	*
TQ	292.5	100.0	100.0	25.0	50.0	3.6	-
1977	1,787.5	500.0	500.0	245.0	490.0	7.0	-
1978	1,822.6	500.0	500.0	260.0	525.0	6.8	-
1979	4,913.0	2,700.0	1,300.0	260.0	525.0	5.1	-
1980	2,146.0	500.0	500.0	260.0	525.0	1.0	-
1981	2,408.4	900.0	500.0	-	764.0	-	-
1982	2,245.5	850.0	550.0	-	806.0	-	-
1983	2,500.6	950.0	750.0	-	785.0	-	-
1984	2,626.6	850.0	850.0	-	910.0	-	-
1985	3,371.7	-	1,400.0	-	1,950.0	-	-
1986	3,658.5	-	1,722.6	-	1,898.4	-	-
1987	3,035.2	-	1,800.0	-	1,200.0	-	-
1988	3,034.9	-	1,800.0	-	1,200.0	-	-
1989	3,039.9	-	1,800.0	-	1,200.0	-	-
1990	3,428.0	-	1,792.3	-	1,194.8	-	-
Total	49,312.2	11,212.5	18,214.9	1,516.5	15,272.4	588.5	94.1

- = None; * = less than $100,000; TQ = Transition Quarter, when U.S. fiscal year changed from June to September. Clyde Mark, see footnote 1.

Table 1. Continued. U.S. Assistance to Israel, FY1949 - FY1989 (millions of dollars)

Year	Export-Import Bank Loan	Jewish Refugee Resettle Grant	Housing Loan Guaranty	American Schools & Hospitals Grant	Other Loan	Other Grant
1949	100	-	-	-	-	-
1950	-	-	-	-	-	-
1951	35.0	-	-	-	-	-
1952	-	-	-	-	-	-
1953	-	-	-	-	-	-
1954	-	-	-	-	-	-
1955	-	-	-	-	-	-
1956	-	-	-	-	-	-
1957	-	-	-	-	-	-
1958	24.2	-	-	-	-	-
1959	3.0	-	-	-	-	-
1960	0.5	-	-	-	-	-
1961	29.8	-	-	-	-	-
1962	9.5	-	-	-	-	-
1963	11.2	-	-	-	-	-
1964	-	-	-	-	-	-
1965	3.4	-	-	-	-	-
1966	-	-	-	-	-	-
1967	9.6	-	-	1.0	-	-
1968	23.7	-	-	6.0	-	-
1969	38.6	-	-	-	-	-
1970	10.0	-	-	12.5	-	-
1971	31.0	-	-	2.5	-	-
1972	21.1	-	50.0	5.6	-	-
1973	21.1	50.0	-	4.4	-	-
1974	47.3	36.5	25.0	3.3	-	-
1975	62.4	40.0	25.0	2.5	-	20.0 Desalt Plant
1976	104.7	15.0	25.0	3.6	-	-
TQ	12.6	-	-	1.3	-	-
1977	0.9	15.0	25.0	4.6	-	-
1978	5.4	20.0	-	5.4	-	-
1979	68.7	25.0	25.0	4.2	-	-
1980	305.9	25.0	25.0	4.1	-	-
1981	217.4	25.0	-	2.0	-	-
1982	6.5	12.5	-	3.0	17.5	- CCC Loan
1983	-	12.5	-	3.1	-	-
1984	-	12.5	-	4.1	-	-
1985	-	15.0	-	4.7	-	2.0 Coop. Aid
1986	15.0	12.0	-	5.5	-	5.0 Coop Aid
1987	-	25.0	-	5.2	-	5.0 Coop. Aid
1988	-	25.0	-	4.9	-	5.0 Coop. Aid
1989	-	28.0	-	6.9	-	5.0 Coop. Aid
1990	-	29.9	400.0	3.5	-	7.5 Coop. Aid
Total	**1,218.5**	**423.9**	**600.0**	**103.9**	**17.5**	**49.5**

cash transfer in 1981, and military aid became all grants in 1985.[3] Moreover, U.S. aid to Israel is made available in lump sum every October in order to allow Israel to invest the funds in interest bearing U.S. Government securities. According to the previously mentioned congressional research report, "Israel also receives $700 million in defense articles to be withdrawn from Europe...$650 million in emergency ESF grants, a $400 million loan guarantee for housing for Soviet refugees, a grant of $7.5 for its foreign assistance program, a $45 million grant for refugee settlement, and shares a $7.5 million program with Egypt for cooperative development programs to promote the Egyptian-Israeli treaty." In addition, the Clinton administration decided in October 1994 to compensate Israel for "redeployment costs" from Gaza and Jericho in the amount of $95 million. That amount was deducted from the $311.8 million settlement penalty, which Rabin's government had agreed to in its accord with George Bush on loan guarantees in August 1992.

The recent twelve-year period of Republican rule witnessed a phenomenal expansion of the special relationship between the U.S. and Israel. That relationship which developed into a strategic alliance was nurtured and upgraded by Clinton, the first president ever to involve the pro-Israel lobby in actual Middle East policy-making. It was consolidated during this period in such a way that no disagreements between the two countries would stand in its way. Only when a conflict related to what Washington perceived as the national interest, expressed in Cold War terms, would the U.S. prevail. Perhaps the 1981 disagreement over the sale of AWACs to Saudi Arabia was the only such example. Otherwise the special relationship shielded Israel from the token condemnation reserved for friendly states, when egregious violations of United States law and international law were involved. Such violations occurred during the Reagan, Bush and Clinton presidencies but they failed to have any adverse effect whatsoever on the special relationship. In fact, the relationship continued to thrive in spite of the violations, and Washington almost always yielded to Israel, no matter how acrimonious these disagreements became.

Between June 7 and July 22, 1981, Israel crossed the borders of four sovereign Arab states and bombed the capitals of two states, causing severe devastation and numerous casualties. The raids on the Iraqi nuclear facility in Baghdad and the residential sections of Beirut as well as the bombardment of the Lebanese coast from Tyre to Damur were carried out by sophisticated American weapons including the F-16.

The principal issues during the Bush presidency were the controversy over loan guarantees to Israel and Prime Minister Shamir's renunciation of his own plan for a Palestinian-Israeli settlement. With Clinton in the White House controversies ceased; Israel tested the special relationship/strategic alliance with the deportation of 400 Palestinians to Lebanon, the closure of Jerusalem and the four-day savage bombardment of Lebanon in March 1993. No protests this time were voiced by Clinton and Secretary of State Christopher, making Bush and Baker, in retrospect, look like the bad boys who kept Israel under check.

Three administrations endeavored consistently to promote the special relationship. The renewed Cold War under Reagan proved to be a fertile environment for its growth, and yet the progress was not impeded by its close or the demise of the Soviet Union.

This chapter will trace the evolution of the special relationship since the Reagan period and will examine the major issues which affected it or were affected by it.

Reagan and the Special Relationship

The evolving strategic alliance, which thwarted the twin objective of the U.S. policy (comprehensive security and comprehensive peace), was particularly enhanced by President Reagan's anti-communist inclinations, his launching of a new Cold War, and his perception of Israel as a "unique strategic asset." Both Reagan and Haig considered Israel as a strategic asset of considerable if not unique significance. It should be recalled that Israel's victory in 1967 spared the United States the trouble of direct intervention to contain the Nasser phenomenon (Arab nationalism, Arab unity, and Arab socialism), which was deemed a threat to U.S. corporate and strategic interests. Lyndon Johnson's memoirs reveal U.S. gratitude for the Israeli victory; similar gratitude was expressed by Reagan during an interview with U.S. journalists on February 2, 1981:

Not only do we have a moral commitment to Israel, [but] being a country sharing our same ideals, our democratic approach to things with a combat-experienced military, [Israel] is a force in the Middle East that actually is a benefit to us. If there were not Israel with that force, we'd have to supply that with our own, so this isn't just altruism on our part....[4]

In fact, after the fall of the Shah, Reagan dismissed the Arab regimes in the Gulf as "weak and vulnerable" asserting that Israel was "perhaps the only strategic asset in the area that the United States can really rely on."[5] Despite their abundant resources, America's Arab allies were viewed as unreliable. They, unlike Israel, were dependent upon U.S. military personnel to keep their military establishments functioning, and on U.S. intelligence to safeguard the stability of their regimes. In his press conference on October 1, 1981, Reagan reaffirmed Carter's pledge to defend Saudi Arabia against outside threats and expanded the Carter Doctrine to cover internal threats as well. No similar worries seemed to have existed with regard to Israel, which merely required the margin of military and technological superiority that had been pledged earlier by Nixon. Reagan's Secretary of State Haig reiterated that guarantee on September 17, 1981, "We are determined to maintain the qualitative edge that is vital to Israel's security."[6] But in the American view, Israel's security and the security of Saudi Arabia were intertwined and linked within the framework of Haig's consensus of strategic concerns.

Israel, however, seemed unconvinced about the efficacy of such linkage. It reminded Reagan during the controversy over the sale of AWACs to Saudi Arabia that Washington's expectation of an interventionary role for Israel might be impaired by the U.S. supply of sophisticated aircraft and weapons systems to Saudi Arabia. But Reagan made sure that the AWACs' capabilities were sufficiently limited to render this argument invalid. He and his staff argued that, far from undermining Israel's security, the sale of AWACs to Saudi Arabia would enhance that security. On October 1, 1981, Secretary Haig told the Senate Foreign Relations Committee:

President Reagan would not have authorized this sale if he believed that it would jeopardize Israel's security. On the contrary, we believe that the risks for Israel are greater if U.S.-Saudi cooperation is disrupted and Saudi Arabia is left insecure or forced to turn elsewhere for equipment.[7]

The same point had already been made by Joseph W. Twinam, Deputy Assistant Secretary for Near Eastern and South Asian Affairs, on September 25, 1981. With regard to the implications of the sales for Israeli security, he said:

Israel enjoys today—and will continue to enjoy after our proposed sales are completed—so decisive a superiority over any combination of regional forces that the practical impact of our proposals [to sell AWACs] on Israeli security would be small.

Twinam went on to describe the efficacy of the particular brand of AWACs planes to be supplied to Saudi Arabia, and left no doubt that, militarily, it left much to be desired:

Contrary to claims, the AWACs cannot collect photographic intelligence. Nor can it collect any intelligence at all on ground targets. The only information it collects is the most perishable kind—aircraft tracks which become useless in a matter of minutes…neither do they have any offensive capacity that could jeopardize Israeli security…it would not significantly improve Saudi ability to assist other Arab nations to do so.[8]

Any remaining doubt about the military value of the AWACS supplied to Saudi Arabia was dispelled by Secretary Haig, who analyzed the Saudi agreement in view of standard arms sales agreements before the Senate Foreign Relations Committee on October 5, 1981. The list of restrictions effectively rendered Saudi sovereignty questionable: no flights outside Saudi borders; U.S. approval of security plans; U.S. inspection; continued U.S. Government ownership of computer software; data exchange only with the United States; and restricted access to equipment and maintenance, etc.[9]

The AWACs affair was, therefore, more a political than a military issue symbolizing the broadening of the strategic consensus. In fact U.S.

arms sales to the Arab world subsequent to that controversy failed to make even the smallest dent in the military balance. Reagan and his two successors were committed to the imbalance in favor of Israel.

Strategic Cooperation

Reagan's adherence to the concept of a special relationship between the United States and Israel was confirmed in an August 15, 1979 *Washington Post* article that he wrote as a presidential candidate. There, he delineated his perception of the Israeli role in U.S. strategy for the region after the downfall of the Shah. Having dismissed the Arab regimes in the Gulf region as "weak and vulnerable," he proceeded to outline his expectations of Israel in three fields of services:

1. Exchange of intelligence;
2. Utilization of the Israeli infrastructure and technological expertise and services;
3. Israeli participation even outside its frontiers in the event of a crisis involving the Soviet Union.

With regard to intelligence, Israel was already sharing information with the United States on Soviet armaments and military technology obtained in the several wars with the Arabs. Moreover, cooperation between the renowned Israeli intelligence services, including the terrorist Mossad, and U.S. intelligence was an ongoing phenomenon.

Utilization of the Israeli infrastructure enabled U.S. military forces in the area to have access to spare parts, repair facilities, and local production. The United States was able to establish in Israel emergency depots run by the Israeli army, a mutually advantageous arrangement since it relieved Israel of a large portion of the cost of maintaining expensive weapons.

In the third area, Reagan wanted to count on Israel's capacity for direct military intervention, and as previously stated, he rebutted charges that the Saudi AWACs would undermine that prospect. Reagan's ideas as expressed in his *Washington Post* article seemed to have contributed to the framework for the U.S.-Israeli agreement on strategic cooperation announced during Menachem Begin's visit to the United States in September 1981, and concluded by the two governments on November 30, 1981. The text of the Memorandum of Understanding (MOU) signed by Israeli Defense Minister Ariel Sharon and U.S. Secretary of Defense Caspar Weinberger revealed their resolve to strengthen strategic cooperation against "threats" to the Middle East "caused by the Soviet Union or Soviet-controlled forces from outside the region." The recognition of a region-wide police role for Israel was formalized in a provision that stipulated the need for the two countries "to provide each other military assistance to cope with threats to the security of the entire region." This need corresponded with Reagan's third expectation, as delineated in 1979, of U.S.-Israeli participation in any crisis involving the Soviet Union.

With regard to his second expectation, i.e., utilization of the Israeli infrastructure, the agreement was not as clear, although it did make reference to cooperation for the establishment and maintenance of "joint readiness activities as agreed upon by the parties." Israel's defense minister Sharon revealed to reporters that the "parties" had agreed upon certain secret clauses.

The November 1981 agreement was followed by yet another agreement on strategic cooperation in November1983 which, together with the June 1985 of the Free Trade Agreement, institutionalized the strategic relationship. The turmoil in Lebanon encouraged the U.S. and Israel to strengthen their ongoing strategic cooperation. In November 1983, President Reagan and Prime Minister Shaniu announced the formation of a joint political-military committee and the implementation of the provisions of the 1981 Memorandum of Understanding. That was followed by joint military exercises in June 1984 and the construction of facilities for stockpiling in Israel. The strategic relationship was reconfirmed and enhanced by yet another agreement signed by the two countries on May 6,1986, which provided for Israeli participation in the Strategic Defense Initiative—Reagan's "Star Wars" project. Israel was awarded the sum of $150 million annually to develop the "Arrow" anti-ballistic missile, under that project. Also, by 1985, U.S. economic and military aid in the form of loans was accordingly converted to outright grants, and was no longer earmarked for special projects.

The elevation and institutionalization of the strategic relationship was used by Israel as a protective shield against international criticism of its violation of international law and as a green light in the face of any misgivings by the U.S. media or public opinion. In the case of the June 1981 Israeli raids on Lebanon, the Reagan administration did not condemn the raid but contented itself with issuing a declaration deploring "all acts of violence," and expressing the usual regret for the civilian casualties adding, however, in deference to the Israeli position, that Israel had been under rocket attacks.

While a great deal was heard from President Reagan and Secretary of State Haig about the need to combat "international terrorism," nothing was ever said about the need to combat terrorism at the level of state policy.[10] In fact the U.S. was supplying and financing Israeli aggression against civilians and providing Israel with a political cover. And yet, under the 1952 Israeli-U.S. Mutual Defense Assistance Agreement, the use of U.S. arms is prohibited in any "acts of aggression against any other state."

By 1985, the strategic alliance had become so strong that U.S. assistance to Israel was no longer dependent upon Israeli willingness to meet Washington's standards or conditions. The suspension of the November 1981 agreement in December 1981, following Israel's unilateral annexation of the occupied Golan Heights, was a form of tokenism not to be repeated. Despite the presumed suspension, the Associated Press reported that the Reagan administration secretly notified Congress of plans to "sell" Israel an additional 75 F-16 fighters for more than $2.5 billion, the biggest arms deal with Israel in four years.[11]

This was arranged just in time for the visit of Israeli Defense Minister, Ariel Sharon, to Washington on May 26, 1982, hardly a week before his troops marched on Beirut with U.S. weapons and diplomatic cover. On the first day of the Israeli invasion of Lebanon, Secretary Haig expressed a measure of identification with Israel when he told reporters "We not only lost an aircraft and a helicopter yesterday, there is a claim that a second aircraft has been shot down...."[12] Even if the "we" was a slip of the tongue, the identification with Israel was readily expressed in the U.S. diplomatic cover, which consisted initially of a U.S. veto of a Security Council resolution calling for Israeli withdrawal and threatening economic sanctions against Israel. As the invasion swept through Lebanon, Reagan and his top aides employed the kind of rhetoric designed to give Israel comfort and confidence by citing the much too familiar phrase of "legitimate self-defense." The contrast between President Carter's attitude during the 1978 Israeli invasion of Lebanon and that of Reagan was indeed very striking. While in 1978 Carter supported his call for Israeli withdrawal with a threat to invoke the Arms Export Control act of 1976 against the offensive use of American weaponry, Reagan's spokesmen cast doubt on the offensive nature of the 1982 Israeli invasion.[13] Israeli and U.S. expectations for the future of Lebanon coincide to such an extent that they are almost indistinguishable.

It was also in the context of this special relationship that the U.S. underwriting of the Israeli occupation of Palestine and other Arab areas must be explained. Occupation means repression, collective punishment, deportation of dissidents, demolition of houses, closing of universities, exploitation of labor and resources, subjugation, and torture of prisoners. The Israeli occupation has meant all of these things with added new dimensions: colonization, atomization of the indigenous society, and de facto annexation. By destroying Palestinian institutions in the West Bank and Gaza, and by attempting to do likewise in Lebanon, Israel was hoping to preempt the formation of a Palestinian state. Lebanon was the principal base of the social, political and military infrastructure of this state-in-waiting, while the West Bank and Gaza were its logical site. The Israeli objective in both areas was undoubtedly in accordance with current U.S. policy. U.S. support for the invasion of Lebanon must be understood in that context of blocking Palestinian statehood. U.S. adherence to that goal remained consistent until the present, as later discussion of the Madrid formula in 1991, Oslo (1993) and the Cairo Agreement of 1994 will reveal.

Not only had Israel's benefactor and partner tolerated violations of international law in the West Bank and Lebanon, but subsidizing Israel's illegal projects, either directly or indirectly, the United States became an accomplice. In fact, by stating publicly that Israeli settlements were "not illegal," Mr. Reagan encouraged and promoted Israeli expansionism and set a dangerous precedent for future U.S. policy towards the occupation itself. It was Israeli's reward for its special role in the U.S. regional strategy for the Middle East.

It can be argued that the more intense the cold war had grown with the Soviet Union, the more committed the United States became toward Israel—and, consequently, the less vulnerable Israel was to U.S. pressure. As the pro-business lobby in the United States counseled even-handedness, in effect giving a boost to Saudi role in strategic calculations in the Middle East, the anti-Soviet militarists focused on Israel as the only reliable gendarme, particularly since the demise of the Shah and Anwar Sadat.[14] As long as the cold war took priority and the "threat" occupied center stage in U.S. foreign policy, Israel continued to be counted on to keep the balance in America's favor.

It is important to recognize the priority that the Reagan administration assigned to Israel's role in "comprehensive security," a fact well-known to Israel's leaders as well as to the American Jewish community. In a letter to the *New York Times* of December 24, 1981, for example, Ivan Novick, President of the Zionist Organization of America, echoed the sentiment of other Jewish leaders when he reminded President Reagan of his own dictum. Reagan had told Jewish leaders at a White House meeting in December 1981 that "Israel's military capability is of great value to the whole Western world.[15] Howard Squadron, chairman of the Conference of Presidents of Major Jewish Organizations, also stressed that the strategic cooperation agreement was a pact of "mutual defense" and "not a favor to Israel." He said that suspending it "will not help defend the cause of freedom in the Middle East, nor will it advance our country's strategic interests." Rather, he said, it will "weaken America's ability to deter and respond to the Soviets."[16] The same cold war emphasis characterized the Anti-Defamation League's reaction. In the words of Maxwell Greenberg, its national chairman, "Let us remember who opposes [U.S.] interests and supports [U.S.] interests...only then will we be able to take appropriate action in the region."[17]

Put in these terms and in a cold war context, there was little that the anti-Soviet President Reagan could do. After all, he could not treat Israel, his chief gendarme against the Soviet Union, as a "vassal state" and a "banana republic," or a "14-year-old who...gets his wrist slapped" for misbehavior.[18] But if he himself were to misbehave, he would be accused of anti-Semitism and may have even risked losing support of the "large and free Jewish community of the United States," as Begin conveyed to the U.S. ambassador on December 20, 1981. It was a stark reminder that the special relationship was a two-way street, in which the client reserved the right to correct the "misconceptions" of the superpower and to critique its policies both on the regional and on the global levels. Ariel Sharon's harsh criticism of what he perceived as a soft and indecisive U.S. posture towards a crisis in Poland in December 1981 illustrates the point: "In the face of Soviet expansionism, they [the Americans] run around like blind men in a chimney."[19]

The Israeli annexation of the Golan Heights was yet another test administered by Menachem Begin to the special relationship with the United States; and, as measured by the U.S. response to the Israeli destruction of Iraq's nuclear reactor and the bombing of downtown Beirut, the special relationship withstood the test. As long as comprehensive security continued to take precedence over comprehensive peace, there was no reason to assume that Israel was going to be deterred from annexing the remaining part of Palestine.

The special relationship, transformed into strategic alliance, was further tested in the Spring of 1988, when Israel rejected the Shultz Plan calling for Palestinian elections and a transitional period of self-rule in the occupied territories to be followed by final status talks between Israel and the Palestinians. The plan was designed to diffuse the Palestinian uprising (the *Intifada*) and to reassert America's role as arbiter in the region. And yet, the American posture towards Israel, before and after the Shultz Plan, was one of excessive generosity. At the time that the Reagan administration was expressing concern about Israeli excesses in dealing with the insurrection(the *Intifada*) in the West Bank and Gaza, it granted Israel a debt relief of approximately $2 billion, and designated Israel a "major non-NATO ally of the United States," which gave Israel preferential treatment in bidding for military contracts and lower prices on U.S. defense equipment. Israel was thus given unique access to U.S. military technology and markets.

To further upgrade the strategic relationship, the two countries signed another agreement on September 8, 1989 providing for Israel's leasing of U.S. equipment and the propositioning of up to $100 million worth of U.S. military supplies in Israel.[20] The administration's request of $3.6 billion in military aid for Israel in fiscal 1989 represented an increase of $1.8 billion. Estimating that the increase matched the direct cost of putting down the Palestinian *Intifada* over a 12 month period, Donald Neff wrote in *Middle East International* that Israel was "already practically assured compensation for its direct costs even if the uprising lasts a full year."

Moreover, a Memorandum of Agreement, which was signed into law by President Reagan on April 21, 1988, after Shamir's rejection of the Shultz Plan, institutionalized the U.S. strategic relationship.[21] A State Department official expressed the dismay of the government officials who disagreed with Shultz's decision by saying that this grant of Shamir's request for the memorandum, "may be seen by his opponents [in Israel] as a reward for not being serious about the peace process." A senior Israeli official confirmed this by saying "it almost looks like Shultz gave him [Shamir] a reward for not cooperating."

By doing that, the Reagan administration had clearly deprived itself of important leverage. The decision to speed up delivery of 75 F-16 jet fighters to Israel, together with acceding to Israel's request for the institutionalization of the strategic relationship, were not linked to Israel's acceptance of the Shultz Plan. It was a sign of changing times and changing relationships, a long way from 1981, when the Reagan administration felt impelled to go through the motion of delaying jet fighter delivery to Israel because of its arbitrary and unilateral decision to annex the Golan Heights. Now, the strategic relationship was institutionalized and it took precedence over all aspects of U.S. policy towards the Arab-Israel conflict.

America's redefinition of the Middle East as a cold war arena, combined with a growing perception of Israel as a bastion against radicalism, manifested as a special relationship and a strategic alliance, has dictated a policy which has remained consistent with the Israeli perimeters of a political settlement. The assumption that Israel was a strategic asset for the United States, entrusted with the task of halting potential forces of change ranging from Nasserism and Palestinian nationalism to Islamic fundamentalism, has rendered the United States as partisan and collaborator rather than as an impartial mediator. The more U.S. policymakers were inclined towards that perception, the less favorable U.S. policy was towards the concept of a peace conference and a comprehensive settlement and the more insistent on direct negotiations and incremental solutions.

The strategic relationship between the U.S. and Israel accelerated the disenfranchisement of the Palestinians from the "peace process." The transformation of Israel from client to surrogate to strategic ally not only reflected the evolving American security policy in the region, but also hastened an ongoing marginalization of Palestinian rights in U.S. policy. By 1983, the Reagan administration had accepted the Israeli view that the Palestine question was not the principal cause of instability in the region. It became secondary, if not indeed tertiary. Henceforth, that issue would not be allowed to interfere in the special relationship between a superpower and its strategic ally.

As long as the anti-Soviet line dominated Washington, and as long as the cold war climate which produced the special relationship prevailed, Israel was insulated from the pressure for a territorial settlement with the Palestinians, and with Syria and Lebanon. Its utility in the U.S. global strategy continued to outweigh its obligations to peace in the region. Thus the persistence of the untenable (from the Arab and Palestinian vantage point) no war-no peace status-quo during the 1980s was linked to heightened conflict in the world and to the intensification of the Cold War under Reagan. But by the same token, the urgency for reconsideration of that status-quo was seen as likely to develop only in the context of the post-Cold War thaw and the Gulf War.

The end of the Cold War and the emerging "New World Order" was expected by many to signal a glimpse of hope for an Arab-Israeli settlement, one that would be congruous with the demonstrable progress already made in Afghanistan, Nicaragua, southern Africa, Cambodia and the Persian/Arabian Gulf. It remains to be seen, however, whether the agreement at Oslo (1993) to include the Cairo agreement of May 1994 will produce a viable peace in spite of the special relationship.

The U.S. and Israel After the Cold War

Although the strategic alliance between Israel and the U.S. remained intact under Reagan's successor, relations between the two governments were not ideal. The major realignments of the strategic and political landscape of the Middle East after the end of the Cold War and the Gulf War provided the U.S. with an opportunity to shape a new structure of relationships in which a settlement of the Arab-Israeli conflict became a U.S. national interest. The views of the Bush administration and those of Shamir's government were not always congruent. Differences over the status of Jerusalem, the Jewish settlements and the occupation itself resulted in crises in the relationship of the two allies. The Bush administration's threat to withhold loan guarantees as a lever to slow down the Israeli colonization of the West Bank was perhaps the major acrimonious event which temporarily divided the strategic allies. In 1991, Israel had requested $10 billion in housing loan guarantees over five years to settle Soviet Jews in Israel. President Bush confronted the pro-Israel lobby head on by taking his case directly to the American people, who supported his position overwhelmingly.

The controversy began in early 1991 when the Bush administration rejected Israel's request for the guarantees to settle Soviet Jews due to Shamir's refusal to halt settlement activites in the occupied territories. By March of 1991, all efforts to reach a compromise had failed because of Shamir's refusal to meet the Bush administration's condition that legislation sponsored by Senator Patrick Leahy (D-Vt.) and Robert Kasten (R-Wis.) which, though conceding presidential authority to suspend guarantees for "inappropriate" new contruction, empowered Congress to override presidential suspension.[22] Bush said on March 17,1991, "We have close, historical relations with Israel.... But we have a difference now, in terms of these settlements."[23] Israel refused to meet Bush's demand for a freeze and Bush took his case to the American people and won their support, dealing a blow to the pro-Israeli lobby. A report by the Government Accounting Office (GAO) stating that U.S. conditions attached to the loan guarantees "had no discernible effect on Israel's housing policies" galvanized a majority of U.S. legislators behind the president.

The controversy over the loan guarantees issue represented a qualitative change in Washington's diplomatic style towards Israel. The concept of Israeli security did not constitute the green light which helped entrench the status-quo in its favor, sometimes at the expense of

America's higher interests and designs. The linkage concept, which the Bush administration labored stubbornly to keep out of the pre-Gulf War diplomacy, was utilized by the Bush administration in its search for an updated basis of its special relationship with Israel. At issue in that process was a possible transformation of Israel from a predominantly global issue to an increasingly domestic matter. The aborted showdowns over the loan guarantees represented an initial victory of sorts for President Bush in an arena in which "humanitarian" values were highlighted by American Jewish activists and their legislative representatives, while strategic considerations were rendered to the sidelines. The U.S. national security sector was more preoccupied then with the Japanese trade surplus "threat" and the new shape and scope of an integrated Europe as well as with America's role in it. These developments entail a reduced leverage for Israel in Washington, hence its tenacious adhesion to the status-quo of "not a single inch," the mad rush to build colonial settlements, and the resultant discord with the United States during Shamir's rule in 1990 and 1991.

By the time of the U.S. presidential campaign in 1991, however, George Bush endeavored to repair the damage and highlight the strategic relationship. The beleaguered incumbent, who trailed his Democratic opponent by more than 20 percent, tried to convince pro-Israel voters that the special relationship was quite alive despite the damage caused by Shamir. But regardless of electoral politics and who was to occupy the White House later on, the future of the special relationship was going to be determined by the strategic establishment in light of the emerging global and regional realities.

The strategic relationship was in fact broadened and deepened, not only during the contentious relationship with the Shamir government, but also after the Bush administration (as will be shown later in Chapters six and seven). This was contrary to the many forecasts based on the simplistic assumption that Israeli services pursuant to the containment policy would be unnecessary, now that the Soviet Union had disintegrated.

The strategic shifts in the region and in the world had two seemingly contradictory effects on Israeli hegemony. Unlike the Arab states, which were left with virtually no leverage, Israeli influence was in fact enhanced. U.S. Defense Secretary Dick Cheney reconfirmed the U.S. commitment to the security of Israel and its military advantage in May 1991, and a new package of military and economic aid was announced during his visit there. And yet, Israel's strategic relationship with the U.S. in the aftermath of the Cold War seemed to require some updating. The Soviet eclipse created a new opportunity for Baker, and produced an added imperative for such a reassessment. A diminished Soviet "threat" was said to be incompatible with the notion of a strategic asset, or a cheap NATO. To some people, Israel has begun to look more and more like an expensive liability.[24] The American public has become less inclined to give foreign aid, after the removal of the "Soviet threat" from Washington's foreign policy lexicon, and as domestic needs have assumed urgent and renewed concern in the midst of recession. A *Wall Street Journal*-NBC public opinion poll, which revealed that the percentage of Americans who would give aid to the Soviet Union (58%) exceeded that of those who would give to Israel (44%), was rather significant.[25]

And yet, the likelihood of an improved strategic relationship remained powerful. An Israeli-U.S. alliance adapted to post-Cold War conditions will not be based on the obsolete "Soviet threat," but on Israel's continued willingness and ability to offer the United States a strategic base in the Eastern Mediterranean to respond to regional conflicts. Israeli strategists suggested in interviews with the *Washington Post* that Israel "will present itself to Washington as a figurative home port in a sea of regional crisis."[26] The Haifa port is gradually and consistently accommodating larger U.S. naval vessels; meanwhile the United States is interested in propositioning enough equipment in Israel for a mechanized battalion. And, already, Israel has served as a testing ground for equipment, a research and development center, and a weapons purchaser and supplier.

Now that the Pentagon has come up with new ideas for American "security policy" in the post-Cold War era, Israeli military planners are at work trying to find a role for themselves and to ensure strategic significance. The concept of "strategic asset"—of which Israel is the prime example—will not only be retained by the U.S., but will also be reshaped and adapted as the Pentagon continues to imagine new enemies to fight. In March 1991, the *New York Times* published a leaked draft policy statement attributed to senior Pentagon officials, that foresaw a single superpower world. The United States is seen as the world's only policeman and no combination of allies or enemies is to be permitted to challenge that role:

> We will retain the preeminent responsibility for addressing selectively those wrongs which threaten not only our interests, but also those of our allies and friends, or which could seriously unsettle international relations.[27]

The Pentagon visionaries apparently imagine a future with a battered Iraq invading Kuwait and other oil states in the Gulf. They anticipate major battles for the U.S. there, in the Korean peninsula, in Panama, and probably the Philippines and Europe. There is practically nothing in the document about taking serious steps towards collective security.

This context will likely prove to be fertile ground for Israel's own military planners, who have long awaited an opportunity to bridge the gap between U.S. global orientation and Israel's regional orientation. In their view, the post-Cold War United States will be more amenable to Tel Aviv's long-standing thesis that regional threats supersede global threats, and therefore Israel's interests in the region and those of the U.S. may coalesce in the coming years. The absence of Soviet-related scenarios could lead both countries to focus on regional problems. With turmoil in Algeria, Somalia and Sudan, uncertainties in Libya, Central Asia and the Gulf, and a full-scale war in Yugoslavia, the Pentagon authors of the future war scenarios might well find an able and willing Israel a suitable platform—"The biggest aircraft carrier in the Mediterranean," as one senior Israeli official put it.

Israel's Regional Role

Israel's strategic relevance for future U.S. endeavors could be enhanced by leaps and bounds in the context of an Arab-Israeli diplomatic settlement. Israel would no longer have to be kept out of Gulf "security" matters. Its regional role would be confirmed and expanded to include the Mediterranean, the Gulf and Central Asia. It would become a vanguard in the coming crusade against what is known in the West as Islamic fundamentalism and extremism. It would be in the forefront in the fight against "terrorism," the spread of nuclear weapons and weapons of mass destruction to countries of the South, and might use its own terrorist methods and nuclear blackmail to achieve U.S.-Israeli mutual objectives. It would also try to seduce the Central Asian states with agricultural technology—the United States is already providing huge amounts of money for an Israeli project involving the export of agricultural and irrigation know-how to Central Asia.

The strategic relationship is also being rebuilt in the area of shared intelligence, as well as servicing U.S. 6th Fleet naval ships and military aircraft stationed in Europe. All U.S. F-15 planes are now serviced by the Israel Aircraft Industries, while the government-owned Israel Shipyards regularly services and repairs U.S. ships at Haifa. The U.S. Navy has allocated funds for expanding the port of Haifa, dredging the harbor and strengthening the piers.

Such joint ventures in military and non-military matters would reconfirm the special relationship and reinforce the strategic alliance. Israel would reemerge as regional enforcer for the sole superpower, and thus continue to be a strategic asset beyond the Cold War and the dissolution of the Soviet Union. On the eve of Rabin's first visit to the U.S. as Israeli prime minister, his foreign minister, Shimon Peres, challenged the view that Israel's strategic importance has diminished:

> If previously we had to confront the Russians, now we have to confront the situation because the best peace paintings, hung on deteriorating walls, will fall down. We need different walls, not just different paintings. And I think it is in the interest of the U.S. to see the Middle East reconstructed.[28]

Such regional "reconstruction" is expected to have a much better chance of success with Rabin at the helm in Israel. His pragmatism and sensitivity to relations with the U.S. qualify him as a more suitable partner for the Pentagon strategists than Shamir, whose obsession with outmoded ideological notions was a serious barrier to such cooperation. Rabin's practical approach is more consonant with Washington's subtle requirements for forging a *pax Americana* under the guise of a "New World

Order." Rabin's August 1992 meeting with Bush at Kennebunkport was pivotal in the creation of a framework for redefining and broadening the post-Cold War strategic cooperation, alluded to by Shimon Peres.

Although this analysis reveals that a new chapter is being opened up in the relationship between the United States and Israel, it by no means implies that Israel in the post-Shamir, post-Cold War era is being given *carte blanche* by its strategic ally. The fact is that while the strategic relationship is being renewed, it is also being clarified. American interests after the Cold War are not exactly the same as during the Cold War. Access to Gulf oil and protection of Israeli security remain, as expected, among the United State's primary interests in the region. Victory in the Cold War and the Gulf War, however, has enabled the United States to establish unrivaled dominance in a previously contested area. American inclinations toward a single superpower world will be enhanced by using that dominance to exercise influence over its principal allies of the Cold War period. The Middle East therefore, becomes a critical testing ground for what George Bush called the "New World Order." Rearranging the regional order under these conditions implies a need for a settlement of the Arab-Israeli conflict. That endeavor also puts the onus on Washington to avoid being blatantly biased. American stewardship in the region is going to require a viable settlement. But how viable that settlement will be is going to depend, not only on American good-will and/or politico-strategic interests, but also on the ability and willingness of the Arab states and the Palestinians to insist that such settlement meet an irreducible minimum of national aspirations and the very basic Arab requirements. So far, this has not happened, and is unlikely to happen in the forseeable future. For the time being, Arab and Palestinian nationalism has been tamed, while the U.S.-Israeli strategic alliance continues to grow and thrive in an increasingly docile Middle East. Ignoring any possible charges of blatant bias during his October 1994 Middle East tour, President Clinton lectured Arafat in Cairo on the need to combat terrorism, but assured the Israeli Knesset that "the survival of Israel is important, not only to our interests, but to every single value that we hold dear as a people."

Notes

1. Clyde Mark, *Israel: U.S. Foreign Assistance Facts*, Foreign Affairs and National Defense Division, Congressional Research Service. The Library of Congress (CRS Issue Brief. Order Code IB85066) September 4, 1991. pp 4–5

2. *Ibid.*

3. *Ibid.*

4. *Christian Science Monitor*, February 2, 1981.

5. When those quotations resurfaced in the German weekly *Welt am Sonntag* on February 7, 1982, the White House quickly denied that they represented current U.S. policy.

6. "Secretary Haig: U.S. Strategy in the Middle East," U.S. Department of States, Bureau of Public Affairs, Current Policy No. 312.

7. "Secretary Haig: Saudi Security, Middle East Peace, and U.S. Interests," Department of State, Bureau of Public Affairs, Current Policy No. 323.

8. Twinam was speaking for James Buckley, Undersecretary for Security Assistance, in an address before the National Conference of Editorial Writers in Providence, Rhode Island.

9. "Secretary Haig: Dangerous Illusions and Real Choices on AWACs," Department of State, Bureau of Public Affairs, Current Policy No. 324.

10. Naseer Aruri and John Carroll, "The Anti-terrorist Crusade," *Arab Studies Quarterly*, Vol. IX No. 2, pp. 173–187.

11. *New York Times*, May 26, 1982.

12. *New York Times*, June 8, 1982.

13. Presidential Advisor Edwin Meese said on June 10, that the Israeli invasion was "suffcently defensible in nature," while Haig brushed aside questions by journalists on this point by saying on June 6 that it was the kind of question Philip Habib might explore.

14. For a description of U.S. strategy following the downfall of the Shah, see President Carter's State of the Union Address to the 96th Congress on January 23,1980. See also the article by George W. Ball in the *Boston Globe*, April 2, 1979.

15. On June 8 and 9, 1982 Pentagon sources expressed gratification for the performance of the Israeli pilots and F-15 fighters against Soviet-sup-

plied Syrian MiGs.

16. *New York Times*, December 21, 1981.

17. *Ibid.*

18. *Ibid.*

19. Associated Press dispatch, *Standard Times* (New Bedford, Mass.), December 26, 1981.

20. Clyde R. Mark, *Israeli-United States Relations.* Foreign Affairs and National Defense Division Congressional Research Service, Library of Congress. September 4, 1991, p.4

21. Text of the Memorandum of Agreement in the Journal of Palestine Studies, Vol. XVIII, No. 1, (Autumn 1988), pp 300-302.

22. See *Report On Israeli Settlements in the Occupied Territories*, Vol. 2, No. 3, (May 1992)

23. *Ibid.*

24. See, for example, Glenn Frankel, "The East-West Warming Trend Has Chilling Implications For Israel," *Washington Post National Weekly Edition,* December 25–31, 1991.

25. *Wall Street Journal*, October 15, 1991.

26. *Washington Post,* July 28, 1992.

27. *New York Times,* March 8, 1992.

28. *Christian Science Monitor*, August 3, 1992.

PART II

MARGINALIZING THE PALESTINIANS

5

The Marginalization of the Palestine Question:

From Carter to Bush and Baker

Carter and Camp David

The marginalization of the Palestine question was a natural consequence of the shifting balance in favor of American unilateralism over nationalism. The "peace process" undertaken under U.S. auspices was always aiming to peripheralize the centrality of the Palestine question and advance the bilateral dimension of the Arab-Israeli conflict. Thus Camp David, which purported to bring about a comprehensive settlement, simply provided cover for a separate peace between Egypt and Israel, while permitting the latter a free hand in the Palestinian territories occupied in 1967. That deal required a tacit reinterpretation of UN Security Council Resolution 242. Given that resolution's broad acceptance as a foundation for a settlement, it was necessary to keep it at the center of the diplomatic stage. Its demotion of Palestinian rights made it attractive to Israel, yet its withdrawal clause contradicted Israeli goals. To reconcile these conflicting components, the real meaning of 242 was effectively floated by the U.S. in such a manner as to allow for a certain accommodation of the Israeli position. For example, despite the fact that the Camp David accords brokered by President Carter promised a comprehensive settlement on the basis of 242, it virtually altered the status of the West Bank and Gaza from occupied territory within the meaning of international law to a disputed territory whose sovereignty became a matter for negotiations. Moreover, the Egyptian-Israeli agreement granted Israel a virtual veto over the final disposition of these Palestinian territories occupied since 1967. Thus Israel's withdrawal from the Sinai Peninsula, which took place in April 1982 in accordance with these agreements, was considered by Israeli leaders as its final territorial "concession," the fulfillment of its obligations under Security Council Resolution 242. "There will never again be a division of Western Eretz Israeli," said Prime Minister Menachem Begin at that time, asserting "eternal sovereignty" over the West Bank and Gaza and consequently blocking off even the Camp David presumed options for these territories.[1]

Together with another separate agreement, brokered by the United States, between Israel and Egypt, Camp David confirmed the quid pro quo. The Sinai Accord of 1975 and the Camp David accords of 1978 embodied the principle that the final settlement of the Palestine question would not be premised on what Carter described as the "faulty assumption" that Israel had violated Palestinian rights.[2] Hence the matter of sovereignty over the West Bank and Gaza was to be included in the category of negotiable items, as required by Camp David. That, in reality, was the true meaning of America's diplomatic blockade against the PLO, which was decreed by Henry Kissinger in 1975 and lifted by the Reagan administration on its way out of office. Columnist David Wilson of the *Boston Globe* correctly observed that the purpose of the Kissinger formula was to "protect Israel and its American ally from having to deal with the 1.7 million Palestinians under occupation."[3]

The marginalization of Palestinian national rights, which was patently revealed in Kissinger's diplomacy, was continued in President Carter's efforts to effect an Arab-Israeli settlement. During his electoral campaign, Carter had spelled out a position on the Palestinians that was consistent with those of the Nixon and Ford administrations. The Palestinians would not be recognized as an independent political entity. Their place in the "peace process" would be merely as adjunct to an Arab delegation, preferably attached to Jordan. No major departures from the ongoing policy of thwarting Palestinian nationalism were signaled by Carter.

The premises of the Carter administration policy in the Middle East were discussed rather candidly in an annual review which was presented by Assistant Secretary of State for South Asian and Middle Eastern Affairs, Harold Saunders, to the Subcommittee on Europe and the Middle East of the House International Relations Committee on June 12, 1978. Working with "moderate" Arab nations, Saunders argued, was essential for achieving a political settlement, assuring a secure and prosperous Israel and securing the economic well-being of the U.S. as well as the capitalist West.[4] The new relationship was described euphemistically as one of "interdependence," and by no means did it imply a tilt toward the Arabs or a reduction of the U.S. commitment to Israel.

Carter's strategy, therefore, was aimed at striking a balance between the Arabs' peace imperative and Israel's security imperative. Israel would have to be taught the virtues of enlightened self-interest; the Arabs would have to be assisted in shaping a consensus linking Jordan to a tamed PLO which would have to effectively qualify its insistence on being the sole legitimate representative of the Palestinian people. President Carter said in his first news conference following the inauguration; "If the Palestinians should be invited to the meeting [at Geneva] as agreed by the other participating nations, along with us, it would probably be as part of one of the Arab delegations."[5] President Sadat, who had already expressed a desire for a formal link between a "Palestinian state" and Jordan, reiterated the same in the presence of Secretary of State Cyrus Vance in Cairo on February 17, 1977, adding that this should be an "official and declared link," i.e., a confederation to be announced *before* a Geneva Conference was convened.[6] Most Arab leaders conveyed the view that the PLO ought to receive an invitation as a full participant in the Middle East conference, but they were willing, at the same time, to exercise pressure on the PLO to accept "any procedural rule—from becoming part of a single Arab delegation to staying away from the conference altogether, letting the other Arabs negotiate for them."[7] The implication of that stand was not lost on Israel's Foreign Minister Yigal Allon, who commented: "This is the first nail in the coffin of the Rabat Conference."[8]

During the spring of 1977, President Carter felt compelled to provide the Arab leaders with a face-saving device regarding the Palestine question. Yet he had to respond to internal and party pressures with regard to Israel and its own definition of peace. His speech in Clinton, Massachusetts on March 16, 1977 revealed this dilemma and hinted at the way out: he would accept Israel's framework of a settlement, providing Israel accepted his obligation to provide that face-saving device to Arab leaders.[9]

Carter's dilemma, however, was intensified when the Likud bloc assumed power in Israel, for the first time, in the summer of 1977. The revisionist Prime Minister Menachem Begin was now publicly imply-ing that the West Bank and Gaza were not occupied territories. "Judea and Samaria" became their official names and the "Arabs of Eretz Israel" his new designation of the Palestinians living there. Carter's plan was now in serious jeopardy. Initially, the president decided to rise to the challenge. When asked if he would find some means of pres-sure or persuasion should the Israeli position at Geneva be quite different from his own, Carter replied:

> I would try to marshal the support of the leader, first of all. Secondly, the opinion of his people back home, the constituencies that might exist in our own country that would have influence around the world, opinion that exists in the European Community, and in the Arab nations as well.[10]

President Carter's "offensive" against Menachem Begin climaxed in the Joint Statement of the U.S.-U.S.S.R. on the Middle East on October 1, 1977, in which the U.S. agreed to associate the U.S.S.R. with the set-tlement in Geneva and used for the first time the phrase Palestinian "legitimate rights."[11] The joint declaration was met with intense oppo-sition by Israel, her constituencies in Congress and the American Jewish community, and was effectively abandoned by the Carter administration. The Dayan-Carter working paper of October 5 ren-dered it ineffectual:

> Acceptance of the Joint U.S.-U.S.S.R. Statement of October 1, 1977 by the parties is not a prerequisite for the reconvening and the conduct of the Geneva Conference.[12]

Meanwhile, Israeli foreign minister Moshe Dayan released a draft of the secret working paper to the Knesset, which reveals that Carter and Vance had not only retreated from their commitment to assure a form of PLO representation at Geneva, but had in fact accepted Begin's def-inition of a settlement regarding the West Bank and Gaza.[13]

The impasse which ensued following Carter's ill-fated "offensive" was interrupted by Anwar Sadat's sudden visit to Israel on November 19, 1977. His interest and that of Begin converged on the need to keep the Soviet Union out of Middle East diplomacy. Thus the focus of attention had shifted away from Geneva to the Middle East.

The next phase of Carter's Middle East policy began with Sadat's Jerusalem visit and ended with the Camp David accord on September 17, 1978. Zbigniew Brzezinski's famous "bye-bye PLO" underscored the administration's abandonment of behind-the-scenes efforts to make the PLO a "qualified" negotiating partner.

Sadat's trip ushered in a new era in the diplomatic history of the modern Middle East, in which the guidelines of a settlement were being formulated mainly by Israel. Carter and Sadat lost whatever initiatives they might have entertained in the past. The Begin Plan, unveiled in December 1977, was advanced as Israel's "contribution to peace," in response to the Sadat trip. It envisioned the formation of an administrative council in the West Bank and Gaza with jurisdiction over local education, religious affairs, commerce, agriculture, tourism, health and policing. Israeli authorities were to remain in charge of "security;" foreign and economic affairs. A committee of representatives of Jordan, Israel, and the Administrative Council was given authority to determine the legality of all acts by the Administrative Council, while Israeli settlements were to continue unabated. The plan itself constituted a reaffirmation of Begin's sovereign claims in the West Bank and Gaza. As such it was at variance with the stated policies of both the U.S. and Egypt. Yet both Carter and Sadat finally accepted Begin's concept of autonomy as a framework for Camp David; they differed with him only on the extent of self-government which it implied. Whereas Begin subscribed to limited autonomy, emphasizing that it was autonomy for the people but not the land, Carter and Sadat favored "full autonomy." A deliberate ambiguity, however, saved the three leaders and facilitated the agreement which was hailed in the U.S. as America's most impressive achievement in the Middle East. But Carter's retreat before Israel and her domestic constituencies, coupled with the Palestinians' resolve to guard their national rights, restricted that achievement to a separate "cold peace" between Egypt and Israel.

The Reagan Period

Special Relationship and Anti-Terrorism

Aside from the 1977 Carter aberration, which was impeded by the Camp David accords, United States policy continued to erode the centrality of the Palestine question until it was completely relegated to a secondary—if not even tertiary—issue during Reagan's presidency. In fact, during the past quarter of a century, Israel was transformed from a U.S. client, to a surrogate in the 1967, war to a partner in the 1982 war, to a strategic ally since that war. That transformation and the corresponding marginalization of the Palestine question made the "peace process" more responsive to the exogenous input of strategic calculation and the exigencies of the Cold War than to the endogenous input of regional harmony and based on international legal principles.

A political settlement thus became intertwined with the United States-Israel special relationship, which was bolstered by the anti-Soviet thrust of the first Reagan administration and in turn reinforced by the anti-terrorist dimension of America's global strategy.[14] The U.S. decree that Israel has not violated Palestinian rights was also at the heart of the terrorism dimension of Reagan's Palestine policy. Together, these salient aspects of American policy since the October 1973 war accelerated the disenfranchisement of the Palestinians from the "peace process" and tried to ensure their national exclusion from the new order that would emanate therefrom. The more intense the Cold War with the Soviet Union grew, the stronger the special relationship with Israel became. The more inroads that were perceived to have been made in the Third World by local revolutionary forces allied with the Soviet Union, the more pronounced became Israel's counter-revolutionary role on a global scale, and consequently the less urgent became a Middle East settlement. By the same token, the more dependent the Arab countries became on the United States for regime security and financial stability and the less coherent the Arab position became, due to inter-Arab strife and Palestinian internecine conflict, the less responsive was the U.S. to their general concerns.

Although the United States' strategic calculations did not totally sidestep the role of conservative Arab states in favor of the special relationship with Israel, the outcome of U.S. policy under Reagan favored hegemony for that relationship and hence gave much greater weight to a more hard-line Israeli position. The special relationship became a principal impediment to an international settlement and a means to the marginalization of the Palestine question and the containment of Palestinian nationalism.

The Reagan Plan of September 1, 1982, which denied sovereignty over the whole of the West Bank and Gaza to both Israel and the Palestinians, exemplified the trend of United States policy, which had aimed, since 1967, to thwart the international consensus and substitute its own "peace process."[15] The plan was spurred on largely by the siege of Beirut, which tarnished Israel's image and at the same time provided an impetus in the world community for linking PLO withdrawal from Beirut to Palestinian statehood. To justify its virtual sole dissent from international will, the Reagan administration felt obliged to launch its own initiative based on the "Jordan option," but the territorial and confederal aspects of the plan evoked a swift rejection from the Israeli cabinet.

The peculiar emphasis which was placed on combatting international terrorism in Reagan's foreign policy reinforced the special relationship as a factor leading towards marginalizing and de-legitimizing the Palestinian national movement. Having been swept into power in part on the strength of anti-communism, the Reagan administration soon launched a new Cold War and equipped its ideological arsenal with anti-terrorism as well. Thus it readily and uncritically accepted Israel's premises about conflict and stability in the region; that Palestinian "terrorism" (rather than legitimate Palestinian rights), together with Islamic fundamentalism, constituted the great scourges in the Middle East. The United States, whose global position was undermined during the 1970s in a second wave of Third World radicalism in Angola, Ethiopia, Iran, Afghanistan, Nicaragua, and Cambodia, allegedly due to a "Vietnam syndrome" which inhibited U.S. military commitments abroad, was declared ready to resume intervention. The Reagan administration proceeded on the assumption that Carter's "wimpish" policies were a mere aberration that would be replaced by a renewed effort to roll back Soviet gains in the

Third World. Hence the pursuit of muscular policies in Grenada, Lebanon, and Nicaragua, as well as the launching of a crusade against international "terrorism," with Libya, Iran, Syria and the PLO as primary targets—all designed to rally a reluctant U.S. public around the resumption of interventionism.

Reagan's perception of Israel as a "unique strategic asset" was reinforced by that foreign policy climate which was dominated by the political thought of neo-conservatives such as Norman Podhoretz, Jeanne Kirkpatrick, Richard Pipes and Irving Kristol. It was also promoted by right-wing journalists like William Safire and George Will and anti-communist politician-ideologues and hawkish strategists like Richard Allen, Robert McFarlane, Alexander Haig, Elliot Abrams, and above all, George Shultz. The foreign policy consensus which they shaped was premised on the notion that a "legacy of restraint," also known as the "Vietnam syndrome," had to be eradicated, lest the United States lose its primary status among the superpowers. The neo-conservatives challenged America to rehabilitate intervention and to "stand tall" against communists, terrorists and would-be challengers of U.S. domination. They attacked the "culture of appeasement," the "isolation" of post-Vietnam America and the detente intellectuals, and they advocated the resurrection of the "rollback" policy towards the Soviet Union. Their anti-terrorist crusade was a manifestation of the "Reagan Doctrine" and its export of counter-revolution which aimed to destabilize governments or political forces deemed close to the "evil empire." Israel occupied a central place in this global strategy. Not only did it share with the United States a common hostility to Third World radical nationalism, but it also shared a common contempt for the United Nation and the role of international law in world conflicts. Israeli rhetoric about terrorism was accepted by the administration without question. Israel also became a conduit for funneling U.S. money, weapons and training to the Contras and other unsavory regimes and movements.[16] Israeli military technology was exported to repressive forces in Central America, southern Africa, and East Asia. The contrast between Washington's quiet approval of Israel's nuclear weapons program and its vigorous scrutiny of similar programs in India and Pakistan as well as its highly publicized opposition to the spread of missiles and chemical weapons in Arab countries can only be understood in terms of the special U.S.-Israeli relationship.

The Palestine question, therefore, paled in significance beside Reagan's global agenda in which Israel's counter-revolutionary role was crucial. Eight years of American deviousness—from the secret mining of Nicaraguan harbors, to the ill-defined military mission in Lebanon, to the double dealings with Iran to subsidize the Contras, to the campaign of disinformation about Libya, to the transfer of advanced military technology to South Africa in contravention of the 1986 U.S. Anti-Apartheid Act—constitute but a modest portion of that global agenda with an Israeli connection. Given, therefore, Israel's role as an activist against communism and a catalyst in Mr. Reagan's post-Vietnam formula for U.S. interventionism, it appeared rather unseemly for the Reagan administration to bring an issue as insignificant as that of the West Bank into the relations of the strategic allies.

As long as that American foreign policy climate prevailed, Israel was insulated from the pressure for a territorial settlement. Its utility in the U.S. global strategy far outweighed its obligations for peace in the regions. Thus the continuation of the untenable status quo in the occupied Arab territories was linked to heightened conflict (the new Cold War) in the world.

The Potential for Change in U.S. Policy

A Missed Opportunity?
The latter period of the Reagan presidency was one of profound change in the world at large, inside the United States, and in the Middle East. That change carried a potential to unfreeze the status quo in the West Bank and Gaza, which had hitherto been guarded by the special relationship and reinforced by Reagan's crusade of anti-communism and anti-terrorism. But although the pressure on the U.S. was growing steadily in the late 1980s to adjust to internal and external developments, a real change in policy continued to be hampered by an utter lack of urgency on the part of the U.S. foreign policy elite. The response to these pressures, therefore, had only occurred in the realm of tactical adjustments, leaving the policy itself quite intact.

The two major developments of 1988 in the United States policy towards the Palestine question—the Shultz Plan and the dialogue with the PLO—came largely in response to these profound changes in the international, regional and local contexts of the Palestine question.[17] Yet Israel's rejection of these developments came strictly in the more orthodox context of the special relationship and the policy of anti-terrorism and anti-communism.

We will first consider the changing realities in the global and domestic arenas, which had a potential for policy change, and then examine the U.S. response (the Schultz Plan and the dialogue with the PLO) and evaluate its impact on the Palestine question.

1. The Global Environment

The three dimensions of the Arab-Israeli conflict, at the local, regional and international levels, had been altered in such a profound manner that the assumptions of the U.S.-Israeli convergence could no longer evade some reconsideration. The anti-Cold War thinking and foreign policy reforms adopted by Mikhail Gorbachev in 1985 were bound to have an impact on the frozen Middle East situation. The new Soviet policies were clearly designed to maximize influence on all sides of major regional issues. The pursuit of a middle ground had given Soviet diplomacy a pragmatic thrust calculated to develop broad acceptability. The emphasis on cooperation, collective security and political instead of military solutions began to give Mr. Gorbachev and the Soviet Union a new international image as arbiters of peace.

Judging that American hegemony in the Middle East was undiminished by Brezhnev's policies, that the Soviet Union lacked any influence in Israel and enjoyed little influence in the Arab world, which remained generally pro-West, Gorbachev decided to redress the imbalance. The Soviet Union, which had been largely absent from the Middle East "peace process" since its 1972 ouster by Kissinger, was beginning to return to the region—not as the sponsor of local surrogates or the archenemy of reactionary Arab states or Zionist Israel, but as a superpower eager to play the role of a moderator rather than collaborator. Moscow had already taken initiatives aimed towards the restoration of diplomatic contacts with Israel, the establishment of diplomatic relations with conservative Arab states in the Gulf, and the improvement of relations with Egypt—all as part of a strategy calculated to broaden its diplomatic options. Moscow was instrumental in bringing about the unity session of the Palestine National Council in April 1988 in Algiers and in persuading the PLO to scale down its position on the nature of the international peace conference and other pre-conditions for peace, such as the controversial issue of Israel's right to exist.[18] Soviet policy under Gorbachev had, in effect, revised the 1981 Brezhnev Plan in order to accommodate U.S. and Israeli demands. Thus, faced with a Soviet policy which began to assign pragmatism a certain priority over ideology, the United States was faced with both a historic opportunity and an obligation to end the Arab-Israeli conflict, a task which would necessitate pressure on Israel and impose a strain on the strategic alliance.

The new Soviet approach was designed to take some wind out of the sails of the U.S.-Israel special relationship, having gone a long way towards meeting the U.S. position and bringing with it a regional alignment, most of whose components were traditionally pro-West. The scenario of the new line-up of Arab forces, including Egypt, Jordan, Saudi Arabia, Iraq and the PLO, was conceived in an exchange of territory for peace, which the U.S., Europe and the Soviet Union had been calling for with varying degrees of emphasis. That rather non-threatening Arab alignment, bolstered by the *Intifada* and combined with the new Soviet approach, began to put the onus on the United States to reassess its policy. Furthermore, the Soviet Union, having just concluded or brokered agreements ending regional conflicts in Afghanistan, Southern Africa, Cambodia and Central America, was seemingly in a strong position to argue that the imperatives for an international settlement in the Middle East were not less urgent than elsewhere. Supporting that endeavor was Western Europe, whose parliament invited Arafat on September 13, 1988, to give a major address to its socialist members on the Palestinian perspective on peace.[19] The invitation to Strasbourg emphasized a new European readiness to participate in a peace process based on the concept of mutual recognition. The question was whether the U.S. was ready to make significant departures from its traditional policy and begin to embrace the global consensus. It simply did not happen—a wasted opportunity.

2. The Domestic Environment

Washington's sudden awakening to the fact that the status quo in the West Bank and Gaza was untenable came in February 1988, after five years of total diplomatic inactivity. Its fifteen-year monopoly of the stalled "peace process" had effectively prevented other actors from participating in a serious search for a negotiated settlement. Consistent with that posture, Secretary Schultz embarked in 1988 on four visits to the region, which failed to produce a settlement. His plan was a confirmation of the U.S. custodianship over the Middle East. It served as a reminder that the region is United States turf, and as such, it was designed to preempt any serious international proposals for peace.

It almost seemed as if Mr. Schultz was trying to save Israel in spite of herself, to protect Israel's tarnished image *inside* the United States, whose citizens and institutions bear the ultimate responsibility for the continued sustenance of the strategic alliance, in which Schultz himself invested so much political capital. He endorsed Israel's right to contain the *Intifada*, but differed slightly with Likud leadership over the proper means of suppression. His assistant secretary for human rights, Richard Schifter, a self-proclaimed Zionist, told a congressional panel:

> In our view, Israel clearly has not only the right, but the obligation, to preserve or restore order in the occupied territories and to use appropriate levels of force to accomplish that end.[20]

This statement, which coincided with unprecedented Israeli repressive measures, including banning the press and sealing off the entire West Bank and Gaza, differed from Henry Kissinger's counsel to Israel only in tone, but not in substance.[21]

While Schifter gave Israel a green light to restore "law and order," the State Department spokesman, Charles Redman, expressed "regrets" over the Israeli restrictions and tried to balance "harsh security measurers" against "violent demonstrations."[22] The State Department's approach reflected an attempt to sanitize Israeli practices, which the U.S. government was no longer able to defend, morally or legally, *inside* the United States. Hence the seemingly erratic reactions of the administration to Israeli excesses, which included soft criticism, reassurances of support, using the veto to protect Israel in the Security Council, and at times abstaining or supporting the universal condemnation. For example, the United States abstained from voting on a Security Council resolution, which, "strongly deplored the opening of fire by the Israeli army, resulting in the killing and wounding of defenseless Palestinian civilians" on the pretext that it was unacceptably harsh.[23] Subsequently the U.S. supported a resolution which called on Israel on January 5, 1988 "to refrain from deporting any Palestinian civilians from the occupied territories," but abstained when a second resolution on January 14 expressed "deep regret that Israel...has deported Palestinian civilians."[24] Two weeks later, the United States vetoed a resolution which called on Israel to "desist forthwith from its policies and practices which violate the human rights of the Palestinian people."[25]

Secretary Shultz warned against drawing conclusions from the previous abstention:

I think it's important for everyone to understand that the United States regards its friendship and the strength of its relationship with Israel as key and unshakable.... Occasionally we disagree, but through all of that, this relationship, as I said, is unshakable—that's what that means.[26]

And yet, the United States warned Israel about possible damage to the "unshakable" relationship when orders were issued on August 18, 1988 for the expulsion of 25 Palestinians in addition to 37 already deported in 1988. Deputy Secretary of State John Whitehead warned Israeli minister Oded Eran that American public opinion did not tolerate expulsions:

You have heard our position before but now the issue has reached the point that an increasing number of Americans are wondering what Israel is doing. If this attitude persists, damage to our bilateral relations will occur. We will oppose Israel in the UN and elsewhere. We urge you to reconsider the expulsion orders, or,...to refrain from carrying them out.[27]

A. Public Opinion
Although public opinion is normally passive, its role in the formu-

lation of public policy in participatory systems can be crucial. There were strong indications that a gap was growing between the requirements of public opinion and the content of public policy in the United States with respect to the Palestine-Israel conflict. The public mood had undergone some change, largely due to the *Intifada*. Yet Palestine, as already shown, had never been high on the official agenda.

A public opinion poll conducted in January 1988 revealed that a substantial 36% of Americans believed that Israel had reacted to the Palestinian uprising too harshly.[28] A June 1987 poll showed that 61%, labeled by the *Los Angeles Times* as a "vast majority," favored the exchange of territory for peace.[29] Another poll conducted in January 1988 found that 31% of Americans favored a Palestinian state federated with Jordan.[30] By March 1988, a Gallup poll determined that 41% favored the "establishment of an independent Palestinian state," without reservation.[31] Prior to the uprising, a June 1988 poll revealed that 50% favored PLO participation in peace negotiations.[32] In January 1988, a general call for peace was endorsed by 74%, of whom 74% favored a PLO role in the negotiations.[33] The same poll showed that 48% favored "direct contact" between the U.S. and the PLO, of whom 56% did not even stake their approval on PLO recognition of Israel's right to exist, as required by the Kissinger formula. This percentage increased in March, when a Gallup poll showed that a substantial 57% of Americans, versus 27% who disagreed, favored direct negotiations between the U.S. and the PLO, while 66% favored direct negotiations between Israel and the PLO.[34] A *Los Angeles Times* poll conducted during the spring of 1988 found that 34% of non-Jews favored a reduction of military aid to Israel and 65% thought that there was "an element of racism in the attitude of Israelis towards Arabs." These figures should not imply that the U.S. government and the U.S. public were on a collision course over a long period.

Analysis of public opinion polls, ranging from a neutral base comparison year of 1981 through mid-1988, reveals a consistent trend of U.S. public support for Israel. When asked in 1981 whom the U.S. should support in the Arab-Israeli conflict, 47% favored Israel and only 11% favored the Arabs. In January 1988, 43% favored Israel, while only 11% favored the Arabs.[35] Although support for Israel held steady even at the height of the *Intifada* in 1988, it actually rose for the Palestinians drastically. A Gallup poll showed that the percentage of those expressing sympathy with Israel was 43% in May 1988 and 46% in December 1988. The corresponding figures for the Palestinians were 20% and 24%, respectively.[36] If we compare these figures with the 11% support for the "Arabs" in January 1988, the roughly 100% increase of support for the Palestinians can be accounted for by the fact that the question which produced 11% support in January referred to "Arabs," while that which produced 20% and 24% later in 1988 referred to "Palestinians." That increase, we should point out, resulted largely from a change in the category of the uncommitted and thus did not reflect an erosion of public support for Israel.

The new factor in the equation, however, was the *Intifada*, which was seen as a non-violent insurrection juxtaposed against Israeli repression that reminded Americans of Chile and South Africa. Moreover, the conflict was beginning to be seen in the U.S. as a Palestinian-Israeli conflict rather than an Arab-Israeli one. After the U.S. decided to open talks with the PLO in December 1988, more than two-thirds (72%) of those polled approved, while only 20% disapproved. And when asked whether these talks between the Palestinians and the U.S. improved the chances for peace, again more than two-thirds (67%) answered in the affirmative, and only 15% expressed the opposite view.

B. The Media

The beginning of a short-lived shift in public opinion was also noticed in media coverage. An ABC *Nightline*'s week-long series from Jerusalem, in which three Palestinians and four Israelis participated in a "town meeting" setting in Jerusalem, was perhaps the first debate of the Palestine-Israeli conflict on national television. (The participants included Dr. Hanan Ashrawi, who three years later became the official spokesperson for the Palestinian delegation to the peace talks in Madrid and Washington, and Dr. Haider Abdul-Shafi, the head of the delegation.) Millions of viewers in the United States saw the Palestinians, perhaps for the first time, as regular human beings with normal feelings and aspirations and a determination to pursue their goals in a reasonable manner, expressing themselves in impeccable English.

The event also underscored the stereotypical assumptions about Arabs, prevalent throughout the U.S. media. Hanan Ashrawi was later profiled by *Time* (May 25, 1992) as follows:

No longer can the world sum up–and dismiss–the Palestinians in the portrait of a stubble-bearded man wrapped in a kaffiyeh. This woman looks civilized...unthreatening...and she speaks with a compelling eloquence...this medieval literature scholar, devoted mother, Christian and woman.

The program highlighted a change in the approach of the American press to the conflict and seemed to set the pace for its coverage. The American press reacted to Israeli repression with uncharacteristic criticism. Some of the rebuke was reserved for the Reagan administration, which was seen by some journalists as responsible for the deadlock. A survey of twenty newspaper editorials revealed this trend during the month of December 1987. One theme of the criticism focused on Israel's special moral obligation, given the history of Jewish persecution. For example, the *St. Petersburg Times* of Florida wrote:

As a nation whose very existence was meant to atone for two millenniums [sic] of persecution culminating in the holocaust, Israel inherited the burden of conducting itself according to high moral principles.[37]

The *Omaha World Herald* said that "Israel, of all nations, should be sensitive about oppression."[38] The *Arizona Republic* went so far as to imply a prohibited analogy with Nazi behavior:

Israel has evolved from a nation founded by the remnants of Hitler's death camps into a country dependent on forced labor.... The inmates have become the guards...who could have imagined that one day the survivors of Auschwitz would...strap young Arabs to the fronts of jeeps as human shields?[39]

Other newspapers compared Israeli behavior to that of the white racist regime in South Africa, normally considered taboo in the discourse on the Middle East. The *Miami Herald* wrote that, "Thoughtful Israelis foresee and shudder at their nation becoming analogous to South Africa."[40]

The *Sun Reporter* of San Francisco made an analogy between the two settler states in rather explicit language:

> South Africa and Israel are both republics, ...both aggressively make claims of being democracies.... The U.S. regards both nations as being firm allies in the secret war against communism.... Both are engaged in hostilities against indigenous people who were already in residence. Arabs living in the West Bank do not live any better than Blacks in Soweto.... The Arabs have no arms. Like the Blacks...they throw rocks.[41]

Some editorials fixed the blame for Israeli intransigence, which led to the present deadlock, on the Reagan administration. For example, the *Grand Rapids Press* accused the administration of having been "almost servile in its deference to the Israeli government," asserting that "the U.S. has let the Mideast peace process sit idle and has done nothing to discourage Israeli provocations in the occupied territories or hasten the establishment of a homeland for the Palestinians."[42] Other editorials reminded Israel of its obligations under the special relationship. The *Charlotte Observer* wrote that "Israel, which depends so heavily on American money and support, must take appropriate steps toward achieving peace so as to maintain its critically important international image."[43]

C. The Jewish Community

Another domestic arena for U.S. policy towards Palestine was the American Jewish community, which supplies the major organized political force behind the U.S.-Israel strategic alliance and against Palestinian rights. Endowed with organizational skills, financial resources, privileged access to decision-making and the mass media, and overlapping membership with business, trade unions and the Democratic Party, the Jewish community supplied the leverage which had enabled the Israeli lobby to assure unquestioning support of Israeli policies over the years.

Israeli supporters, however, seemed rather troubled by the consequences of Defense Minister Rabin's policy of "might, force and blows," which had tarnished Israel's image in the United States and throughout the world in such a drastic manner. For example, senators who were known to be ardent supporters of Israeli policies, such as Carl Levin (D) of Michigan and Rudy Boschwitz (R) of Minnesota, initiated the process which led thirty of their colleagues to sign a letter critical of Shamir's summary rejection of Shultz's initiative, in the spring of 1988. The letter expressed the view that "...peace negotiations have little chance of success if the Israeli government's position rules out territorial compromise."[44]

Another group of well-known supporters of Israel in the House of Representatives, such as Barney Frank of Massachusetts, James Scheur of New York and Howard Berman, Henry Waxman and Tom Lantos of California, attempted to follow up with another letter, which did not materialize despite the positive sentiment for such action.[45]

Apparently, Shultz himself intervened so that the administration would not appear to be behind these efforts to pressure Israel. The *New York Times* quoted a State Department official as saying that "what we don't want is the appearance that we are orchestrating pressure, because we're not."[46]

Expressions of discontent with Israeli practices began to surface in the U.S. Jewish community in the latter part of 1987 and became somewhat more frequent in 1988. The American Jewish Congress adopted a resolution in September 1987 which labeled the occupation as "benign" but warned that its continuation would lead to:

repressive measures that, in the long run, cannot but distort and corrupt the values we associate with a Jewish state.... The Jewish commitment to personal dignity, to human freedom, to social justice and to the rule of law all argue against the permanent governance of another people by a Jewish state.[47]

Rabbi Alexander Shindler, President of the Union of American Hebrew Congregations, cabled the Israeli President, saying that his government's policy was "...an offense to the Jewish spirit" and it "...threatens to erode the support of Israel's friends here in the U.S."[48] Albert Vorspan, the senior vice-president of the organization, warned Shamir that "...Israel should not always expect reflexive support from

American Jews."[49] Vorspan wrote that "…American Jews are trauma-tized by the events in Israel" and that the occupied territories have become "…Israel's Vietnam, Kent State and Watts rolled into one."[50] S. Hyman Bookbinder, a spokesperson for the American Jewish Committee, expressed similar sentiments and concerns about an anti-Israel backlash in the United States when he said that Rabin's policy of might, power and blows "has caused great chagrin, great dismay among their best Jewish supporters."[51] In a letter to the *New York Times*, promi-nent Jewish intellectuals Irving Howe, Arthur Hertzberg, Michael Walzer and Henry Rosovsky called upon Israel to express readiness "to end the occupation in such a way that, with necessary territorial adjustments, Israeli security and Palestinian national aspirations can be satisfied."

Progressive groups like the Jewish Peace Fellowship and the New Jewish Agenda held many demonstrations outside the Israeli Embassy in Washington and many Israeli consulates around the country. The split in the Jewish community over Israel was dramatized by the New York conference sponsored by *Tikkun* in December 1988. Among the themes voiced in that meeting were: "Wake up Israel; negotiate now; break the lock of AIPAC and create J-PAC, A Jewish Peace Action Committee, that would support Israel by affirming the Palestinian right to establish an independent state."[52] What was interesting was the absence of any campaigns by the Israeli lobby in the U.S. in sup-port of Israel's opposition to the opening of a dialogue between the U.S. and the PLO. The public remarks of representatives of the major Jewish organizations were rather low-key and reticent in their acqui-escence in the U.S. decision. This was a marked departure from their vigorous opposition to the Reagan administration's decision to sell AWACs to Saudi Arabia in 1981.

Clearly there were altered realities in the global and domestic con-texts of U.S. policy in the Middle East. These realities, however, while having afforded an opportunity for change, had actually failed to pro-duce any significant change in U.S. policy. To many, it was a missed opportunity.

The Shultz Plan

The Shultz Plan was the instrument used to obviate a policy change in the face of international and domestic pressures. It was introduced to reaffirm U.S. custodianship over the Middle East, to elbow out other serious plans for settlement and to protect Israel's image in the U.S., which had been tarnished by its brutal methods of suppressing the *Intifada*. Mr. Shultz, who endorsed Israel's attempt to contain the *Intifada*, invited the Palestinians to explore a solution based on the Reagan Plan and Camp David. The framework consisted of "full autonomy," transitional periods, elections for a "self-governing authority," and some kind of association with Jordan, none of which was likely to incur serious Israeli opposition.

Shultz's proposals for a "comprehensive settlement" in the Middle East envisioned a final resolution of the Palestine question that precluded the exercise of the inalienable rights of the Palestinian people to "self-determination without external interference," to "national independence and sovereignty," to "return to their homes and property" and to select and designate their own representatives.[53] It referred to these basic issues in vague terms. For example, it stated that "Palestinians must achieve control over political and economic decisions affecting their lives." These categories fall neither into the realm of sovereignty nor into that of administrative autonomy. Likewise, it added that "Palestinians must be active [but not independent] participants in negotiations to determine their future." Also, "Legitimate [but not national] Palestinian rights can be achieved in a manner which protects Israeli security."[54]

Most of the outstanding issues, such as borders, water resources, Jewish settlements and security, were deferred. Israel could veto any agreement that did not accord with its own view of a proper settlement and thus maintain the status quo on these issues in its favor. Such would have been the logical result of leaving these issues open for "negotiations" beyond the three-year transition period and of depriving the international peace conference of its supervisory role. The conference could not impose solutions or veto agreements reached bilaterally.

Shultz's proposals represented a blend of previous U.S. plans, falling largely between Camp David and the Reagan Plan, but lagging behind both in certain basic aspects. The Shultz Plan promised the Palestinians autonomy but not the "full autonomy" of Camp David. It reiterated Camp David's call for "final status" talks to determine the sovereignty issue in the West Bank and Gaza, despite the fact that the Reagan Plan of September 1, 1982 had subsequently denied that sovereignty to Israel and to the Palestinians in favor of the anticipated Jordanian-Palestinian confederation. In that sense, the Shultz Plan was regressive. It came too late and promised too little, even by U.S. standards, not to mention the global consensus, which required Israeli withdrawal from the West Bank and Gaza and recognition of the right of the Palestinian people to self-determination.

The ingredients of failure were so built into the Shultz Plan that none of the principal parties to the conflict gave it a serious hearing. Neither Washington's Arab friends and "full partners" nor its "authentic" and "moderate" Palestinians inside the occupied territories nor even its strategic and only "democratic" ally in the Middle East who had expressed enthusiasm about the plan. King Hussein realized that an interim settlement which promised the Palestinians autonomy rather than self-determination was doomed, particularly after the four-month-old *Intifada* had rendered the Jordan option unacceptable. Under the circumstances created by the uprising he decided to maintain a low profile, while allowing Israel's prime minister, Yitzhak Shamir to be the first one to turn it down. President Mubarak, who had launched his own proposal during a late January 1988 visit to Washington, retracted his earlier call for a six-month "cooling off" period in the occupied territories and expressed reservations about the concept of interim settlement and a Camp David framework. But he later described the Shultz Plan as "encouraging," and he appealed to Arab leaders not to reject it outright. Since Israeli Prime Minister Shamir had already declared "Shultz's signature" as the "only acceptable" part of the plan, which he also denounced as "bad," "unwelcome" and "impractical," Mubarak was in no need of appearing as the rejectionist.[55] Meanwhile, Shultz's invitation to Palestinians in East Jerusalem to meet with him had been rebuffed. But despite all the skepticism expressed throughout the region about the plan, the Reagan administration tried to keep it alive through an adjunct mission by Philip Habib and a second visit in April to the region by Secretary Shultz himself.

The real aim of the American mission was to defuse the situation on the ground, to arrest the momentum created by the uprising in order to forestall political and social instability in a region which the U.S. regarded as its own turf. The Reagan administration perceived the uprising as a political threat to its hegemony in the region and endeavored to check its potential for extension beyond the occupied territories into Arab countries ruled by conservative regimes. The administration was also concerned about Israel's repressive image in the United States, which could threaten their strategic relationship. Hence the sudden awakening to the fact that the unresolved Palestine-Israeli conflict was a threat to the status quo. An erosion of U.S. public support for American policy towards Israel was seen as a strategic step backward, which Washington could not afford. Shultz's endeavor turned out to be a series of diplomatic shuttles not only between Arab capitals and Israel but also between the two heads of the Israeli government (Shamir and Peres). His diplomacy seemed to have been operating on the assumption that the crucial choices were between Israel's Likud preference for functional autonomy (which keeps "Greater Israel" intact as the Palestinians in the West Bank and Gaza are enfranchised in the Jordanian state) and Labor's "territorial" autonomy, which is a diminutive version of the Jordan option. His diplomacy also assumed that the choices were between Labor's cosmetic international conference and Likud's direct negotiations without a fig leaf. The fact that the Jordan option was dead for the time being, that the concept of a Palestinian-Jordanian delegation was unacceptable, and that the Camp David formula was discredited throughout the Arab world had neither discouraged Mr. Shultz nor constrained his diplomatic efforts.

Upon completion of his second visit during the first week of April 1988, he delivered some very unequivocal "no's": "no" to an independent Palestinian state; "no" to a return to the 1967 situation; "no" to PLO representation.[56] At least the second "no" alone was capable of barring any serious Jordanian consideration of the Shultz Plan, since the recovery of a quarter or one-third of the West Bank could not induce King Hussein to risk pulling a Sadat. Hence whatever basis may have existed for a convergence between the positions of Jordan and Israel's Labor party could not even be matched with the exigencies of the Shultz Plan. Although these exigencies were more in consonance with the perspective of Israel's Labor party than with that of Likud, Mr. Shultz showed a complete lack of willingness and ability to engage in a serious attempt to pressure Shamir. In fact, despite Shultz's tendency to lean more towards the position of Peres than that of Shamir, there seemed to be a remarkable agreement between him and Shamir on fundamental issues: upon completing his April 1988 "shuttle" to the region, Shultz told reporters that his session with Shamir on April 3 had concentrated on the need for direct negotiations between Israel and the Arab states. He said that a Palestinian state was "absolutely" out of the question and that it "does not make sense." When asked by a reporter whether he were saying "no" to a Palestinian state, he replied: "No to a Palestinian state, no to a return to the borders."

Remarkably, Shultz and Shamir were not that far apart; they both coalesced on the need to marginalize the Palestine question and Palestinian national rights. Their differences were procedural but not substantive. For example, when Shamir was asked whether Israel was ready to exchange land for peace, he replied:

We have to leave it for the future. At Camp David, Begin and Sadat agreed to postpone this. We made an agreement with the full cooperation of the U.S. to solve the problem in two stages: First, full autonomy for the Palestinians in the territories for a transition period of five years; then in the third year of autonomy, start negotiations about the final status of the territories.[57]

The difference between the two was over the length of the transition period, but both ruled out Palestinian statehood and a return to the 1967 borders. Moreover, the outcome of Shultz's diplomacy worked for the benefit of Shamir. The latter's visit to the United States in mid-March, ostensibly to discuss peace with the administration, enabled him to respond to U.S. critics of Israeli repression in the occupied territories, to raise funds in the American Jewish community and to solidify and upgrade the U.S. strategic alliance.

The Shultz initiative, therefore, provided Shamir with the context to deflect the kind of criticism which Israel considered potentially harmful to the viability of its special relationship with the United States: criticism from "fair-weather friends" in the American Jewish community, from the U.S. media, and from Congress, as Shamir put it. Having already made his position clear on the Shultz Plan, Shamir directed his attention during his visit in March 1988 to the real mission. In his quest to remove Israel from the defensive corner to which it had been driven by the policy of "might, force and blows," he adopted Henry Kissinger's advice on how to suppress the *Intifada*.

Shamir's second theme was that Israel had already fulfilled its international obligations under UN Security Council Resolution 242 by withdrawing from the Sinai. He particularly emphasized this point in a letter which he directed to Senators Rudy Boschwitz and Carl Levin in response to criticism by thirty U.S. senators of his negative attitude towards the Shultz Plan.[58]

His third theme was that an international peace conference (despite the fig leaf character assigned to it, in deference to Israel's Labor Party preference) was objectionable because it invited Soviet and Chinese communists to a "peace process" which bore the imprint of the United States. As Shamir prepared to depart, Mr. Reagan assured him that, despite the impasse which his rejection had created, "no wedge will ever be driven between us."[59] Ironically, he seemed to be rewarding Israel for non-compliance by speeding up delivery of 75 F-16 jet fighters to Israel and upgrading their strategic alliance.

The "Dialogue" with the PLO

When the PLO recognized Israel's "right to exist," "renounced terrorism" and called for a two-state solution, the Reagan administration had merely agreed to no more than talking to the PLO sporadically at a fairly low level and on the basis of a constricted agenda. Both developments were greeted with the same rejection previously accorded by Israel to the Rogers Plan and the Reagan Plan.

In response to the second major development of 1988—the U.S. decision to open contacts with the PLO—Israel was even more adamant in its rejection. The prime minister's office reacted by saying: "We will continue to look at things the way they are even if all the world is against us... we have been isolated in the past...the United States is one country, we are another."[60] The statement, however, expressed confidence that the special relationship would remain unaffected: "We disagree as friends... we hope this is a passing phase. We hope this is a slip—a short one."[61] This position was indeed vindicated by the subsequent termination of the "substantive dialogue" that George Shultz had authorized on December 13, 1988 and by the demonization of the PLO after the Iraqi invasion of Kuwait. At best, the American opening to the PLO had temporarily draped the PLO with a measure of respectability which Israel had been struggling for so long to deny it.

The major developments in U.S. Mideast policy during 1988 went far beyond the abilities of Shultz and Arafat to bridge the gap in semantics and pinpoint the proper boundaries between clarity and ambiguity. Surely Arafat's famous declarations in December 1988, in which he recognized Israel's right to exist and renounced all forms of terrorism, gave Shultz no choice but to terminate the "no talk" policy. The United States had done no more than agree to talk to the PLO, and George Shultz emphasized that "the first item of business on our agenda in that dialogue will be the subject of terrorism."[62] Reaffirming the U.S. position on direct negotiations and the role of the PLO in these negotiations, he said:

> We hope that dialogue may help bring about direct negotiations that will lead to peace. How those negotiations are structured, who is there to speak on behalf of the Palestinians, is a subject that's a difficult one; we've worked on it a long time, and I imagine it will continue to be difficult.[63]

From the American point of view these talks constituted a forum from which to lecture the PLO on the requirements of acceptable behavior in the hope that the PLO would replace Jordan, for the time being, as interlocutor for the Palestinians of the West Bank and Gaza. It should be made clear that the PLO paid a high price for the dialogue, having met not only Kissinger's conditions for it but also Reagan's codicils. The latter included Israel's "right" to exist rather than merely the right "to live in peace," as well as the "renunciation" rather than the "condemnation" of terrorism. Both of these additions, which impelled Shultz to boast that "I did not change my mind, they changed theirs," were immediately used by the legal minds of the new governments in Washington and Tel Aviv to extract new concessions from the Palestinians; if Israel had the moral and legal right to exist, then why had the Palestinians waged a "war" against it for forty years? By the same logic, the Zionist movement would have to be seen not as a colonial settler phenomenon which resulted in Palestinian dispersal and dispossession, but as a national liberation movement. A further implication was that the *Intifada* was a form of violence and would have to be "renounced" along with the National Charter, which negates Israel's "right" to exist. In fact, according to the first disclosure in the West of the classified protocol of the initial negotiations between the United States and the PLO in Tunis, the United States apparently considered the *Intifada* a form of terrorism. The *Jerusalem Post*, citing the Egyptian magazine *Al Musawwar* as its source, quotes the U.S. delegation as saying to the PLO:

Undoubtedly, the internal struggle that we are witnessing in the occupied territories aims to end the security and stability of the State of Israel, and we therefore demand cessation of those riots, which we view as terrorist acts against Israel. This is especially true as we know you are directing from outside the territories those riots which are sometimes very violent...we want to emphasize that the world "terrorism," as we understand it, includes all Palestinian military action against Israel, whether against Israeli targets, installations or people. This concept includes military action undertaken by Palestinians inside the occupied territories.[64]

Conflict and Convergence in U.S.-Israeli Relations

Having rejected both initiatives of the Reagan administration, Israel had placed itself in a seemingly adversarial position vis-à-vis its ally and benefactor. The irony, however, was that what the U.S. had devised as a short-term remedy and a tactical adjustment, Israel perceived as a mortal danger. Such divergence in the perception of the 1980s realities between the U.S. and Israel, however, had not developed into a crisis. The recent diplomatic history of the region reveals a number of so-called reassessments, undertaken by successive administrations, including Reagan's. They served, in effect, as reminders to Israel that occasional historical changes often alter the context and forces operating on U.S. and Israeli interests in the region, which might provoke divergence in their styles, conceptions of security and the cost and nature of alliances. Such divergences are not untypical of those occurring between colonial settler regimes, which must survive on the land, labor and resources of indigenous people, and the more mobile and flexible metropolitan interests, which must accommodate shifting alliances and emerging political and economic forces. In a word, the United States is more capable of adapting to shifting alignments than Israel, whose margin of maneuver is constrained by national and religious myths, which inhibit flexible policy reactions to social change. The United States, as a superpower, was also called upon to deal with its increased diplomatic isolation in the Middle East. Israel, on the other hand, acting under the impetus of a fortress mentality, had become more accustomed to defiance and obstruction of the international consensus and rather oblivious to the cost of defending Israel's territorial acquisitions and colonialist projects.

The rhetoric of U.S. policy towards Israel began to shift in response to this emerging perceptual gap between the two countries and as an acknowledgement of the *Intifada*. For example, in response to this emerging gap between the U.S. and Israel, which was brought to the surface by the *Intifada*, the Undersecretary of State for Near Eastern and South Asian Affairs, Richard Murphy, raised the cost of suppressing the *Intifada* on June 11, 1988 in an address before the New York Council on Foreign Relations. His speech was appropriately titled "Middle East Peace: Facing Realities and Challenges."[65] He found a glaring disparity between Israel's defense expenditure, which amounts to 19% of the Gross National Product, and the average for other countries in the world, which is 5%. Such a disparity could only be maintained by a permanent U.S. subsidy, which would impose severe burdens on an economy that was already burdened by the largest budget and trade deficits in U.S. history and by a defense budget approaching $300 billion a year. Israel's diplomatic rigidity and lack of sensitivity to altered realities was succinctly described by Hebrew University professor Yaron Ezrahi in the following words:

Israel has been jarred into reality...our leaders were living in the most incredible and unrealistic universe, constructed entirely by their own hands. In this universe, American support was treated as though it were a divine right. Israel did not invest seriously in political initiatives vis-à-vis the Palestinians, and it was indifferent to the changes in American public opinion. Now we are paying the price.[66]

Divergence between Israeli and American perceptions of security, which contrary to Ezrahi's conclusion was of no cost to Israel, continued to strain relations between the two allies, but failed to cause any rupture, inasmuch as the divergence was limited to the verbal level. Thus Secretary of State Shultz appealed to Israel on June 5, 1988, upon his arrival there to save his ill-fated plan, to reassess its concept of security: "The location of borders is less significant today in ensuring security than the political relations between neighbors. Peace is the real answer to the problem of security."[67] He urged Israel and the Arabs to re-examine their definitions of political rights, boundaries and sovereignty, which he considered as "outdated" in view of emerging global realities: "Borders today are permeable and porous, indifferent to the ballistic missile, and indifferent to the desire of any sovereign to shut out the outside world."[68]

The same message was also conveyed by Richard Murphy, who asked rhetorically: "Are peace and normalization essential to satisfy the necessity for security? The answer is yes, because geography and conventional military strategy can no longer ensure security."[69] He also challenged Israel to "accept and act upon the understanding that legitimate political rights and democratic self-expression for Palestinians are compatible with Israeli security;" adding that "In the long run, they are the key to real security for an Israel at peace with its neighbors."[70]

The altered realities of that era have also moved the United States towards a public re-examination of the conception of rights. That, in addition to a belated discovery of the damaging consequences of an impasse that was allowed to widen, impelled Washington to sound the proper warning about prolonged occupations. Thus, Secretary Shultz counselled Israel on June 5, 1988 that "continued occupation of the West Bank and Gaza and frustration of Palestinian rights is a dead-end street."[71] The phraseology of his three 1988 shuttles, while conforming to the linguistic parameters of diplomacy, did not conceal U.S. anxiety about the consequences of the impasse. He promised an "equitable settlement of the land issue" and tried to assure the Arabs that Resolution 242 calls for the "exchange of territory for peace."[72] The settlement must address "legitimate Palestinian political rights" so that Palestinians and Israelis "learn to treat each other decently, respect their mutual right to live in security, and fulfill their political aspirations." Palestinian-Israeli accommodation was not consistent with a "winner-take-all" approach, he said. Israelis and Palestinians "will realize that the fulfillment of their own dreams is impossible without the fulfillment of the other side's dream." While Shultz promised the Palestinians "control over political and economic decisions that affect their lives and active participation in the peace process," he spoke of the necessity to call off their uprising: "For Palestinians, the challenge is to forge an effective political program to replace slogans and violence."

If we judge the emerging U.S. approach to the Palestine-Israel conflict by Mr. Shultz's prose, we might conclude that we were approaching a new chapter in United States Middle East diplomacy—one that was more credible and more even-handed. Although it signified some departures from the uncritical support of the general Israeli position, deemed necessary because of strategic considerations, it still maintained opposition to fundamental Palestinian rights and to real international supervision of the negotiations. And yet the Reagan-Shultz legacy to George Bush included some kind of an adjustment. Undersecretary of State Richard Murphy, for example, had this to say about Camp David:

Can these people [the Israelis] really believe that the clock can be turned back to 1978 and that negotiations can start from a basis which Jordan, Syria, and others rejected categorically? This is an illusion which cannot and will not be fulfilled.[73]

Murphy added the factors of "demography, tools of war and extremism" to the emerging realities which were changing the diplomatic landscape of the Middle East.

In summary, the Reagan-Shultz legacy to the Bush administration contained considerable rhetoric about the need for change, but it had certainly failed to usher the way towards real change. The firm commitment of the Reagan administration to the strategic alliance with Israel had superseded the need to bridge the perceptual gap regarding the limits of the special relationship and the objective determinants of U.S. policy. The *Intifada* had reshaped the Palestine-Israel conflict in 1988; the challenge to George Bush was to reconcile the varying responses of the U.S. and of Israel.

The Bush-Baker Strategy
Round One

The last two months in office for the Reagan-Bush adminstration were very busy in terms of Middle East developments. A historic recognition of Israel by the PLO in November 1988 and a reunification of terrorism by Yaser Arafat obliged the administration to suspend its no-talk policy and to start a dialogue with the PLO at the ambassadorial level.[74] The seriousness with which the world reacted to the Palestinian peace initiative was demonstrated in a myriad of actions, not the least of which was the removal of the entire session of the United Nations General Assembly to Geneva to hear the speech by Arafat, who was barred from New York by the U.S. Secretary of State, George Shultz.[75] Suddenly, the dipomatic ball was thrown into Israel's court, and the United States was challenged to produce an initiative. After all, Washington had offered its diplomacy as the alternative to the UN framework and imposed itself as sole conciliator in the Middle East. It was time to deliver.

And yet, the incoming administration of George Bush seemed to be in no particularly hurry to produce a new initiative in the Middle East. The lack of action by the new administration during its first five months in office was reflective of its world view and its sensitivity to domestic realities. Mr. Baker, who viewed the world through the prism of American domestic politics, expressed apprehension along with the president about major initiatives that might lead to doing "dumb things." Not only did the Middle East have a low priority on their policy agenda at that time, but it also suffered from the absence of a constituency of pressure against Israel. Consequently, they spent the first five months waiting for things to "ripen" on the Palestinian-Israel front, in accordance with counsel supplied by the pro-Israel think tank known as the Washington Institute for Near East Policy. And when it became clear that the Middle East could no longer be ignored, they moved with characteristic caution and timidity. The fear of doing the wrong thing appeared to haunt this administration to the extent that it began to look for surrogates who would sponsor its ideas. Shamir and Mubarak were persuaded to attach their imprimatur to the plan that Baker would later declare as "the only game in town." It was vintage for an administraiton that continues to pay lip service to the "vision thing" but lacked a necessary measure of conceptualization and the will to forge ahead with commensurate courage.

The diplomatic void was filled by the so-called elections plan supplied by Shamir, a rather safe issue for the Bush administration, which had introduced it and elevated it to the centerpiece of its Mideast diplomacy. The plan itself, which Israeli Defense Minister Rabin had earlier conceived as a means to stop the *Intifada* and to provide the U.S. Congress with the necessary justification to maintain the status quo, received approval of the Israeli cabinet on May 4, 1989.[76] It was decorated with slogans and buzzwords designed to grant it easy access to the American political arena. Phrases such as "free democratic elections" (a sacrosanct concept in liberal America), "lull in violence" and "interim phases" were safe enough issues for the administration to extend approval.

The substance of the Twenty Point Program, however, was totally rejectionist. Consider the four points which constitute its "Basic Premises":

1. Direct negotiations based on the Camp David accords.
2. "No" to negotiations with the PLO.
3. "No" to a Palestinian state.
4. "No" to "any change in the status of Judea, Samaria and Gaza other than in accordance with the basic guidelines of the Government."

The administration, however, continued to try to "play it safe" with a major address by Secretary Baker to the American-Israel Public Affairs Committee (AIPAC) on May 22, 1989.[77] It was filled with rhetoric but short on substance, carefully avoiding the label of a U.S. plan. Its list of "do's" and "don'ts" placed the administration in the position of arbiter, albeit an active bystander whose intense scrutiny would fall short of producing a verdict. Shamir dismissed it with a mild rebuke as "useless," despite the fact that Baker's demands from the Palestinians and Arabs were more substantially specific than those made on Israel. He urged them to produce a "constructive" response to the initiatives which the "Israeli government *has* offered." He commanded the Palestinians to "renounce the policy of in all languages…. Amend the Covenant. Translate the dialogue of violence in the *Intifada* into a dialogue of politics and diplomacy." He asked them to accept a transitional period of autonomy prior to a final settlement. He warned them not to "distort international organizations" by seeking admission to membership in the United Nations' specialized agencies. He wanted them to convince the Israelis of their peaceful intentions, to accept as a real opening the elections proposed by the Shamir government and to "understand that no one is going to deliver Israel for you."

As for Israel, the new element in Secretary Baker's AIPAC speech was not merely the language:

> Now is the time to lay aside, once and for all, the unrealistic vision of a greater Israel…. Forswear annexation. Stop settlement activity. Allow schools to reopen. Reach out to the Palestinians as neighbors who deserve political rights.

Mr. Baker clearly placed the onus for breaking the impasse on the Palestinians and the Arab world, which he admonished to "take concrete steps towards accommodation with Israel," and he insisted that such steps could not be taken outside the framework of the "peace process." He therefore ignored previous Arab efforts on behalf of accommodation, which spanned two decades, beginning with UN mediator Gunnar Jarring in 1970 and including the numerous resolutions adopted by Arab summit conferences calling for mutual recognition. He bade the Arabs to "…end the economic boycott, stop the challenges to Israel's standing in international organizations, repudiate the odious line that Zionism is racism." He then turned to the Soviet Union, which, unlike the United States, was committed to the right of self-determination for both Arabs and Jews in Palestine, and challenged it to extend the "new thinking" to the Middle East.

On the whole, the first major policy statement of the Bush administration introduced very little, if any, in terms of substance. But the sensational phraseology, reaffirming the U.S. perspective on Israel's obligations under Resolution 242, marked a stylistic change in Washington's dealing with Israel. The only new element in the speech, however, was Washington's open support for Shamir's elections plan. And yet the speech was widely interpreted in the U.S. as the first major policy pronouncement of the Bush administration and was generally described as even-handed.

If sponsoring elections through Israel was the first phase of the Bush-Baker diplomacy, selling the plan to the Palestinians through Egypt was the second phase. Washington's secondary proxy in the region would sweeten the bait and try to camouflage its *diktat* character.[78] But Mubarak's ten-point plan was rejected by Israel, notwithstanding its capitulatory character. Consider the procedurally-oriented amendments it offered, with no mention of Palestinian independence, or its accommodation of the Likud by creating a new legitimate representative of the Palestinian people—figures from the West Bank and Gaza.

Baker's response to its recalcitrant ally was five "suggested points," again carefully avoiding the impression that there was any American plan and keeping the U.S. away from the center of the negotiating process.[79] The intent of the "suggested points" was to hold a meeting of the foreign ministers of Egypt, Israel and the U.S. in order to decide who was the legitimate representative of the Palestinians. After all, Mr. Shamir not only rejecting the PLO in that role; he also expressed objections to a broad range of Palestinians from Jerusalem, the diaspora and those involved in the uprising in the occupied territories. He said in response to Mubarak's earlier invitation to an Israeli and a Palestinian delegation to Cairo the following: "Who will come to Cairo? The leaders of the *Intifada* will come. Were we to sit together, it would not be for negotiations but surrender talks."[80] Israeli rejectionism of its patron's suggestions had become so untenable that it disturbed traditional supporters in the United States. "Bleak Rejectionism" was the title of a *Washington Post* editorial on October 9, 1989, accusing Shamir of making a decision "to greet the new president in his first year...with a hard line in order to set the tone for the rest of his term." A *New York Times* editorial (October 4, 1989) titled "Is Coaxing Enough?" stated that Shamir and his allies were "tough customers" who were "unlikely to budge unless Washington makes clear, at least privately, its determination to get talks underway."

That the Shamir government was stalling and perpetuating the impasse was indeed very clear. But the important thing was that Shamir had renounced his own proposal, under pressure from new extremist allies in the Likud coalition who believed the plan would ultimately lead to a Palestinian state. Hence the crisis in U.S.-Israeli relations. And yet none of the other parties would rock the boat; Baker would not push Shamir into a corner and risk a collapse of his fragile "national unity" government. Mubarak, with a vested interest in a settlement that would vindicate Egypt and present Camp David as the way for the future, was not ready for a confrontation with Shamir either, and the PLO, with the most to lose, since it would be formally disenfranchised, decided against rejecting what amounted to a repackaged Camp David in order not to be seen as the spoiler. It obliged Baker by providing the green light for Palestinian leaders in the occupied territories to meet with Israeli officials and with the Bush administration's first high-ranking delegation in May 1989. Such accommodation took place even when Washington's own contacts with the PLO, under guidelines established by the outgoing Reagan administration, were limited to the level of U.S. functionaries in Tunis. The PLO had emerged, in effect, as the silent non-public interlocutor who would deliver acceptable Palestinian leadership from the occupied territories in order to keep Baker's diplomatic endeavor viable. It was the only alternative left for Baker, after all means were exhausted by Washington, to promote Jordan as the Palestinian interlocutor.

After Jordan decided to sever constitutional links with the West Bank under the impact of the *Intifada* in August 1988, the PLO made the hard choice of scaling down even its minimal position outlined in the November 1988 Declaration of Independence in which it recognized Israel,[81] in return for having acquiesced in a "peace process" with self-government rather than statehood on the active agenda. The PLO had hoped to salvage as much as possible of the ever-vanishing land in the West Bank and Gaza. But even that limited objective proved unattainable, given Mr. Baker's reluctance to assume the role of "catalyst for peace" and in view of the absence of any international authority to insist on the implementation of United Nations resolutions.

Meanwhile Baker's first round was dealt a crushing blow when Shamir renounced his own plan despite its potential to produce a settlement favorable to Israel. Given the administration's excessively cautious approach bordering on timidity, and given the uncritical attitude of U.S. legislators beholden to the pro-Israel lobby, any meaningful pressure on Shamir was simply not in the offing.[82] The closest to an exercise of a daring act on Baker's part was flashing the State Department's telephone number on the television screen followed by the statement: "If interested in peace, call us."

In the meantime, the PLO had not only played Arafat's "last card," i.e., recognition, but the *Intifada's* card as well, which produced a meager dialogue with Washington. From Washington's perspective, the Palestinians, who have been marginalized, would have to develop new cards or make yet new concessions in order to warrant substantive U.S. moves beyond the dialogue, which itself was terminated a few months later. The Israelis, on the other hand, would have to be persuaded that their security was not compatible with the status quo and that U.S. global interests would have to supersede Israel's interest in keeping *all* the occupied territories. Some sort of a land-for-peace exchange was beginning to look more and more necessary from Washington's vantage point. Shamir would have to be prevailed upon to resurrect his plan and to rethink his total and irrevocable opposition to a comprehensive settlement that would entail withdrawal, even if it were to be confined effectively to the Golan. Such a "grand design," however, had to wait for a major regional or international development; the Gulf War was a convenient catalyst.

Notes

1. *New York Times*, May 4, 1982.
2. Jimmy Carter's phrase as reported in the *New York Times*, April 1, 1976.
3. *Boston Globe*, December 20, 1988.
4. Annual Review of U.S. Middle East Policy (Washington: Department of State); based on a statement by Harold H. Saunders, Assistant Secretary for Near Eastern and South Asian Affairs, before the Subcommittee on Europe and the Middle East of the House International Relations Committee, June 12, 1977, p. 11.
5. *New York Times*, January 14, 1977.
6. *New York Times*, February 19, 1977.
7. *New York Times*, February 15, 1977.
8. *The Economist*, January 8, 1977, p. 63.
9. Text of the speech in the *New York Times*, March 19, 1977.
10. Interview in *Time*, August 8, 1977.
11. Text in the *New York Times*, October 2, 1977.
12. Text in the *New York Times*, October 6, 1977.
13. Text in the *New York Times*, October 14, 1977.
14. For a discussion of Reagan's anti-terrorist policies, see Naseer Aruri and John Carroll, "U.S. Policy and Terrorism," *American-Arab Affairs*, No. 14 (Fall 1985), pp. 59–70; also, by the same authors, "The Anti-Terrorist Crusade," *Arab Studies Quarterly*, Vol. IV, No. 2 (Spring 1987), pp. 173–187.
15. For a discussion of the Reagan Plan, see Naseer Aruri and Fouad Moughrabi, "The Reagan Middle East Initiative," *Journal of Palestine Studies*, Vol. XII, No. 2 (Winter 1983), pp. 10–30; also Naseer Aruri et al., *Reagan and the Middle East* (Belmont, Mass.: AAUG Press, 1983), pp. 49–86.
16. On Israel's role in the U.S. global strategy, see Noam Chomsky, *The Fateful Triangle* (Boston: South End Press, 1983); Jane Hunter, *Israeli Foreign Policy: South Africa and Central America* (Boston: South End Press, 1988); Israel Shahak, *Israel's Global Role: Weapons for Repression* (Belmont, Mass.: AAUG Press, 1982); Milton Jamail and Margo Gutierrez, *It's No Secret: Israel's Military Involvement in Central America* (Belmont, Mass.: AAUG

Press, 1986).

17. See highlights of the plan and texts of speeches by Shultz explaining the plan in "U.S. Policy in the Middle East," U.S. Department of State, Bureau of Public Affairs, No. 27 (June 1988).

18. For a text of the PNC resolutions dated April 26, 1987, see *Journal of Palestine Studies*, Vol. XVI, No. 4 (Summer 1987), pp. 196–204.

19. Text of Arafat's address in *Journal of Palestine Studies*, Vol. XVIII, No. 2 (Winter 1989), pp. 206–213.

20. David Ottoway, "State Department Official Defends Israel's Use of Force," *Washington Post*, March 30, 1988, p. A–21.

21. According to a confidential memorandum by Julius Berman, a former Chairman of the Conference of Presidents of Major American Jewish Organizations, Henry Kissinger told eight Jewish leaders at a breakfast in early February 1988:

> Israel should bar the media from entry into the territories involved in the present demonstrations, [should] accept the short-term criticism of the world press for such conduct, and [should] put down the insurrection as quickly as possible—overwhelmingly, brutally and rapidly.

Letter dated February 3, 1988 typed on stationary imprinted with Kaye, Scholer, Fireman, Hays & Handler. Also news story by Robert McFadden in *New York Times* March 5, 1988.

22. Ottoway,

23. Resolution 605, December 22, 1987.

24. Resolutions 607 (January 5, 1988) and 608 (January 14, 1988).

25. Resolution s/19466 (January 29, 1988).

26. Donald Neff, "Diplomatic Isolation," *Middle East International*, January, 23, 1988, pp. 7–8.

27. *Jerusalem Post*, August 24, 1988.

28. Mark J. Penn and Douglas E. Schoen, "American Attitudes Towards the Middle East," *Public Opinion*, May/June 1988, p. 47.

29. *Los Angeles Times*, June 3, 1987.

30. Penn and Schoen, p. 46.

31. Gallup Organization, "A Gallup Survey Regarding the West Bank and

Gaza Conflict between Israel and the Palestinians," Princeton, N.J., March 11, 1988.

32. *Los Angeles Times,* June 3, 1987.
33. Penn and Schoen, p. 46.
34. Gallup Organization, op. cit.
35. Penn and Schoen, p. 45.
36. George Gallup, Jr., and Alec Gallup, "Talks with PLO Support," *San Francisco Chronicle,* January 16, 1989.
37. *St. Petersburg Times,* December 29, 19887.
38. *Omaha World Herald,* December 21, 1987.
39. *Arizona Republic,* December 17, 1987.
40. *Miami Herald,* December 21, 19887.
41. *Sun Reporter,* December 23, 1987.
42. *Grand Rapids, Press* December 25, 1987.
43. *The Charlotte Observer,* December 28, 1987.
44. *Washington Post,* March 8, 1988.
45. *New York Times,* March 25, 1988; see also Rob Wright, "Rep. Frank Urges Israel to Withdraw from Territories," *Boston Globe,* March 9, 1988.
46. *New York Times,* March 11, 1988; see also Joseph Harsch, "Shultz's Slow Steady Mideast Moves Builds on U.S. Jews' Support," *Christian Science Monitor,* March 18, 1988.
47. "Resolution of the Jewish Congress on the Middle East Peace Process," *American-Arab Affairs,* No. 22 (Fall 1987), pp. 120–23.
48. *New York Times,* January 25, 1988.
49. *New York Times,* March 21, 1988.
50. *New York Times,* May 8, 1988.
51. *New York Times,* January 26, 1988; see also James Franklin, "U.S. Jewish Leader Criticizes Israelis for Crackdown on Press," *Christian Science Monitor,* March 5, 1988. Reference is to Theodore Ellenoff, President of the American Jewish Committee; see also Linda Feldmann, "U.S. Jews in Turmoil over Violence in Israel," *Christian Science Monitor,* March 4, 1988.
52. See article by Mark Muro, "And Now: A Jewish Intifada," *Boston Globe,* (Focus Section), December 25, 1988, p. A–24.
53. For an analysis of the Shultz Plan, see Kathleen Christison, "The Arab-Israeli Policy of George Shultz," *Journal of Palestine Studies,* Vol. XVIII, No. 2 (Winter 1989), pp. 29–47.

54. From "The statement by Secretary of State George Shultz addressed to the Palestinians in the occupied territories in East Jerusalem," February 26, 1988, Washington, D.C., Department of State, Bureau of Public Affairs (Current Policy No. 1055). (see Appendix)

55. *Boston Globe,* March 12, 1988, p. 4.

56. *Boston Globe,* April 6, 1988; also Associated Press dispatch in *Standard-Times,* (New Bedford, Mass.), April 5, 1988.

57. *U.S. News and World Report,* March 21, 1988.

58. Text of letter from Shamir on criticism from 30 U.S. senators in *New York Times,* March 10, 1988.

59. *New York Times,* March 17, 1988.

60. *Boston Globe,* December 16, 1988.

61. *Ibid.*

62. *New York Times,* December 19, 1988.

63. For a text of Shultz's news conference, see *New York Times,* December 15, 1988, p. 18–A.

64. *Jerusalem Post,* January 6, 1989.

65. Richard W. Murphy, "Middle East Peace: Facing Realities and Challenges," U.S. Department of State, Bureau of Public Affairs, Current Policy No. 1082.

66. *New York Times,* December 19, 1988.

67. "U.S. Policy in the Middle East," no. 27, op. cit., p. 8.

68. *Ibid.*

69. Richard W. Murphy, "Middle East Peace: Facing Realities and Challenges," op. cit.

70. *Ibid.*

71. "U.S. Policy in the Middle East," No. 27, op. cit.

72. Secretary Schultz, "The Administration's Approach to Peacemaking," a speech before the Washington Institute for Near East Policy, Wye Plantation, Queenstown, Maryland, September 16, 1988, U.S. Department of State, Current Policy No. 1104.

73. Richard Murphy, op. cit., p. 3.

74. *New York Times,* December 16, 1988.

75. The Palestinian initiative was received warmly at the official level in Europe. The socialist members of the European Parliament invited Arafat to address the Parliament in Strasbourg. Even British Prime Minister

Margaret Thatcher said that the initiative qualified the PLO to participate in a peace conference (*Boston Globe,* December 16, 1988) and the
British Foreign Office issued a statement welcoming the fact that "The
Americans share our analysis that the PLO has moved to positions that
represent real progress" (*Ibid.*).

76. "A Peace Initiative: Document," *The Jerusalem Post,* May 15, 1989.

77. Secretary Baker's "Principles and Pragmatism: American Policy toward
the Arab-Israeli Conflict," Washington: U.S. Department of State, Bureau
of Public Affairs, Current Policy No. 1176; also see *New York Times,* May
23, 1989. (see Appendix)

78. For a text, see "Mubarak's 10 Point Plan," *Boston Globe,* October 8, 1989;
also see Abba Eban, "Mubarak's Offer: A Dramatic Test" *New York Times*
September 28, 1989, and Joel Brinkley, "New Israeli Thicket," *New York
Times,* September 27, 1989.

79. Thomas Friedman, "Advance Reported on Middle East Talks," *New York
Times,* December 7, 1989, and Mary Curtius, "Shamir Is Seen Accepting
Egypt View of U.S. Plan," *Boston Globe,* December 8, 1989.

80. Brinkley, op. cit.

81. Several articles on the subject in *New York Times,* December 15, 1988.

82. Naseer Aruri, "America's Passive Approach," *Middle East International,*
No. 636, November 7, 1989.

6

Further Marginalization

The Impact of the Gulf War

The conflict in the Gulf had a profound effect on the Palestinian people, their economic and social institutions, their relations with Arab countries and with the international community, on the status of the PLO, and on the prospects for realizing their minimal goals. The conflict and its aftermath have created serious disruptions in the lives of Palestinian communities living under Israeli occupation, in the Gulf countries, in Jordan, Egypt, and in Lebanon. It is safe to state that for the overwhelming majority of these communities, the new situation has not been less than calamitous. This chapter will examine the social, economic and political implications of the Gulf crisis and the postwar conditions for the Palestinians, the PLO, their cause and continued struggle for self-determination. It will probe the relationship between these largely negative implications and the political stance of the Palestinian leadership during the impasse, and will analyze the evolving strategy for resolution of the Palestine-Israel conflict.

The Gulf War and the Israeli Right-Wing

A debate between the Israeli left and right was taking place as the Iraqi Army tried to consolidate its occupation of Kuwait. Twelve prominent Palestinians and sixteen Israeli Knesset members issued a joint statement at the Notre Dame Hotel in Jerusalem on August 5, 1990 calling for a "just resolution" of the Arab-Israeli conflict. The principles of the settlement included the right of the Palestinians to self-determination in accordance with UN General Assembly Resolution against colonization (1960), and to designate their own representatives to an international peace conference that would convene under UN auspices in accordance with UN Security Council Resolutions 242 and 338. The statement emphasized that "no side can decide for the other who will represent it in the negotiations.[1]

On the other hand, the Israeli right-wing was beginning to make its presence felt more than ever in the wake of the failure of Secretary of State James Baker in March 1990 to dissuade Prime Minister Shamir from disavowing his own plan for elections in the West Bank and Gaza. Knesset member Rehavam Ze'evi of the extremist Molodet party told the Knesset Foreign Affairs and Defense Committee that "we should take the Palestinians and place them in front of the Arab forces."[2] He also urged that Israel announce the immediate expulsion of Palestinians in the event of an Iraqi attack.[3] The debate had already been proceeding in favor of the superhawks, who made their entry into Shamir's new cabinet in March 1990, well before the Iraqi invasion of Kuwait. In mid-September, elements from the "peace camp" were calling for an end to the ongoing dialogue between Palestinians and Israelis, and by December, their meetings had all but ceased.[4] Central to that debate was the issue of the *Intifada* and the best ways to end it. The faint voices of the "peace camp" were drowned by the avalanche from the right, now fueled by increasing violence in the *Intifada*, which they attributed to the radical appeal of Saddam Hussein. Their analysis conveniently side-stepped other crucial factors such as the massive immigration of Soviet Jews, the massacres of Rishon Le Zion in May and of Al-Haram Al Sharif in October 1990.

The Gulf Crisis provided the Israeli government with a natural pretext to clamp down more violently on the *Intifada* in an atmosphere of near total freedom from international scrutiny. While the attention of the media and international human rights agencies was focused on Kuwait, the U.S. and her Arab partners were engaged in crisis management to keep the coalition intact, and the Israeli "peace camp" was paralyzed.

The new draconian measures applied by Israel in the occupied territories during the Gulf crisis were the culmination of a determined and systematic effort which began in March of the same year when Shamir terminated Baker's effort to salvage his own plan and publicly embraced the position of the super-hawks. Under the Gulf cover, Israel embarked more aggressively on the "destruction of all the achievements of the *Intifada* over the past three and a half years in health, education, and economy, in addition to the political achievements."[5]

The unfolding conflict in the Gulf and the Arab world provided yet another opportunity for crippling the Palestinian infrastructure under occupation.

Impact on the Economy Under Occupation

1. The Agricultural Sector

Since the inception of the Gulf crisis, new restrictions were imposed on Palestinian agricultural exports to the Gulf. These measures were adopted in time for the olive oil harvest, which was abundant in the 1990 season. The harvest, which is a major source of livelihood for Palestinian farmers, generates an income of $50 million, and it usually far exceeds the requirements of local consumption. The rationale for these measures was the prevention of trade with Iraq, although Tahseen Al-Faris, chairman of the Federation of Cooperatives for Agricultural Marketing, testified before the so-called Civil Administration, i.e., the Israeli military government, that "Iraq does not import any products from us."[6] Another casualty was the citrus fruit export from Gaza, which normally nets $10 million. Of 174,000 tons produced in 1989, 48,000 were exported to Arab countries through Jordan.[7] The halt of exports to the Gulf posed a severe problem for citrus growers as similar difficulties affecting Jordanian exports forced a competition with Palestinian produce in Jordan. The Agricultural Relief Committees of the occupied territories estimated that 30–40 percent of agricultural produce is exported to Arab countries through Jordan. In the case of bananas, however, that ratio is 90 percent.

Not only did Israeli authorities ban Palestinian farm exports to the Arab world, but they also began to enforce previous measures adopted early in the *Intifada* banning Israeli markets to Palestinian produce. Israeli juice factories, for example, bought 55% of their production from Gaza in 1989. Instead, in 1990, the authorities confiscated enormous amounts inside Israel as part of the measure to enforce regulations, and even banned trade between the West Bank and Gaza leading to the accumulation of huge surpluses and a glut of perishable seasonal fruits and vegetables. Still newer measures were adopted by Agriculture Minister General Rafael Eitan, who once vowed to "squeeze the Palestinians like drugged cockroaches in a bottle." Agricultural boycott of the occupied territories would end the "…sale of fertilizers, cows, chicks, seeds and seedlings to farmers in the West Bank and Gaza…to the extent that it is used to support the *Intifada*."[8]

As if such measures, amounting to a war against Palestinian agriculture, were not sufficient, the authorities declared a 24-hour indefinite curfew on the entire occupied territories starting on January 17, 1991, the day George Bush started the air war against Iraq. Israel Knesset member Abd al-Wahab Darawsheh of the Arab Democratic party accused the government of using the Gulf War as a pretext to punish the Palestinians.[9] At a January 23rd news conference, the Coordinating Committee of International Non-Governmental Organizations in the occupied territories said that 1.7 million Palestinians are being subjected to "…in effect, house arrest."[10]

The agricultural sector was severely hit by the curfew, primarily because people were unable to tend to their farms. Approximately 30,000 farm workers were unable to go to the work place. According to Dr. Abd al-Fattah Abu-Shukr, Dean of Faculty of Economics at Najah University, some 100,000 *donums* (4 *donums* to an acre) of irrigated land in the West Bank were damaged during the first ten days of the curfew, which lasted 37 days.[11] During the same period losses suffered in greenhouse production which depends on irrigation, amounted to $19 million during the same short period. The West Bank was losing $45 million per week and Gaza was losing $15 million as a result of the curfew.

The Non-Governmental Organizations (NGO) committee reported in its news conference that "Palestinian farmers are prevented from irrigating, spraying, harvesting, or marketing their crops."[12] The curfew's effect on the agricultural sector differed depending on land topography and climate conditions. In the highlands which depend on rainfall the impact was severe. The curfew was imposed after a period of drought which has already had a devastating effect on the fruit and olive harvest and caused the grain harvest a loss of 60 percent, grazing was also limited. Coincidentally, there was substantial rainfall during the curfew, but because of the curfew, farmers were unable to plow and sow the seed, causing a loss of a whole season of grain, and depriving animals from grazing, thus denying many farmers their usual livelihood, in addition to causing a negative impact on the following fruit season. In the highlands of the West Bank, the land must always be cultivated and readied for the production of olives, grapes, and almonds. Meat and dairy products fluctuate according to winter grazing season.

As to the plains in the Jordan Valley, Tulkarem area and Gaza, where farmers depend on irrigation, the produce consists of citrus fruits, bananas and vegetables. Here, thousands of farmers were unable to pick, market and spray with insecticides. Similar damage occurred in the intensive farming in greenhouses. Thousands of acres were destroyed. In the Tulkarem region, for example, where thousands of *donums* of citrus were left to rot on the ground during the curfew, the loss was estimated at $4.5 million per week. The January 1991 memorandum of the Palestinian Economic Coordinating and Planning Committee summed up the loss to the agricultural sector, which employs 42,000 people and contributes 35% of the GNP in a good season, this way:

> It should be evident by now that the curfew strikes a heavy blow to all aspects of the agricultural production processes. The most relevant loss however, is the one resulting from the decline in the level of the consumption for agricultural plant animal products which lowered their prices. Now with the curfew entering its fifth week the farmers will be forced to get rid of their herds. This poses a direct threat to future years. The most significant damage in this sector will fall on the sheep and goat breeders and following them the cattle breeders, then the vegetable farmers, especially the small ones, and finally the citrus and banana farmers, in descending order.

2. The Industrial Sector

The industrial sector which employs 30,000 workers and accounts for 15 percent of the Gross Domestic Product, is itself based primarily on agricultural inputs. It was adversely affected by the same problems which caused enormous damage to the agricultural sector, including distribution blockages of both raw materials and finished goods, reduced demand and the inability to operate due to the restriction on movement, especially during the curfew. Even some of the food and medicine factories which received special permits to open were unable to operate because the farms that provided them with milk and other raw materials or the tin factories which provided containers for olive oil were shut down. Only a small percentage of their workers obtained curfew passes. The frequent curfews and bans on travel created irreparable economic damage the effect of which was not only felt in the short range but will also be felt in the medium and long range as well. Curfews limit the production of items due to a shrinkage of demands and an effective closure of markets, causing a ripple effect because of the organic link between all the different sectors (industrial, trading, agricultural and service.) It is noteworthy however, that shoe factories in the West Bank which supply Israel with 90 percent of its needs at a low cost, were allowed to operate without any interruption.

3. Wage Laborers

From the very inception of the 1967 occupation, Israel pursued an anti-development strategy calculated to prevent any evolution towards economic independence in these territories. The aim was to integrate them into the Israeli economy as perpetual dependencies. Concurrently with land acquisition and colonization, Israel embarked on a policy of tapping other resources, including water and labor. By 1990 some 120,000 Palestinian workers were absorbed into the Israeli labor market, comprising 7% of the total labor force in Israel. This constituted 44% of construction workers, 17% of agricultural workers, 6% of service workers, and 4% of industrial workers.[13] Those plus 170,000 workers in the West Bank and Gaza have been the most severely hurt by the various restrictions in movement during the Gulf crisis and particularly by the prolonged curfew in January and February 1991. Unable to work and dependent on daily wages, many of them experienced drastic reduction in their purchasing power and some were forced to sell or mortgage what little jewelry they have in order to buy food. By the latter part of 1990 with Soviet immigration at an all-time high and violence on the rise by the army, settlers and the *Intifada*, the Gulf crisis provided another opportunity to attempt a crippling of economic life in the occupied territories.

A plan to reduce Palestinian workers by 50% was officially adopted by the Israeli Economic Ministry in November, and new restrictions on Palestinian entry into Israel proper began to take a toll on Palestinian workers who traveled to their work place. Judith Winkler wrote in *Ha'aretz*: "There is by now, an established process of expelling the Arab workers from their work places in Israel."[14] Given that some 70,000 Palestinian workers had no permits to work in Israel under the new plan, the fines for employers was from $250 to $1000 for each violation of labor laws along with a fine of $450 for each day an illegal worker is employed. The Minister of Economy, David Magen, estimated that some 60,000 Palestinian workers would lose their jobs under this plan. To effect this the Israeli army issued green cards to all Palestinian s deemed "security risks." Those were automatically barred from entry into Israel. Any Palestinian caught working or sleeping illegally in Israel was to be arrested and taken back to his place of residence to stand trial.[15] Even Jerusalem is out of bounds to green card holders. Indeed, many workers already lost their jobs to new Soviet immigrants and joined the army of unemployed, already on the rise due to Israel's anti-development strategy.

Economist Abu-Shukr told *Time* magazine that a total ban on Palestinian Labor in Israel would raise unemployment from 20% to 55% in the West Bank and from 25% to 60% in Gaza.[16] He estimated that about 75% of the West Bank population are considered to be either poor or living under the poverty line (a monthly income of approximately $260).[17] Another economist, Samir Haleileh reported that studies in the hill regions of the West Bank reveal that six percent of the families in the region were at "starvation level" in February 1991. An additional 50% owed significant debts which curtailed further borrowing for essential food purchases.[18] Another Palestinian economist Fawaz Abu Sitta, told the Associated Press that about 65,000 Gaza workers, who constitute half the labor force, worked in Israel. With the layoff in effect, the future of 40,000 of them who had no work permits was in great jeopardy, particularly in view of the fact that 70% of Gaza's 750,000 people are refugees.[19]

The dependent economy of the occupied territories is almost devoid of any significant absorptive capacity under restrictive occupation policies. The 60,000 who lost jobs in Israel constitute 20% of all Palestinian workers in the West Bank and Gaza. To those, we must add another 25,000 who were forced to leave Kuwait and other Gulf countries. Not only were their remittances or externally generated income lost, but they became a burden on the already fragile economy.

That forced dependency of the Palestinian community on its Israeli occupier did not constitute the only source of damage inflicted on Palestinians during the Gulf conflict. The Gulf countries, where 700,000 Palestinians lived and worked, were a source of grants, remittances and marlets for exported produce from the occupied territories. Annual flows from all Arab sources were estimated at $700 million.[20] Much of that amount was halted due to the conflict. The more than 400,000 Palestinians in Kuwait were reduced to 150,000 by war's end and to a mere 20,000 now. Their remittances have virtually stopped. The Gulf Cooperation Council countries interrupted their contributions to Palestinian institutions in the West Bank and Gazas as well as to the PLO. The *Economist* estimated the total loss for the occupied territories resulting from the layoffs, lost remittances, and taxes at $1.4 billion.[21] That is the equivalent to only one-tenth of the income per capita in Israel where the cost of living is the same.

The Palestinian community in Jordan was also severely hit by the Gulf conflict. Having already suffered from a general decline during the past three years and from the 50% devaluation of the Jordanian *dinar* in 1989, they were particularly harmed by the trade embargo during the Gulf crisis due to their predominance in the private sector. Palestinian economist George Abed estimated their losses at $2.5 billion during 1990 and 1991, and those of the Palestinian community in Kuwait at $10 billion.[22]

Impact on Social Services

A further burden on the impoverished population was a decision by the occupation authorities to unleash on Palestinian cities and towns tax officials with authority to arrest and confiscate property and identity cards for non-payment. For example, in the village Nahalin, Salah Abdullah Fanoun offered to sell his kidney in order to pay NIS 400,000 in taxes (NIS is the Israeli Shekel; three Shekels equal one dollar).[23] He was threatened by the authorities, while in Dahriyeh prison for non-payment, that his house would be confiscated.

Additional punitive measures were applied against residents and whole towns for non-payment of utility bills. Hebron, the second largest city in the West Bank, and Haloul suffered blackouts between March 4th and 7th. The Israeli-appointed mayor of Hebron estimated a loss of NIS 20 million to local laboratories and factories. Water supplies were also cut to a number of villages and towns for non-payment.

The entire Palestinian population had to face the possibility of war without protection against chemical warfare. They were not provided with gas masks which were made available to Israelis, and most Palestinian health professionals had no access to such masks. There was a total absence of a war emergency system in the Occupied Territories. Prisoners were particularly vulnerable as they were left without access to shelter or any protection while their Israeli guards were provided with gas masks. The health and medical facilities serving the Palestinian community were totally incapable of handling emergencies arising from potential effects of the use of mass destruction weapons. Provisions for vital medications and adequate preparations of hospitals for war emergencies were totally lacking, while permissions for medical personnel to travel to their places of work during the repeated curfews were not always available. Palestinian Jerusalem hospitals reported that between 25% and 50% of their medical staff were prevented from reaching the work place during January 1991.[24] Moreover, during the long 24 hour curfew there was a cessation of basic medical care services such as pre-and post-natal care and immunization programs. Heart and cancer patients, diabetic patients, patients on dialysis and women in labor were severely hit by the curfew as many others who also suffered from shortages of medicine and pharmaceutical supplies. The prolonged curfew also threatened a deterioration in the nutritional status of the population, especially those at risk, such as children, pregnant women, the elderly and the disabled.

At a press conference held on January 31, 1991, the Union of Palestinian Medical Relief Committees (UPMRC), which comprises some 1000 medical volunteers, the Maqasses Hospital Medical Center, and Israeli Physicians for Human Rights issued an urgent appeal for lifting the curfew. Their statement reads, in part:

> The curfew situation and the fact that mobility of people is in the hands of the army has effectively meant that decisions regarding health and sickness needs are made by officers that have no understanding of what medical needs constitute nor of what is urgent and what is not.[25]

In a subsequent appeal issued on February 14, the UPMRC complained of the lack of clear directives regarding the transport of patients for treatment. The fact that people were shot during the curfew made many others hesitate to leave their homes in order to apply for permits to transport patients. "As a result disease conditions were complicated by the delay in the receipt of medical care."[26]

Education continued to suffer during the Gulf impasse. Most universities were closed in 1988 when the *Intifada* was in the early stages and continued to be closed until after the Gulf war. The elementary and high schools that were allowed to open in 1989 and 1990 were closed again during the gulf impasse and the war. A report issued by the Israeli Information Center on Human Rights, B'Tselem, accused the army of "heightening tensions issuing closure orders where there had been no violence, not offering a scheduled reopening date, and not revealing who ordered the closure." The report also accused soldiers of "provoking violence by entering school premises at will and humiliating school staff in front of the children."[27]

In addition to using the curfews, bans, export restrictions, layoffs, closure of educational, social and charitable institutions to cripple the economy and interrupt the daily lives of people, the army used the cover of the Gulf Conflict to violate its already disreputable system of justice. The normally quick trials became even quicker as lawyers were unable to reach their clients due to travel restrictions. In fact, the Occupied Territories were virtually divided into four regions, and travel between these "regions" was restricted by red tape and ever-changing regulations. The refugee camps were all surrounded by wire and high walls made of cement-filled barrels, with army checkpoints all over.

The Gulf War had enabled Israel to make a serious effort for undoing

much of the *Intifada's* accomplishments along the road of self-sufficiency. The draconian methods applied towards that end revealed how
vulnerable a community which has not been allowed international
protection can be. Regardless of how resourceful this community has
been, the cumulative effect of a prolonged occupation has made its
economic, social and cultural institutions so intertwined with and so
dependent on Israel that the latter could inflict irreparable damage on
the vital structures and immobilize them whenever the opportunity
presented itself. The Gulf Conflict, which provoked demonstrations
of support for Iraq by the disenfranchised Palestinians and evoked fear
of Iraqi scud missiles by Israelis, afforded that very opportunity; it was
a windfall for the Likud government.

The Palestinians in Kuwait

The suffering of Palestinians in human rights terms was no less than
the suffering in socio-economic terms. While repression under Israeli
occupation was increased by leaps and bounds, a new threat to the
Palestinians had arisen in a most unlikely place. Prior to the entry of
U.S. forces into Kuwait in late February 1991, graffiti could be seen on
many buildings predicting yet another ordeal for the Palestinians:
"Amman 1970; Beirut 1982; Kuwait 1991." Reports from American and
British journalists indicated that the Palestinians in Kuwait were subjected to abuses including torture, beatings, shootings, and shooting
deaths from single bullets to the head; as well as incommunicado
detention of individuals seized from their homes on suspicion of col-
laboration with the Iraqi occupation authorities.[28] Torture victims
were assigned to secret hospital wards only accessible to Kuwait physicians and some were beaten while still in the emergency room. Some of
the freelance vigilante work was carried out by young members of the
ruling Sabah family. Middle East Watch revealed that as many as 2000
people, mostly Palestinians, were rounded up and detained in the first
three weeks since the reconquest of Kuwait.[29] Many were tortured and
in several cases summarily executed. The report added that the
Palestinian community suffered from collective punishment. Kuwaiti
security forces were reported to have used lit cigarettes and lighters to
burn people, knives to carve words into the flesh, and glass bottles had

been forced into rectums. In a news statement which contains the findings of an Amnesty International fact-finding team to Kuwait, it was stated that the range of violations was extensive and that abuses by "resistance" squads and armed forces personnel included the use of electric current, sulfuric acid and severe beating.[30]

The Palestinians were in effect being given a message to leave, as there was no longer a future for themselves and their families in Kuwait. In fact, several thousands of the less than 150,000 who remained during the Iraqi occupation were rounded up and expelled from the country in March and April 1991.[31] A *New York Times* correspondent was told by Kuwaitis that the anger against Palestinians was such that there was little chance that most of those who left during the Iraqi occupation could ever come back and relatively few of those remaining would be able to stay.[32] Expulsions of Palestinians were also carried out by other Gulf states and new restrictions on renewal of work permits and residencies were adopted by some of the Gulf Cooperation Council countries.

The consequences of the Gulf War for the Palestinian community in Kuwait were devastating. A politically conscious, affluent and coherent community, which has been an asset to the Palestinian cause at the political, social and economic levels, had nearly ceased to exist. The Palestinian cause was deprived of its political and informational network and the *Intifada* missed its financial support. Along with other Palestinian communities in the Gulf/Peninsula region, it was no longer the pillar which sustained the struggle, but a fragmented community undergoing dispossession and dispersal for the second or third time.

The Gulf War and the Political Future of the Palestinians

The Palestinian stance on the events in the Gulf and the post-war conditions have affected international reactions to the Palestinian cause, and Arab attitudes towards that cause as well as internal Palestinian politics.

The suspension of the "peace process" in the summer of 1990, after the failure of Mubarak's "ten points" and Baker's five points, in bridging the gap between Israel and the United States, led the PLO to shift its primary diplomatic focus in the Arab world from Egypt to Iraq.

Frustrated by the breakdown of the U.S.-Egyptian endeavor to prepare for direct Israeli-Palestinian talks, and angered by the fact that it had to communicate with Washington regarding these talks, through Egypt, despite the dialogue, which was later suspended anyway, the PLO began to pin its hopes for a diplomatic settlement on a perceived Iraqi potential for mutual deterrence vis-à-vis Israel.

The failure of the U.S. and Egypt to effect a diplomatic settlement coupled with the failure of Iraq to develop military and political leverage for a settlement based on mutual recognition had clearly placed the Palestinians at the mercy of the new balance of power in the region. The conventional wisdom prevailing then in the West, in general, and in the United States in particular, was that the Palestinians had done their cause irreparable damage by identifying too closely with Iraq. President George Bush stated in Martinique in March 1990 that the Palestine Liberation Organization had "backed the wrong horse;" implying that it should not, therefore, expect an invitation to the post-war negotiations.

Long before Bush unleashed the Allied bombers and cruise missiles against Baghdad, media analysts in the U.S. and abroad pronounced the Palestinian struggle for a homeland as a principal casualty of the Gulf conflict. "Whoever the winner may be in the coming cataclysm, there was certain to be one big loser: the Palestinians…," wrote the *New Statesman*.[33] In a column titled *Desperation and Folly*, Anthony Lewis ventured that "over many decades Palestinian nationalism has made crucial political mistakes. This may be the worst."[34] Lewis then proceeded to quote Professor Walid Khalidi, a prominent Palestinian intellectual:

> The principles violated by Saddam in his invasion of Kuwait were the very principles from which the Palestinian cause drew its moral strength. The terrorist image that Arafat was desperate to shed was only reconfirmed by a close association with Saddam after [his] invasion of Kuwait…."[35]

The *New York Times* editorial in the same issue agreed saying; "By embracing Saddam Hussein, the Palestinian Liberation Organization has injured its cause in every imaginable direction."[36]

A cartoon by Szep depicted Arafat laying on a couch with psychiatrist Saddam Hussein by his side saying; "Other than feeling universally hated, detested and unwanted, what's your problem?"[37] Much of the same feeling was reiterated by television's alternative voice, Bill Moyers, to say nothing of the numerous mainstream journalists who made the same conclusions with monotonous regularity.

This is not to say that the conclusions were utterly lacking in validity. Palestinians in the occupied West Bank and Gaza and in Jordan took to the streets to demonstrate their opposition to the U.S. military deployment during the autumn of 1990. They were certainly in tune with much of Arab public opinion, which feared the unstated objective of U.S. policy, which had been largely achieved—the destruction of Iraq and its elimination as a regional power. Neither their external representatives in Tunis nor their internal leaders of the *Intifada* offered blessings to the Iraqi occupation of Kuwait. The PLO took the position that while Iraq had violated a basic tenet of the Arab political order, the inviolability of state sovereignty, Saudi Arabia and her Gulf allies in the Gulf Cooperation Council (GCC) have also challenged the institutionalized rules of conflict resolution within the "Arab family" by acquiescing in U.S. military intervention. Arafat's efforts to mediate reached a dead end when the very concept of an "Arab solution," which he pursued together with other members of the Arab League, was discredited and discouraged by the Bush administration, which was opposed to any settlement that would have left Iraq's military and industrial capability intact.[38] Meanwhile Saudi Arabia refused to accept anything short of a PLO endorsement of the U.S. military deployment as the price of reconciliation.

As for the leaders of the *Intifada* inside the occupied territories, being even less constrained by the exigencies of diplomacy, they delivered an unequivocal condemnation of the Iraqi and Israeli occupations. In a statement issued on August 15, 1990 in Jerusalem, they affirmed "the non-legitimacy of the acquisition of land by force and the unacceptability of resorting to military options in solving conflicts among states, which may involve the occupation of Arab lands and the Iraqi invasion of Kuwait."[39] Their statement also affirmed "the inadmissibility of the fragmentation of international legitimacy and the recognition of double standards." That meant that the United States, which demanded Iraqi withdrawal from Kuwait, had condoned Israeli occupation of Arab territories.

In practical terms, however, neither the PLO's hopes for mediation, nor the *Intifada's* insistence on a single standard against aggression, territorial acquisition and the application of UN resolutions, would improve Palestinian fortunes in the U.S. political arena. What did count was the fact that they were seen on the "wrong" side.

Would a more compliant attitude have yielded a viable remedy for the plight of the Palestinians? The question wrongly assumes that there had existed diplomatic progress, which would be consequently abandoned as a form of punishment. As we have shown previously, genuine hopes for peace in Palestine-Israel have not been justified, given that the U.S. had marginalized Palestinian rights for decades, and obstructed an international settlement.

In any case, U.S. policy in the aftermath of the Gulf conflict was not going to be determined by a perceived Palestinian stand on that conflict. Rather it was bound to reflect the new global balance and shifting regional alignments. Accordingly, it was unlikely to deviate from the dictates of a solidified U.S.-Israeli alliance, and from the exigencies of domestic politics, which continued to prevent U.S. diplomacy from achieving a real peace in the Middle East. It was significant that President Bush reaffirmed the three "Nos" of his election campaign platform after the Gulf War: "No" to an international peace conference; "No" to PLO representation in any negotiations on the Palestine question; "No" to a Palestine state.[40] These "Nos" paralleled the "Basic Premises" of the Israeli plan of May 4, 1989, known as the Shamir Plan.

Not only had the United States been working in tandem with Israel since the Gulf War, but after Iraq was defeated and America's Arab clients were rescued, the U.S. became less constrained by the previous pretense of fairness and the presumption of even-handedness. In fact, U.S. *rejectionism* was not only strengthened; it had gained more support among the Arab members of the war coalition. Egypt and some of the family regimes in the Gulf began to signal an unsubtle retreat from the Arab consensus on Palestine, which had previously envisaged a settlement on the basis of Israeli withdrawal from the occupied territories and mutual recognition. That consensus, which was enshrined in the Arab summit conferences in Rabat, Morocco (1974), Fez (1982), Amman (1987) and Algiers (1988) began to disintegrate. Saudi Arabia, for example, floated the idea of a Palestinian state in Jordan, an idea which approximated the Reagan Plan of 1982; the Egyptian and Syrian agreement to a non-substantive, regional conference, instead of the international conference, which the Arab states had always insisted was another nail in the coffin of the consensus. Also significant was the absence of any reference to the PLO in official Arab declarations after the Gulf war, starting with the Damascus Communiqué issued by the Arab members of the war coalition in March 1991.[41] Moreover, Kuwait, together with other Gulf states and Egypt, joined the United States and Israel in the re-demonization of Yasir Arafat and the delegitimization of the PLO.

The erosion of official Arab support for the PLO began to result in a clear distancing from Palestinian national rights including self-determination. The combined resources marshalled by the United States and its strategic ally, together with those of its Arab war partners to produce a post-war settlement, were to prove no less than catastrophic for Palestinian national and human rights, as will be shown in the next two chapters.

Notes

1. *Al-lttihad* (Haifa), August 6, 1990.
2. *Al-Quds* (Jerusalem daily), August 21, 1990.
3. *Al-Fajr* (Jerusalem daily), August 21, 1990.
4. Jackson Diehl, "A Radical Shift In The Intifada," *Washington Post*, December 8, 1990.
5. From a memorandum prepared by the Palestinian Economic Coordinating and Planning Committee published in *Attalia,* (Jerusalem weekly in Arabic), January 21, 1991; also in Jerusalem Media Communication Center (JMCC), Feb. 17–23, 1991.
6. *Al-Fajr* (English Edition), October 8, 1990; JMCC, September 30, 1990–October 6, 1990.

7. "Alarm Bells for Palestinian Economy and Society," *Tanmiya* (Geneva: Welfare Association), December 1990, p. 6.

8. *Ibid.*

9. *Al-Sha'ab* (Jerusalem daily), January 26, 1991; also JMCC, January 20–26, 1991.

10. *The Guardian*(London), February 6, 1991.

11. *Attali'a,* January 31, 1991.

12. *An-Nahar* (Jerusalem daily), January 26, 1991.

13. Jon D. Hull, "No Palestinians Need Apply," *Time,* November 26, 1991, p. 47.

14. Judith Winkler, "The Devil Came Out of the Fire Bottle", *Ha'aretz,* November 25, 1990.

15. *Jerusalem Post,* March 8, 1991.

16. *Time,* November 26, 1990.

17. *Attali'a,* January 31, 1991.

18. *Jerusalem Post,* February 28, 1991.

19. *Boston Globe,* December 21, 1991.

20. George Abed, "The Gulf's Toll on the Palestinians, *The Christian Science Monitor,* November 29, 1990, p. 18.

21. *The Economist,* February 2, 1991, p. 20.

22. Abed. *op.cit.*

23. *Al-Quds,* March 5, 1991, JMCC, March 3–9, 1991.

24. Union of Palestinian Medical Relief Committees (UPMRC), *Appeal Number 5,* January 26, 1991, Jerusalem.

25. UPMRC, *Appeal Number 6,* February 4, 1991.

26. UPMRC, *Appeal Number 7,* February 14, 1991.

27. JMCC Newsletter, September 30–October 6, 1990, p. 5.

28. See for example: "Terror For Innocent Palestinians As Kuwaitis Resistance Fighters Run Wild," *New York Times,* March 6, 1991; Donatella Lorch, "With Iraqis Gone, Kuwaitis Turn Wrath On Palestinians, *New York Times,* March 4, 1991; Richard Cohen, "Lynch Law in Kuwait," *Washington Post,* March 7, 1991; William Brannigin and Nora Bustany, "Right Officials: Kuwaiti Soldiers Commit Abuses," *Washington Post,* March 17, 1991; Nora Bustany, "Kuwaiti Hospital Said To Cover Up Torture," *Washington Post,* March 22, 1991; Ken Fireman, "Kuwaiti Abuse Repeated," *New York Newsy,* March 22, 1991; Andrew Whitley, "The Dirty War In Kuwait," *New*

York Times, April 2, 1991; Tim Kelsey, "Saddam Has Left, But the Horrors Are Not Finished," *The Independent,* March 3, 1991; John Kifner, "Kuwaitis Urged To Halt Attacks On Palestinians," *New York Times,* April 3, 1991; Robert Fisk, "Kuwait Palestinians Face Gunmen's Revenge," *The Independent,* March 4, 1991; Ian Glover-James, "Terror Rules the Street As Kuwait Takes Revenge," *The Sunday Times* (London), March 24, 1991; Virginia Sherry, "Purging Kuwait," *The Nation,* March 18, 1991, pp. 328–329.

29   Andrew Whitley, "The Dirty war In Kuwait," *New York Times,* April 2, 1991. Author was Executive Director of Middle East Watch reporting on the findings of an 18-day mission to Kuwait.

30   Amnesty International, "Kuwait: Amnesty International Calls On Emir To Intervene Over Continuing Torture and Killings," News release, April 18, 1991.

31   *New York Times,* April 3, 1991.

32   Youssef Ibrahim, "Palestinians In Kuwait Face Suspicion and Probable Exile," *New York Times,* March 14, 1991.

33   Stephen Howe, "The Palestinians, Back To the Wall," *New Statesman,* August 24, 1990.

34   *New York Times,* January 21, 1991.

35   *Ibid.*

36   *Ibid.*

37   *Boston Globe,* March 27, 1991.

38   Even President Carter was quoted as saying "…when we prohibited any sort of resolution of the issue in a peaceful fashion, then we make it inevitable that Saddam would not yield at all…thus eliminating all alternatives to the complete conquest and destruction of Iraq." *Boston Globe,* February 2, 1991.

39   *Al-Quds,* August 16, 1990.

40   Text of the 1988 Republican Party platform in Journal of Palestine Studies, Vol. XVIII, No. 1 (Autumn 1988) pp. 304-306.

41   George Church, "The Saudis Seize the Day," *Time,* March 18, 1991, and Mary Curtius, "Saudi Arabia Has Halted Funding of the PLO, Baker is Told," *Boston Globe,* April 12, 1991.

7

The Road to Madrid and Beyond

Baker and the Palestinians

In light of the damage suffered by the Palestinians during the Gulf War, why did the U.S. bother to invest so much political capital in the Madrid conference convened in September 1991? Why was a diplomatic reflection of the military victory so important for the consolidation of U.S. gains? Why did the various parties to the conflict agree to participate, and what means of pressure and persuasion were employed to guarantee their involvement? What impact did Washington's pursuit of stability have on the "peace process," and how did that affect the future prospects?

The Global and Regional Setting for a Settlement

The Imperatives for "Peace"

It will be recalled that Baker's first initiative for a Palestinian-Israeli settlement was thwarted by Israeli Prime Minister Shamir, who had renounced his own plan after Baker called that plan "the only game in town." Thus, Baker felt that he had lost an opportunity. Less than a year later, however, he was to have yet a second "window of opportunity," now bolstered by objective and material changes occurring at the regional and global levels. It was not dependent, as before, on the imperatives of Israeli domestic politics and Shamir's shifting moods. The strategic imperatives for a negotiated settlement, largely on U.S. terms and under U.S. auspices, were created by the effective collapse of the Soviet Union and the destruction of Iraq. The Soviet Union was transformed from chief diplomatic backer and arms supplier of the Arab states to U.S. appendage in the "peace process." Iraq was reduced from the champion of strategic balance with Israel to an impotent nation preoccupied with the preservation of its sovereignty and territorial integrity. Thus, with deterrence having suddenly vanished at the global and regional levels, the U.S. was left without any serious opposition for the first time since Nasser. Ironically, the major source of irritation for its diplomatic efforts was its own regional ally.

The dramatic transformation of the strategic and political landscape of the Middle East in the aftermath of the Cold War and the destruction of Iraq paved the way for George Bush to shape a new structure of relationships in which an Arab-Israeli settlement became a U.S. national interest. U.S. strategic planners now envisioned a post-Cold War redivision of the world in which economic rather than military power would be the catalyst for change and in which the Middle East, as a potential source of capital, would rest securely in the North American sphere. Given that U.S. relations with Japan and the EU (European Union) would have to consume the larger portion of American energies during the next phase, a settlement of the Arab-Israeli conflict became not only desirable but also necessary from the U.S. vantage point.[1]

The wartime alliance in which Arab active participation combined with Israeli passive support proved to be a mere battle convenience. Translating that convergence of interest into a viable anchor for regional stability required a negotiated settlement capable of freeing the conservative Arabs to fully embrace Washington's new political order in the region. The settlement would also free U.S. taxpayers from the huge burden of subsidizing the Israeli treasury in the name of security, a fact which itself continues to fuel anti-American sentiments in the region.

Moreover, as long as America's energy policy remained dependent on the military option, and whereas the flow of oil to the industrial world on exceedingly favorable terms remained vulnerable to national self-assertion, an unsettled Arab-Israeli conflict would constitute a potential threat to the desired stability. Add to this the fact that America's enhanced hegemony in the Middle East, at a time of relative economic decline and anticipated competition from Europe and Japan, required the kind of political settlement that would improve a sagging credibility. If the U.S. hoped to assume the leadership in shaping the "New World Order," it must demonstrate not only its commitment to crush the detractors but also its willingness and ability to broker a viable peace after a prolonged impasse. To the extent that the Middle East has become more firmly entrenched in the American sphere than at any other time in the past, U.S. unilateralism came under an urgent scrutiny. The world began to look at how the United States was conducting itself in the Middle East, wondering whether the self-styled chief arbiter would finally deliver. This performance somehow became a litmus test of U.S. leadership in the post-Cold War.

Altered Relationships
1. The Arab States

The Gulf War effectively demolished the official Arab consensus on Palestine, eroded Arab solidarity and exposed regime insecurity in the Gulf/Peninsula region. The illusion of Arab defense and the higher Arab interest was eclipsed by the spectacle of kings, sheikhs and presidents ingratiating themselves with Washington, enabling it to deal with them bilaterally and on the basis of narrowly construed interests rather than as a solid bloc with a nationalist and Palestinian agenda.

The Arab world became more divided than at any time since the establishment of the Arab League. Arab solidarity against Israel had broken down and an important source of pressure for Israeli concessions thereby eliminated. Moreover, the indebtedness of the poorer Arab countries, as well as the virtual protectorate status of the richer Arab states, seemed to translate into a loss of relative sovereignty and leverage.[2] There was hardly any economic or diplomatic leverage left for these countries, and with the destruction of Iraq as a regional power the military leverage was also eliminated for the foreseeable future.

These developments dismantled the joint Palestinian-Arab strategy developed at the Rabat summit in 1974, whose pillars consisted of Arab economic and diplomatic leverage and Palestinian "moderation;" i.e., a two-state solution rather than the secular democratic state concept. That enabled the Bush administration to obtain Arab and Palestinian acquiescence in its framework for negotiations, tilted heavily against the Arab side.

The Gulf War also removed the question of Palestine from the top of the Arab agenda. The conventional wisdom prevailing in the West— that the Palestinians had done their cause irreparable damage by identifying too closely with Iraq—was conveniently adopted by the Arab members of the war coalition.[3] Not only was the Palestinian leadership demonized for its political stance, but the institution itself, which became the embodiment of Palestinian nationalism, was peripheralized and the cause itself further marginalized. Moreover, the rapidly growing importance of the internal Palestinian leadership, a trend underway since the 1982 Lebanon war, was exploited by the U.S. and Israel to further marginalize the external leadership in Tunis and consequently to devalue Palestinian national rights.

An example of that marginalization was the U.S. refusal to allow the PLO a meaningful diplomatic gain in exchange for its historic concessions of 1988. It will be recalled that the Algiers Declaration of Independence and Arafat's subsequent "renunciation" of terrorism, rather than "denunciation," as well as his recognition of the "right" of Israel to exist, rather than his recognition of its actual existence, satisfied not only Kissinger's well-known conditions of 1974 but Reagan's additions as well.[4] And yet Washington managed to "suspend," or more accurately terminate, its dialogue with the PLO. In doing so, Washington set a trend which proved diplomatically costly for the PLO in Europe and even in the Arab world. The PLO was no longer insisting on representing the Palestinians in diplomatic negotiations, let alone refusing to share that role with anyone else; it became reconciled to merely naming the negotiators within Israeli-set limits and was committed to the concept of a joint delegation.

Another consequence of the Gulf War was the apparent triumph of U.S. unilateralism over the international approach after a struggle lasting nearly a quarter of a century.[5] The allied victory in the war signalled the effective demise of the idea of an international conference and a settlement under the auspices of the UN It consecrated U.S. diplomacy as the sole agent of an Arab-Israeli settlement and signaled a visible shift in decision-making, a role which had seemed to be limited largely to the U.S. and Israel. Secretary of State Baker not only succeeded in replacing the international conference with a symbolic regional parley whose main function was to legitimize the bilateral talks, which Israel so much desired, but he also secured Soviet and Syrian acquiescence.

2. Israel

The Gulf War consolidated the hardline forces in Israel, placing the Israeli peace camp on the defensive and causing its faint voices to drown in the avalanche from the rapidly rising right-wing forces, fueled by a violent shift in the *Intifada*. The crisis also provided the Israeli government with a natural pretext to clamp down on the *Intifada* in an atmosphere of near total freedom from international scrutiny.[6] Under cover of the Gulf crisis, Israel would simply embark upon the destruction of *all* the achievements of the *Intifada* over the preceding three and a half years in the diplomatic, political, and economic fields and in health care and social organization. It was an "opportunity" to cripple the evolving Palestinian infrastructure, which had already been dealt a serious blow a decade earlier in Lebanon.

The Gulf War also provided Israel with an opportunity to impose its diplomatic framework on any negotiations that it was expected to join. In fact, it was the only party whose demands were not scaled down for the sake of a compromise, but were elevated instead. Consider Israel's refusal to entertain Baker's suggestions for a freeze on building illegal settlements in occupied territories rather than the suppression or cessation of such activities, as mandated by international law. Israeli demands did not encounter significant U.S. opposition. The emerging U.S. strategy in the aftermath of the war was to shift the emphasis away from the Palestine/Israel dimension, which characterized previous plans such as that of Reagan (1982), Shultz (1988) and the Shamir-Baker-Mubarak proposals of 1989, and pursue instead a "two-track" solution. Although this was defined as a simultaneous pursuit of Arab-Israeli and Palestinian-Israeli agreements in parallel negotiating tracks, Shamir argued that only after Israel had peace with the Arab states would it feel confident enough to discuss the West Bank and Gaza.[7] That in fact represented a change from his earlier insistence on Arab recognition of Israel as a pre-condition for entering peace talks which would ultimately lead to peace talks between Israel and the Palestinians.[8] But the two-track approach, which provided for multilateral negotiations on environmental issues, water, refugees, economic development and arms control, along with the bilateral talks, assured Israel a *de facto* recognition from the Arab states attending the "multilaterals," such as Saudi Arabia and other Gulf states. Such de facto recognition would not even be contingent on the fulfillment of Israeli obligations to the Palestinian people or to Syria and Lebanon.

The second idea was the replacement of the international peace conference, which was called for in Security Council Resolution 338, with a regional conference hosted by the U.S. and the U.S.S.R. Not only did this strange concept diminish the importance of Resolution 242, but it effectively floated its real meaning and value and rendered a 45-year-old legal record, enshrined in countless UN resolutions, virtually irrelevant to the framework of the negotiations. Unlike the peace processes in El Salvador and Cambodia and the previous negotiations to solve the Iran-Iraq conflict and the Afghanistan problem, Middle East negotiations were governed by ground rules totally outside the context of the United Nations. A token UN presence was assured at the conference, but the observer was committed to humiliating silence.

In addition, Israel set a number of other conditions which were accepted by Baker, sold to the Arabs and incorporated into what became known as the Madrid framework. Salient among these are the following:

1.) The Soviet Union would have to establish "full diplomatic relations with Israel and agree to the meeting ground rules demanded by Israel" in order to qualify as co-sponsor.[9] These ground rules included Israel's insistence that "all that would be discussed at first with the Palestinians is an interim settlement involving self-government." Final status talks would begin three years later.

2.) An opening statement at such a conference by the U.S. must refrain from delineating any plan for settlement.[10] In fact, Secretary of State Baker was already on record as opposing the presentation of a plan. It will be recalled that he went out of his way to emphasize that his "Five Points" of 1989 were simply a "proposal," not a "plan."

3.) In view of the limited purpose of the conference, which would be a one-time event to launch direct negotiations and pave the way for discussing Israel's autonomy plan, participation would be limited to Palestinians living in the West Bank and Gaza and would exclude those living in East Jerusalem, in Israeli jails and the four million living in the diaspora.

Israel further expected the U.S. to persuade the Arab states to agree that the regional conference led immediately to direct negotiations in the two tracks; that the meeting have no power to impose solutions on the parties, or to pass judgment on agreements reached in bilateral negotiations[11]; that Resolutions 242 and 338 not determine the outcome of the process; and that the U.S. promise that the PLO would have no role at any point in the process, a position which the U.S., the Arab states and even the PLO itself accepted. Had the PLO insisted on representing the Palestinians, the United States and the Arab states were ready and willing to promote an alternative leadership in the occupied territories to negotiate a peace based on the new balance of power in the region. The tools intended for that scheme included Israeli measures to ease conditions and 'improve the quality of life," Saudi petrodollars, and U.S. orchestration. The deteriorating economic conditions in the occupied territories created by Israel's draconian measures during the Gulf crisis were counted upon by the three parties as the catalyst that would prod the Palestinians toward their scheme. A U.S. official traveling with Baker on one of his early shuttles in the region was rather unsubtle about the utility of Saudi money and Israeli measures:

> There are political ways, ways designed to sort of create more of a sense of political support for Palestinians who would be stepping forward. There are financial ways, especially given the level of economic deprivation and difficulties in the territories now.[12]

The Gulf War was clearly viewed by Israel and the Zionist movement as a historical juncture that could associate a number of Arab states with its long-standing objective of removing the national rights and grievances of the Palestinian people from the diplomatic agenda. Disqualifying the PLO from the process was calculated to be the first significant step towards achieving that goal.

An "Opportunity" for James Baker

These consequences of the Gulf War provided Mr. Baker with a favorable climate for the kind of negotiations which he thought were possible, largely because of the victor-vanquished dichotomy. Having just emerged in the post-Cold War period as the uncontested superpower in a militarily unipolar world, the U.S. seemed even more determined than ever to use whatever force was necessary to maintain the regional balance in its favor. The carnage in Iraq was meant to underscore a determination that American hegemony in the Middle East and Israel's military superiority over *all* its Arab neighbors combined would not be challenged. For the United States, this was the first "opportunity" to reshape the strategic balance in the Middle East without the countervailing influence of the Soviet Union and in the absence of a single Arab power professing responsibility for mutual deterrence vis-à-vis Israel. As for Israel, this was also the first time since the peace treaty with Egypt in 1979 that a number of Arab states seemed ready to conclude peace with it outside the framework of an international peace conference, in direct bilateral negotiations, and not subject to Palestinian approval.

The dramatic transformation of the strategic and political landscape of the Middle East, which led to a virtual recolonization of the Arab East, provided George Bush with an opportunity to shape a new structure of relationships in which an Arab-Israeli settlement became a U.S. national interest.[13] The major task then facing the U.S., as the hegemonial power in the region, was how to convert what it viewed as opportunity into a concrete diplomatic achievement.

The strategic imperatives for a modified U.S. policy in the Middle East, which derive from the end of the Cold War and the Gulf War, may not have been sufficient in themselves to produce a viable peace and the required stability. The unfolding relationships of the U.S. in the region are entangled and complex. While those imperatives exacerbated the ongoing imbalance of power in the region, the imbalance itself created a new dynamic which impelled the sole superpower to redefine its own national interest against the backdrop of the new realities. In that context, the U.S.'s enhanced preeminence could conceivably take precedence over Israel's own aspirations for regional dominance.

Washington had the option of dusting off previous strategic blueprints of the Baghdad Pact and the "consensus of strategic concern," which would help incorporate some of the active Arab components of Desert Storm and the passive Israeli partner into a new Middle East order. The Arab parties which refrained from extending blessings to the destruction of Iraq (Jordan and the Palestinians) were differentially placed on probation.

All of this implies that Washington's advantageous position vis-à-vis the Arabs and Israel would offer it a new flexibility which could enhance the desired regional stability. That prospect was linked to America's perception of the roles which Israeli security and Palestinian activism were likely to play in the next phase.

Palestinian Vulnerability

As for Palestinian activism, U.S. strategic planners have already made corresponding reassessments of their estimates of its potential for regional destabilization. The major difference, however, is that, unlike the revised estimates of Israel's value, which is subtle, Washington's estimate of the Palestinian "threat" was rather unequivocal. Deprived of a solid and unified Arab backing in the negotiations, isolated from its constituencies in the occupied territories, the Gulf, Syria, and Lebanon, and faced with economic, ideological, leadership and governance crises, the PLO was seen by the Bush administration as the weakest link. This low estimation was seen in the structure, framework and style of Baker's diplomacy, which treated the Palestinians as unequal. A deliberate ambiguity left the various parties considerable room for personal interpretation and even self-delusion; it was designed to secure a unanimous consent for attending the conference. But after the opening speeches, the urge towards specificity began to replace the ambiguity. The vague boundaries between substance and procedure which kept Baker's mission alive were in need of more close definition. Many substantive issues were thinly camouflaged as procedural arrangements. A few examples suffice:

1.) The issue of Palestinian representation was not a matter of procedure; it was and is substantive par excellence. Baker's acquiescence in Israel's exclusion of the diaspora and the Jerusalem Palestinians rendered Palestinian national rights questionable and negotiable, including their internationally recognized rights of return and self-determination.[14] It also lent a certain credence to the Israeli claim on Jerusalem, despite the well-established international position to which the U.S. was committed.

2.) The numerous encumbrances on the peace conference, including its designation, participants, the limits of speech and the frequency of meetings, among others, were also substantive inasmuch as they rendered the very issue of a belligerent occupation—a recognized status under international law—to the sidelines.[15]

3.) The much-publicized two-track approach represented a disingenuous attempt to sidestep the central issue in the Arab-Israeli conflict. Issues of arms control, water resources, economic development, regional security and the environment, which made up the agenda of the multilateral talks, did not arise out of an ideological conflict between the Arabs and Israel. They derived naturally from the central issue, Palestine, which is the root cause of the Arab-Israeli conflict. The two-track concept, therefore, was not a procedural issue, but a substantive one, packaged in procedural wrappings, intended to entice a reluctant Israel. Whereas the bilateral track represented the "give" for Israel, the multilateral track held the plums. Israel expected to reap the benefits in the latter.

4.) The transitional period represented another substantive issue packaged as procedural. A thin layer of one segment of five and a half million Palestinians, carefullychosen to satisfy Israeli requirements and meticulously screened for their willingness and ability to operate within specific and well-defined constraints, would sit, after an interim period of limited autonomy, across the table from an Israeli team free of any constraints to negotiate the final status of the occupied territories. They would have a smaller chance of success than a delegation from Tibet facing China.

Baker's Shuttles and Assurances

The outcome of the Gulf War had consecrated U.S. diplomacy as the sole agent of an Arab-Israeli settlement and signaled a visible shift in decision-making, a role which now seemed to be limited largely to the U.S. and Israel. Not only had Secretary of State James Baker succeeded in replacing the international conference with a symbolic regional parley whose main function was to legitimize the bilateral talks, which Israel so much desired, but he also secured Soviet and Syrian acquiescence during eight shuttles to the region between March and September 1991. Baker's shuttle diplomacy was successful in bridging the gap between the Arabs and Israel on terms largely prescribed by the latter yet incorporating cosmetic changes which created the illusions of a compromise. The Arab position, which was based on the necessity of an international conference, was gradually watered down with each shuttle. On April 12, 1991, Syria and Jordan indicated their willingness to attend an international conference with the additional proviso that it should be based on UN resolutions. At the same time Israel was insisting that the conference would not exceed a single brief session, followed by direct talks. On April 19, just one week later, King Hussein said that "Jordan would be very flexible when it came to the terms of [a] conference." Syria, on the other hand, stood by its position insisting on UN participation in a conference that had a permanent structure and demanded that Israel commit itself to the exchange of land for peace.

On his next shuttle, on May 8 1991, Baker proposed a "compromise" whereby the conference would be sponsored by the U.S. and Russia and would reconvene every six months. A UN envoy would be present but would remain passive. Although the meeting would be based on UN Resolution 242, Baker proposed that each side be free to bring in its own interpretation of 242 with regard to Palestinian representation. Baker's "compromise" saw the Palestinians as part of a joint Jordanian-Palestinian delegation. Even that "compromise" proved to be unacceptable to Israel and was also rejected by Syria, thus prompting Baker to return to Washington and blame both parties. He did, however, emphasize that Israel's continued settlement policy was "the biggest obstacle to peace." In the meantime, President Bush hinted that invitations could be issued, implying that those who failed to attend would be considered as standing in the way of peace. On July 14, President Assad accepted the U.S. "compromise," stating that the plan was "…an acceptable basis for achieving a comprehensive solution." This prompted Baker to return to the area to look for additional conciliatory moves by the Arabs to entice Israel. But despite a firm Syrian commitment made to Baker by Assad in Damascus plus a call by President Mubarak to the Arabs to end the economic boycott of Israel in return for an Israeli suspension of settlement building, Prime Minister Shamir could tell Baker upon his arrival in Israel on July 21, only that he needed time to consider the matter. On the same day, Jordan announced its acceptance of Baker's proposal and together with Egypt and Saudi Arabia offered to suspend the economic boycott.

With Arab concessions mounting in this manner, Israel became concerned about the outcome of the public relations battle, particularly as it had developed a posture of rejectionism under Shamir. Israeli approval was thus finally extended on July 24, but the familiar conditions were repeated; Palestinian presence at the regional conference would be limited to non-PLO, non-Jerusalem, non-diaspora Palestinians. This exclusion amounted to about 75% of the Palestinian people.

The Arab concessions were incorporated into a letter of invitation signed by the United States and the Soviet Union on October 18, 1991. The letter effectively replaced the United Nations resolutions as a framework for settling the Arab-Israel conflict. It was accompanied by a "letter of assurances" to the protagonists, which largely defined United States (not Soviet) understanding and intentions concerning the negotiations. The main principles in the letter of invitation are:

1.) Peace would be grounded in Security Council Resolutions 242 and 338 and the principle of territory for peace, in accordance with President Bush's address to Congress on March 6, 1991. It would provide for Israeli security and recognition, for legitimate Palestinian political rights, and for Palestinian control over political and economic decisions which affect their lives.

2.) The venue for the peace negotiations would be a regional conference that would lead, after four days, to direct bilateral negotiations. The conference would have no power to impose solutions, veto agreements reached by the parties, or make decisions for the parties. It could reconvene only with the consent of the parties.

3.) The negotiations would be conducted in phases, beginning with talks on interim self-government arrangements. The interim self-government would last for five years, and during the third year negotiations would begin for final status.

The letter of assurances to the Palestinians reiterates these principles and added a few specific points:

1.) The Israeli occupation would have to come to an end, but that could be accomplished only through negotiations that would be comprehensive and would proceed along both, a Palestinian and an Arab track, (i.e. two tracks).

2.) The United Nations would be represented by an observer. Agreements would be registered with the UN Secretariat and reported to the Security Council. As long as the process went on, the United States would not support another process in the United Nations.

3.) The Palestinians could choose their own delegation. Although the U.S. claimed it did not seek to determine who speaks for the Palestinians, it stipulated that the delegation members would be residents from the occupied territories who agreed to the two-track concept, in phases, and who were willing to live in peace with Israel. No party could be forced to sit with anyone.

4.) Jerusalem would never again be divided and its final status would be decided in negotiations. The U.S. would not recognize Israel's annexation of East Jerusalem or the extension of its municipal boundaries. Palestinians from Jerusalem would be excluded from the delegation but a Palestinian resident in Jordan with ties to a prominent Jerusalem family would be eligible to join the Jordanian delegation. Palestinians from East Jerusalem would be able to vote in the election for an interim self-governing authority. Together with diaspora Palestinians, these could also negotiate on final status.

The proximity of these parameters to Israel's conditions is very striking. The similarity can be attributed to the extent to which Baker's eight shuttles incorporated the Israeli position. Thus the ground rules of Madrid not only supplanted the United Nations framework but earlier U.S. proposals as well. The self-proclaimed catalyst for peace had to conduct its brokering in Madrid and subsequently in Washington and Moscow largely in accordance with Israeli standards. This in itself reflected a disparity in Washington's post-Gulf estimates of Israeli and Palestinian/Arab potential influence as well as strategic significance in the post-Cold War period.

The Real Challenge and the Prospects

While the objective conditions, which rendered Baker's shuttles and his mission in general necessary in the first place, implied a reduction of Israeli influence, the concessions, which permitted the procedural packaging of substantive issues, were made solely by the Palestinians and the Arabs. Such asymmetry initially caused Syria to boycott the multilateral talks on the grounds that no progress was made during the second phase of bilateral negotiations on the territorial question. The imbalance was bound to raise the indignation of the Arab people sooner or later, despite their leaders' docility and subservient demeanor at the present time.

While moral and legal considerations were secondary to the strategic nature of Baker's diplomacy, the obvious lack of an attempt to give them minimal attention constituted a basic flaw in the initiative. The fundamental moral issue which Baker's diplomacy ignored is the wrong done to the Palestinians: dispossession, dismemberment, disenfranchisement, subjugation—ills which George Bush's declared tenets of a "New World Order" promised to remedy. Hence the responsibility for the plight of the Palestinian refugees was arbitrarily transferred from Israel to the world community despite UN Resolution 194 of 1948 and the fact that its fulfillment by Israel was made a condition for Israel's own admission to the United Nations. Also, the principal legal element which Baker's approach neglected is the Fourth Geneva Convention Relative to the Protection of Civilians in Times of War of 1949. Security Council Resolution 681 unanimously declared in 1991 that the convention protects the Palestinian people in the occupied territories from being coerced into illegal agreements. It guards against the renunciation of their rights under the convention and restricts Israeli practices in the manner of a de facto sovereign. Moreover, the interim period, which precedes the final status negotiations, can only be accepted after the Israeli position regarding the occupation becomes legal. This is but a small list of the provisions of the convention, which the U.S. government has a legal obligation to enforce as signatory. These provisions, however, stood at variance with the spirit of Baker's framework.

These shortcomings of the Madrid agreement and the deliberate ambiguity of Baker's diplomacy prevented the parties from making the kind of progress needed to meet deadlines. Self-government for the Palestinians was scheduled for implementation one year from the Madrid conference; in October 1992. This did not happen, in view of Israel's refusal to come to terms with its status as occupier and to commit itself on the controversial issue of the colonial settlements. The right-wing sector, which was in power in Israel at the time, viewed the Madrid process as an investment to buy a few more years in which Soviet immigrants and expanded settlements would help assure an effective foreclosure on a territorial peace. Shamir put it succinctly; "This mass immigration aims at forming a greater Israel...will make Israel bigger, stronger and better...in the space of five years you will not be able to recognize this country. Everything will change, everything will be bigger. The strongest of the Arabs around us will be in a state of desperation and panic as they will not be able to stop the natural flow of Jewish people into their land."

Not surprisingly, the Madrid process seemed to go nowhere after eleven rounds of talks in Washington, Rome and Moscow, as Israel clung tenaciously to the policy of building settlements, thus forfeiting any kind of a territorial solution. For the Palestinians, it was an uncertain path, if not in fact a blind alley. Negotiations constitute a process of conciliation with a possible outcome already in place. In this case there was neither an outline nor a vision of the final outcome. All fundamental issues involving borders, refugees, Jerusalem and indeed the occupation itself were deferred. Self-government, as the sole concern of these negotiations in the immediate term, was seen by the Palestinians as the necessary link towards independence; Israel, on the other hand, had ruled out independence and viewed what it calls self-government as a mechanism to ratify the occupation under a new and different label. Any doubt about this strategy was dispelled by the text of the Israeli plan, entitled "Ideas for Peaceful Coexistence in the Territories during the Interim Period," submitted during the March 1992 round of negotiations in Washington.

The premise of that plan seemed to be consonant with parameters enunciated by then Israeli Deputy Foreign Minister Benjamin Netanyahu in December 1991: "Maximum security for Israel and minimum intervention in Palestinian life." The text of the plan made it very clear that the concept of Israeli security disallowed the Palestinians any notion of an overall central authority, geographical space, independent economic planning, real legislative authority or judicial review, not to mention defense, foreign affairs or natural resources. Minimum intervention in Palestinian life would remove direct Israeli control of fragmented municipalities. The Palestinians would have enclaves on about 5 percent of historic Palestine, exactly the same amount of land owned by Jews on the eve of the establishment of Israel.

The outcome of the Gulf crisis had so radically altered the balance of power in the region that it was nearly impossible for the Palestinians to achieve their minimal goals under U.S. diplomatic auspices. The United States has, after all, used its Security Council veto or abstained in the voting on nearly all of the 43 UN resolutions critical of the Israeli occupation since 1967 . The new world order of George Bush did not regard international legality as indivisible, nor did it set a single standard for the application of human rights. Bush's vocal defense of the human rights of the Kuwaiti people, in which he included self-determination and the restoration of the unelected emir to power, was not matched by a call upon Israel to allow the Palestinians to choose their own representatives, elect their own government and enjoy self-determination, as required by UN resolutions.[16]

The real challenge to Baker and Bush acting as "catalysts for peace" was to bridge the gap between the Arabs and Israel with definite proposals, a task which Israel considered taboo and Washington approached with extreme caution bordering on timidity. The material conditions which propelled U.S. diplomacy towards Madrid and the quality of change Madrid was expected to produce had to be synchronized. That was dependent on the pace at which specific proposals would replace the necessary ambiguity. Mr. Bush's espousal of the Madrid process was not followed by the transfer of the well-known substantive positions of the U.S. from the realm of the abstract to that of the tangible and the applied. Hence a crippling impasse rendered the Washington diplomatic rounds an exercise in futility. That situation persisted until the deadlock was resolved at Oslo in September 1993.

Notes

1. On the relationship between the U.S., Europe and Japan, see Lester C. Thurow, "Money Wars: Why Europe Will Own the 21st Century," *The Washington Post* (Outlook C—April 19, 1992), p. c1; also Steven Greenhouse, "U.S. and the World: A New Economic Order is Ahead," *New York Times*, April 29, 1992.

2. Yahya Sadowski, "Revolution, Reform or Regression? Arab Political Options in the 1990 Gulf Crisis," *Brookings Review* (Winter 1990/91), pp. 17–21.

3. For a sample of Western media opinions, see Stephen Howe, "The Palestinians: Back to the Wall," *New Statesman* (August 24, 1990); Anthony Lewis, "Desperation and Folly," *New York Times*, January 21, 1991; also see editorial in the same issue under the title of "Sure Losers: The Palestinians."

4. For a discussion of this subject, see Naseer Aruri, "The United States and Palestine: Reagan's Legacy to Bush," *Journal of Palestine Studies*, Vol. XVIII, No. 3 (Spring 1989), pp. 3–21.

5. For a discussion of this see Naseer Aruri, "The United States Opposition to an International Peace Conference," *International Journal of Islamic and Arabic Studies*, Vol. II, No. 1 (Winter 1985).

6. See the weekly bulletin of the Jerusalem Media and Communication Center for that period.

7. *Boston Globe*, March 4, 1991.

8. Peter Waldman, "Israel Drops Recognition as Peace Talk Condition," *Wall Street Journal*, March 6, 1991.

9. Thomas Friedman, "Israel Backs Plan for Single Session on Mideast Peace," *New York Times*, April 10, 1991.

10. *Ibid.*

11. Mary Curtius, "Israel Says It Would Meet Arab States, Palestinians," *Boston Globe*, April 10, 1991.

12. Mary Curtius, "Saudi Arabia Has Halted Funding of the PLO, Baker Is Told," *Boston Globe*, April 12, 1991.

13. On the question of recolonization, see Naseer Aruri, "The Recolonization of the Arab World," *Arab Studies Quarterly*, Vol. II, Nos. 2 & 3 (Spring/Summer 1989), pp. 273–285; also "Recolonizing the Arab World," *Middle East International*, No. 385 (October 9, 1990).

14. UN General Assembly Resolutions 2535 of December 10, 1969, 2672 of December 8, 1970, and 2787 of December 6, 1971 recognize the status of the Palestinians as a colonized people entitled to "independence" and possessing "inalienable rights." Resolution 3210 of October 14, 1974 recognizes the PLO as representative of the Palestinian people. Resolution 3236 of November 22, 1974 reaffirms the inalienable rights of the Palestinian people to self-determination and to national independence and sovereignty. See *United Nations Resolutions on Palestine and the Arab-Israeli Conflict, 1947–1991* (V. 1-4), (Washington: Institute for Palestine Studies, 1992).

15. See W. Thomas Mallison and Sally Mallison, *The Palestine Problem in International Law and World Order* (New York: Longman, 1986); Raja Shehadeh, *Occupiers Law: Israel and the West Bank* (2nd ed.), (Washington: Institute for Palestine Studies, 1988).

16. For a discussion of the double standard, see Norman Finkelstein, "Israel and Iraq: A Double Standard in the Application of International Law," *Monthly Review* (July/August 1991), pp. 25–53.

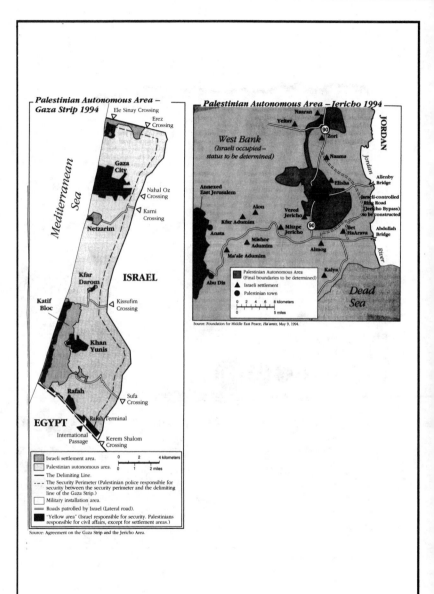

Palestinian Autonomous Area – Gaza Strip 1994

Ele Sinay Crossing

Erez Crossing

Mediterranean Sea

Gaza City

Nahal Oz Crossing

Karni Crossing

Netzarim

ISRAEL

Kfar Darom

Katif Bloc

Kissufim Crossing

Khan Yunis

Rafah

Sufa Crossing

EGYPT

Rafah Terminal

International Passage

Kerem Shalom Crossing

0	2	4 kilometers
0	1	2 miles

Israeli settlement area.

Palestinian autonomous area.

— The Delimiting Line.

--- The Security Perimeter (Palestinian police responsible for security between the security perimeter and the delimiting line of the Gaza Strip.)

Military installation area.

Roads patrolled by Israel (Lateral road).

"Yellow area" (Israel responsible for security. Palestinians responsible for civil affairs, except for settlement areas.)

Source: Agreement on the Gaza Strip and the Jericho Area.

Palestinian Autonomous Area – Jericho 1994

Naaran

Yeitav

Zori

JORDAN

West Bank
(Israeli occupied –
status to be determined)

90

Naama

Jordan

Elisha

Allenby Bridge

Annexed East Jerusalem

Alon

Vered Jericho

Israeli-controlled Ring Road (Jericho Bypass) to be constructed

Kfar Adumim

Mizpe Jericho

Abdullah Bridge

90

Bet HaArava

Anata

Mishor Adumim

Almog

River

Ma'ale Adumim

Kalya

Abu Dis

Dead Sea

Palestinian Autonomous Area (Final boundaries to be determined)

▲ Israeli settlement

● Palestinian town

0	2	4	6	8 kilometers
0		5 miles

Source: Foundation for Middle East Peace; *Ha'aretz*, May 9, 1994.

Population — Occupied Territories

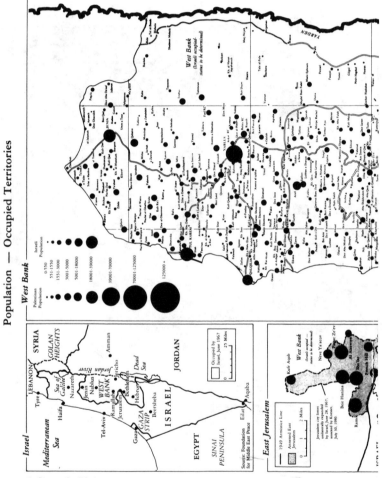

West Bank

Israeli Population

		0-550
		551-1550
		1551-5000
●		5001-5000
●		5001-18000
●		18001-19000

Palestinian Population

●		19001-70000
●		70001-125000
●		125000 +

Israel

Mediterranean Sea

LEBANON
Tyre
Haifa
Sea of Galilee
Nazareth

SYRIA
GOLAN HEIGHTS
Amman

Jenin
Nablus
Jordan River
Jericho
Ramallah
Jerusalem
Bethlehem
Hebron
Beersheba

WEST BANK
Dead Sea

JORDAN

Tel-Aviv
Gaza
GAZA STRIP

ISRAEL

EGYPT
SINAI PENINSULA
Eilat
Aqaba

Occupied by
Israel, June 1967

0   25 Miles

Source: Foundation
for Middle East Peace

East Jerusalem

1949 Armistice Line

Kafr Aqab

West Bank
(Israeli occupied:
status to be determined)

Neve Ya'acov
Pisgat Ze'ev
Al Qaram

Beit Hanina

Ramat
Shu'fat
French Hill

Jerusalem city limits
unilaterally expanded
by Israel, June 28, 1967;
annexed by Knesset,
July 30, 1980.

Armistice East
Jerusalem

0   2 Miles

❖   Report on Israeli Settlement

188

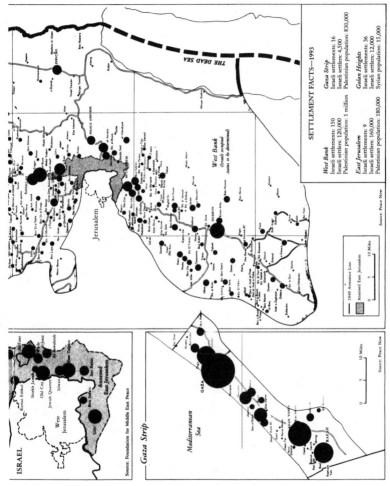

SETTLEMENT FACTS—1993

West Bank
Israeli settlements: 150
Israeli settlers: 120,000
Palestinian population: 1 million

East Jerusalem
Israeli settlements: 9
Israeli settlers: 160,000
Palestinian population: 180,000

Gaza Strip
Israeli settlements: 16
Israeli settlers: 4,500
Palestinian population: 830,000

Golan Heights
Israeli settlements: 36
Israeli settlers: 12,000
Syrian population: 15,000

Source: Peace Now

THE DEAD SEA

West Bank
(Israeli occupied;
status to be determined)

Jerusalem

RAMALLAH

MAALE ADUMIM

BETHLEHEM

HEBRON

1949 Armistice Line

Annexed East Jerusalem

0   5   10 Miles

Source: Peace Now

ISRAEL

West Jerusalem

Annexed East Jerusalem

Ramat Eshkol
Shiekh Jarrah
Old City
Jewish Quarter
Silwan
Gilo
Beit Safafa

Source: Foundation for Middle East Peace

Gaza Strip

Mediterranean Sea

GAZA

KHAN YUNIS

RAFAH

0   5   10 Miles

Source: Peace Now

November 1993

Foundation for Middle East Peace ❖

189

8

The Clinton Administration and the Israeli-Palestinian Accords

A Historic Handshake

For the first time ever, PLO Chairman Yasir Arafat and Israeli Prime Minister Yitzhak Rabin were hosted on September 13,1993 by the President of the United States. The occasion was a White House ceremony of the signing of the Declaration of Principles (DOP), known also as the Oslo accords.[1]

The accords must be viewed in the context of the recently achieved total American hegemony over the Middle East, resulting from the collapse of the Soviet Union and the consequences of the Gulf War. These accords represent a PLO surrender to the power of the U.S. and its ally Israel. Arafat and the PLO were in a weakened position, but the catalyst was the Clinton administration, which, during the first six months, had acquiesced in Israel's closure of the occupied territories, massive bombardment of Lebanon, and expulsion of 413 Hamas supporters, all carried out without any semblance of due process. The act which precipitated Arafat's acceptance of the Oslo accords, however, was Warren Christopher's "Declaration of Principles" of June 30, 1993, which repudiated long-standing American policy by implying that the West Bank and Gaza were "disputed" rather than "occupied" territory; by making reference only to authority over people but not over territory.

The accords created a fundamental change in the political terrain on which the struggle for a diplomatic settlement had begun nearly twenty years before. The "Declaration of Principles" and the "Mutual Recognition" statements, which were signed in an atmosphere of euphoria and exultation, are said to have signaled a turning point in the Arab-Israeli conflict.[2] The reluctant handshake between Arafat and Rabin was seen as the start of a new chapter that would convert a perpetual conflict to a new peaceful co-existence.

There was little to be gained in reflecting on the real significance of these accords as the media appeared fully mobilized to produce instant analysis—optimistic analysis to be sure—and to summon at short notice a standing army of so-called Middle East experts who would overwhelm a stunned audience with an endless variety of explanations for the miraculous event. One would announce that the "deal" was a real coup for President Clinton, the domestic policy president, who had the good fortune to reap diplomatic capital at almost no cost. Another would have you believe that the agreement was well-crafted, sophisticated and mindful of the protagonist's major concerns, but that "the devil is in the detail". Still a third would have us believe that while the agreement did not grant the Palestinians independence, it nevertheless represented the first and necessary step towards Palestinian statehood.

Ardent believers said that provisions such as the West Bank and Gaza constitute "a single territorial unit" (Article IV), ignoring the fact that such a unit is, in reality, a collection of cantons and sub-cantons severed by permanent Israeli settlements and their infrastructure. They would also tout Article I, which states that "…the transitional period of interim self-government shall lead to a permanent settlement based on Security Council Resolutions 242 and 338," again ignoring the widely-known Israeli claim that Israel had already met its obligations under 242, when it made the Sinai withdrawal after Camp David.

To understand the agreement, we must place it in its proper context. This would help us answer the question of "why now?" Why, after more then twenty years of active but futile diplomacy and after twenty-two months of a crippling impasse in the Madrid process, was this agreement finally reached in Oslo with the involvement of a few trusted aides and in an atmosphere of total secrecy? The second question we need to answer is how much of a breakthrough this agreement represents, and how much of a departure from the existing situation it signifies. Are we really on the threshold of a new situation?

The Context
The key to the context of the PLO-Israel agreement is the new political

reality which resulted from the collapse of the Soviet Union and the destruction of Iraq. That reality permitted the United States to effectively emerge as the only arbiter and sole peacemaker in the Middle East. The hegemonic ambitions it was pursuing in the region for a quarter of a century were not only achieved, but also accepted by all the Arab states, irrespective of whether they were pro-West or presumed to be vanguards of Arab liberation and previous spokespersons of the South in the earlier struggle for a new economic world order. The collapse of the Soviet Union ended the Cold War, and thus terminated whatever leverage might have been achieved; the Gulf War signaled an important victory of the North over the South in the battle for resources. It was the start of a new era, a militarily unipolar world order.

These dramatic transformations convinced Washington that an Arab-Israeli settlement had become a vital U.S. national interest. That impelled Washington to "seize the opportunity" and pave the road to Madrid and beyond. The Oslo accord, which was said to have surprised Washington, was the logical extension of Madrid and the culmination of America's foreign policy goals.

With deterrence having suddenly vanished at the global and regional levels, the U.S. and Israel were both left without any serious opposition, hence Madrid, Washington and Oslo, leading to a virtual Palestinian surrender. The question, however, is why did Arafat opt for an open-ended agreement which did not promise to meet the minimum aspirations of his people? What steered him towards Oslo while his own delegation, struggling in protracted talks in Washington, was left in the dark?

During twenty-two months of negotiations (November 1991–August 1993), the major concern in the Palestinian street was whether the negotiations would lead to genuine independence or to a fractured entity of unconnected bits and pieces in which the people's destiny would be determined by others. Having participated in the Madrid conference under conditions dictated largely by Israel (bilateral negotiations, transitional arrangements, UN dislodgment, and virtual sole U.S. sponsorship of the process), the Palestinians were acknowledging the bitter realities of the post-Gulf, post-Cold War period. Consequently, they expected to make major concessions consonant with the shifting regional and global balance.

The conclusions of Washington and Tel Aviv were not one and the same, but they were basically similar. Bush and Baker had differed somewhat from Israel on the real meaning of UN Security Council Resolution 242, the exchange of land for peace, the question of colonial settlements and the status of Jerusalem. But U.S. strategic influence, combined with the total absence of any Arab pressure on Washington, prevented the American "catalyst" from bridging the diplomatic gap between the Arabs and Israel with any specific proposals. At issue were the following basic matters: whether the Occupied Territories are occupied or not, illogical though it sounds; whether the projected Palestinian self-governing entity has any geographic definition, a land dimension or only a people's dimension; whether its jurisdiction is derived from the popular will of the Palestinians or conferred and limited by the occupation regime, making it an agent of an occupation that would continue to exist under a different label; whether Israel could continue to exclude Jerusalem from negotiable items during the transition; and finally, what really lies beyond the transition.

Throughout the period of Bush and Baker, the Palestinians kept hoping to resolve these issues, particularly after receiving a set of written U.S. assurances conveyed to them just prior to Madrid on the exchange of land for peace, termination of the Israeli occupation, and reaffirmation of the U.S. position that Jerusalem is occupied territory. What is really significant is that this scaled-back position was sustained by a solid consensus in the Palestinian community of six million world-wide and throughout the larger Arab World. Madrid signified a turning point in the Arab-Israeli conflict. Not only did the Arabs and Palestinians accept the reality of Israel, but they also recognized its legitimacy as a state, even prior to an explicit acknowledgment by Israel of its occupation of their land, a statement which has never been made yet.

The important legal issue involved here is that unless Israel came to terms with its status as occupant within the meaning of international law, it would be able to render any agreement regarding withdrawal, security, sovereignty and human rights completely superfluous. And that is what led the Palestinian delegation under the leadership of

Haider Abdul Shafi to stand firm, despite eleven rounds of negotiations. Without acknowledging its status as occupant, Israel would be able to shrug off its responsibility to the people while it controls their land. It would be able to set aside, as it has been doing since 1967, the 1949 Geneva Convention Relative to the Protection of Civilians in Times of War.

The applicability of the Geneva Convention to the occupied territories was reaffirmed by Security Council Resolution 681, which was adopted unanimously in 1990. The convention protects the Palestinians from being coerced into illegal agreements; that is, agreements which violate their rights. It also guards against the renunciation of their rights; and significantly, it restricts Israeli practices in the manner of a de facto sovereign.

The applicability of the convention is also recognized by the United States. The Country Report on Human Rights Practices for the year 1987 recognizes the applicability of both the 1907 Hague Convention and the 1949 Geneva Convention to the Israeli Occupation. So did James Baker's letter of assurances, though in a somewhat watered-down form.

The prospects for a negotiated settlement based on the Madrid framework began to look more grim with the ascendancy of Bill Clinton to the presidency. For Yasir Arafat and a handful of decision-makers, that event was to mark a juncture. Israel had never had a more loyal friend in the White House. Rabin's government had promised the electorate that a settlement would be reached in nine months. Gaza had become a major nuisance with hardly any benefits to Israel. According to members of the Palestinian delegation to the Washington talks, Israel had actually made a unilateral offer to vacate Gaza and dispose of it if the Palestinians were willing to assume the burden. The offer was not accepted unless it was to be part of a total rather than partial interim accord.

The struggle for Palestinian national rights would soon be refocused on municipal rights. The interests of Arafat and Rabin began to converge. Islamic resistance was on the rise, threatening both Arafat and Rabin. Arafat has become, together with his organization, increasingly irrelevant. The *Intifada* had given him a reprieve after his ouster from

Lebanon in 1982, and now he was looking for an extension of that reprieve.

The irrelevance of his organization and the erosion of his leadership were further accentuated by the growing prominence of the West Bank-Gaza negotiators who were admitted to the Washington talks by the Madrid process. While Haider Abdul Shafi led his delegation to the State Department and as Hanan Ashrawi articulated the Palestinian position to the press on a regular basis, Arafat's overseer Nabil Sha'ath had to take a backseat. He was seldom able to venture beyond his Washington hotel in which he was in constant touch with his boss in Tunis. The Oslo venue made a dramatic change by providing Arafat a welcome exchange of his proxy role in favor of direct on-the-spot involvement. He felt that he had been rescued despite the heavy cost in terms of national rights, which were subordinated to his narrower interests. It was ironic that he would be rescued by the only two nations that voted "no" on the General Assembly resolution in favor of mutual recognition in the Geneva session in November 1988. Arafat's rush to Oslo was pushed along also by mounting crises facing his leadership; financial crisis, governance crisis and outright corruption. The U.S. and Israel were now more than ready to drop their reservations and objection; terrorism was no longer an issue. A revised and updated renunciation (first stated in 1988) by Arafat would do, particularly when the new edition would also imply a virtual renunciation of internationally recognized rights, or at least a deferral of these rights. As soon as these conditions were met by Arafat, the road to Oslo was opened.

The Clinton Administration
1. Zionists at the Top

The policies of the Clinton administration convinced Arafat that the crippling diplomatic impasse would become worse unless he was to give in. The venue was Oslo. We might ask, what exactly the new administration did to intimidate Arafat? With the ascendancy of self-described Zionists into top foreign policy positions, the role of the pro-Israel lobby has been transformed from merely pressuring Congress and the Executive Branch to conceptualizing and articulating

Washington's Middle East policy. The range of controversy regarding Middle East policy extended between AIPAC, the main pro-Israeli lobby, and Americans For Peace Now. The *Washington Post* put it this way: "This keeps the Clinton Kitchen debate on the Middle East a peculiarly Jewish Family Affair."[3]

Having established himself during the campaign of 1992 as the truly pro-Israel candidate, Clinton began to build up a team of advisors to fashion a Middle East policy.[4] The names on that team are very revealing both in terms of their positions across the Jewish spectrum and their broader world views. These are Stuart Eizenstat, Steven Spiegel, Michael Mendelbaum, and Martin Indyk. The latter was assigned the task of drawing up the main position paper on the Middle East for the transition team.

Zionist influence in the Clinton administration was discussed candidly by the Israeli journalist, Avinoam Bar-Yosef in the Tel Aviv daily, *Maariv*. Such influence is seen as existing "at all levels" of government, and not only in the mideast arena of decision-making. He writes:

In the National Security Council, seven out of eleven top staffers are Jews. Clinton had specifically placed them in the most sensitive junctions in the U.S. security and foreign administration. The situation is not much different in the president's office, which is full of warm Jews.[5]

Bar-Yosef's list of "warm Jews" is rather extensive, including several cabinet positions and a variety of top-level advisors, directors of various program and projects and the deputy chief of staff, among others.

It is significant that Clinton's consensus building within the Jewish community seemed to assign tasks proportionately, according to his assessment of the power configurations in the Jewish community and his own conception of the United States interests. While the Jewish Peace Lobby was given access to Clinton and a hearing, in addition to positions in the transition team and in the administration, the mainstream and AIPAC operatives were assigned both positions and policy-formulation functions. For example, the four persons commissioned to set the tone of Clinton's Middle East policy came from the AIPAC-mainstream axis. The key person on that panel, Martin Indyk, is an Australian Jew whose naturalization as a U.S. citizen had to be completed in time for his appointment as the top Middle East "expert" in the NSC. Prior to his founding of the Washington Institute for Near East Policy in 1985, he served as assistant research director for AIPAC. Although he does not like to be identified with AIPAC and makes it a point to describe the Washington Institute as a non-partisan scholarly think-tank, his pro-Israel character is undeniable. He is reported to have said that the purpose of the Institute is to "counter Arabist views."[6] Eizenstat comes from the mainstream of the Jewish community with a position close to that of AIPAC now Rabin's policy. Spiegel, a UCLA political scientist, is also close to AIPAC, as is Mendelbaum, a Johns Hopkins political scientist, who is generally a foreign policy hardliner.[7]

Thus, the four people entrusted with the premier task of drawing up the main position paper for Clinton's transition team included none of the so-called doves from the Jewish peace lobby. It is also significant that Indyk's input into policy had already reflected the positions which the Washington Institute has been developing since 1985. In 1988, Indyk expressed the mission of his institute, which was established with seed money from foundations and contributions from American Jews, as consisting of the effort to inject a "balanced and realistic voice" into Washington's Middle East policy debates. He said on April 30, 1988: "We thought there was a balance problem…a feeling that the Arabists were in the heroic phase."[8]

He thought at the time that U.S. policy was "confronting Israel", causing it to suffer serious setbacks. He began to invite the "Arabists" from Defense and State for lunch once a month to hear speakers, and to interact with think-tank "experts." He also invited congressional staff, and diplomatic correspondents and began to publish policy papers and newsletters. The institute convened numerous study groups, seminars and symposia. Among those was a forty member study group held in 1988 to make recommendations on Middle East policy for the incoming Bush administration. While some of the ideas emanating from Indyk's "ready talents" showed up ultimately in Baker's diplomacy four years later, the cumulative findings and recommendations of the Washington's Institute's seminars, under Indyk's guidance and leadership, became the centerpiece of Clinton's Middle East agenda. Of course Indyk tried to involve in the study groups a broad segment of the establishment and the pro-Israel community, both inside and outside the government, in order to gain credibility. His second study group produced a publication entitled "Pursuing Peace: An American Strategy for the Arab-Israeli Peace Process." It was released on September 25, 1992, at a most convenient time, when Indyk was already serving on the four-member panel charged with drawing up the main paper for Clinton's transition team.

Others from the Jewish establishment and AIPAC who played important roles in the transition include Morris Amitay, a former AIPAC director, and Richard Schifter, a Reagan democrat, extremely hawkish, neo-conservative, who served, ironically, as Assistant Secretary of State for Human Rights in the Reagan and Bush administrations. Reuter reported (Jan 21, 1993) that he used to personally screen the entries on Israel in the State Department's annual report on human rights in an attempt to repair Israel's image and conceal its egregious human rights violations in the occupied territories. When Schifter left the Bush administration in 1992, it was apparently due to differences with Baker over policy on Israel. Israeli deputy Foreign Minister Yossi Beilin was quoted by Reuter (Jan 21, 1993) that Schifter told him that Israel's expulsion of 413 Palestinians to Lebanon on December 17, 1992 did not constitute a violation of international law. Meanwhile Dennis Ross, who served as Baker's right arm in Middle Eastern Affairs, was replaced by Samuel Lewis, who was Ambassador to Israel from 1977 to 1985. As the new director of policy planning in the State Department, Lewis, whose tenure in Israel coincided with the development of a strategic alliance under Reagan, has already had a great deal of influence over U.S. Mideast policy. He was described by the Israeli newspaper *Hadashot* as a "long-time friend of Israel". Another newspaper, *Yediot Aharonot,* said the appointment "strengthens hope for a continuation of the special relationship." It is interesting that his position was first offered to Michael Mendelbaum, who played a major role on the Middle East during the transition, but he turned it down.

2. The Jewish Peace Faction

As for the peace faction in the Jewish community, a number of people associated with Americans for Peace Now, with close ties to the Clinton administration, were offered senior positions, but none was included in the formal bodies working on the Middle East, either during the campaign or after. In fact, people associated with the peace faction like Peter Edelman, Eli Segal, Stanley Sheinbaum and others have no Mideast positions in the administration. Sheinbaum, one of the five Jewish activists who met with Yasir Arafat in Stockholm in 1988, had to submit his memoranda to Clinton during the campaign, through Steven Spiegel, Clinton's Mideast policy consultant.[9] Peter Edelman, on the other hand, the Georgetown professor who headed the transition team for the Justice Department and who is chairman of Americans for Peace Now, submitted directly to Clinton a number of memoranda advocating a more active U.S. role in the "peace process." The *Washington Post* described his connections to Clinton as going "beyond the professional; they first met through Edelman's wife, Marion Wright Edelman, the President of the Children's Defense Fund, who was Hillary Clinton's mentor."[10] Another member of the board of Americans for Peace Now, Eli Segal, served as financial officer in the transition, but had no Mideast-related assignment.

3. The Range of the "Controversy"

Given that the competing views on Middle East policy in the Clinton administration are fairly limited to the American Jewish community, it seems that a real controversy does not exist. Perhaps the single most important difference between the peace camp, represented by Edelman-Sheinbaum and others, on the one hand, and the mainstream-AIPAC group on the other, is the extent to which the U.S. government should be involved in the negotiations. While the former group's memoranda to Clinton advocated a much stronger participation to salvage the "peace process", the Indyk group called for continued U.S. involvement as a high priority, but emphasized the need for the parties to advance substantially before Washington could intervene with "bridging" proposals. The latter group also expressed strong opposition to any modification of the Madrid framework. Upon releasing a blue-ribbon study on September 25, 1992 by the Washington Institute for Near East Policy, Martin Indyk had this to say:

The current rules of the game should be maintained. There may be circumstances in which one or the other party may try to change the rules of the game, to test the resolve of a new administration...the whole thing will start to come apart if you start with that.

Other than this issue, differences between them are fairly subtle. Symbolically, members of the peace camp have gained a reputation for being close to the PLO, having had meetings with its top leaders and having advocated, previous to Madrid, a direct PLO role in the negotiations. The Washington Institute, on the other hand, had taken a position back in 1986 against giving the PLO any role whatsoever unless the PLO was willing to divest itself of the attributes of self-determination, which was exactly what Arafat had, in effect, agreed to in Oslo. Long before Baker devised his formula for Palestinian representation, which sidestepped the PLO, Indyk had the following to say on this issue in April 1986:

The United States should abandon its efforts to draw Yasir Arafat and his Palestine Liberation Organization into Middle East Peace efforts and concentrate on cultivating a new group of moderate Palestinians.... The United States has spent the past nine years pursuing the option of transforming Arafat without the slightest measure of success.[11]

Significantly, Indyk claimed that by involving the PLO in negotiations, the U.S. would have to face the "bleak options" of Palestinian self-determination and an international peace conference. In fact, these ideas paralleled and may have influenced Baker's diplomacy two years later. Although the Jewish peace camp in the Clinton circles had entertained divergent views on Palestinian rights, the realities of the Madrid process made the pace of negotiations and the proper U.S. role into the major issues in the controversy, a task that hardly offered a serious challenge to Clinton. Thus, for the first time in forty-five years, consensus building on the Middle East in the official U.S. arena had become a Zionist concern. The various constituencies (church-peace groups, African-American, and "oil lobby" and the "Arabist" groups), who have traditionally argued for some restraint of U.S. uncritical support of Israel, were virtually absent. Meanwhile, Clinton, who was elected mainly on domestic rather than international issues, was quite disposed to remove Mideast policy from the realm of controversy.

Having witnessed Clinton's embrace of Zionists throughout the presidential campaign and after victory, Arafat drew his own conclusions and hastened to secure his own tenure even at the expense of Palestinian national rights. The stark choice before him was to be involved in the "peace process" without the attributes of national rights, or to risk being bypassed altogether. The road to Oslo implied a role for and recognition of the PLO, but only in form and not in substance.

4. Israel Tests the Clinton Administration: Mass Expulsions

Israel began to test the new administration rather early in January of 1993. Three major escalations by Rabin simply elicited acquiescence in Washington. The expulsion of 413 Palestinians to Lebanon in December 1992 led the Clinton administration to shield Israel from imminent UN Security Council sanctions. The closure of the Occupied Territories, in March 1993, rendering them into four unconnected districts; and creating enormous economic hardships for their Palestinian residents failed to produce even a nudge from the self-styled arbiter normally concerned about confidence-building measures. The bombardment of Lebanon in July 1993 with the declared objective of depopulating the south causing numerous civilian casualties; and the destruction of some 70 Lebanese villages demonstrated how far Israel can go without antagonizing the "honest broker."

The range of Israel's discourse on the plight of the Palestinians whom Rabin expelled to Lebanon on December 17,1992 was between those who viewed the expulsion as a preemptive measure designed to prevent further attacks by Islamic activists on Israeli soldiers, and others who saw it as a form of retaliation and/or a show of force by the Rabin government to appease the Israeli public. In either case, the assumption was that there was an underlying threat—"terrorist" to be sure, but a special kind, bearing the new label of Islamic fundamentalism. Such a "threat" continued to provide the ideological framework for Israeli retaliation and intervention. The syndrome is firmly entrenched in the political culture, and the two dominant blocs—Likud and Labor—usually try to outdo each other in meeting the challenge.

Responding to criticism by right-wing members of the Knesset, and aware of public opinion polls showing that 78 percent of Israelis supported the expulsion,[12] Prime Minister Rabin boasted on February 8, 1993 to a BBC correspondent:

> We knew we were making an unprecedented move. Which government in the past 20 years was prepared to expel or remove temporarily 25, not to mention 400, people? I felt at the time a need to level an immediate, tough blow against Hamas that went beyond everything done previously. I achieved that aim, whether it involved 300 or 400.

That statement hardly masked the siege mentality, which Rabin himself had asked Israelis to shed, when he assumed office only seven months earlier, in July 1992. "We must overcome the sense of isolation that has held us in its thrall for almost a half a century," he said. The statement also reflected a grotesque sense of proportion, whereby 400 Palestinians are summarily ejected to a makeshift mountain camp in the middle of winter in retaliation for the killing of four Israeli soldiers. Worse yet was that during Rabin's first six months in office, the death toll among Palestinians killed by Israelis was on the increase. According to the Israeli human rights organization B'tselem, security forces shot dead 76 Palestinians between August 1992 and January 1993, in contrast to 63 dead during the first six months of 1992. During the same period the number of Palestinian children killed soared from 6 to 17. [13]

Applying Rabin's criteria for retaliation and/or preemption, one could speculate about the number of deportees required to placate Israeli public opinion—40,000 or perhaps 400,000—had these death statistics during Rabin's latest tenure been Israeli not Palestinian. Or one could also speculate, as did the *Houston Chronicle*, about the world's reaction to a similar atrocity committed against Israelis by Palestinians:

> What would have happened if the Palestinians had held 415 Israelis hostage for over a month in a cold and barren no man's land with nothing but tents to shelter in? What would Israel have done if the Palestinians had their

hostages over holidays and said they would not be allowed to go home unless they agreed to end their occupation of Arab land? What would those in human rights circles have done, from Washington to London, if not one of these hostages had been given any sort of trial before being deported from their land and dumped in the cold? What would the press have said if they were submitted to intermittent showers of snow and artillery?[14]

The Demographic Battle

That 1,600 Palestinian natives can be quickly rounded up and in a few hours 413 of them are blindfolded, handcuffed and bussed to the Lebanese boarder, without charge, trial or any semblance of due process, is ominous enough. But the act itself represented a new dimension of Israel's expulsion policy, and was intended to set a precedent in Israel's demographic battle with the Palestinians. Unlike the mass expulsions of 1948 and 1967, which took place under the cover of armed conflict, and unlike those of 1989–1990, which were executed bureaucratically on the pretext of improper residency, the December 1992 expulsion was the first mass expulsion to be carried out explicitly in the name of security. On December 16, 1992, Prime Minister Rabin, who also holds the defense ministry portfolio, issued Authorization No. 97 granting military commanders in the occupied territories the authority to expel "inciters." Almost simultaneously, the required "legal" machinery was set up with the issuance of Military Order 1086, and the expulsion was carried out in accordance with the instant legislation. This "legislation" had amended a previous rule, which allowed those subject to expulsion orders the right of appeal to a military committee and then the Supreme Court. In fact such appeals never succeed; the Israeli Supreme Court had never overturned an expulsion order by the government.

Surely Yitzhak Rabin, himself a veteran of expulsions, having "removed" some 55,000 residents of Ramleh and Lydda in 1948 (a small portion of the 800,000 Palestinians who became refugees) and having served as the Army Chief of Staff in 1967, when about 300,000 were "removed" to Jordan, was seeking new horizons in the policy of acquiring more land and less people. The cumulative impact of such expulsions on the political future of the Palestinians would be devastating. The 413 who were expelled in December 1992 included a high number of career professionals, businessmen, and students. In addition, the thousands of Palestinians who were expelled since 1967 represent a high percentage of qualified people. An escalation of this mass expulsion for security reasons, as Rabin threatened, could deprive the Palestinians of a large number of their future administrators, engineers, scientists and even negotiators.

U.S. Complicity in Israel's Expulsion Policy

The expulsion of December 17,1992 provided President Clinton with his first opportunity to embark on the road of Middle East diplomacy. His decision became a defining event for the Clinton administration. Not only did that act represent a new and more dangerous dimension of Israel's expulsion policy, ongoing since 1948, but it may have also signaled a new American attitude towards the admissibility of expulsions from occupied territories under international law.

For Israel, establishing a right to carry out mass expulsions for "security reasons" is designed to enhance its demographic goals. Demography, like land and water, is at the core of the Arab-Israeli conflict, and was central to the controversy over the expulsions. The damage which this policy has inflicted on the Palestinian people was likely to be further compounded by implicit American acceptance of Rabin's latest acts. In fact, Rabin wasted no time in claiming a major victory when he struck a deal with the Clinton administration on February 1,1993. According to what Secretary of State Warren Christopher described as a "compromise", Washington agreed to shield Israel from imminent sanctions in the Security Council in exchange for Israel's agreement to allow 101 of the deportees to return immediately, while keeping the other 295 in exile for one year.[15] Environment Minister Yossi Sarid, who represents the supposedly dovish Meretz Party in the Israeli cabinet, confirmed U.S. support: "We are getting full backing from the United States…there is no more fear that sanctions will be imposed."[16]

Sarid was simply reacting to what became common knowledge in late January 1993. According to Elaine Sciolino of the *New York Times* (January 29, 1993):

Despite the Security Council vote in favor of the immediate return of the deportees, neither Mr. Clinton, nor Mr. Christopher explicitly repeated that demand when they spoke with Mr. Rabin in separate telephone conversations last weekend, according to Israeli officials.

The Clinton administration had also succeeded in blocking separate efforts by the UN Secretary-General and by the PLO to press for some type of sanctions against Israel. After Christopher announced the agreement, saying that Israel's move should end UN involvement in the issue, and promising that the U.S. "will prevent any decisions in international forums that would have operational significance against Israel", Rabin described the agreement as a "package deal", and asserted that it preserved "the principle of our ability to remove for a limited time hundreds of inciters, leaders and organizers."[17] Although the Clinton administration did not cherish being characterized as an accomplice by Rabin, no U.S. official has disavowed the attribution.

Worse yet from Washington's standpoint were Rabin's boasts that he was able to hoodwink the Americans. According to Agence France Presse (7 February, 1993) Rabin boasted: "I've made a great deal with the Americans." When asked about the Palestinian's rejection of the deal, he was reported to have said: "It's no longer my problem… Now it's Clinton's problem. He can stew in his own juices. I wanted a deal with the Americans and I've got one…the reaction of the expelled Palestinians does not interest me, it never has."[18]

Having taken the Israeli-U.S. special relationship for granted and having callously dismissed international law as irrelevant, Rabin in fact succeeded in convincing the Clinton administration to supply the necessary pressure to get the Arab states and the Palestinians to fall in line and return to the so-called "peace process". With the ninth round of negotiations underway in Washington, neither the Arab parties nor Washington was demanding to place the expulsion matter on the active agenda. In short, Israel has succeeded in enlisting U.S. implicit support for the claim that it has a right to expel civilians from the occupied territories.

Having succeeded in getting the Clinton administration to acquiesce in a new dimension of Israel's expulsion policy was unprecedented.

This is not to imply that the Reagan and Bush administrations were promoters of peace and justice, but they did adhere to the principle that expulsion from occupied territories was illegal. The U.S. departure from this principle, which the Rabin-Christopher "compromise" of 1 February implied, explains the Israeli prime minister's glee.

This first action on the Middle East by the Clinton administration reveals not only a collaborative attitude towards Israel but a deviation from international law, which was touted repeatedly in the conflict with Iraq. During the year 1992, the U.S. government expressed its position on this question at least on two occasions. Voting in favor of Security Council Resolution 726 on January 6, 1992, the U.S. ambassador to the UN Thomas Pickering said:

> The U.S. government believes that deportation of individuals from the occupied territories is a violation of Article 49 of the Geneva Convention.... Any persons charged with wrongdoing should be brought before a court of law based on the evidence and be given a fair trail, which would afford a full judicial process.

As late as December 18,1992, then Secretary of State Lawrence Eagleburger reaffirmed the U.S. position, which considered expulsion a violation of the fourth Geneva Convention of 1949. Article 49 prohibits absolutely "individual or mass forcible transfers, as well as deportations...regardless of their motive." Deportations are also a form of collective punishment which is expressly forbidden by Article 33 and are specifically cited as a "grave breach", or a war crime punishable under the convention in Article 147. Moreover, Article 146 places specific duties on states party to the convention to suppress grave breaches by prosecuting the perpetrators. The latter requirement is significant in light of the U.S.-Israeli "compromise" of February 1, which makes the U.S., a party to the convention, an accomplice in an illegal act.

Contrary to the claim made by Christopher that the Israeli offer to repatriate 101 out of 400 Palestinians was "consistent with Security Council Resolution 799," that resolution in fact made no exceptions or exemptions. The resolution did not establish new categories of permissible expulsion, partial expulsion, or temporary expulsion, as absurdly implied in that process, which in Christopher's view made it "unnecessary for the matter to come before the Security Council for further action." It demanded the "immediate repatriation" of all deportees. The prohibition of deportation in international law is categorical. Therefore, the departure of the Clinton administration from the requirements of international law, as well as from long-standing U.S. policy, amounted to rewarding Israel for carrying out an illegal act. So much for the U.S. as guardian of international legality.

For Yasir Arafat, it began to look like his negotiators were likely to face not only a recalcitrant Israel, but a more Israelized American policy. If the U.S. was unwilling to enforce Resolution 799, would it ever help in the enforcement of Resolution 242? This was the question which he began to ponder. Obviously, it was another factor which hastened his capitulation.

Clinton "Bridges" the Gap

The real catalyst, which reinforced the ongoing secret affair in Oslo, was the crucial decision of the Clinton administration to break the impasse with so-called bridging measures—something which Bush and Baker were reluctant to undertake. The Washington negotiations between Israel and the Palestinians, which began after the Madrid conference, failed to yield results despite eleven rounds over a period of 22 months. The impasse, which was created by Israel's refusal to come to terms with its status as occupier and by U.S. unwillingness to give concrete meaning to its letter of assurances, was finally resolved at the expense of the Palestinians. A proposed "Declaration of Principles" was announced by Warren Christopher on June 30, 1993.[19] In particular, three elements in that declaration upheld the Israeli position. First, the implication that the West Bank and Gaza are disputed rather than occupied territory. Second, the conspicuous absence of any reference to the exchange of land for peace, or to Israeli withdrawal or even redeployment, implying that Israel has an equal right to lay claims to the land. Thirdly, the U.S. declaration committed the Palestinians to agree, beforehand, that all matters relating to sovereignty are outside the scope of the negotiations for the interim phase, hence discussion of Jerusalem, the still expanding settlements and the land issue are to be deferred for several years. Also, because the issues of land and the nature of authority on that land are treated separately in the U.S. declaration, the focus of negotiations would be limited to authority over the people but not the territory, with the people reduced to the status of inhabitants or a minority rather than a people with national rights. This manifest departure in U.S. policy, which effectively modified the Madrid framework and the context of the U.S. letter of assurances, is the real catalyst for the PLO-Israeli agreement, known as the Declaration of Principles (DOP).

The Declaration of Principles: Issues and Implications

The Oslo accord, which was confirmed by the historic handshake between Arafat and Rabin on September 13, 1993 at the White House, signified a critical juncture in the Palestine-Israel conflict.[20] For the first time in history, the Palestinian leadership endorsed a settlement which kept the Israeli occupation intact on the premise that all the outstanding issues in the conflict would be subject to negotiations during a period of three to five years hence. The assumptions of the accord (DOP), however, and the political environment in which it was drawn, precluded a brighter outcome in the future. A few observations about the accord suffice:

1. There is a conspicuous shortage of principles in this "agreement to reach agreement". Contrary to the initial pronouncements of a number of U.S. journalists that "the devil is in the detail," a major deficiency, in fact, was not the lack of details, but the desertion of principles. The text of the agreement makes no mention of the occupation, the exchange of land for peace, the inadmissibility of conquest by force, or the national rights of the Palestinian people or other principles, some of which are endorsed by the United States and some of which are universally accepted.

There is no reference whatsoever to the human rights of the Palestinians at a time when the need for guarding against abuse is more urgent then before. During the transitional period of "self-governance," the Palestinians would have to contend with a new Palestinian administration in addition to the occupation regime. Dissidents who oppose the agreement would be vulnerable to abuse, especially in view of the total absence of clear and effective means of accountability, with two authorities looking over each other's shoulders.

The urgency is further accentuated by the already demonstrated lack of respect (to put it mildly) for the human rights of Palestinians not only by Mr. Rabin but by Arafat himself and Clinton as well. President Clinton had telephoned President Assad of Syria on September 15, 1993 requesting that he silence critics of the agreement.[20] The following quotation from Rabin illustrates the point rather well:

> I prefer the Palestinians to cope with the problem of enforcing order in the Gaza (strip). The Palestinians will be better at it than we were because they will allow no appeals to the Supreme Court and will prevent the (Israeli) association for civil rights from criticizing the conditions there by denying it access to the area. They will rule there by their own methods, freeing–and this is most important–the Israeli army soldiers from having to do what they will do.[21]

The PLO chief of security, Hakam Balawi, told Israeli television: "We will crush the opposition."

2. As for the issue of recognition, Israel recognized in the preamble of the declaration "mutual legitimate and political rights" but not national rights or the right of return, enshrined in UN resolutions. In fact, the only UN resolutions Israel recognizes are 242 and 338, but that applies to the form and excludes substance; and in the exchange of letters, Israel recognizes the PLO but not the Palestinian people.

For Palestinians, that recognition has a psychological and political importance but it does not denote legal recognition because the declaration does not envision a sovereign entity. Moreover, the so-called mutual recognition is asymmetrical and non-reciprocal. The agreement is predicated on the faulty assumption that the Palestinians, who were subjected to dispossession, dismemberment, disenfranchisement and subjugation, are the party which has done wrong and must apologize for their legal resistance to a military occupation as if it has been an act of random violence. Nothing is said about the Israeli practices, which fill thousands of pages in numerous reports of the most reputable human rights organizations in the West and in Israel itself.

Arafat's men in Oslo did not or could not extract a simple statement from Rabin's representatives pledging that Israel refrain from practices which have been described as crimes of state in the Nuremburg sense. Human Rights Watch reminded Warren Christopher that deportations, as a form of collective punishment, prohibited by article 33 of the 1949 Geneva Convention and specifically cited as a "grave breach", are a war crime punishable under the convention in Article 147. [22]

3. Regarding the issue of withdrawal, the declaration provides for an Israeli withdrawal from the Gaza Strip and Jericho Area, but only for a redeployment from population centers in the West Bank. Moreover, this partial and limited withdrawal will not abolish the military government. And the fact that Israel did not acknowledge its status as occupier will mean that its military government will remain the body in which sovereignty is vested under international law even in Jericho and Gaza. It also means that the code of military orders which constitutes the basis for the legal system in the West Bank and Gaza will remain in force in the six spheres enumerated in Article V, No. 2; education and culture, health, social welfare, direct taxation and tourism.

Even before the signing of the DOP, Israel's Chief of Staff, Mordechai Gur and Prime Minister Rabin expressed their interpretation of the clauses which deal with withdrawal and redeployment. Their statements revealed no ambiguity whatsoever. Gur said; "This is redeployment not withdrawal. Anything that happens, the IDF will be there." [23] Rabin's statement on this subject was even more explicit:

> The forces of the Israeli army will be redeployed on locations determined only by us, unlike the Camp David agreements which mandated a withdrawal of the Israeli armed forces. In the agreement we reached, we didn't consent to use the formula 'withdrawal of Israeli army forces' except when it applied to the Gaza Strip. In application to all other places the only term used is 'redeployment'. [24]

In fact, Article XIII, No 3 of the DOP makes further Israeli redeployment contingent only on the ability of a strong Palestinian police force to control the situation.

4. The source of authority is clearly the occupation regime. The Palestinian Council has legislative power, but only relating to the six areas in Article VI and in Annex II of the DOP. That excludes the Israeli settlements and the network of roads connecting these settlements with each other and with Israel proper. It also excludes settlements, Jerusalem, military locations and Israelis. Article VII-5 of the DOP's "Specific Understandings and Agreements" solidifies Israel's claims as final authority: "The withdrawal of the military government will not prevent Israel from exercising the powers and responsibilities not transferred to the Council."

The implication of this article is that Israel claims what is known as "reserved powers" or inherent powers. Such broad construction is deliberate and makes no secret of who is really sovereign. The Palestinian Council, unlike a real legislature, can exercise powers and responsibilities merely in the spheres which have been "transferred" to it by the agreement. Its powers are purely "delegated," not by the Palestinian people or their representatives, but by the occupation regime.

Moreover, the so-called self-government arrangements described in the DOP can only be altered or amended during the final status talks. Hence the Palestinians will be unable to adopt their own constitution and enact their own laws, inasmuch as these must conform to the spirit and the letter of the DOP. Article IX ensures that the Israeli military orders of the past 27 years and the relevant Jordanian laws remain in effect until amended by both parties, Israel and the Palestinian council; "Both parties will review jointly laws and military orders presently in force in remaining spheres..." (that is, other than the authorities transferred to the council.) The term "jointly" means by agreement; Israel will be able to exercise a veto over such amendments.

The occupation regime remaining as the source of authority was reconfirmed in the subsequent agreement which was signed in Cairo by Israel and the PLO on May 4, 1994.[25] The Cairo Agreement, also known as Gaza-Jericho First, has enabled the PLO to set up a governing apparatus with a police force and a judiciary in Gaza and Jericho, but it did not end the occupation despite the confusing language in Article VII-5 of the DOP: "After the inauguration of the council, the Civil Administration will be dissolved, and the Israeli military government will be withdrawn."

A careful reading of this clause reveals that unlike the Civil Administration which is being "dissolved," the military government remains and will be redeployed to other areas of the occupied territories, away from population concentrations. The continuation of the military government, and therefore the occupation, is further assured by Article XXIII-7 of the Cairo agreement:

The Gaza Strip and Jericho Area shall continue to be an integral part of the West Bank and their status shall not be changed for the period of this agreement. Nothing in this agreement shall be considered to change this status.

One of the principal authors of the DOP and the Cairo Agreement, Joel Singer, a legal advisor to the Israeli Foreign Ministry, put it frankly as follows: The Palestinian entity "will not be independent or sovereign in nature, but rather will be legally subordinate to the authority of the military government."[26]

Conclusion

Given these few observations, the level of jubilation which greeted these agreements was truly out of place. For the Palestinian people, the Oslo agreement may very well be a "done deal" and the "only game in town". And yet, it is also an uncertain path, if not a blind alley. Negotiations usually constitute a process of conciliation with a possible outcome already in place. For example, the negotiations in South Africa were expected to lead to the termination of apartheid and the realization of majority rule. That has already been realized. In the case of Palestine however, there is neither an outline nor a vision of the final outcome. All fundamental issues involving borders, refugees, Jerusalem and indeed the occupation itself are deferred. "Self-government", as the sole concern of these negotiations in the immediate term, is seen by the Palestinians as the necessary link towards independence; whereas Israel views that concept only as a mechanism to ratify the occupation under a new and different label.

That outcome seemed to have been assured by the accumulated effect of U.S. Middle East policy during a period of more than twenty-five years. The persistent efforts exerted by succeeding administrations finally have come to a full fruition under President Clinton. His predecessors had resolved to deal with the Palestine question on the basis of autonomy according to the Camp David formula. George Bush and James Baker were holding out for a Palestinian entity whose status would fall somewhere between autonomy and statehood. The twenty-two month impasse was, in part, a reflection of the search for a point in that range. It did not happen; Baker and Bush were timid, reluctant to interfere in their roles as catalysts. Israel, on the other hand, was adamant against changing the status-quo. Being skillful in riding the waves and buying time, Israel procrastinated throughout 1992—an election year in the United States. The beleaguered Bush was in no position to rock the boat. Meanwhile the delegations went back and forth and wasted precious time.

Not until the Clinton administration put forth its own formula for bridging the gap did things begin to move away from dead center. That move produced Oslo, which reconfirmed the occupation, yet reorganized it, repackaged it and obtained Palestinian consent for it. So far, the aftermath of the Oslo agreements, the Cairo agreements I, II,and III, and "early Empowerment"shows no sign whatsoever that the "peace process" is leading towards a meaningful autonomy, let alone statehood for the Palestinians. Not only does Israel stand firmly against any kind of parity for the Palestinians, but the Clinton administration is unwilling to nudge Israel. Feeling secure as the world's only superpower and the sole hegemon in the Middle East , the United States under Clinton will continue to pursue the peace, but it will be a Pax-Americana, Pax-Israelica.

Unlike post-Cold War agreements, such as those in El Salvador, Cambodia, and Afghanistan, which were held under UN auspices, and unlike the South African agreement, negotiated by the parties themselves as equal partners, this was thoroughly an American "peace". The Middle East was reconfirmed as America's own turf, in which there was a victor—America's surrogate and partner, promoted to strategic ally—and a vanquished, whose leadership agreed to give up the struggle for national rights and abide by the rules of the game—the rules of the New World (dis)Order.

Notes

1. Text of the Israel-PLO Draft Agreement on Palestinian Self-Rule appeared in the *New York Times,* September 1, 1993.

2. Exchange of letters between Arafat and Rabin appeared in the *New York Times,* September 10, 1993.

3. *Washington Post,* December 13, 1992.

4. See the detailed study by Avinoam Bar-Yosef, "The Jews Who Run Clinton's Court," *Maariv,* September 2, 1994.

5. *Ibid.*

6. *National Journal, Inc.,* April 30, 1988.

7. *Washington Post,* December 13, 1992. See *The New Republic,* October 12, 1992.

8. *National Journal, Inc.,* April 30, 1988. For Indyk's views on the Middle East see his article in *Foreign Affairs,* December 1991.

9. *Washington Post,* December 13, 1992.

10. *Ibid.*

11. States News Service, April 11, 1986, obtained through Lexus-Nexus.

12. *Washington Post,* February 7, 1993.

13. As reported by Agence France Presse, February 8, 1993, through Lexus-Nexus.

14. *Houston Chronicle,* February 7, 1993.

15. Clyde Haberman, "Israel to Return 100 Palestinians It Had Deported," *New York Times,* February 1, 1993.

16. *Ibid.*

17. Clyde Haberman, "Deportees' Return Defended by Rabin," *New York Times,* February 4, 1993.

18. Agence France Presse, February 7, 1993.

19. Text in *Mideast Mirror,*.July 5, 1993.

20. Middle East Watch, "Report on Lebanon" Vol. 5 (September 7, 1993), p.2

21. *Yediot Aharonoth,* September 7, 1993.

22. Letter to Warren Christopher signed by Aryeh Neier, Executive Director of Human Rights Watch and Patricia Derian, Member of the Board of Middle East Watch, dated February 4, 1993.

23. *New York Times,* September 3, 1993

24. *Ibid.*
25. Text of the Cairo Agreement of May 4, 1994 in Journal of Palestine Studies. Vol. XXIII, No. 4 (summer, 1994), pp. 118-126.
26. Joel Singer, "The Declaration of Principle on Interim Self-government Arrangement: Some Legal Aspects," *Justice*, February 1994, p. 6.

9

From Oslo to Cairo and Beyond

Repackaging the Occupation

I. The Cairo Agreements: A Synopsis
Gaza/Jericho—First or Last?

The road from Madrid to Washington to Oslo and beyond to Taba and Cairo has spelled disaster for the Palestinian people. Much has been said and written about the Oslo deal, the DOP, its pitfalls, short-comings, and manipulative phraseology. But clearly, the Cairo agreements which followed Oslo (Feb. 9, April 4, and May 4, 1994) have secured Palestinian acquiescence in Israeli unilateral acts taken in the course of the occupation. The agreements on the questions of juris-diction, security, economics, and settlements, for example, offer insight into the outlook for the future, when the final status of the occupied territories is expected to be resolved.

The agreements, call them Cairo I, II and III, have demonstrated that their "Gaza-Jericho First" model, under which the Palestinian Authority (PA) was set up in Gaza and the "Jericho Area," is not likely to produce an improved version during the next phase. After all, there is no ambiguity about the fact that during the interim period, the sta-tus of the Gaza Strip and the "Jericho Area" will be identical to that of the West Bank, despite the dissolution of the Civil Administration and the withdrawal of the Israeli army. In fact the Israeli army is still in the Gaza Strip but it has been redeployed to the settlements and other adja-cent areas. The status of the Gaza Strip and Jericho is, therefore, essentially the same as that of the West Bank, despite the establishment of the PA. Both areas are still under occupation. Annex II, Number 6 of the DOP makes this quite clear:

Other than these agreed arrangements, the status of the Gaza Strip and Jericho Area will continue to be an integral part of the West Bank and Gaza

Strip, and will not be changed in the interim period.

Cynics have been saying, since the historic handshake on September 13, 1993, that the "Gaza-Jericho First" will also be last. Now, after the three Cairos, the question is what kind of a "first" do we really have, and what kind of precedents have been set? The questions of security and jurisdiction have clearly been decided in accordance with Israel's interpretation of Oslo, reflecting a dangerous imbalance, which has already ruled out an honorable compromise.

The Oslo accords had put an end to the ambiguity of Camp David regarding the nature of Palestinian rights, inasmuch as they are based on personal rights and not on territorial rights. Camp David spoke of the military government being "replaced" by the Palestinian Authority. Now, it is crystal clear that there is no replacement. The PLO role in the West Bank is a "functional extension rather than a territorial extention" of Palestinian rule, as Shimon Peres put it.

The Cairo Agreement is, moreover, based on the notion that the West Bank and Gaza are disputed territory and that their status will not change, inasmuch as the military government will exercise all powers not transferred to the Palestinian Council, which will be legally subordinate to its authority. Israel will continue to exercise de facto sovereignty, and the occupation law will continue to be the principal legal basis for governing the West Bank and Gaza. The PLO is simply charged with administering occupation law. It was not surprising therefore, that the results of the negotiations in the Cairo agreements have simply ratified the status-quo.

The balance sheet of the Cairo agreements reveals that the outcome was consistent with the terms of the Oslo Declaration of Principles (DOP). Cairo I was already determined and pre-ordained by the DOP, despite nearly five months (September 1993–February 1994) of a fruitless struggle by Yasir Arafat to obtain a better deal. Such exertion of energy and utilization of diplomatic resources might have made a better investment in Oslo rather than in Taba and Cairo. Lacking even the simplest attempt at a legal strategy, Arafat's negotiators at Oslo gave away the essence of the Palestinian position, on the basis of which Palestinian rights gained world-wide recognition during the past quarter of a century. The position which Haider Abdul Shafi's team had adhered to, upon Arafat's own instructions between October 1991 and August 1993 and during eleven rounds of negotiations, was squandered in Oslo. The DOP is not predicated on the crucial principle that Israel is an occupant within the meaning of international law. Hence Israel would be able to claim and exercise de facto sovereignty not only over the illegal Jewish settlements but over Gaza, Jericho and the whole West Bank, including Jerusalem, as well.

The Issue of Security and Border Control

When the deadlock was finally resolved in Cairo on February 9, 1994, regarding the control of border crossing, the relative size of the "Jericho Area" and the question of security, Rabin felt vindicated while Arafat appeared despondent. The former had only to invoke Article VIII of the DOP: "Israel will continue to carry the responsibility for defending against external threats, as well as the responsibility for overall security of Israelis…."

Therefore, Palestinian demands for control of traffic over the Jordan River bridge and at the Rafah crossing to the Sinai Peninsula were more in the realm of supplication rather than negotiation. Had Arafat employed strategic planning at Oslo, rather than his more familiar petty tactics of conflict resolution, (which he used over the years to remain arbiter in a factious movement), he would have known the serious implications of the provision in Article VIII.

That implication is exactly what he accepted: actual Israeli control of the border and symbolic Palestinian presence bestowed gratuitously in deference to a presumed Arab lust for honor and prestige. The Orientalist experts of Israel's colonial departments came up with the tools; flags, guards with uniforms, immigration officials armed with ineffectual entry stamps and even special arrangements for a "VIP crossing."

Meanwhile, the three-wing terminal is managed by an Israeli director while inspection of passengers entering the Palestinian wing is a joint responsibility. Foreigners and Israelis pass through a separate terminal managed by Israel and totally off limits to Palestinian agents. Israeli staff can still prevent passengers to Gaza and Jericho from entering if they consider them undesirable. They exercise this function while hidden inside a booth behind two way windows which enable them to see out while not being seen. They receive passenger documents from Palestinian agents through a narrow drawer. They scrutinize them and pass them back. Thus even Palestinian jurisdiction over travelers to the "autonomous" areas is restricted. Meanwhile, Israeli officers will continue to be responsible for Palestinians, Israelis and other travelers destined for the West Bank, just as they have been for nearly 28 years. Refugees wishing to return home will not be helped by so-called Palestinian immigration officers or their entry stamps. Their fate is to be decided during final-status negotiations by a tripartite committee consisting of Israel, Jordan and the PA, and all decisions will be reached "by agreement."

Palestinian officers at the border crossing are ultimately responsible to the Israeli director-general. Their authority is restricted to the extent that their real task becomes effectively clerical under their Israeli "counterparts." At the conclusion of the checking processes, Palestinian officers are assigned to providing the passenger "...with a white card issued by the Israeli officer." At the exit, another Palestinian officer will collect these cards "with indirect and invisible Israeli checking." So much for control at the border. It was confirmed as an Israeli responsibility in Cairo I as a derivative of the external security clause in Article VIII of the DOP.

Security and the Two-Stage Concept

The division of the "peace process" into interim phase and final status, which is rooted in the Shultz and Baker Plans of 1988 and 1989 as well as in the Israeli "election plan" of 1989, has been utilized by Israel to gain virtual PLO acquiescence in its position on security, settlements and jurisdiction.

The security reasoning, which Rabin used to insure Israeli control of crossings in Cairo I, was later claimed to confirm Israeli responsibility for overall security, even in Jericho and Gaza during the interim phase. This is what Cairo II had in fact resolved, and what Rabin had announced on the BBC on April 1994:

Only one party must retain overall responsibility for security. Israel will retain sole responsibility for security in Hebron… [and] throughout the Gaza Strip as well as in that area of Jericho where the Palestinian self-administration body will be established.

Consequently, the entry of the Palestinian police into Gaza and Jericho in May 1994 did not relieve Israel of that "responsibility." Rabin stated, "While there is redeployment, on the one hand, we continue to bear overall responsibility for whatever happens in the Gaza Strip." He made it clear that a vacuum of power will not be allowed, and therefore no Palestinian police units will be deployed until they are "thoroughly ready to undertake their responsibility to uphold law and public order." No doubt, he was speaking of Israeli occupation law and the kind of public order that leaves no room for dissidence. Again, by virtue of Article IX, the DOP insures that reviewing existing law is a joint responsibility, hence giving Israel a veto on such review, and assuring survival of the Israeli military rules at this stage.

Clearly, security and public order mean, in effect, security of Israel and Israelis. The Hebron massacre on February 25, 1994 and the blood trail of its aftermath demonstrate how lax security procedures can be when it comes to the Palestinians. The mass killer Dr. Baruch Goldstein was able to enter a presumably guarded mosque with sufficient arsenal to kill and maim dozens of worshipers before he was finally subdued and killed by survivors of the massacre.

Cairo II had already closed the files of the Hebron massacre. The absence of an impartial investigation, and the revelations that Israeli soldiers and police are not allowed to shoot at settlers, even if the settlers shoot at Palestinians with the intent to kill, rendered the security provisions of Cairo II completely one-sided. Not only did the PA assume the role of Israel's enforcer, but it also deprived itself of enforcing security for its own constituents.

Every demand touted by the PLO in the wake of the massacre (international protection, dismantling of Hebron settlements and placing settlements immediately on the interim phase agenda) was mere posturing; these demands were predictably surrendered in Cairo II. Again Israeli responsibility for overall security was reconfirmed as the token force of 160 observers from Norway, Denmark and Italy was declared a substitute for the requested international force; Rabin assured his constituents that the Temporary International Presence in Hebron (TIPH) did not constitute a "force," not even "entirely an observer group," since some of them were assigned administrative duties at the Hebron municipality. The observers were hemmed in by unusual, if not unprecedented constraints: they have no military or police functions and their sole weapons consisted of pistols which could be used only in self-defense; their freedom of movement was restricted by Israel and the renewal of their mandate was subject to an Israeli veto. They were not made responsible to the UN secretary-general, but to the joint Hebron committee (JHC) consisting of two Israelis and two Palestinians.

The make-up and functions of TIPH made a mockery of the concept of international protection. In this case that presence was effectively removed from the context of the UN, despite the qualified condemnation of the massacre by Security Council Resolution 904, which was linked to the Oslo accord upon insistence by the U.S. and Israel. That also happened in spite of Resolution 681 of 1990, which reconfirmed the applicability of the 1949 Geneva Convention to the occupied territories. As the centerpiece of Cairo II, this new and strange dimension of international protection was enshrined as a provision which effectively supersedes the Geneva Convention protection.

Given Israel's long-standing policy against the admission of any international commissions or forces into the occupied territories, there was no reason to assume that the Hebron massacre would change that policy, particularly when it was designed to serve a strategic goal. From the very inception of the occupation in 1967, Israel was able to sidetrack all actions and initiatives by the United Nations, particularly when they had a supervisory, investigatory or mediating role, that would infringe on Israel's implicit or explicit claims of sovereignty in the occupied territories.

The strategy of manipulating the two-stage concept was also applied by Israel in Cairo I to establish another precedent for and to gain PLO acquiescence in a long-standing Israeli position on settlements. Again, playing on the concept of security in Article VIII of the DOP, in conjunction with the two-stage formula, Israel realized a startling achievement regarding settlements in Gaza. Sixteen settlements occupying 18 square kilometers, which seemed dispensable to Israel during the Washington rounds, not only obtained a new lease on life, but were also provided with an additional twenty-two square kilometers of land to provide them with a "security zone" and a measure of contiguity. Article VII (5) of the DOP, referred to earlier, was also utilized to gain this tantamount acknowledgment by the PLO that settlements constitute an Israeli internal matter.

Thus, the division of the negotiations into two phases has already inflicted irreparable damage on the Palestinian position by the two parties which invented the concept and insured its incorporation into the ground rules of the "peace process." In their haste to demonstrate some success to constituents whose opposition to the DOP began to surface in the wake of the massacre, Palestinian negotiators allowed themselves to be diverted into the Israeli agenda, thus sacrificing the crucial principles which govern negotiations.

The Trappings of Statehood

Cairo III, which was signed on May 4, 1994, is replete with make-believe elements of statehood as are its predecessors Cairo I and Cairo II. Just as Cairo I invented the symbolic entry stamps and use of immigration officers, Cairo III invented such ornaments as a passport which would have the familiar phrase "laissez-passer" inscribed on the cover. As stateless people, the Palestinians have gotten accustomed to the laissez-passer granted to them by Egypt and Jordan, and since 1967 by Israel. Now, "residents" of the Gaza Strip and Jericho "area" will be receiving Palestinian laissez-passer documents instead, but for those with selective perception the document might be called "passport" since the word would appear on the cover under the inscription "laissez-passer." The Palestinian postal stamps, which carry the phrase "Palestinian Authority," are not valid for international use. International callers to Jericho and Gaza will dial a separate area code but will go through the Israeli telephone system. And the list of embellishments goes on and on; yet Israel did not hesitate to draw red lines where the trappings could conceivably be construed as symbols of sovereignty. Thus, Yasir Arafat was made to understand in no uncertain terms that his five year old title "President of Palestine" would be dropped and exchanged for the earlier title "Chairman of the PLO," in view of the fact that Israel had recognized the PLO and not Palestine or its people in the September 1993 exchange of letters.

Likewise, the Palestinian monetary authority which was created in the Paris economic accord on April 29, 1994, is presumed to be something of a central bank, but the Palestinians were denied the right to issue their own currency.[1] Meanwhile, the phrase "economic cooperation" which appears frequently in the DOP is being utilized by Israel to insure the continued dependency of the Palestinian economy on that of Israel. "Cooperation" is hardly the description of a relationship between an economy with $63 billion Gross Domestic Product and another with a mere $2.5 billion GDP, two-thirds of which is derived from work in Israel. This kind of cooperation will be used by Israel to safeguard against Palestinian economic independence and to reinforce the solid restrictions on political independence as well.

Palestinian misfortunes are not the result of a poor negotiating strategy; in fact the term negotiations as it applied to the Oslo and Cairo talks may have been a misnomer. The Palestinian position has actually suffered from a frame of reference which has allowed them little room for real negotiations. The Oslo frame of reference, which was prepared by the legal staff of the Israeli Foreign Ministry in accordance with a long-standing position, has dictated the provisions of the Cairo agreements. The imbalance in terms of power, strategies, and consistency is appalling. Not only did Israel act in accordance with a coherent strategy, but it also adhered to a consistent policy, supported by domestic consensus and sustained by tangible power and international backing. Israel's position is now bolstered by an accord whose every word, phrase, concept, and even commas and semi-colons, are checked to insure its correspondence with the Zionist consensus—that there is room for *only* one nation-state in the area lying between the Jordan River and the Mediterranean Sea, and that is Israel. Hence the significance of the peace treaty between Jordan and Israel signed on October 27, 1994 which reconfirms Israel's control of external security along the Jordan River. Likewise, the Israeli-Egyptian Peace treaty of 1979 confirms Israel's control of external security along the old Palestine-

Egypt border in the southwest.

By contrast, the Palestinian side had already wasted its recognition card and, in effect, disavowed resistance as a form of terrorism, thereby removing the *Intifada* from the calculus of the negotiations. In return for recognition of Israel's right to exist, the Palestinians were simply allowed to live in scattered portions of the West Bank and in Gaza as residents in greater Israel but not as citizens in the future state of Palestine. This is the pattern which seems to be emerging from the Cairo agreements. The DOP has become the legal foundation for *all* subsequent agreements. There is no reason to believe that the final status agreement, when and if it is concluded, will prove to be an exception.

II. Early Empowerment; The Burden, Not the Responsibility

On August 24, 1994, Israel and the PLO signed the fourth major agreement since the Oslo accord was concluded on September 13, 1993.[2] This is an agreement on the Preparatory Transfer of Powers And Responsibilities in the West Bank, better known, however, as "early empowerment"—not to be confused with the limited "self-rule" extended by the Cairo agreement to Gaza and Jericho.

A. A Subordinate Role

In the Gaza-Jericho transfer, Israel retains control of external security and ultimately of internal security. Under "early Empowerment" in the West Bank, it retains total control over *all* types of security and any responsibility for public order. Under the new agreement, the Palestinian Authority (PA) does not have any police functions or powers relating to criminal matters, such as investigation, law-enforcement, or adjudication.

Israel's de facto sovereignty is protected by numerous provisions, which relegate the PA to a mere functionary apparatus, existing and operating in total legal and political subordination to the occupation regime. Any powers or new responsibilities delegated to the PA are so carefully defined and, indeed, circumscribed as to guard against any misinterpretation or exaggeration of the limited transfer. The spheres which will be affected by this transfer are five: education and culture, health, social welfare, tourism and direct taxation. Palestinian responsibility for the management of these spheres will be not only curtailed by "security" considerations, but also by sovereignty considerations. Autonomous decision-making, therefore, will be excluded in education, health and tourism on security grounds, while taxation authority will have to be shared with Israel for sovereignty reasons. With regard to legislation in the five spheres in which a transfer has been effected, the agreement grants the PA "secondary" authority. Article VII-1 states that "the Palestinian Authority may promulgate secondary legislation regarding the powers and responsibilities transferred to it." That legislation, however, must be submitted to Israel for determining whether "…it exceeds the powers and responsibilities transferred to the Palestinian Authority" (Article VII-3-(1)). In the event that such legislation is declared invalid, the PA can appeal the verdict to the joint legislative subcommittee established under the Gaza-Jericho agreement, which reaches its decisions "by agreement," implying in turn an effective Israeli veto.

B. A New Jurisprudence

This agreement is, of course, based on the Oslo Declaration of Principles (DOP) and on the Cairo agreement of May 4, 1994, known as the "Gaza-Jericho First," neither of which made any reference to the implementation of UN resolutions. Israel and the Clinton administration are now trying to establish a new global consensus based on the supremacy of these agreements as the effective jurisprudence of the Arab-Israeli conflict. After decades of vigorous attempts by Israel to render UN resolutions on Palestine ineffectual, the Clinton administration has finally decided to join the endeavor, saying that the UN no longer has any role with regard to the status of Jerusalem, the settlements, the refugees and the question of Palestinian sovereignty. Ambassador Madeleine Albright's letter to UN member to that effect on August 1994 was an ominous addition to the U.S. first abstention on the 1993 vote in the General Assembly, reaffirming Resolution 194, which established the right of return or compensation for the Palestinian refugees in 1948.

Given the PLO's negotiating "strategy," which presently lacks a United

Nations dimension, and given the Clinton administration's determination to supplant the body of the UN resolutions, which it calls "contentious" and "obsolete," the Palestinian people are in great danger of losing their international cover. They would be at the mercy of the architects of the Oslo process and the Israeli interpretations of that process, which precludes their internationally recognized rights.

Therefore, it is important to analyze the legal implications of the latest agreement for the political future of the Palestinian people. For regardless of the division of negotiations into two stages, interim and final status, the modalities of these agreements and the legal principles on which they are based are bound to supply the crucial precedents that would influence the shape of the final status. The basic premises which govern the "early empowerment" agreement are the following:

1. Continuity of the Israeli occupation: no substantive change is effected or contemplated in the status of the West Bank. That reinforces the U.S.-Israeli view, in which Arafat's leadership has acquiesced, that the area is disputed rather than occupied. Occupation law remains in force, and Israel retains an effective veto over any amendments to the existing military orders and regulations (Article VII).

Unlike the situation in Gaza, where the civil administration has been dissolved, here in the West Bank both the civil administration and the military government remain intact. The military government's authority in the spheres which have not been transferred is fully retained, while its responsibilities for security and public order in the five spheres, in which the Palestinians are "empowered" are preserved (Article VI-5).

To underscore the importance of these security functions, Article VI-4 obligates the PA to inform the occupation regime about any "planned" public large-scale events and "mass gatherings" within any of the five spheres. Thus, the freedom of assembly, were it to be exercised by students, welfare recipients or disgruntled taxpayers, for example, could be suppressed by the Israeli military, with open and legal PA participation. Israel will continue to possess powers of curfew and closure of Palestinian schools and universities in the name of security. This kind of a collective punishment has inflicted severe damage on Palestinian education and resulted in curtailments of essential services in the fields of health, welfare, commerce and industry. "Early empowerment" would not alleviate the suffering which Palestinians endure under extended curfews when access to the place of work, the pharmacy or the grocery shops is impeded.

The PA is also obligated to inform the occupation authorities of any person wounded by any kind of weapon upon his/her admission to a hospital, and of "…any death from unnatural causes." (Annex II-8). The PA is further expected to provide for the transfer of "…the corpse of any deceased from unnatural causes, for an autopsy in the Institute of Forensic Medicine." (Annex II-9).

The PA has no power whatsoever in the area of law enforcement pertaining to the five spheres, but certain employees, approved by Israel, are authorized to act as "civilian inspectors" to monitor compliance with laws and regulations in these spheres, providing they act separately, without uniforms and not in a central unit (Article VIII-2). Thus, even the unlikely presumption that these monitors may constitute an embryonic police force on Palestinian territory is completely ruled out. As the head of the civil administration General Gadi Zohar, said: "We are transferring the control of issues but not of territory." *(Al-Hamishmar* July 15, 1994).

2. Consolidation of the apartheid system: the existence of two separate entities with separate legal standards for the indigenous population and for the Israeli settlers is not only preserved, it is legitimized with a legal framework and Palestinian approval. Moreover, that legal separation is solidified by the formalization of a hierarchy with categories; including West Bank Gaza and Jericho Area, settlements, Jerusalem, and Israelis. The last three are totally excluded from the PA jurisdiction; while the status of the West Bank is separate from that of Gaza and Jericho, thus Article VII-9 decrees that "legislation regarding the West Bank shall be published as a separate part of any publication of legislation regarding the Gaza Strip and the Jericho Area issued by the Palestinian Authority."

The dangerous consequence of this arrangement is the possible transformation of the Palestinian occupied territory into a Jewish terrain dotted by scattered Palestinian communities. That terrain would consist of an expanded greater Jerusalem (already more than 1/5 of the West Bank), settlements and military installations (occupying more than 50 percent of the West Bank), and "Israelis," defined as "Israeli statutory agencies and corporations registered in Israel," and operating in the West Bank (Article I-d). The remaining area, designated as state land, would be used by Israel to further entice the Palestinians and secure their commitment to the evolving project, which excludes independence and sovereignty.

The confirmation of legal separation in the West Bank also implies a system of "separate but not equal." Borrowing from the discourse of extra-territoriality, a relic of European relations with the Ottoman Empire and with the Manchu Dynasty in the 19th century, the agreement empowers Israel to use force as a measure for collecting land taxes from Palestinians, but forbids the PA from using any force to collect income tax from Israelis under its jurisdiction (Appendix B-5).

Consistent with extra-territoriality and with Menachem Begin's dictum, "autonomy for the people not for the land," the taxing authority will be split between Israel and the PA, with the former continuing to tax the entire Palestinian land within the PA's sphere, while the PA can only collect income tax and Value Added tax (VAT). (Article XI and Annex V). Moreover, the agreement entitles Israel to collect income tax, not only from Israelis working in the settlements in which it exercises jurisdiction anyway, but also from Israelis working in the West Bank, providing that the "business or service" in which they work "accrues or derives an annual turnover...exceeding $7,000 U.S." (Annex V-3-6). Needless to say, the PA does not have a corresponding privilege.

3. Exemption of Israel from all liabilities, obligations and omissions with regard to acts occurring prior to the transfer: consistent with the unusual provisions of the Cairo Agreement of May 4, 1994, Israel is again exempted from legal responsibility for acts committed during 28 years of a brutal occupation. Thus, the families of civilian victims of Israel's death squads or the numerous owners of the vast land, which

Israel expropriated during all these years, will have no right whatsoever to redress grievances against Israel.

Worse yet is that such grievances of financial claims against Israel, were they to arise, must now be "referred to the Palestinian Authority." (Article IX, 1-a and b). And in the event that an award is made against Israel and subsequently paid by Israel, the PA is obligated to "reimburse Israel the full amount of the award." (Article IX, 1-e). These provisions are tantamount to a blanket amnesty granted to the perpetrator by the victim, even prior to a peace agreement and while the victim has no assurance that his legal subordination can be altered under this agreement.

Conclusion

The historic handshake, which was expected to usher in a kinder and gentler political terrain in the Middle East, has not resulted in the anticipated change, which was triumphantly forecast in September, 1993 by a euphoric U.S. media. Very few, if any, traces of the post-Oslo, post-Cairo euphoria were still evident by the end of 1994. There is a diplomatic paralysis despite the Cairo agreements and "early empowerment." The persistent deadlock in Israeli-Palestinian negotiations is not surprising, in view of the built-in conflict over the meaning, objectives, and the desired eventual outcome of the Declaration of Principles.

As expected, the Palestinian negotiating strategy is predicated on the goal of a nation-state as the end result, despite the lack of the necessary pillars for independence in the declaration. The Israeli strategy, by contrast, is grounded in the firm belief that under no circumstances should a Palestinian state emerge. Consequently, the elections for a Palestinian self-governing council, which were planned for July 1994, in accordance with the Oslo and Cairo agreements, had not been held by mid-1995. While the Palestinians anticipate the election of the equivalent of a national legislature based in universal suffrage, Israel has insisted that the council would consist of only 25-30 members, to render administrative and secondary legislative functions. Israel further insists that the religious opposition, mainly Hamas, and other groups opposed to the Oslo Declaration must be disenfranchised.

The impasse, therefore, is not over means but rather over ends as well as means. Apparently when the Palestinian negotiators initialed the Declaration at Oslo, their hope was that the *spirit* of the agreement, as they conceived it, would ultimately overcome disagreements over the *letter* of it. It was a groundless hope, at best, which reflects a political naiveté, unwarranted optimism, and a garbled knowledge of the constitutional nomenclature.

Given these conflicting visions of peace and the peculiar premises of the peace accords, one can only wonder whether terms such as "empowerment" and "peace process" have some other meanings after all. Even the minimal aspirations of the Palestinian people for a dignified existence on a sovereign and contiguous fraction of their national patrimony have been effectively dashed by these accords, which force Palestinians to assume the burdens, but not the responsibilities. These agreements and their antecedents represent an attempt to regularize the Israeli occupation and to consolidate the unilateral and illegal acts undertaken in the course of the occupation. Accordingly, it becomes occupation by consent. The so-called Jericho-Gaza option might be first and last, and the occupation thus would not be terminated, but merely relabeled.

1. Text of the Agreement in *Journal of Palestine Studies,* Vol. XXIII, No. 4, (Summer 1994), pp. 102-118.
2. Text of the August 24, 1994 *Agreement in Journal of Palestine Studies*, Vol. XXIV, No. 2 (Winter 1995), pp. 109-126.

10

Oslo and the Crises in Palestinian Politics

Discord in Palestinian Society

The two documents, one signed in Washington on September 13, 1993 and the other in Cairo on May 4, 1994 created a fundamental change in the Palestinian political terrain and in the very nature of the struggle for a diplomatic settlement, which began more than twenty-five years ago. The Oslo and Cairo accords have already shattered the Palestinian consensus based on a two-state solution subsequent to the termination of the occupation. That consensus had remarkably survived Madrid and Washington during twenty-two months of negotiations due to a profound commitment by the Palestinians and their negotiators that these negotiations must yield a genuine independence rather than a fractured entity composed of scattered pockets, enclaves, and "autonomous zones" surrounded by blocs of Jewish settlements.

The crucial legal issue is that unless Israel came to terms with its status as occupant, within the meaning of international law, it would be able to render any agreement regarding withdrawal, security, sovereignty and human rights completely superfluous. Not only did Israel refuse to make such a commitment, but the Palestinian leadership has also acquiesced in the refusal, thus giving credence to the claim that the West Bank and Gaza are *disputed* rather than *occupied* territory. Hence, Israel assumed an equal right to lay claims to Palestinian land occupied since 1967, while the status of Jerusalem, the still expanding colonial settlements, the land issue and refugees were deferred for several years.

This manifest departure by the PLO from the Palestinian consensus, which Haider Abdul Shafi's team had managed to keep intact throughout the Washington negotiations under utterly unfavorable odds, is the nexus of the shocking discord in Palestinian society. Rebuilding that consensus amidst increasing pressures on the Palestinians to make further compromises, as if their concessions had not bottomed out back in Madrid, has already proven to be an arduous task. It will require from the leadership rigor, tenacity, and uncommon foresight. It will require placing the public interest above power politics, personal ambitions and partisan obsessions. So far, that prospect seems to be remote indeed as Palestinians face a crisis of governance, economic crisis and a clash of political cultures, all enmeshed and interlaced. The Palestinian body politic is currently in a state of flux. Also at issue are the political, social, and economic implications of the expected trans-formation of the PLO from a "revolutionary" organization to a political entity.

Crisis of Governance and Leadership

The task of nation-building, widely-discussed and eagerly contemplated in the wake of Oslo, is experiencing severe strains. Palestinian high-level human power, which had been a major factor in state-building through-out the Arab world, particularly in the Gulf during the past four decades, might have made the task easier. The building of the Palestinian polity, however, is being hampered by crippling factors inherent in the PLO body politic, which is being transplanted into the politics of the Gaza/Jericho enclaves, and by external encumbrances dictated by the guarantors of peace. Internally, that task remains a casualty of *ad hoc* methods of governance by the Palestine Authority, including archaic decision-making practices, haphazard appointments, lack of account-ability at both the political and economic levels, a deliberately foggy and confused structure for division of authority and lines of responsibility in order to guarantee control at the top, and a total absence of the basic elements of a rational, efficient and consultative policy-making process—clearly a missed opportunity, if ever there was one.

The widespread concern among Palestinian ranks, shared by sectors of the establishment, the upper bourgeoisie, the liberal reformers, and the religious bloc about *ad hoc* decision-making and cronyism, is beginning to threaten further schisms in the Palestinian movement. This time, however, it affects the loyal opposition. Press accounts and reports by mainstream PLO leaders revealed that half of the negotiators appointed at the eleventh hour to the Taba talks which produced the Cairo agreements, were basically unqualified loyalists who hadn't read the text of the declaration. That and other accounts of incompetence came as a shock to Palestinian constituencies already uncomfortable about the caliber of their leadership. Yet the mechanisms of repair and amelioration continue to be retarded, as much of the energy, talents and resources are being invested in the ongoing power play and the jockeying for position, some of which takes place in the open, and some under the cover of pluralist demands.

Palestinians, who earned world-wide respect for resourcefulness, considerable achievements in education, perseverance in the face of an incredibly tenacious, aggressive and highly-endowed enemy, and a just cause with an unusual claim on the world conscience, are extremely embarrassed and clearly stymied. From Madrid to Oslo to Cairo to the latest so-called "early empowerment" in the West Bank the much advertised self-governance has failed to materialize in a way that would auger well for a basic dignified existence. The military occupation still continues with its daily humiliations to the Palestinians throughout the occupied territories (40 percent of Gaza is still under direct Israeli control); the PA is totally absorbed in the task of attracting funds to establish control; and the donor community continues to insist on financial accountability and rational management of public funds as a pre-condition for the release of money.

Lacking the willingness and/or ability to develop fiscal responsibility and, therefore, political credibility, the PA continues to fall prey to economic blackmail and political strangulation by the Western donors and by Israel. A pattern of exchanging political concessions for money (not for development purposes but for operating expenses) has already been established. It will be recalled that the price for returning to the negotiations table after the Hebron massacre in February 1994 was the money to pay the salaries of the Palestinian police. Likewise, the price for the release of reallocated funds for the PA was a major Palestinian concession on the question of Jerusalem. The Arafat-Peres agreement of September 13, 1994, which was reached after serious pressure from the U.S., the EU and Japan, states that neither Israel nor the PLO "shall bring before the donor community those political issues that are of disagreement between them. They will deal with such issues between themselves, based on the [Oslo] Declaration of Principles and subsequent agreements." This was a clear concession by Arafat to drop his insistence that some international donor assistance be designated to fund Palestinian institutions in East Jerusalem, which Israel regards as a section of its capital in which the PA has no jurisdiction. Having agreed to Israel's demand that Jerusalem is out of bounds even for symbolic Palestinian development, the PA was rewarded with funds to support its expanding bureaucracy for the next six months and pay the police force, which relieved Israel of upholding "law and order" in Gaza.

The Israeli conquest of Jerusalem, therefore, which has been considered illegal by the entire world, with the exception of the banana republics of Costa Rica, El Salvadore and lately Guatemala, is being steadily legitimized by Oslo, Cairo and their codicils. The pattern of deferral in these agreements (on Jerusalem, borders, sovereignty, and refugees) has effectively removed the Palestine question from its national context, reducing it to the status of an instrument to regularize the Israeli occupation. The focus is no longer on the national and human rights of the six million Palestinians everywhere, but on the rearrangement of living conditions for less than one-third of the Palestinians, in a way that would stabilize a status-quo, which most of the world considered unacceptable for more than twenty-seven years. The ingredients for this undertaking consist of carrots and sticks: donor funds to support the civilian and police apparatus necessary for pacification, and investment funds to make living conditions less intolerable. So far, most of the allocations have been for governance and for consolidation of Arafat's authority.

The establishment of "self-rule" in Gaza and Jericho has not improved the living conditions of the 200,000 Gazans and the impoverished 650,000 refugees who live in Gaza, which became worse than before: less jobs, a rising inflation rate (18–20 percent), phenomenally higher rents and a 12 percent increase in the price of basic commodities. With Gaza and the West Bank "separated" from Israel following the suicide bombing of January 22, 1995, more than 50,000 Palestinian workers have lost their jobs in Israel, pushing the unemployment rate in Gaza to 52 percent. Arafat's Palestine Authority was able to come up only with 4000 substitute jobs in Gaza by the end of February. Even posting letters becomes a problem, with Palestinian postage being unacceptable in most of the outside world. There is confusion in the legal system, with Jericho applying Jordanian law and Israeli military rules, while Gaza implements the British mandate law (called by many "Palestinian law") together with Israeli military orders. Granted, "self-rule" was only implemented since May 1994, not a long time, but the trends are not encouraging.

Meanwhile, the "carrots" remain meager, and they apppear in an erratic fashion, given the lack of an economic development plan and the squabble between politicians for control of projects. It is also not clear whether the vision is one which calls for an export-based productive economy that will insure a measure of self sufficiency, or a Caribbean style economy based on squeezing more money from Gazan cheap labor. Palestinian leaders keep repeating that their model is Singapore rather than Somalia. It is hoped, however, that Gaza will not become the *maquilladora* of Israeli firms and expatriate Palestinian partners.

Crisis of Legitimacy and the Opposition

The much scaled-back endeavor of rearranging living conditions is stalled, and criticism is rampant. It is, however, diffuse, uncoordinated and cynical. The absence of political parties which would channel it towards alternative policy proposals, and the failure to hold elections that would establish a legitimate government have effectively placed the PA in a state of political limbo. It no longer derives its legitimacy from the crumbling PLO, the "sole legitimate representative" of the Palestinian people, and is seen largely as the product of the Oslo accord, which itself has two contradictory interpretations, an Israeli and a Palestinian. The crisis of governance is therefore aggravated by a crisis of legitimacy. Edward Said has written in this regard the following: "As the peace process unravels in "autonomous" territories, many Palestinians now feel that non-cooperation with the Palestine Authority is the only responsible political position to take. Arafat, they surmise, will soon outlive his usefulness, even to Israel and the United States.[1]

The public discourse in the occupied territories in 1994 reveals that whatever mandate had been accorded to the negotiations with Israel (neither the Palestine National Council nor the PLO Central Council had ratified the Oslo and Cairo accords) it is now non-existent. Yet Arafat continues to conduct business as if the United States and Israel are the present source of his legitimacy. Having in effect accepted the Israeli interpretation of the Oslo accord, Arafat has clearly shattered the post-Madrid Palestinian consensus.[2] Moreover, having renounced resistance as a form of terrorism and having accepted Washington's dictates as to which acts deserve commendation and which require condemnation, Arafat has effectively abdicated his role as leader of a dispossessed, disenfranchised and dismembered nation.

Opposition to the Oslo accords, which surfaced in the occupied territories during the latter part of 1993, gained momentum in the aftermath of the Cairo signing in May 1994. It began with an initiative by the West Bank-Gaza-based "Movement for Reforms and Democracy," which indicted the Cairo agreements as having conferred legitimacy on illegal measures undertaken by Israel during the occupation. Initial signatories of the declaration dated April 25, 1994, including a number of former negotiators and the delegation chief, Haider Abdul Shafi, appealed to the Palestinian people to consider the Cairo agreement as "not-binding" on them and as "null and void." The declaration also called for pluralist governance, rational decision-making and respect for human rights and the rule of law. The Movement for Reforms and Democracy was hoping to emerge as a third stream offering Palestinians in the occupied territories an alternative to Arafat's leadership and to the religious sector, but as of the spring of 1995, it seems to be lacking direction, leadership and organization.

Never before, since the formation of the PLO, has the question of Arafat's leadership and his ability to govern been such a crucial issue. Misgivings, long suppressed in the interest of national unity and other such noble principles, are now coming up to the surface. Dissatisfaction by the Damascus-based ten-group coalition, which rejects the declaration in toto as a sellout by Arafat himself, was of course expected. But that opposition has not been manifested in a clearly defined program and a plan of action. The Islamists, on the other hand, who had been promoted by Israel during the *Intifada* as a counterbalance to the secular forces of the PLO, have now emerged as the only opposition which practices armed struggle. Their vision of the future society, however, is fuzzy, and their cadres are divided among purists and pragmatists. Despite that, they seem to have replaced the secular left as the principal opposition.[3]

A more important point, is that Arafat's leadership is being questioned by the very coalition which helped him win approval for the declaration—the People's Party (formerly Communists), elements of FIDA, a breakaway faction from the Democratic Front for the Liberation of Palestine, and a number of independent political figures. The Peoples Party (formerly Communists), which had supported the Madrid process, rejects Oslo and cooperates with the yet to be formed "Movement for Reforms and Democracy".[4] Moreover, a segment of high ranking politicians from Arafat's own group, Fateh, appears to be alienated, including Mahmoud Abbas, who signed the document at the White House Rose Garden ceremony and Ahmad Qurei (Abu-Ala'a), his chief negotiator in Oslo. But while Qurei holds a "ministerial" post in Arafat's government, other so-called historic leaders of Fateh, such as Farouk Kaddoumi and Hani al-Hasan have become open critics and would not move to Gaza.[5] Opposition was also voiced initially by a large number of intellectuals, journalists, businessmen and most of the diplomats who participated in the eleven rounds of negotiations in Washington .

Although some of the dissidents are not ardent critics of the accords themselves, they nevertheless view Arafat as the main obstacle to a strategy that would build on what they see as the positive aspects and contain the negative aspects of the accords. In general, they are concerned about the future of what they call nation-building (al-Amaliya al-Wataniya), which involves translating the provisions of the accords into reality and constructing a democratic national authority capable of achieving independence in the next phase.

The dissidents, who were hoping to become a nucleus of a popular protest movement, but who are yet to be organized under a broad umbrella of reforms, are nevertheless actuated by a common impulse and a common denominator: a genuine fear that Arafat's ability to meet the most serious challenges which Palestinian society has ever faced is now seriously impaired. Given the flawed nature of the accords and the herculean efforts it would take to salvage what little remains of Palestinian rights under unfavorable regional and global conditions, the disparate group of reformers have good reason to worry. In fact, Arafat's bunglings are beginning to be viewed by them as "clear and present danger." His personal style of governance is seen not only as embarrassing and incompatible with accepted norms, but also as counter-productive in terms of nation-building. He exercises more than sixty functions, which include not only those of a chief executive and chief of state, but also extend to many mundane chores. The fact that those functions include several chairmanships of newly established boards, and no less than twelve new committees of the transitional authority in the occupied territories has convinced the dissidents that the national project is in trouble. Such unprecedented concentration of power is at variance with the requirements of efficiency and rational decision-making. The danger is even greater as the Palestinians face an efficient post-modern protagonist, which has proven its ability to recruit, mobilize and assimilate talents from numerous countries around the world.

When viewed in terms of governing potential, the results are appalling. Arafat's "shadow government" is more involved in symbols and jockeying for position than with the actual business of governing. For many in the ruling faction, the "revolution" has become, over the years, a source of employment and livelihood, when ruling used to mean no more than running a bureaucracy whose function was to arbitrate conflicts and cater to the needs of organized constituencies. The many factions of the revolution were kept in the fold by a system of patronage over which Arafat presided almost alone. His personal control of the power of the purse, which continues until today, enabled him to co-opt the factions and reduce a seemingly ideological conflict into one over power and money. Now that the money supply has dwindled after the Gulf massacre, and the concept of power is being redefined to suit the requirements of a more complex political entity as opposed to managing the revolution, his traditional methods of conflict resolution are seriously strained.

Yet, in the face of mounting opposition, he continues to prevail even with a divided ruling party, a fractured coalition, an alienated upper bourgeoisie, as well as skeptical donors like the World Bank and the U.S. State Department. He has been able to turn his weakness into an asset by convincing Israel and the U.S. that he is their best bet in the Palestinian camp. His demise would simply disrupt their plans. His security apparatus, which sometimes operates in the style of mobsters and gangs, and his proclivity to suppress the opposition, who he now calls "terrorists", have won him praise from Rabin and Vice-President Al Gore. The emergence of Hamas and Islamic Jihad as the major Palestinian opposition group serves as a principal catalyst for the U.S., Israel, PA alliance during this juncture.

The political conflict within Arafat's mainstream faction, Fateh, is complex and multi-dimensional.[6] First, there is the division between the "inside" and "outside" cadres. The former claims for power and position are based on their physical presence on the land where the new entity is to be placed. The expatriates claims are based on long association with the liberation movement that became the embodiment of Palestinian nationalism.

Second, there is the rivalry between senior leaders, which Arafat has so far been able to control. A main priority for him is to insure that no credible potential rivals for the power at the top emerge during the next phase. Thus Abbas' aspirations for a vice-presidency are easily blunted by Arafat, who relies on an old technique of playing one man off against the other, while trying to marginalize those who seem capable of making a serious bid for real power. While Fateh seniors like Farouk Kaddoumi and Abu-Maher Ghoneim have developed a reputation for a harder line than Arafat, having voted against the Madrid process and occasionally criticized the Oslo accord, they are pitted against the "moderate," Mahmoud Abbas, who signed the Oslo accord. The latter (who has lent name to a tough worded petition) of the reform movement is doing his best to undermine Arafat while leaving some opening for a possible reconciliation. His qualified support for the dissidents may well prove to be a tactical move. These and other examples of political expediency illustrate the drastic shift in Palestinian politics away from issues and ideology and increasingly towards the pursuit of power and position.

In the face of this shift, an important sector of Fateh, particularly in the middle and upper middle ranks, is beginning to sympathize with dissidents and identify themselves with their reformist demands. Yet the Fateh skeptics have much more at stake (their own livelihood) in the status-quo than do the non-Fateh and independent dissidents. A split of Fateh will deprive its undifferentiated membership—loyalists and dissenters—of positions in the future authority. Such fear constitutes an important barrier to an easy coalescing of Fateh and non-Fateh critics in a solid oppositional front, which could infuse the Palestinian body politic with the kind of spirit and ethos of reform which produced the new political landscape in eastern and central Europe.

The "Millionaires" of the Diaspora

An additional grumbling was also voiced by the so-called millionaires of the diaspora, who sent Arafat a memorandum in December 1993 which, while reiterating their support for the "peace process," raised alarm about the cavalier manner in which decisions were being made. They expressed dismay that "the logic of the revolution has prevailed over the logic of nation-building." They wrote:

> While the revolutionary era permits, on certain occasions, a measure of personal decisions and certain excesses, the task of nation-building can only rest on solid pillars of democracy, which create opportunities for diversity of opinion and the input of those who possess intellect, knowledge and skill.

Appointments by Arafat based on "personal loyalty and confidence" rather than "experience, proficiency and know-how" are particularly bothersome to businessmen, who are concerned about the credibility of the "national project" and the apprehensions expressed by the World Bank and the U.S. State Department about the leadership's ability to handle the complex tasks involved in receiving, spending, reporting and keeping records of grants and loans. The fact that Arafat had initially appointed himself as head of a newly created Board of Development and Reconstruction, to be assisted by other politicians,

impelled the businessmen to urge that the board be set up as an independent body run by qualified professionals.

The memorandum, whose signatories constituted a "Who's Who"
among Palestinian capitalists (Shouman, Sabbagh, Masri, Qattan, etc.),
urged Arafat to step aside from the day-to-day operations. The signers' antipathy to Arafat's rule was derived from a concern for efficiency
rather than a commitment to participatory politics. In fact, the memorandum called for replacing the Palestine National Council with a
consultative assembly pending elections in July 1994. A transition committee of up to ten could then be formed from that assembly to
commission international consulting agencies to supervise the creation
of an efficient bureaucracy and recruitment of Palestinian high-level
personnel. Their ideal would be a situation in which the leadership was
restricted during the transitional phase to overseeing the administrative
operations, but would refrain from any involvement in actual implementation "unless there is an absolute necessity and dire need to
correct the path."

By the spring of 1995, however, Arafat had been able to placate the
millionaires, many of whom anticipate doing business with the PA after
limited redeployment of Israeli troops from parts of the West Bank.
At a business conference held in Amman, Jordan during the last week
of May 1995, Arafat was featured as the principal speaker. Many of the
critics among the wealthy businessmen were in attendance and there
was no mention of Arafat's autocratic style or his cronyism.

Clash of Political Cultures

The Oslo accords have not only generated new conflicts inside the
Palestinian body politic; they have also created additional divisions in
an already segmented Palestinian society. There is now an additional
hierarchy of areas (Jericho "area," West Bank, Gaza, Jerusalem), of people (insiders and outsiders); and of layers of decision-making. Should
the accords become a "done deal," it could mean the permanent dismemberment of the Palestinian people once and for all. If negotiating
the size of Jericho had taken several months then negotiating the return
of three million refugees could take decades. The one area that needs to
be addressed in the immediate term during transition is the challenge

of integrating what have become two different Palestinian political cultures—that of the occupied territories inside, and the one outside in Tunis. A highly developed civic society which came to flourish during the *Intifada*, inside the West Bank and Gaza, stands in sharp contrast to and in contradiction with the forms of autocracy and paternalism, which became the hallmark of the PLO leadership in recent years.[7]

A new, dynamic and vibrant society has developed in the occupied territories, where the challenge of facing a ruthless occupier and right-wing vigilante settlers has endowed it with creative abilities to withstand the pressure. It was left largely to fend for itself, and it consequently developed a progressive and pluralistic political culture and had to cultivate its own grassroot structures. The popular committees, the self-help projects, the independent health care system created by volunteers, and the legal assistance programs were all the people's initiative. Merging these institutions, which reflect norms of voluntarism and associational values, with institutions that reflect inertia and bureaucratization, will not be an easy task, particularly when the deficient culture is endowed with the political power. How can the dynamic and democratic segment passively accept a takeover by the patronage bosses with autocratic style? It is not a coincidence that much of the impetus for reforms and pluralism springs out of the occupied territories, and that the "pro-democracy" movement itself is in part a product of the clash of political cultures.

It is no wonder that the freedom of press and assembly had to be curtailed by the PA and that the logic of "security," a hallmark of the Israeli occupation, is preponderant under Palestinian self-governance. The Jerusalem daily, *al-Nahar*, the first casualty of press restrictions, is back in circulation, after being banned in Gaza and Jericho, but clearly it has been tamed. And there is yet another draconian measure, decreed by the Palestinian chief of police on September 9, 1994, banning all "political meetings" of "whatever coloration," without a prior written permission from the chief himself. Most disturbing was the brutal armed attack by Arafat's police on Hamas demonstrators on November 18, 1994, which recalls the worst Israeli massacres of Palestinian civilians. The establishment of the Higher Court for State Security headed by a military judge on February 7, 1995 upon urging from the U.S. and

Israel, has been criticized by the Palestinian human rights organizations Al-Haq in the West Bank, and by the Gaza Center for Rights and Law.[8] The director of the Gaza Center, Raji Sourani, a prominent lawyer who had been awarded the Robert Kennedy human rights award, was detained for sixteen hours by Arafat's police on February 14, 1995 after issuing a statement saying that the establishment of the State Security Court "appears to undermine the basis of democracy, the independence of the judiciary, and the separation of powers between arms of government."[9] Sourani was subsequently fired from his position by a hitherto inactive board of directors of the Center, which was somehow reactivated when Arafat decided that Sourani must go.

The hegemony of the culture of security is also illustrated by the existence of seven branches of intelligence service, which is bound to give the emerging Palestinian polity one of the highest per capita intelligence organizations in the world. With the notorious Israeli Shin Bet and the Mossad watching, the climate for participatory politics and human rights remains sad indeed. Intolerance of dissent and the omnipotence of political authority are sources of great worry for many activists in the occupied territories.

Notes

1. Edward Said, "The Palestinian Case against Arafat", *The Washington Post*, (C-4), December 25, 1994.

2. For some insight on the post-Madrid consensus, see Hanan Ashrawi, *This Side of Peace: A Personal Account*, Simon and Schuster, 1995, Old Tappan, N.J.

3. For insight into Islamist politics, see Mouin Rabbani, "Israel and the Palestinian Fundamentalists", *Middle East International*, No. 488, (November 18, 1994), pp 15-16, also Lamis Andoni "Palestinian Opposition Dominated By the Right", *Ibid*, No. 489, (Dec. 2, 1994), p. 18.

4. See article by PPP leader Mustafa Barghouthi, "Democracy: A Precondition For Palestine Survival", *Middle East International*, No. 496 (March 17, 1995), pp 16-17. Also by Barghonthi, "Make Way For A Clear Mandate", *Los Angeles Times*, December 21, 1994.

5. Lamis Andoni, "Fateh's Deepening Rift", *Middle East International*, No. 497

(March 31, 1995), pp. 4-5.

6. Lamis Andoni, "Arafat Falls Back on Fateh", *Middle East International*, No. 489 (December 2, 1994), p. 5, Also Graham Usher, "Keeping Up the Crackdown", *Ibid*, No. 495 (March3, 1995), pp. 5-6.

7. Naseer Aruri, "Oslo and the Crises in Palestinian Politics", *Middle East International*, No. 467 (January 21, 1994), pp. 16-17, see also Graham Usher, "The Struggle For Palestinian Civil Society", *Ibid*, No. 498 (April 14, 1995) pp. 18-19.

8. Text of the decree establishing the military court in *Palestine Report*, Vol. 8, No. 18 (May 16, 1995).

9. Violations of human rights by the PA are documented in Human Rights Watch-Middle East. *The Gaza Strip and Jericho: Human Rights Under Palestinian Partial Self-Rule*, Vol. 7, No. 2 (February 1995); also Lawyers Committee for Human Rights, "Rule of Law Under Threat in Gaza and Jericho." Advocacy Alert No. 2 (February 16, 1995).

Part III

United States Middle East Policy and American Politics

11

United States Policy and Electoral Politics

A unique characteristic of United States Middle East policy is that it has never been substantively debated in the political arena. Other than a spate of articles in the mainstream press during occasional disruptions in U.S.-Israeli relations, there has always been an absence of a sustained and thorough-going debate in the media. The same thing can be said about Congress, where bipartisan support for Israel has been the norm during most of the period of Israel's existence as a state. Whatever debates may have taken place in Congress, they were seldom focused on the substance of U.S. Middle East policy, but rather on the process by which that policy is made, particularly as it affects the relationship between the legislative and executive branches.

Nor has a genuine debate ever taken place during presidential elections, when matters relating to domestic and foreign affairs are usually placed on the public agenda and issues and candidates are subjected to the electoral scrutiny. Unlike Vietnam, El Salvador, Nicaragua and the issue of human rights, where dichotomous positions were generally assumed by hawks and doves, interventionists and revisionists, declinists and revivalists, idealists and realists, Middle East policy has been relatively free of conceptual and ideological controversies.

Democratic candidates in the presidential primaries have frequently tried to outdo each other in supporting Israel's concerns and catering to its needs. The platforms of both parties on the Middle East have differed only in terms of emphasis and nuances, but seldom in relation to core and content. This pattern has persisted ever since the 1944 presidential elections, when both parties' platforms endorsed the 1942 Biltmore Program, calling for unrestricted Jewish emigration to and colonization of Palestine so that a "free and democratic Jewish commonwealth" would be established. That pattern continued to the 1992 elections, in which both parties platforms pledged to broaden and deepen the strategic relationship with "the only true democracy" in the Middle East. The real test , however, would ultimately focus on which candidate did Israel and its Zionist lobby in the U.S. really trust and feel most comfortable with, since both parties normally endorse Israel's economic and military needs as well a Israel's stance in the Arab-Israeli conflict.

This chapter will explore these themes and shed some light on the relationship between U.S. Middle East policy and domestic American politics, including political parties, candidates, and lobbies. An exhaustive treatment of the subject is not what is intended here. A few case studies will cover the period beginning with the 1976 presidential campaign between Jimmy Carter and Gerald Ford. They will also include conflicts between Carter and Begin over the convening of an international peace conference in 1977, between Reagan and Begin over the sale of AWACS to Saudi Arabia in 1981, and between Bush and Shamir over loan guarantees.

Democrats and Republicans: What Difference Does it Really Make?

Long before the creation of Israel, Jewish immigrants in the U.S. who were largely blue-collar urban people with inclinations towards the left, supported the politics of social change. Those who came to the United States in the 1880s from Central Europe were poor and unskilled, unlike previous immigrants from Germany, who were affluent and fairly well-established. Although Jewish voters began to gravitate towards the Democratic party during the 1890s, more Jews actually gave their votes to Republican presidential candidates during much of the first three decades of this century. In 1948, a Democratic president and a Democratic Congress lobbied for the UN partition resolutions, which led to the creation of Israel. But Republicans in the Congress viewed Israel as a bastion of the West against the Soviet Union. From those days, when Senator Robert Taft championed Israel as a first line of defense for the Suez Canal in the early fifties to the time when candidate Nixon pledged to guarantee Israel a "margin of military and technological superiority" over all the Arab states combined, neither political party in the United States could afford to write off even the smallest percentage of the Jewish vote.

American Jews, concentrated in the big urban states with sizable electoral votes, have had much more than average participation in elections, and have shown a great deal of skill in political organization and mobilization. Their most important lobby, the American-Israel Public Affairs Committee (AIPAC) is generally regarded as one of the most effective in Washington. It has been referred to as "The Lobby," not only by Edward Tivnan, the author of a book by that title, but by senators and representatives who had to endure their lack of approval or enjoy their financial and electoral support.[1]

Congressional support for Zionist projects dates back to 1922, when Congress adopted a resolution in favor of a national home for the Jews in Palestine, a sort of U.S. Balfour Declaration.[2] Such support often ran counter to administration policy, setting off conflicts between the lobby and its congressional allies, on the one hand, and the White House and the State Department, on the other. A 1944 congressional resolution supported by 411 representatives endorsing the Biltmore Program was in keeping with both parties' platforms, but it was followed during the next year by a letter initiated by Senator Robert Wagner signed by 54 senators and 250 representatives asking him to prevail on Britain for the admittance of Jewish immigrants into Palestine. Although President Truman was opposed to both resolutions on the grounds that the war effort would be harmed, he, nevertheless assured the sponsors that support would be given after the allied victory. He kept the promise, despite opposition from his own advisors.

Truman's successor, however, was less susceptible to organizational pressure by the pro-Israel lobby. A number of Israeli unilateral acts, deemed at variance with international legality, had angered the Eisenhower administration, creating a rift with Israel and its U.S. supporters. Among these were the transfer of the Israeli foreign ministry from Tel Aviv to Jerusalem in July 1953 and the moving of settlers into the demilitarized zones in the Jordan Valley.

The Eisenhower administration, which did not feel beholden to the Jewish lobby, had already been asserting, in the words of Secretary of State Dulles, that it was elected by an overwhelming vote of the

American people as a whole. Henry Byroade, the Assistant Secretary of State for Near Eastern Affairs, urged Israelis in 1954 to look to themselves "as a Middle Eastern state" and not "as headquarters…of a world-wide grouping…who must have special rights within and obligations to the Jewish state."[3] Administration officials were reluctant to meet with the Israeli lobby. After receiving a request to meet with the Chairman of Presidents of Major Jewish Organizations, who was a European-born rabbi, Secretary Dulles said:

> Why should I waste my time meeting with Rabbi X when I can hear the same arguments directly from Israeli Ambassador Abba Eban and in much better English at that.[4]

The posture of the U.S. government during the Suez invasion in 1956, when Israel, Britain and France were branded by the UN as aggressors, and were ordered to withdraw from Egypt, was never to be repeated. It remains as a unique event in five decades of a relationship that developed into a strategic alliance.

By contrast, the War of 1967 was a watershed and a landmark event signifying closer U.S.-Israeli relations. Israel was perceived as tough and forceful in a way which Americans across the liberal-conservative divide found rather appealing. In only six days, Israel was able to do what U.S. clients in Vietnam, their U.S. advisors, Green Berets and even ground troops were unable to do in years. Israel continued to have it both ways because for U.S. doves and liberals, it was seen as a humanitarian and a liberal cause; for hawks and conservatives, it was a cornerstone for anti-communism and an anchor for a status-quo based on United States hegemony. Thus, Israel and its Washington lobby derived crucial support from Cold Warriors like the Democratic Senator Henry Jackson, who linked trade and aid to Jewish immigration from the Soviet Union, as well as from liberal Democrats, who supported détente and detested the cold war in the 1970s. Israel continued to enjoy the support of both factions as long as her needs for money and arms did not include American GIs. Israel's military prowess was seen as a vindication of liberal sentiments against direct military intervention, yet at the same time it appealed to the Rambo mentality of "kick-butt" and shed blood, which U.S. generals were unable to do in Vietnam. Israel was, therefore, seen as a cost-effective enterprise. U.S. economic aid to Israel was a modest premium on an insurance policy.

Economic aid, which was decreased during the Eisenhower period, was increased after 1967 beyond the levels requested by the Johnson administration. President Johnson complained about a pacifist attitude, which he thought American Jews had displayed towards Vietnam, and which stood in contrast to their interventionist posture in the Middle East. But his green light, which later provided Israel with Phantom jets, signaled the start of a shift that made the U.S. replace France as the mainstay of the Israeli airforce.

American Jews supported LBJ's vice-president, Hubert Humphrey in the 1968 campaign against Richard Nixon, who, like Humphrey, supported the sale of Phantoms to Israel. Ninety percent of the Jewish vote went to the Democratic loser, but Nixon, with a reputation for having a streak of anti-Semitism, was to emerge as the first U.S. president, not only to view Israel as a strategic asset, but to grant it the necessary ingredients in economic, military and diplomatic terms, and hence to enable it to set the pace in the only region where U.S. preeminence was not seriously challenged. Henceforth, it became immaterial whether Democrats or Republicans were at the helm. In fact, for Israel and its Washington lobby, the best combination during the largest portion of the next quarter of a century was a Republican White House and a Democratic-run Congress. The Carter interlude was an added bonus, with Democrats dominating both, and by the time Clinton assumed the presidency, Israel's *carte blanche* was institutionalized. For the duration of the Cold War Israel was protected, on the "left", by the Democratic alliance with Jewish voters, and on the right, by the militant anti-communism of the Republican party.

The Elections of 1976

While the percentage of the Jewish vote for the losing Democratic presidential candidate, George McGovern, had decreased from 90 percent in 1968 to 60 percent in 1972, that percentage went up in 1976 to 75 percent in favor of Jimmy Carter. The vote reflected Jewish disenchantment with President Ford's opposition to anti-boycott legislation in Congress and his threat to "reassess" U.S. Middle East policy in the face of Israeli intransigence in the negotiations on the Sinai Peninsula. Despite the unprecedented level of support for Israel under the stewardship of Nixon and Kissinger, Israel's dissatisfaction constituted a measure of a rapidly growing expectation, which became difficult to fulfill despite U.S. uncritical support.

Henry Kissinger insured a continuity in Middle East policy after Nixon's humiliating resignation from the presidency. American Jews, however, seemed much more willing to trust Jimmy Carter than Kissinger and Ford. About 63 percent of Carter's campaign money was contributed by Jews, but only one-third of that percentage was deemed sufficient for his campaign during the primaries, when one of his opponents was Senator Edward Kennedy. By his own admission, Carter's stand against the Arab boycott "was one of the things that led" to his election.[5] The Jewish vote helped him defeat Ford in key electoral college states, and yet he was not the first choice of American Jews. According to Mitchell Geoffrey Bard, former editor of *AIPAC's* newsletter *Near East Report*, Carter's strategy, in part, prepared by Representative Benjamin Rosenthal's office, "paid off because ... if only one in nine of the New York Jews who voted for Carter had voted for Ford, he would have lost New York and the presidency. As a result, Carter theoretically had a campaign debt to repay."[6] Yet tensions continued to mark Carter's relations with Israeli supporters, despite Camp David, which had underwritten the Likud Plan to allow the Palestinians a limited autonomy in the West Bank and Gaza instead of independence and self-determination, as sanctioned by the international community.

Carter's remarks in the heat of the campaign regarding his expectations from Arabs and Israelis for the sake of peace were explicit. He asked the Arabs for a change of attitudes, which would be reflected in "tangible and concrete actions, including first of all the recognition of Israel; second, diplomatic relations with Israel; third, a peace treaty with Israel; fourth, open frontiers with Israel's neighbors; last, an end to the embargo and official hostile propaganda against the State of Israel."[7] He stated his position on the Palestinians in a manner which recalled that of the Nixon and Ford administrations:

> I would not recognize the Palestinians as a political entity, nor their leaders until after those leaders had first recognized Israel's right to exist…ultimately, I believe that we will see the legitimate interests of the Palestinians met. My preference would be that, if they are granted territory by Israel, that it would be on the West Bank of the Jordan, administered by the nation of Jordan.[8]

But in reply to a question on the matter put to him by the *Jewish Telegraphic Agency*, Carter expressed a position which paralleled that of Israel:

> The PLO is not the group to deal with in solving the Palestinian problem. The PLO is an alliance of guerrilla organizations, not a government in exile. The PLO is unrepresentative of the Palestinian problem. The PLO should not participate as an equal partner in any resumed Geneva's peace conference because the PLO's stated aims are diametrically opposed to any peace which envisions the continued existence of Israel.[9]

As for his expectations from Israel, Carter found it unnecessary to go beyond what the Israeli government was willing to concede: "Israel must withdraw from some of the territories occupied. I would not try to force the Israelis to relinquish control of the Golan Heights or Old Jerusalem."[10] He called for a general settlement, perhaps in Geneva, to be reached by direct negotiations between the parties. He absolved Israel of any wrongdoing by saying that such settlement would not be based on the "faulty" premise that Israel caused the Palestine problem.[11]

Borrowing from Woodrow Wilson's rhetorical idealism, he denounced balance of power politics and the secrecy, which characterized Kissinger's style of diplomacy, which, in his view, compromised Israel's "security needs." Emphasizing a stronger commitment to such needs, he said that "Israel must feel secure in the support that it expects from America in order to take the necessary risks for peace." Thus, he maintained that Israel cannot be counted upon to make territorial concessions if "aid should be used in a carrot-and-stick fashion." The implication of this assumption was that Ford's publicized threat to "reassess" U.S. relations with Israel in 1975 had forced Israel to agree to the Sinai Accord with Egypt including withdrawal from the Mitla and Giddi Passes. He denounced Kissinger's step-by-step diplomacy, which led to the Sinai Accord claiming that the "underlying threat to Israel" remained "unresolved." He conveniently set aside the fact that Ford, in his two years in office, delivered $4.5 billion worth of sophisticated and lethal weapons to Israel, and that on the eve of the elections, new credits and weapons systems, including the deadly cluster bombs, were approved for Israel by the Ford administration.

During the presidential foreign policy debate of October 6, 1976 Carter reminded his audience that under the Johnson administration, Israel received 60 percent of all weapons destined for the Middle East. Now, he said 60 percent went to the Arab countries (forgetting that Iran is not Arab), and this, he said, was a "deviation from idealism." Earlier he told a group of Jewish leaders that his administration would give Israel "undeviating, unequivocal" support, asserting that "...this is not just a political statement. As a Christian myself, I think that the fulfillment of Israel, the coming of that nation, is fulfillment of Biblical prophecy."[12]

Carter never ceased to turn a liability into an asset with American Jews. As a "born-again" Christian, he was initially a source of worry to many in the Jewish community, but he used his religion and employed moral slogans to underline his commitment to Israel. The God of Jews and Christians was the same God, he told Jewish audiences. He also said in a campaign speech on June 6, 1975 that "...the survival of Israel is not just a political issue, it is a moral imperative." He made a moral issue out of the boycott question when during the October 6, 1976 debate he said, "I'll do everything I can as president to stop the boycott of American business by the Arab countries."[13] He described it as "an absolute disgrace" only because it affects companies that "trade with Israel or because they have American Jews, who are owners or directors."[14]

The two main controversies during the 1976 campaign over boycott and the sale of weapons to Arab nations did not reflect differences in ideologies between Ford and Carter or between Republicans and

Democrats. For in the real world of politics, these were political and economic issues, not moral issues. After all, the U.S. had for a long time maintained boycott policies of its own toward countries like Cuba, Vietnam, China, and North Korea, and it still applies these policies at the present. Unlike the situation in the Middle East, some of these U.S.-boycotted countries were not even in a state of war with the United States.

The arguments presented by the Ford administration against anti-boycott legislation were largely based on the notion that such legislation would be harmful to U.S. trade with the Arab world. Surely President Ford and the Republican party were closer to that sector of the business community, which was presumably the principal loser in the event of retaliation by the Arab League. But no chief executive, Carter included, could afford to neglect the interests of the business community.

It is important to note that President Ford did not oppose anti-boycott legislation *per se*, but rather the form in which it was presented in Congress during Ford's last days in office. That is why the Carter administration decided to step aside while negotiators from the business community and the Jewish lobby proceeded to draw up a compromise which preserved the basic interests of both parties. Such interests, together with Carter's electoral strategy, and presidential leadership, rather than any genuine party differences, were responsible for the final outcome, which reflected a retreat from the congressional version, that had been approved by Ford. Interestingly, such a retreat came at the behest of none other than President Carter, who had championed the anti-boycott side during the election campaign. For president, rather than candidate Carter, a compromise was deemed essential to the success of what had become known as the peace process. Such were the dynamics of electoral politics.

That outcome was reminiscent of an earlier episode when George McGovern in 1972, made the freedom of immigration for Soviet Jewry a campaign issue on moral grounds. Nixon, whose détente policies toward the Soviet Union would have been substantially harmed by the espousal of the kind of proposals made by McGovern, felt impelled to match McGovern's promises but *not* to translate them into real policy. When it came to the "national interest," both candidates and both parties often closed ranks.

This pattern of electoral politics also characterized the second main Middle East issue in the Carter v. Ford campaign of 1976—the sale of weapons to pro-Western Arab regimes. Again, candidate Carter was extremely critical of Ford's willingness to sell advanced fighters to Saudi Arabia and Egypt on the usual grounds that it would "undermine our commitment to Israel."[15] President Ford had been favorably disposed to Saudi Arabia's request for F-15s and to Egypt's interest in the F-Es, but as in the boycott issue, there was no time to act. Upon Carter's succession to the presidency, it remained clear that the assessment of the U.S. strategic establishment of the Middle East politico-military equation had not been altered since Ford's departure. Candidate Carter's assessment, therefore, had to be reconciled with President Carter's updated position, which, in turn, had to be congruent with that of the politico-strategic establishment.

The electoral concept of "our commitment to Israel "was now amended to read "we must keep our commitments;" i.e. Ford's commitment to Saudi Arabia and Egypt; and our commitment to U.S. defense contractors who were in danger of losing business to French weapons companies. Also, the Carter administration added our commitment to "moderation in the Middle East, with respect to peacemaking and other regional initiatives and more broadly in world affairs, as in petroleum and financial policy."[16] Moreover, by selling these planes to Saudi Arabia, Egypt and Israel, the Carter administration was not in reality deviating from earlier U.S. policy. The sale, in the words of President Carter, represented a discharge of a commitment "to the military balance in the Middle East."[17] Of course, none of this multiplicity of varying, yet presumed harmonious, commitments was deemed in conflict with the earlier overriding commitment by Richard Nixon to enable Israel to defeat any combination of Arab military forces. So in the end, the sale would be presented as being in the best interest of the United States, and would even promote the national interest, irrespective of whatever campaign rhetoric about commitments that might have been entered into the campaign discourse. President Carter expressed it this way at a press conference, in March 1978:

I have no apology at all to make for this proposal.... I can say without any doubt that the superior capabilities of the Israeli Air Force, compared to their neighbors, is maintained, and at the same time, it reconfirms our own relationship with the moderate Arab leaders and nations for the future to insure that peace can be and will be maintained in the Middle East.[18]

Again, no real differences had existed between Carter and Ford on the military balance in the Middle East and the requirements of the "national interest." It would be simplistic to presume that Ford was the anti-Israel candidate and Carter was the pro-Israel one. In fact, Carter's National Security Advisor, Zbigniew Brzezinski, was considered by AIPAC as an enemy of Israel. He was reported to have said that American Middle East policy could not succeed until the pro-Israel lobby had been confronted on a major issue and defeated, and that the F-15 vote would "break the back of the Israeli lobby."[19] The F-15 vote was for selling planes to Saudi Arabia, Egypt and Israel. Although the Israeli lobby lost by 54-44, the F-15s were to be stripped of their offensive capabilities—bomb racks and missiles. That same controversy over weapons sales carried through to the Reagan administration, when the sale of AWACS to Saudi Arabia became a trying issue.

It was interesting that both Carter and Reagan were committed to selling advanced airplanes to Saudi Arabia. But that issue was not to be found prominent in the 1980 campaign, which was actually characterized by unqualified support for Israel by both Carter and Reagan. Unlike the 1976 campaign in which the Jewish vote was crucial for Carter's success, Reagan's victory in 1980 was attributed largely to the broad perception that Carter's "wimpish" foreign policy had threatened to erode America's global standing vis à vis the Soviet Union and third world reassertion. Significant, however, was the erosion of Jewish support for the Democratic party and its presidential candidate, who took credit for Camp David. In contrast to 1976, when Carter obtained 75 percent of the Jewish vote, his 1980 share was only 44 percent, while Reagan's share was 39 percent, a high proportion for a Republican. The upgrading and institutionalization of the special relationship by President Reagan was in fact attributed to his virulent attitude toward the Soviet Union and third world revolution and had little to do with the Jewish vote. It was for that reason also that Reagan supported the sale of AWACS to Saudi Arabia, much to the chagrin of Israel's Begin and the pro-Israel lobby in the United States.

These episodes illustrate the constraints on the Israeli lobby influence over U.S. foreign policy towards the Middle East. While the Jewish vote can be instrumental in ushering a candidate into the White House, electoral promises are not necessarily destined to become foreign policy, particularly when they fall under the rubric of national security. In that case, Congress, which has been traditionally more susceptible to organizational pressure from the Israeli lobby, was inclined then to defer to the president. Meanwhile, the president would be acting primarily in his capacity as commander-in-chief and chief diplomat rather than as party chief; his principal input would, therefore, reflect assessments by the executive branch and the strategic establishment.

The Presidential Campaign of 1984[20]

The 1984 campaign was, in many ways, a repeat of earlier campaigns in terms of the rituals of devotion to Israel's past, present and future needs, which are regularly expressed by the principal presidential contenders. It was different, however, in that lesser candidates from the Democratic party attempted to place the question of Palestinian statehood on the political agenda.

Ronald Reagan and Walter Mondale staked out familiar grounds on the Middle East; a firm commitment to a militarily strong Israel, opposition to Palestinian statehood, and a reconfirmation of the no-talk policy with the PLO. While President Reagan exalted his own record of vigorous support for Israel (even when Israel's policies under Menachem Begin and Yitzhak Shamir were profoundly expansionist), Walter Mondale and Geraldine Ferraro, in a concerted effort to win back the traditionally Democratic Jewish vote, pledged to transfer the American Embassy from Tel Aviv to Jerusalem. So intent were the Democratic candidates on winning Jewish support that the Mondale campaign felt compelled to return $5000 in contributions from Arab-American donors, a decision reminiscent of former Democratic contender Gary Hart's haste in repaying a $700,000 loan from First

American Bank when he discovered that the bank was owned by Arab investors. Similar precautions were repeated in more recent times by Congressman Joe Kennedy (D-Mass) who felt it necessary to return a campaign contribution from the former Arab-American senator, James Abourezk.

Scrambling for the Jewish vote, as well as hostility to Arab-Americans, is nothing new in U.S. presidential campaigns. Harry Truman's well-known rhetorical question to advisors who urged even-handedness, "How many Arab constituents do I have?," has described the attitude of presidential aspirants since the 1940s.

Both parties were competing to fulfill the five major goals adopted by the 1984 Annual Policy Conference of the American-Israel Public Affairs Committee (AIPAC, the official pro-Israel lobby). While Mr. Reagan took credit for the fulfillment of AIPAC's goal of converting all direct official U.S. aid to Israel to a grant basis, Democrats in the House passed the $2.6 billion foreign aid bill, which gave Israel $439 million more than Reagan had requested. According to the *Washington Post,* Reagan proposed to spend "six times more on aid to Israel in 1985 than on energy conservation in the United States, twice as much as on domestic consumer and occupational health and safety programs, and about the same amount as the combined worldwide spending of the State Department and the Peace Corps plus all U.S. contributions to the United Nations and its agencies."[21] The Reagan administration agreed to AIPAC's demand for the cancellation of the Stinger missile deal with Jordan, while the Democrats used the foreign aid bill to allow the sale of sophisticated weapons systems to those Arab countries which acquiesced to the Camp David "peace" formula. AIPAC's third and fourth goals, were the development of strategic cooperation and a U.S.-Israel free trade area. Only with regard to the Mondale-Ferraro promise on Jerusalem did the Reagan administration lag behind, and the Democratic promise to move the U.S. embassy from Tel Aviv to Jerusalem should be viewed in light of a 1980 Carter-Mondale commitment that was not honored.

Despite the traditional positions taken by the party nominees, however, the situation in the Middle East was a major topic of debate during the Democratic primary campaigns. This made 1984 a novel election year, for it was the first time in memory that America's anti-Palestinian policies had been criticized by serious candidates for the presidency.

1. Seeking New Coalitions

An effort was made in 1984 to forge a progressive coalition that would challenge many of the old assumptions about American foreign and domestic policies. For example, the very premise of the Cold War was questioned during this campaign, and with it Israel's role in the U.S. global strategy. In the past, attempts to forge a progressive coalition have occurred largely outside the dominant two-party structure, as in the Citizen's Party, for example. In 1984, however, efforts were made by Jesse Jackson and George McGovern to forge Democratic primary victories around the so-called "new" issues of the environment, feminism, international peace, and nuclear disarmament. Reverend Jackson's vision was the more powerful of the two because he attempted to create a multi-racial coalition of persons active on the "new" issues as well as those concerned about social justice and civil rights. As part of their campaigns, both McGovern and Jackson launched outspoken attacks on the one-sidedness of America's pro-Israel stance.

The strategies of McGovern and Jackson sought to take advantage of changing electoral patterns, including the weakening of the Democratic party's alliance with Jewish voters. The strength of that alliance was demonstrated by the fact that for the past half-century successful Democratic candidates for the presidency have attracted support from 70 percent or more of Jewish voters. But between the mid-1970s and mid-1980s increasing numbers of Jews have crossed party lines to vote for Republican presidential candidates. In 1980, President Carter became the first Democrat to win less than half of the Jewish vote when he attracted only 44 percent, against 39 percent for Reagan and 17 percent for John Anderson. At the same time, Jews became uneasy with parts of the Democratic platform. Many Jews were becoming critical of Democratic support for "affirmative action" policies designed to increase employment among Blacks, Hispanics, and women; and they were critical of the non-interventionist sentiment among left-wing Democrats, preferring instead a hard line toward the

Soviet Union and the Arab world. The trend reflected a shift away from liberalism towards neo-conservatism.

Some Democrats on the left began to argue that their party should attempt to form a new electoral coalition in which, by implication, Zionist support would be of marginal significance. These Democrats began to seek alliances between the increasingly powerful women's lobby, environmentalists, opponents of nuclear power and nuclear weapons, and Blacks. In 1984, Jesse Jackson and his "Rainbow Coalition" provided the ideological base and attempted to reach out to these groups as they began an organized movement for a new Democratic left. The progressive, international coalition they were attempting to form was not likely to be attractive to militant Zionists whose constant quest for arming Israel was a contributory factor in the Cold War. At the same time, the Reagan brand of right-wing populism had attracted many conservative Democratic voters, in the South and West particularly, those who admired the President's emphasis on "traditional" values, his willingness to cut social programs, and his hard line abroad.

The early 1980s had also seen a slight but significant erosion of American public support for Israeli policies. By the end of 1982, one-quarter of Americans expressed themselves to be more in sympathy with "the Arab nations" than with Israel, compared with one in ten in 1977; and half the nation preferred that the United States talk directly with the PLO as the representative of the Palestinian people. And there had been an increase in the militancy of Arab-American groups, who have become increasingly outspoken and visible in the public media and in Washington.

2. The Jackson and McGovern Positions

These adjustments in the American partisan climate were reflected in primary debates among the contenders for the Democratic nomination. On the central issue of the Palestine-Israeli conflict, the Reverend Jesse Jackson and George McGovern, the former senator and 1972 Democratic presidential nominee, dissented from the historic party consensus. Both supported a peaceful settlement based on mutual recognition. "I do not believe that peace will come to the Middle East until Israel recognizes the legitimate rights of Palestinians to an independent homeland of their own," said McGovern at an Arab-

American gathering in Los Angeles in November 1988. On another occasion, the International Day of Solidarity with the Palestinian People, McGovern told a Washington audience that "the Palestinian people have been victims of one of the world's great tragedies by being denied their legitimate rights of self-determination and statehood." Jesse Jackson repeated this theme on the same occasion, saying that "...the quest by the Palestinian people for self-determination must ultimately be respected by all the nations in the world." And unlike Mondale, who shunned association with Arab-Americans, Jackson told the American-Arab Anti-Discrimination Committee's convention in March 1984, "No longer will Arab-Americans be locked out."

While recognition of the national rights of the Palestinian people was a departure from Democratic policy, Jackson and McGovern continued to support Israel's "right to exist." Jackson, for example, drew the distinction between "supporting the right to exist" and "supporting the right to occupy." In addition, Jackson viewed Israel in an economic and military context. He advocated open trade relations between Israel and the Arab states and predicted that this would make Israel the "commercial hub" of the Middle East. Remarkably, Palestinian self-determination was articulated in this campaign for the first time by major contenders for the American presidency. Despite the novelty of his views, national polls showed that Jesse Jackson was running strongly among white as well as Black voters in early February 1984. His sizable support made him the target of systematic harassment by the Jewish Defense League, which disrupted Jackson's speeches and picketed his headquarters. Jackson also came under attack in the press, which accused him of accepting "Arab money" to support his civil rights work, and which reported his use of an anti-Semitic word ("Hymietown") in conversation. As a result of the latter controversy, Jackson's campaign was put on the defensive, and white support began to fall away. In May, Jackson was targeted by mainstream Jewish leaders, who exerted tremendous pressure on regular Democrats to distance themselves from Jackson's views on the Third World and from his support for Palestinian self-determination. The occasion of that campaign was Jackson's association with Black Muslim minister Louis Farrakhan, who was reported to have threatened a Black reporter and

Jews who criticized Jackson. Leaders of major Jewish organizations threatened to punish the Democratic party by withholding votes unless Mondale and other Democratic officials pressured Jackson to disavow Farrakhan. Initially, Jackson dismissed that demand as a "diversion away from issues of substance in this campaign," and stated that his campaign was reaching out to get support from Black, Hispanic and Arab-American voters as well as whites and Jews.

3. Black-Jewish Relations

The gap between the Jackson coalition and the Jewish community remained despite Jackson's eloquent apology at the San Francisco convention. Their differences transcended Farrakhan and Jackson himself, and his well-publicized "Hymietown" remark and were rooted in differences over domestic and international policy. At the core of the disagreement was the fear among militant Zionists that the Jackson campaign would change the political landscape in substantial ways. It was significant that the most vehement attacks against Jackson came from conservative leaders of the Jewish community, such as Norman Podhoretz and Irving Kristol, who was leading a "neo-conservative" movement among American Jewish intellectuals. On the other hand, George McGovern, who espoused similar positions to Jackson, ran rather poorly and largely escaped criticism.

The Jackson campaign demonstrated again the tensions within the Democratic party between Blacks and Jews. Throughout this century, Blacks in the United States have identified with the plight of the "Hebrew children of the Old Testament." Both groups have been victims of bigotry. Blacks appreciated the funding and active support rendered by Jewish groups and individuals during the civil rights movement in the 1950s and 1960s. They marched together, held sit-ins together and went to prison together. But while many whites, including some Jews, thought that Blacks have been the principal beneficiaries of federal "give-away programs," many Blacks considered the old civil rights alliance as having failed to meet their social and economic expectations.

However, a dialogue redefining Black-Jewish relations had been going on since the forcible resignation of United Nations Ambassador Andrew Young over his unauthorized contacts with the PLO. The

Andrew Young affair helped bring to the surface submerged differences over issues relating to jobs and quotas. While Blacks considered job quotas as a vehicle for social mobility, Jews, who had increasingly been moving away from the working class into the upper socio-economic categories, and who had traditionally viewed such quotas as a means for their own exclusion, began to see them now as placing a ceiling on their own social mobility. Thus Jewish intellectual and legal opposition to Black upward mobility in the U.S. Supreme Court case of De Funis, Bakke and Weber, which helped popularize the phrase "reverse discrimination," i.e., discrimination against whites, was and remains a source of friction. The special relationship between the Israeli government and the apartheid regime in South Africa was another source.

The transformation of the civil rights movement from a judicially oriented movement seeking legal integration, to a militant political and economic movement seeking the redistribution of power, created yet more distance between these former allies in the Democratic party coalition. Jesse Jackson explained this phenomenon in 1979: "When there was not much decency in society, many Jews were willing to share decency. The conflict began when we started our quest for power." Andrew Young reiterated the theme: "Jews historically made all the decisions in the coalition. When Blacks began to think for themselves and challenge liberal views and leadership, things changed." That this perception became widespread in the Black community was demonstrated by a 1982 study by the public opinion research firm Yankelovich, Skelly and White, which showed that 40 percent of Blacks believed that Jews held too much power.

The challenge by Andrew Young in 1979 to Kissinger's dictum against contact with the PLO, which had become one of the sacred cows of U.S. Middle East policy, and Jesse Jackson's successful venture into Middle East diplomacy with Syria, signaled a new phenomenon: no longer would Black's be confined to ghetto politics and excluded from the seemingly complex arena of international affairs; nor would they accept the Zionist-imposed taboo on discussion of the Palestine question. Henceforth the Palestine question was not inappropriate for rational debate in the U.S. political arena. A call for reassessment of United States Middle East policy was implicit in that transformed relationship between the two pillars of the Democratic coalition.

The 1988 Presidential Campaign

In a synoptic comparison of the two presidential candidates on a broad range of domestic and international issues, the Sunday *New York Times* (September 25, 1988) had the following entries for George Bush and Michael Dukakis on the Middle East:

Bush: Opposes a separate Palestinian state; Against negotiations with Palestine Liberation Organization unless it abandons terrorism and its call for Israel's destruction.

Dukakis: Would not recognize a declaration of a Palestinian state; Against a PLO role in negotiations unless it renounces terrorism in word and deed.

Needless to say, these positions could not be more similar, and yet the Middle East was high on the candidates' agendas. George Bush was hoping to build on the Reagan record, which included the strategic alliance and the trade agreements. It was an uphill struggle for him, however, despite the tangible benefits, which Israel derived during eight years of the Reagan-Bush administration. In fact, the term "strategic cooperation" was introduced by the Reagan administration in November 1981 when Secretary of State Alexander Haig and Israel's then Defense Minister Ariel Sharon signed a "Memorandum of Understanding on Strategic Cooperation." Accordingly, Israel was charged with supplying pro-western third world regimes with the technology of repression, which the U.S. itself could not advance because of congressional and public opinion scrutiny. The world views of Israel and the Republican party were fully *in sync* during the 1980s. In the words of one Israeli:

"Israel, in a sense, earns its special status and relationship with the United States by giving aid and arms to regimes that Washington supports but cannot overtly assist because of concerns about its international image, U.S. public opinion, or congressional prohibitions."[22]

Israel of course was compensated handsomely for its performance of surrogate function to hold up unsavory regimes, from which the U.S., for public relations reasons, had to keep some distance. The package of rewards included increased U.S. aid, access to advanced weapon technology, free trade arrangements, a U.S. market for Israeli weapons and a stronger diplomatic alignment with Israel at the expense of the Arab world. This was a vital component of Bush's electoral arsenal aimed against Michael Dukakis. But despite all that, and despite Dukakis' image as the anti-Cold War, peace candidate, which conservative American Jews normally felt uncomfortable with, Bush was the target of attacks by both conservative and liberal Jews. The right-wing *New York Times* columnist, William Safire, for example, accused Bush of having led a campaign, when he was vice-president, to withhold arms shipment to Israel as a punishment for its 1981 attack on Iraq's nuclear research facility. The *Jewish Times* published a report in April 1987 accusing Bush of having convinced Reagan to vote against Israel when the latter invaded Lebanon in 1982. Bush was viewed by the publication as the least friendly to Israel among all possible Republican candidates. Also, *Jewish World* (Vol. 7, #37 September 9-15, 1988) printed an article by Larry Cohler titled "Bush Campaign Riddled With Fascists, anti-Semites." The article charged a number of people in leading roles in the Bush campaign of heinous acts, such as denial of the holocaust, defense of John Demjanjuk, membership in several pro-Nazi cliques and other associations which would repel not only Jewish voters but all decent people as well. Bush's ethnic outreach campaign leaders were accused of having undermined the Office of Special Investigations, the Justice Department's Nazi hunting unit, and of having received Bush's blessing for it.

Dukakis, by contrast, came very "clean" for Jewish voters with the prospect of ushering in the first Jewish first lady to the White House. He was certified by Israel's then Foreign Minister Shimon Peres as a loyal friend of Israel, whose support was "one hundred percent." [23] A photographer was brought to the Dukakis home in Boston where Peres was a guest in August, 1987 to produce electoral tools for later use in the campaign.

Although Dukakis was soundly defeated, having carried a small number of states, he was able to rally about 70 percent of the Jewish vote.

American Jews, who continued to vote Democratic and liberal, apparently concluded that strategic cooperation with Israel, although a Republican achievement anchored in a conservative anti-Communist world view, would not be objectionable to the liberal Dukakis. For it was known that Dukakis' liberalism in foreign policy stopped at the doors of the Middle East. Being a "dove" throughout the world but a hawk in the Middle East was not something new. In a speech at Georgetown University on September 25, 1987, Michael Dukakis declared at the start, "I am an internationalist," and proceeded to say that national security and the significant cuts in defense spending, which he was proposing, were not incompatible.[24] Threats to U.S. security, U.S. allies and to world peace, "do not all emanate from the Soviet Union," he added. There was the threat of international terrorism, the Persian Gulf war and nuclear proliferation. Though he named Israel, India, Pakistan and South Africa as being on the threshold of joining the five nuclear powers, only Pakistan and Libya were singled out for the scolding.

His position on the Middle East was outlined in a one-page campaign brochure, and it hardly differed from that of his Republican opponent. In fact the closing statement read as follows:

> There is no dispute among Republicans and Democrats that the United States has vital interests in the Middle East and the Persian Gulf. I look forward to working with leaders of Congress from both parties to develop a strong policy that will protect our interests; guarantee the security and well-being of Israel; and improve the prospects for long term peace and stability throughout the region.[25]

His stated precondition for that kind of peace and stability "has been and remains a decision by Arab leaders to recognize Israel's right to exist and to enter into formal, direct negotiations with Israel."[26] And to that end, he promised that as president, he would do the following:

—strengthen strategic cooperation between the United States and Israel;
—maintain generous levels of economic and military assistance to Israel and Egypt;

—oppose arms sales that would endanger the security of Israel;

—encourage direct negotiations between Jordan and Israel aimed at resolving the Palestinian/West Bank issue within the framework of the Camp David accords; and

—oppose negotiations with the Palestinian Liberation Organization until that group renounces terrorism (both in practice and in word), recognizes the right of Israel to exist, and accepts the text of UN Resolutions 242 and 338.[27]

Of course, much of that package had already been delivered by Reagan and Bush. Moreover the Republicans did not have to contend with a Jesse Jackson problem—either regarding his views on the PLO or his acrimonious debate with New York ultra-Zionist Mayor, Edward Koch, over the "Hymie town" remark. Additionally, they did not have to prove their macho image regarding the Soviet Union and its perceived allies. Their principal problem with Jewish voters was the latter's loyalty to the Democratic party, and that was precisely what the less-experienced (and presumably less-assertionist at the global level,) Michael Dukakis, capitalized upon.

He told the B'nai B'rith International convention that he was "…the first governor to sign a comprehensive agreement with Israel to encourage joint economic development projects;" and that he was the first governor to insist that "any company doing business with Massachusetts must reject the Arab boycott of Israel."[28] He reminded his audience that he spoke out against the UN resolution equating Zionism with racism, and that Bush's campaign manager, John Sununu, an Arab-American and a former governor of New Hampshire, was the only governor who refused to condemn that resolution.[29]

Dukakis' appeal to Jewish voters throughout the country was met with overwhelming support in the Jewish community. A nationwide poll conducted between October 10-13, 1988 revealed that American Jews favored Dukakis over Bush by a margin as high as four to one.[30] His campaign targeted nine metropolitan centers, where 75-80 percent of the country's Jewish population reside: New York and northern New Jersey; Long Island; Miami and southern Florida; Los Angeles and Long Beach, California; Philadelphia, Trenton, New Jersey;

Wilmington, Delaware; Chicago; Boston; and Washington-Baltimore. Of 647 American Jews of voting age living in these areas who were contacted by telephone one month prior to elections, 60.6 percent said they would vote for Dukakis, 15.5 percent said they would vote for Bush, and 22.5 percent were undecided.

A Dukakis campaign worker wrote the following:

> During six months of campaigning for the primaries in Florida "the Jewish vote was our primary target." Approximately 95 percent of South Floridians are Jews, many of whom are retired and are members of condominium associations and Democratic clubs. They meet regularly, voice their concerns, articulate their interests and expect politicians to address their interests and concerns.[31]

Not only did Dukakis address these concerns but his troops were also in full force at the Florida State Convention with a "kosher New England fish chowder luncheon for all delegates, and three Greek chefs flown in from Boston's Noname Restaurant to prepare and serve the crowd in a Yankee style."[32]

But Dukakis had to contend with Jewish disenchantment with Jesse Jackson and his sympathies for Palestinian rights. According to his campaign worker, Eileen Parise, several leaders of the Jewish community were so enraged with this situation that they contemplated throwing their support toward George Bush, as the lesser of two evils. The Dukakis strategy, however, avoided reference to Jesse Jackson even though Jewish voters were seeking assurances that Jackson would have no role in a Democratic administration. Instead, the Dukakis campaign kept emphasizing a difference between Dukakis who "shared the values of the Jewish community," and George Bush, whose values were supposedly not the values of the Jewish community.[33] For example, Bush was accused of supporting the radical right's call for school prayers, public aid to parochial schools, and a ban on abortion, in contrast to Dukakis who upheld the separation of church and state. Also Bush's running mate, Dan Quayle, was accused of opposing aid to Israel and supporting Arab arms deals, and of the claim that neither he nor Bush had "the same gut feeling toward Israel as President

Reagan." Moreover, Kitty Dukakis was utilized to assuage Jewish public opinion and to mollify constituents angered by the Jesse Jackson factor. A speech to some 2000 in a North Miami Beach temple was typical of her attempts at persuasion:

> George Bush doesn't acknowledge Israel's sovereignty over its capital—an undivided Jerusalem. Michael Dukakis does.
> We cannot, and should not try to impose a solution on the region….
> No settlement that is unacceptable to Israel will be acceptable to the United States.

Having thus assured her audience that Israel would exercise a veto on any negotiated settlement and indeed over U.S. choices for a settlement, a rather novel idea for any candidate to express, let alone a spouse, she proceeded to speak to the crowd as one of them:

> I know how many of you have devoted your lives to helping Soviet Jews. Over the years, Michael and I have been grateful for the opportunity to work with you; to do our part; to be inspired by the courage and to rejoice in the freedom of people like Benjamin Charny and the Fuch-Rabinovich family. We will never forget the joy in our hearts at Mishka's long over-due Bar Mitzvah, where I was called to the Bimah for an aliyah.

In the end, however, Michael Dukakis was able to reclaim the Jewish vote for the Democratic party, but he lost the election to George Bush, who as president did much of what Dukakis had pledged to do in the Middle East anyway. Again, the American Jewish community was able to have its cake and eat it too. The Republican party continued to equate world order with American paramountcy, and continued to view Israel's role as crucial for that order. Electioneering around Middle East issues in 1988 seemed, in retrospect, an unavoidable exercise.

The 1992 Presidential Campaign

1992 was a problem year for incumbents. The Cold War had just come to an end. The world seemed to be militarily unipolar but economically multipolar. American voters were focused on domestic issues—jobs, health care, budget and trade deficits, housing and crime. The communist bogeyman was yet to be replaced, and the euphoria of Desert Storm had just about vanished. It was an opportunity for the domestic-minded Democrats to stage a comeback after a quarter of a century of Republican control of the White House, interrupted only by the Carter interlude.

1. Bush and the Jewish Community

In the Middle East, the Bush administration was having a trying relationship with the Likud government of Yitzhak Shamir, which expressed its intransigence by renouncing its own peace plan, which Secretary of State James Baker had earlier described as "the only game in town." Their disagreement reached new dimensions when President Bush telephoned Shamir on February 10, 1990 urging him to start talks about elections in the West Bank and Gaza. Moreover Shamir's insistence on building settlements in the occupied territories had incurred the wrath of Baker and Bush, who subsequently threatened to withhold loan guarantees to Israel. The acrimony resulting from the controversy made the special relationship look anything but special during the beginning of the 1990s. It was not surprising, therefore that the ascendancy of Yitzhak Rabin to power in July 1992 was greeted with widespread approval in the United States among American Jews, who were disheartened by the acrimony.

The U.S. media hailed Rabin's victory as a vote for the U.S.-sponsored "peace process." In the midst of the 1992 U.S. presidential campaign, in which George Bush trailed his Democratic opponent in the public opinion polls, two occasions in August were seized by the beleaguered incumbent and the Republican party to make a serious bid for the Jewish vote; the well-publicized visit of Israeli Prime Minister Rabin and his wife to the home of George and Barbara Bush in Kennebunkport, Maine, and the Republican party national convention.

Bush and Rabin had hoped to gain political capital from the Kennebunkport visit; whereas Rabin was counted upon to deliver a diplomatic feat for George Bush, he himself was hoping to demonstrate to the Israeli electorate that he and his party were capable of repairing the damage caused by his predecessor, Yitzhak Shamir, to the special relationship with the U.S. By the same token, Bush was hoping to demonstrate to Israeli supporters in the U.S. that the special relationship with Israel was intact, and that his differences were not with Israel, but with Shamir's inflexible policies.

After nearly two years of opposition to loan guarantees for Israel, President Bush recommended on October 10, 1992 (one month before the elections) that Congress pass the loan guarantees legislation, providing the money be used within the pre-1967 Israeli borders. There were suficient loopholes in the legislation, however, which pleased Israel, its U.S. lobby and congressional supporters. So intent was the Bush administration on reassuring the American Jewish community of its support to Israel that only one day after the Israeli elections, Edward Djerejian, Assistant Secretary of State for Near Eastern Affairs, told the House Subcommittee on Europe and the Middle East: "The U.S./Israel relationship remains rock solid. It is based on the firmest of foundations [including]...an unshakable U.S. commitment to Israel's security."[34]

Bush's futile panderings also included statements updating and revising positions he had taken earlier. Only three weeks after the Israeli elections, he revised his position on Jerusalem and the Palestinian refugees in response to a June 30th letter sent by members of the House of Representatives to Secretary Baker expressing concern about what they considered as "ambiguous" remarks by the administration on these issues. In a meeting with the American Jewish leaders, a senior administration official cited a 1970 memorandum sent to Golda Meir by President Nixon.[35] The relevant portion states that the United States "shall not press to accept a solution to the problem for the refugees which will basically alter the Jewish character of the State of Israel and endanger its security." The right of return for the refugees, enshrined in General Assembly Resolution 194, which has been reaffirmed annually by the assembly since 1948 with the U.S. voting in the affirmative, had thus been undermined in the heat of the campaign.

The *Washington Jewish Weekly* (June 25, 1992) quoted from a letter by Bush to the Rabbinical Council of America in which he made a "commitment to maintaining basic foreign and military aid to ensure Israeli security." Improved relations with Israel was indeed a White House priority during the summer of 1992 because, according to one official, it could give the president "a lift before the [Republican] convention." And according to *Forward* magazine (July 24, 1992) the Bush campaign team intended "to remove the venom [that] GOP officials acknowledge has poisoned ties between the administration and the American Jewish Community."

Although Republican presidential candidates have never received more than 39 percent of the Jewish vote, George Bush was in no position to forfeit even the slightest segment of that vote. He was keenly aware that Jewish voters, who are concentrated in states with large populations and who regularly turn out at the polling booths, could make a crucial difference. The Rabins' visit was an occasion for the president to try to salvage what was left of the much eroded Jewish support for the Republican party. He used the visit to reaffirm the U.S.-Israeli strategic relationship and to lay to rest speculation that Israel's strategic importance had diminished with the end of the Cold War.

The Republican national convention was the second occasion for an investment in Jewish votes to shore up Bush's sagging popularity. The platform repeated the substance of the president's earlier pledge to Rabin at the conclusion of his visit to Kennebunkport:

> ...Consistent with our strategic relationship, the United States should continue to provide large-scale security assistance to Israel, maintaining Israel's qualitative military advantage over any adversary or coalition of adversaries.... we will continue to broaden and deepen the strategic relationship with our ally Israel—the only true democracy in the Middle East.

2. Clinton and the Campaign

Rabin was courted by both Bush and Clinton, and no matter who was going to win the election in November 1992, Israel and the United States were to embark on a second honeymoon. Early in the campaign, Clinton resorted to the familiar pandering which U.S. politicians engage in at least once every four years. The confrontation between Bush and Israel seemed a ready-made issue for a Democratic candidate in pursuit of votes. He challenged Bush's linkage of loan guarantees to the territorial issue: he told the Jewish Leadership

Council, "The lack of positive vision has led to miscalculations and missed opportunities," and, while he praised Bush and Baker for convening the peace talks, he added: "…but they have chosen to brow-beat Israel, the region's sole democracy, while nurturing ties to Syria's despotic regime." In an interview with the French quarterly *Politique Internationale*, which was published on the eve of the elections, he accused Syrian President Hafez Asad of "territorial ambitions." Following up on the Democratic party's 1992 Platform, he declared Jerusalem the capital of Israel and declared his opposition to the establishment of a Palestinian state.[36] He said in an interview with *Middle East Insight* (November-December 1992) that he "would not move the American Embassy from Tel Aviv to Jerusalem during negotiations."

His attitude towards Palestinian self-rule was spelled out in a June, 1992 speech to the Jewish Leadership Council. He said:

> The Palestinians should have the right…to participate in the determination of their own future. But they do not have the right to determine Israel's future, and for that reason, I oppose the creation of an independent Palestinian state.[37]

Unlike the Republicans, who had to minimize the damage and "remove the venom," in their assiduous efforts to reassure the Jewish community, Democrats had only to stress positive relations between the U.S. and Israel. And rather than courting the pro-Israel lobby, which Republicans had to do, AIPAC, the lobby itself, was facilitating the Democratic campaign in various ways. At the Democratic convention, for example, AIPAC featured Hillary Clinton at one of their receptions. *Near East Report*, AIPAC's newsletter ran a headline: "Clinton: Friend and an Ally." The newsletter also featured Al Gore with praise for his relentless opposition to U.S. negotiations with the PLO, and for leading Christian Zionists to Israel, among other chores normally expected of office seekers in the United States.

The religious dimension of the Clinton-Gore campaign was also manifested in a speech by Clinton, in which he added a mystical quality to his relationship with Jews and Israel. It was reminiscent of Jimmy Carter's earlier exploitation of his religion to attract Jewish voters.

According to the *Jerusalem Post* (November 6, 1992), after describing a visit to Israel in 1981 as "fundamentally religious rather than political," Clinton recited to his Jewish audience in June 1992 a segment of a conversation, which he supposedly once had with his pastor on the latter's death bed, in an emotional tone:

He [the pastor] said to me that someday I would have a chance to run for President, but that if I ever let Israel down, God would never forgive me...I think he is looking at me, and if I am elected President, I will never let Israel down.

Clinton's overall posture on the Middle East was not fundamentally different from that of the previous Democratic candidate, Michael Dukakis, or from that of George Bush, for that matter. Having recognized the importance of the Jewish vote, Bill Clinton recruited staffers and advisors from across the Jewish spectrum. Jewish staff and fund-raising operations as well as get-out-the-vote campaigns were set up in major cities across the United States. A principal goal of his strategy was to switch 10 to 20 percent of the Jewish vote from Bush to himself. In fact, he added 10 percent of the Jewish vote to Dukakis' 70 percent. According to the *New York Times* (January 5, 1993), 80 percent of Jewish voters supported Clinton and 60 percent of Clinton's non-institutional contributions came from Jewish donors. What is novel about Clinton's Middle East policy team is that the semblance of impartiality, which is generally regarded as necessary for the role of honest broker and catalyst for peace, is totally absent. The Washington Institute has succeeded in transforming itself from a peripheral pro-Israel organization to a source of Middle East policy and personnel for the Clinton administration. As the sole "expert" on the Middle East at the White House, Martin Indyk, the former director of the Washington Institute, played a significant role in formulating Clinton's Middle East policy during the campaign. His subsequent appointment, as the key Middle East officer in the National Security Council, placed him strategically for translating some of the center's ideas into policy. At no other time in the past had a lobbyist for Middle East policy been admitted directly into the echelons of policy-making. In February 1995, Indyk was nominated by Clinton for the post of U.S. Ambassador to Israel.

Given the parameters of Middle East policy, defined largely, if not exclusively, by hawks, doves and mainstream Jewish groups, the Clinton approach to the issue was vintage Clinton. It is no secret that the new president sees himself as a consensus builder. That makes him predominantly sensitive to the needs of the organized groups whose approval counts; it goes without saying that Arab-Americans are outside the contest.

Concluding Remarks About the 1992 Elections

Not unlike previous election campaigns, the differences between the two parties' positions on the Middle East in 1992 were subtle. There were no substantive or dramatic differences, either in the content or the meaning of the candidates' statements, or in the tenor of the parties' platforms. Both expressed categorical opposition to an independent Palestinian state, which had been recognized by a vast majority in the UN General Assembly, while they insisted that Iraq abide by UN resolutions. Both acknowledged the right of Soviet and other Jews to leave their countries of origin, travel to Israel and move freely; but while invoking half of the relevant phrase in the Universal Declaration of Human Rights, they left out the other half, which also acknowledges the right of people to *return* to their country of origin. While Clinton reiterated Dukakis' position that Jerusalem is Israel's capital, the Republican platform made a thinly-veiled reference to Israel's right to establish settlements in and around Jerusalem: "Jerusalem should remain an undivided city, with free and unimpeded access to all holy places by people of all faiths. No genuine peace would deny Jews *the right to live anywhere* in the special city of Jerusalem."

Both parties endorsed the Israeli position that negotiations should be direct (i.e. without UN involvement), even after their sudden rediscovery of the United Nations as the natural instrument for the pacific settlement of disputes in the post-cold war period. Their leaders lectured widely and sanctimoniously about the virtues of the United Nations. They preached about the importance of complying with UN resolutions on Iraq but failed to see any need for applying the compliance issue to Israel. On the contrary, Israel was given an exemption, a special waiver. Just as the United States had immunized itself to the judgment of the International Court of Justice in the dispute with Nicaragua, Israel would also be immunized by the Republican party's platform against the need to respect an international settlement: "We do not believe the U.S. should attempt to impose a solution on the parties…. Israel should not be forced to negotiate with any party." Total acquiescence in the Israeli interpretation of Resolutions 242 and 338 was also made by the Republicans. Again the platform stated: "The basis for negotiations are UN Security Council Resolutions 242 and 338…it will be up to the negotiators to determine exactly what is required to satisfy these resolutions."

As if this formulation did not grant Israel sufficient leeway regarding withdrawal of its forces from occupied territories, the next half of the sentence, though meant to be subtle, really represents an unambiguous endorsement of expansionism: "…but we firmly believe Israel has a right to exist in secure and recognized boundaries."

It is interesting to note that the only other Republican candidate, Pat Buchanan, had not only dissented from the Republican party's platform, but was the only presidential hopeful in favor of exerting pressure on Israel to exchange land for peace. He supported the establishment of a Palestinian state, arguing that the *Intifada* had changed his mind:

It was clear to me…that these were people who had reached a level of political maturity, that were willing to stand up to guns and assert their right of peoplehood and nationhood.[38]

Buchanan was in fact the only candidate for whom the U.S. commitment to Israel did not necessarily contradict a similar commitment to the Palestinian people. His campaign headquarters answered questions on this subject by the *Boston Globe* this way:

The U.S. has a moral commitment to guarantee the security and survival of Israel…[but that] there will be no lasting peace in the region until the longing of the Palestinian peole for a homeland is satisfied.[39]

Buchanan was also skeptical about the mounting U.S. aid to Israel:

> At a time when many Americans are losing their homes or having trouble meeting the mortgage or the rent, taxpayers should not be forced to subsidize Israeli settlements 10,000 miles away.[40]

Such a position, expressed by a right wing conservative who felt that even George Bush was not sufficiently conservative for the Republican party, stood in contrast to those of stalwart liberals, such as Paul Tsongas, who said that a Palestinian state would destabilize the region, but for some unexplainable reasons limited self-government would not! It stood in contrast to the positions of Senators Tom Harkin and Bob Kerrey, as well. The other Democratic hopeful, Jerry Brown, did not commit himself to a position on this subject.

The conservative-liberal dichotomy has come to mean very little in the Middle East context. Liberals are not necessarily the champions of the underdog and the downtrodden; not the champions of progressive change and self-actualization, not the champions of fairness and social justice, whatever these slogans really mean. Republicans are not always on the side of military intervention; not always alone in the forefront of the onslaught by the mighty against the underclass. But America's dominant parties share a consensus on the Middle East; the negotiated settlement will not be even-handed, will not be international, will not rock the boat, will not diminish Israeli hegemony, will not empower the Palestinians, will not sacrifice old friends, allies and surrogates, no matter these parties' record on human rights.

The mid-term elections of 1994 have confimed that consensus. The Republican victory was widely considered as worrisome to Israel and to the Jewish community, which gave Democratic candidates 87 percent of the Jewish vote. The *Jerusalem Post* headlined "Earthquake in Washington," while the *Washington Jewish Week* (November 17,1994) reported "Jews Wary of GOP Victories." Such concern was undoubtedly attributed to Republican opposition to foreign aid in general, and more specifically to Senator Jesse Helms' well-publicized opposition to the stationing of U.S. troops on the Golan Heights as part of an Israeli-Syrian settlement. Jesse Helms, a staunchly pro-Israel senator, is the new chair of the Senate Foreign Relations Committee. His remarks, which paralleled the position of the right-wing Likud, were of concern even to Rabin and to the Clinton administration.

Headlines aside, however, the concern about the GOP victory is certainly unwarranted. The new Republican Speaker of the House, Newt Gingrich, was quick to dissociate himself from the Golan stand of his Senate colleague, Jesse Helms. He also went out of his way to assure Rabin, during the Washington visit in November 1994, that Israel's aid will not be affected. Moreover, Israel has more influential friends in the new Congress at almost no cost because most Jewish voters have supported Democratic candidates. The Republican senator Mitch McConnel of Kentucky, who replaced Robert Byrd (D-VA), the outspoken critic of U.S. aid to Israel, as chair of the Foreign Operations Appropriations Subcommittee, has promised to cut foreign aid by 20 percent, but to increase aid to Israel.[41] Representative Benjamin Gilman (R-NY) has replaced Lee Hamilton (D-IN) as chair of the House International Relations Committee (formerly called House Foreign Relations Committee). He has recently dissolved the Middle East and Europe sub-committee in order to maintain his control over Middle East policy in the House. Under the new Republican rule, he would not have been able to chair the subcommittee. Along with Senators Connie Mack (R-FL) and Joseph Lieberman (D-CT), Gilman has urged that the PLO be denied the $500 million in U.S. aid promised by Clinton over a five year period unless it amends the Palestine National covenant and clamps down against all acts of violence against Israel.

In addition to the expanded influence of Israel's supporters in Congress from both parties, most of the incumbent supporters were reelected. Israel's non-partisan image was accentuated by AIPAC's *Near East Report:*

> Many Republican congressional leaders are long-time champions of the U.S.-Israel relationship...and many new members have already laid out strong pro-Israel positions.[42]

The 1994 mid-term elections demonstrated, once again, the uniqueness of Israel as a factor in U.S. domestic politics.

Notes

1. Edward Tivnan, *The Lobby: Jewish Political Power and American Policy* (New York: Simon and Schuster, 1987).

2. Irwin Oder, "American Zionism and the Congressional Resolutions of 1922 on Palestine," *Publications of the American Jewish Historical Society* No. 45 (1955).

3. Quoted in David Schoenbaum, *The United States and the State of Israel* (Oxford: Oxford University Press, 1993), p. 95.

4. Quoted in Mitchell Geoffrey Bard, *The Water's Edge and Beyond* (New Brunswick, N.J.: Transaction Publishers, 1991), p. 125.

5. Bard, *op. cit.*, p. 103.

6. *Ibid.*, pp. 103–104.

7. *New York Times,* April 1, 1976.

8. *New York Times,* April 1, 1976.

9. *Jewish Telegraphic Agency,* October 18, 1976.

10. *New York Times,* April 1, 1976.

11. Jewish *Telegraphic Agency,* October 18, 1976.

12. *New York Times,* April 1, 1976; *U.S. News And World Report,* May 24, 1976.

13. "Carter Moves Cautiously on Anti-Boycott Proposals," *Weekly Report* (Congressional Quarterly) March 12, 1977. p. 437. Quoted in Mitchell Geoffrey Bard, *The Water's Edge And Beyond.* op. cit., p. 102.

14. *Ibid.*

15 Bard, *op. cit.*, p. 37.

16. *New York Times,* February 15, 1978.

17. *Department of State Bulletin,* April 1978, p. 22.

18. *Ibid.*

19. Quoted in Bard, *op. cit.,* p. 42.

20. Much of this section appeared in an article co-authored with John J. Carroll, "Reflections On American Politics and the Middle East" *Mideast Monitor,* Vol. 1, No. 2 (October 1984), a publication of AAUG, Belmont, MA.

21. *Washington Post,* September 23, 1984.

22. Yagil Weinberg, "The Iran-Contra Crisis and Its Impact on U.S.-Israeli Counterterrorism Cooperation," Neil Livingstone and Terrell Arnolds (eds.), *Beyond the Iran-Contra Crisis,* Lexington, Mass., 1988, p. 175.

23. *Boston Globe,* August 22, 1987.

24. Michael S. Dukakis, "The Elements of Our National Security," speech given at Georgetown University

25. "Mike Dukakis, On the Issues: Towards Peace and Security In The Middle East." n.d; see texts of both U.S. parties platforms in *The Journal of Palestine Studies,* Vol. XVIII, No. 1, Autumn 1988, pp. 303-306.

26. *Ibid.*

27. *Ibid.*

28. Michael Dukakis, speech delivered at the B'Nai B'rith International Convention, Baltimore, Maryland, September 7, 1988.

29. *Ibid.*

30. "American Jews Favor Dukakis by Four to One Margin, Poll Finds," *Ohio Jewish Chronicle,* October 27, 1988. p. 1.

31. Eileen Parise, "Evolution of the Dukakis Policy On The Middle East." Term paper Dec. 19, 1989.

32. *Ibid.*

33. "Which Presidential Candidate Shares Our Values," a political advertisement which appeared in several U.S. newspapers.

34. Quoted in *Breaking the Siege,* Newsletter of the Middle East Justice Network, Vol. 4, No 3, August–September, 1992, p. 3.

35. *Ibid.*

36. Text of platform in *Journal of Palestine Studies,.* Vol XXII, No. 1, Autumn, 1992, pp. 166-168.

37. *Near East Report,* July 13, 1992.

38. James Zogby and Peter Tiniko, "Profiles On The Middle East Positions of the 1992 Presidential Candidates," Washington, Arab American Institute, 1992. p. 4.

39. H.D.S. Greenway, "Sounding Out the Candidates on Israel" *Boston Globe,* February 13, 1992.

40. *Ibid.*

41. *Washington Jewish Week,* December 22, 1994.

42. *Near East Report,* November 21, 1994.

12

The Campaign of Delegitimization in Congress

The decision by the Reagan administration to engage in a "substantive dialogue" with the PLO on December 14, 1988, after Arafat's pledge on the same day to "renounce terrorism" and recognize Israel's right to exist, was hailed by optimists and feared by detractors as an important step towards U.S. recognition of the organization. They both saw the no-talk policy, which was instituted by Henry Kissinger on September 1, 1975, as approaching its end. But did that dialogue portend a new relationship of reciprocity and mutual respect? Were the Palestinians about to be removed from the roster of terrorists and added to the roster of honorable parties who endorse the world view espoused by Washington?

The PLO was not lacking in legitimacy; by the time the dialogue decision was made, the number of states that had recognized the PLO and allowed it diplomatic representation was larger than that which recognized Israel. There was hardly a more eloquent testimony to PLO international legitimacy than the U.S General Assembly's decision to interrupt its session in New York and reconvene in Geneva in December, 1988 in order to enable Yasir Arafat to address the assembly, after he was denied an entry visa by the Reagan administration.

And yet, in a world dominated by the U.S., the Reagan administration's decision to talk to the PLO was seen as the *real* sign of legitimacy, despite the fact that the U.S. itself was isolated from the global consensus on the whole question of Palestine. Suddenly, and after a consistent pattern of demonization and relentless marginalization of the PLO by the U.S. government and mainstream media, the potential for PLO credibility inside the U.S. began to appear a bit higher on the horizon.

Rather than giving consideration to the unilateral Palestinian initiative, which was made without any reciprocation from Israel, many of Israel's supporters in Congress embarked on a determined course to undermine the administration's dialogue policy and to perpetuate the delegitimization of the PLO. They endeavored to "nip in the bud" any possible potential for serious political and diplomatic gains for the Palestinians.

1. The PLO and International Organization:
The Politics of Blackmail

By the time the Palestine National Council (the PLO's parliament-in-exile) declared the independent state of Palestine in November 1988 in Algiers, the PLO was already a member of a growing number of international organizations, including some of the UN specialized agencies. The respectability which that affiliation had conferred on the PLO, while Israel was largely considered as a pariah state, was a source of profound concern and anguish for Israel's supporters on Capitol Hill. The administration's decision to start the dialogue had added urgency to their concerns and exacerbated their fury. To arrest any possible momentum for PLO credibility, Representative Tom Lantos (D-CA) together with Christopher Smith (R-NJ) and Larry Smith (D-FL) introduced H.R. 2145 on May 16,1989 prohibiting U.S. contributions to the United Nations or any of its affiliated organizations if full membership was granted to any organization or group that did not have the "internationally recognized attributes of statehood."[1] This bill, which passed the House on May 18, 1989 aimed to prevent the PLO from becoming a member of the World Health Organization (WHO). A similar bill (875) was introduced in the Senate by Senators Robert Kasten (R-WI) and Patrick Leahy (D-VT), along with 25 other sponsors.[2]

Ironically, Representative Lantos, who often speaks on human rights in the Congress, and who later became chair of a human rights sub-committee, saw no contradiction between his professed commitment to human rights and the implied denial of such rights in the bill which he had sponsored. In addition to the political advantage which the WHO membership would bring to the Palestinians, there were tangible health benefits for 1.8 million Palestinians living under Israeli military occupation. Prior to the 1982 Israeli invasion of Lebanon, the PLO operated a healthcare system for one-half million Palestinian refugees, which was the envy of many in the Arab world.[3] Through membership in WHO it could have contributed to alleviating the abject health conditions in the occupied territories where Palestinians are totally outside the Israeli healthcare system.[4]

Not only did this U.S. policy contribute to the denial of healthcare for Palestinians under occupation and in the diaspora, but it also had a negative implication for Palestinian agricultural development and food resources. In November 1989, the U.S. government, prodded by Congress, threatened to cut funds to the United Nations Food and Agricultural Organization (FAO) if the latter cooperated with the PLO in agricultural projects in the occupied West Bank and Gaza. But despite that threat, the FAO voted 96-2 to strengthen its ties with the PLO. The two dissenting votes were cast by Israel and the U.S.

In addition, Congress lobbied to deny the PLO membership in the World Tourism Association (WTA). Representative Tom Lantos (D-CA), whose dedication to and uncritical support for Israel remain among the highest in Congress, deemed the WTA affiliation sufficiently threatening as to warrant adding it to the congressional list of PLO denials.

The endeavor to accelerate PLO de-legitimization was also stepped up by Israel's supporters on Capitol Hill when Representative Barney Frank (D-MA), an avowed liberal and anti-interventionist, gathered twenty-six signatures for a letter dated July 21, 1989 to the Swiss ambassador in Washington, urging his government to deny the PLO request for accession to the 1949 Geneva Convention Relative to the Protection of Civilians in Time of War.[5]

It was ironic that most of the signers, who were members of the House Foreign Affairs Committee and Judiciary Committee, predominantly liberal and civil libertarians, were largely tolerant of Israel's violations of the provisions of the 1949 Geneva Convention, despite Israel's formal accession to the convention. As if the fact of accession in itself was equivalent to actual adherence, the signers wrote:

We believe signatory status to the Geneva Convention is reserved for legitimate states as recognized by international law. The PLO in no way meets this requirement.

Again, ignoring Israel's record of state terrorism against Palestinian and Lebanese civilians, as documented by Israeli and Western human rights organizations, the signers wrote:

> By requesting formal status in the Geneva Conventions, the PLO is blatantly attempting to achieve a political victory to further its political agenda which, despite protestations to the contrary, includes the promotion of terror in the furtherance of its objectives against Israel.

Ignoring the PLO's unilateral recognition of Israel as an important precedent towards reconciliation, at the time that Israel persisted in its refusal to acknowledge its status as occupier under international law, Barney Frank and his colleagues shrugged off the positive side of the PLO recognition act and focused instead on a procedural precedent of no real significance:

> PLO accession would create a dangerous precedent that could make PLO membership in the International Red Cross and other international organizations, reserved for legitimate and responsible members of the international community, more difficult to prevent.

The implications of PLO membership in international organizations became a matter of such concern to the pro-Israel activists in Congress that they resolved to oppose membership by all possible means. Their perseverance was due to an apprehension that such membership was an important step towards Palestinian sovereignty. Senators Patrick Leahy (D-VT) and Robert Kasten (R-WI) initiated a letter signed by 38 senators on April 13, 1989 commending Secretary of State James Baker for his opposition to a Palestinian state.[6] And in June of the same year, another letter initiated by Senators Rudy Boschwitz (R-MN) and Frank Lautenberg (D-NJ), carrying 95 signatures, was sent to Baker urging him to accept the Israeli plan for elections in the occupied territories.[7] That plan, which explicitly ruled out Palestinian statehood and Israeli withdrawal, envisaged limited self-government for the Palestinians, hence the senator's approval:

> It is our conviction that Israel's offer is both sincere and far-reaching.... We must keep in mind that Israel will be asked to give up politically what it won militarily by defending itself against attacks from outside Israeli borders in which thousands of Israelis died.

That was the Shamir Plan, once called by Baker "the only game in town," and to the dismay of Baker, it was later renounced by its own author, as has been previously stated. So much for the plan's "sincerity" and "far-reaching" character. Another sad commentary on congressional foreign policy-making was the fact that 95 out of 100 Senators would attach their signatures to the document, casually arguing that the Israeli occupation was the result of a defensive war. It was no secret that a number of Israeli generals, who fought in that war, have been on record stating that Israel's existence had never been threatened. But after all, manufacturing reality about the Middle East is not a difficult task in the United States.

2. PACs and Lobbies

Members of Congress, by and large, obtain their catechism on the Middle East from the Israeli lobby. That catechism, however, has its own price. The Israeli lobby is well-equipped not only in terms of organizational capabilities, but also in terms of financial resources. AIPAC itself is not a PAC (Political Action Committee), but has developed a network of PACs devoted to funding Pro-Israel candidates. These PACs spent $3,870,052 in direct contributions to the campaigns of 453 candidates for the Senate and the House just prior to the 1988 elections.[8]

The PACs with names that appear to have no connections with the Middle East, such as Hudson Valley PAC, Washington PAC, and Desert Caucus PAC, have officers represented on AIPAC's board of directors, thus making AIPAC informally the umbrella organization for all of them. At the end of the 1990–92 election cycle, 76 active pro-Israel PACs reported collecting $14,015,509 and donated $4,704,051 directly to candidates.[9] During the current election cycle the figures are dramatically lower. Thirty-nine PACs raised only $1.2 million between January 1993 and June 1994. By September 1994, eighty percent of the funds were given to Democratic candidates with an overall total of $1,066,274 distributed to all congressional candidates.[10] According to figures compiled regularly by the *Washington Report on Middle East Affairs*, the pro-Israel activists in Congress were predictably among the top recipients of pro-Israel PAC contributions. For example, in the 1984 elections, Senator Paul Simon, Democratic challenger to Republican Senator Charles Percy, who incurred the wrath of the lobby by his vote on the Reagan administration sale of AWACS to Saudi Arabia and a statement mildly favoring a Palestinian state, topped the Senate list with $235,000. In 1988, Simon was near the top with $104,351. Although Simon received a mere one thousand dollars in 1994, he remains the number one recipient on a cumulative basis with a total of $581,794. He is followed by Senator Frank Lautenberg (D-NJ) with a total of $388,242 including $92,992 during 1994. The overall ranking of the top ten recipients, in descending order, continues as follows:

	Career-Total
Senator Arlen Specter (R-PA)	$351,823
Senator Robert Kasten (R-WI)	$341,249
Rep. Samuel Gejdenson (D-CT)	$237,344
Sen. Jeff Bingaman (D-NM)	$202,675
Rep. Mel Levine (D-CA)	$199,730
Sen. Robert Packwood(R-OR)	$176,850
Sen. J. Robert Verry(D-NE)	$173,500
Rep. Howard Wolpe (D-MI)	$173,175

Other pro-Israel members of Congress, who are not among the cumulative top ten recipients, received generous contributions during earlier years. They include, for example, Carl Levin (D-MI), who totaled $295,083 from the time of his election in 1979 until 1989; Senator Rudy Boschwitz received $207,775, during the same period. Senator Howard Metzenbaum's share of pro-Israel PAC money between 1977 and 1989 was $327,460. Senator Joseph Lieberman (D-CT) ranks number 13 on cumulative basis with a total of $141,508. His share for the current cycle is $76,750, which makes him second to Senator Lautenberg.

By contrast, senators who were inclined to support more even-handed resolutions and who refrained from giving automatic support to the letter-writing campaign, were either opposed to all PAC contributions, on principle, or were the recipients of meager amounts from the pro-Israel PACs. Senators Mark Hatfield (R-OR) and John Chafee (R-RI) received zero sums, while Senator James McClure (R-ID) received a bare $500, and Senator Nancy Kassebaum (R-KS) totaled only $4000.

This pattern was consistent with the situation in the House, except that the amounts allocated for the latter were understandably much less than those for the Senate. The amount of $145,730 for former Representative Lawrence Smith (D-FL), a frequent sponsor of pro-Israel resolutions between 1983 and 1989, for example, is considered a high contribution. Dante Fascell, the Florida Democrat whose influence as Chairman of the House Foreign Affairs Committee was crucial for the Israeli lobby, received $156,500. Other frequent sponsors of resolutions and letter campaigns included Tom Lantos (D-CA), Benjamin Gilman (R-NY) $45,950, Robert Torricelli (D-NJ) $120,500, Edward Feighan (D-OH) $136,950, and Peter Kostmayer (D-PA) $142,750. The top five House recipients of pro-Israel PAC contributions for 1993-1994 are:

	1993–94	Career Total
Newton Gingrich* (R-GA)	$14,500	$ 71,250
Nita Lowey (D-NY)	$10,640	$ 59,540
Peter Deutsch (D-FL)	$10,000	$ 15,000
Samuel Gejdenson** (D-CT)	$9,290	$ 237,344
Charles Wilson (D-TX)	$9,000	$59,550

*As new Speaker of the House, Gingrich has already made his uncritical support for Israel well-known.

**Gejdenson won over his opponent in 1944 by a mere four votes. The political activism of PACs and lobbies is legitimate, and is a recognized aspect of the American political system; yet Arab-Americans tend to be excluded from that participatory function for reasons relating to defects within their community, such as poor organizational skills and financial resources and lack of a real will to develop coherent strategies for political action. Such effective disenfranchisement, however, is not only self-inflicted; it is also promoted by anti-Arab racism, which is manifested in the folklore, movies, books, magazine articles, cartoons, as well as appointments and dismissals of various staffs.[11] Campaign contributions to political candidates from Arab-Americans are often returned after reminders and implicit threats by pro-Israel activists. Altogether, these liabilities were combined to create real barriers between the Arab-American community and Congress.

3. Commitments and Compliance
A. Congress and the U.S.-PLO Dialogue

The steadiness of Israel's supporters on Capitol Hill was further demonstrated by additional efforts to minimize the significance of the U.S.-PLO dialogue, and to prevent it from becoming a substantive factor in the U.S., Middle East policy. Senator Connie Mack (R-FL), the third top recipient of pro-Israel PAC contributions during 1993-94, introduced Senate Resolution 1160 on June 12, 1989, which became known as the PLO Commitments Compliance Act of 1989. Originally introduced as S.763, it was later incorporated as Title VIII, into the Department of State Authorization Bill S.1160, which was later amended to the House version, H.R. 1487. The Act required the president to report to Congress, three times each year, on the extent to which the PLO was complying with its commitments to move towards peace, by monitoring the actions and statements of PLO members.

Given the loose organizational structure of the PLO and the presence within it of varied groups and constituents whose affiliations were more tenuous than real, it would not have been difficult to produce quick indictments. The scarcely-hidden agenda of that legislation was to cast aspersion on the credibility of the PLO in order to disqualify it as a possible negotiating partner at a later stage unless of course it agreed to negotiate a limited self-rule. And yet the legal arsenal against the PLO was already loaded. In addition to Kissinger's Memorandum of Agreement of September 1, 1975, there was also the International Security and Development Cooperation Act of 1985 which stipulated: "No officer or employee of the United States government and no agent or other individual acting on behalf of the United States government, shall negotiate with the PLO or any representative thereof unless...."

There were also official statements by Reagan and Shultz which had already reinforced the ban. For example, the State Department issued a statement on November 26, 1988 saying that "the United States has convincing evidence that PLO elements have engaged in terrorism against Americans and others."[12] And subsequent to the dialogue, President Reagan warned that "the PLO must demonstrate that its renunciation of terrorism is pervasive and permanent," and threatened to "break off communications" if the PLO reneged on its commitments.

In addition to all this, the PLO Commitments Compliance Act of 1989 introduced a list of demands from the PLO, which were so humiliating as to make it impossible for the PLO—irrespective of whether it complied or not—to gain any measure of respectability, not only in the U.S. but also among its own constituents. Hardly any self-respecting Palestinian would continue to view the PLO as the sole legitimate representative of the Palestinian people and the embodiment of Palestinian nationalism if the PLO were to comply fully. The requirements, in themselves, were tantamount to a finding that the PLO was an instrument of terror, and not a vehicle for legal and moral redress and for national restitution. Consider a sample of the long list of requirements:

1. Disbanding units which have been involved in terrorism.
2. Ceasing the intimidation of Palestinians who advocate a cessation of or who do not support the unrest.
3. Calling on the Arab states to recognize Israel and to end their economic boycott of Israel.
4. Amend the PLO covenant to remove provisions which undermine Israel's legitimacy, and which call for Israel's destruction.

The PLO Commitments Compliance Act required the president to report to Congress, every 120 days, a detailed description of acts and statements which constitute hostile declarations and/or acts, or that can be considered as positive step by the PLO towards compliance. These requirements undermined the *raison d'etre* of the organization, if not threatened its very existence and the cause it represents. Among the information sought by the congressional activists in the president's report are such things as whether Arafat's "Force 17" had been "disbanded and reconstituted under different names." Also requested was information relating to possible PLO intimidation of collaborators in the occupied territories. The euphemism for collaborators is Palestinians "who advocate a cessation of or who do not support the unrest," i.e., the *Intifada.*

The law also requested information on whether the PLO intended to extradite certain alleged terrorists and to compensate American families who are victims of alleged PLO terrorism. The law put the onus on the PLO to persuade Arab governments to end the economic boycott of Israel, to publicly recognize Israel and to end all their efforts to expel Israel from international organizations.

The most astonishing aspect of this act was its grotesque lack of proportionality and gross imbalance. In return for the privilege of having a low-level dialogue with the United States, whose primary purpose was to allow the U.S. a forum from which to lecture the PLO on terrorism, the PLO was expected not only to acknowledge that it is a terrorist organization, but also to embark on a remedial and rehabilitative course, prescribed by the United States through the dialogue.

From Israel's vantage point, the dialogue did not constitute a serious threat; in fact, Rabin was quoted as having told a delegation of Peace Now leaders that is was a delaying tactic to buy Israel time to crush the *Intifada*, both militarily and economically.[13]

Following disclosure that U.S. Ambassador to Tunisia Robert Pelletreau had met with the number two man in the PLO, the late Salah Khalaf, legislation was proposed in Congress ostensibly aimed at limiting the U.S.-PLO dialogue. The language, in that legislation was bound to eliminate any possibility of continuing the talks. Senators Jesse Helms (R-NC) and Charles Grassley (R-IA), supported by 23 other senators, attached a proposed amendment to the State

Department Authorization Bill on April 7, 1989 forbidding discussion with any PLO member unless the president certified that the member had not participated in any way in any terrorist operations against Americans.[14] Moreover, the sponsors of the proposed amendment tried to derail the dialogue by linking the PLO directly to nine "terrorist acts" allegedly taking place between December 26, 1988 and March 15, 1989. President Bush reacted to this proposed amendment by saying that it "would interfere significantly with, if not destroy, the ability of the United States to promote a viable peace process in the Middle East."[15] Although this amendment, coupled with similar action in the House proposed by Representative Chuck Douglas (R-NH) failed to find wide support in the Congress, it nevertheless reflected the determination of the pro-Israel lobby to render the dialogue superfluous and to prevent any possible transformation in the PLO image in the U.S. While the Helms-Grassley amendment was eventually defeated, a "compromise" amendment, proposed by Senators Dole and Mitchell, accomplished the same objective by stipulating that the PLO members prevented from participating in the dialogue were "known" to have committed terrorist acts.

Meanwhile, in the House of Representatives, Edward Feighan (D-OH) and Mel Levine (D-CA) introduced H.R. 3005 containing language similar to the Helms amendment:[16]

(1) No funds made available by any Act or joint resolution may be made available for the conduct of negotiations or dialogue with any representative of the Palestine Liberation Organization unless the president certifies to the committees specified in paragraph (2) that he has determined that, based on all available United States government intelligence information, the representative did not directly participate in the planning or execution of a terrorist activity which resulted in the death, injury, or kidnapping of a United States citizen.

(2) The certification required by paragraph (1) shall be submitted to the Committee on Foreign Affairs and the Permanent Select Committee on Intelligence of the House of Representatives and the Committee on Foreign Relations and the Select Committee on Intelligence of the Senate.

These identical resolutions demanded that the administration obtain a full accounting from the PLO on the nine incidents in the event of any further talks with the PLO. When a rogue operation by the Arab Liberation Front, a fringe group led by Abu Al-Abbas took place on May 30, 1990 on the Israeli coast, the opportunity had finally arrived for the anti-dialogue lobby. The abortive raid provided them with much needed ammunition. Senator Frank Lautenberg (R-NJ) initiated a letter to James Baker dated June 1, 1990, which was signed by 44 senators, saying that "the U.S. must be firm in insisting that Yasir Arafat renounce terrorism and publicly denounce those who continue to commit terrorist acts."[17] On June 7th, 1990, Senate Concurrent Resolution 138 requested that the U.S. suspend its dialogue with the PLO until the PLO condemns the raid of May 30, 1990 and expels Abu Al-Abbas from its executive committee.[18]

In that regard, it is important to recall that the May 30th raid on the Israeli coast came in the wake of the May 20, 1990 massacre at Rishon Le zion, when an Israeli soldier, Ami Popper, went on a shooting rampage killing seven Palestinian workers at the "slave market." That was followed by a U.S. veto of a UN Security Council resolution, which called for the dispatch of a UN investigative team to the occupied territories to prepare a report by the following week to the council. That resolution had been supported by 14 council members, leaving the U.S. as the sole dissenter. The despair following this demonstration that Israel was still firmly in Israel's camp was the context for the Abu Al-Abbas raid.

Although Arafat condemned the raid, he found it politically unfeasible to expel Abu Al-Abbas, and he consequently lost his dialogue with the United States. The anti-dialogue lobby in the Congress undoubtedly felt vindicated. Their relentless efforts to suspend the dialogue finally succeeded, ironically, with the help of an undisciplined, yet peripheral Palestinian leader.

Similar actions were taken in the House. Representative Mel Levine (D-CA) initiated a letter to Baker with ten signers, which was followed by a second letter initiated by James Saxton (R-NJ) with 29 signatures. House Resolution 4995 was also initiated by Lawrence Smith (D-FL) on June 7, 1990, with 36 co-sponsors requesting the administration to "declare that further negotiations between the United States and the Palestine Liberation Organization are prohibited by section 1302 of Public Law 99-83 because the Palestine Liberation Organization has failed to adhere to its renunciation of the use of terrorism."

The congressional campaign to demonize the PLO and halt any momentum for a change in U.S. policy toward the Palestine question also included attempts to deny Yasir Arafat a visa to attend the UN session on Palestine. Congressional letters to the Secretary of State were initiated in both the House and the Senate. A Senate letter dated September 21, 1989 and circulated by Connie Mack (D-FL), Pete Wilson (R-CA), Carl Levin (D-MI) and Joseph Lieberman (D-CT) was signed by 68 senators (34 Democrats and 34 Republicans).[19] The letter accused the PLO and Arafat of "condoning terrorism," "terrorizing Palestinians," "opposing dialogue," and introducing resolutions calling for escalation of the armed struggle. It opposed any steps by the U.S. "that could be seen as generally rewarding the PLO," including the reversal of "current policy of denying a visa for Arafat …or elevating the PLO dialogue to higher levels." A similar letter was circulated in the House by James Saxton(R-NJ) and others.

B. Congress And Palestinian Education

While all this campaigning was going on in the Congress to undermine the Palestinian cause, a number of senators and representatives introduced amendments to the State Department Authorization Bill, putting Congress on record as opposing Israel's policy of denying education to Palestinian children. The closure of Palestinian schools and universities by the Israeli occupation authorities was a standard punishment during the 1980s.[20] There were concerns that an entire generation of Palestinians would be severely harmed by such a policy. While anti-Palestinian moves seemed to be reaching a new height in the late 1980s, Representative Howard Nielson (R-UT) circulated a letter on May 17, 1989 to his colleagues soliciting co-sponsors for a concurrent resolution.[21] He stated in the letter that "the school closures have created an entire generation of 8 year-old illiterates and have dealt a severe blow to the Palestinians who pride themselves on being the most educated group in the Arab world." He added, "As we prepare to vote on a new $3 billion aid package to Israel in the coming weeks, it is time to let Israel know that Americans value the right of all people to an education and that we believe reestablishing a more normal educational environment" on the West Bank would be an important step toward creating a climate which is more conducive to achieving peace in the region.

Nielson then introduced Concurrent House Resolution 124 urging Israel to "reopen schools in the West Bank."[24] The resolution stated that all 1194 schools and kindergartens were closed on January 20, 1989 "until further notice" and all universities were closed "for over one year" affecting 300,000 pupils and 18,000 university students "or roughly 40 percent of the population of the West Bank." It further stated that the "denial of instruction…leaves serious gaps in their cognitive development which is very difficult to correct at a later stage." It reminded Israel of its obligation under Articles 50 and 33 of the Geneva Convention to facilitate education and to refrain from collective punishment.

Shortly before the Nielson resolution could be put forward as an amendment to the House Foreign Operations Appropriations Bill, Israel announced the reopening of schools, undoubtedly at the behest of its supporters in Congress. That cleared the way for the latter to introduce a compromise amendment commending Israel for its decision; but Congress was on record as opposing the denial of the right of education of occupied people as a violation of the 1949 Geneva Convention.

A similar amendment was introduced in the Senate on May 18 , 1989 by Senators John Chafee (R-RI), Nancy Kassebaum (R-KA) and Mark Hatfield (R-OR) as part of the State Department Authorization Bill. [23] The *Washington Jewish Weekly* (August 4, 1989) described the outcome as "one of Israel's biggest human rights beatings on the Senate floor this year."

C. Accelerated Commitments and More Compliance, 1991–1994

After the Gulf War was over, and following an address to Congress by President Bush on March 6, 1991, in which he called for an exchange of land for peace and pledged to "close the gap between Israel and the Arab states...and between Israel and the Palestinians," a few voices were raised in Congress echoing the president's initiative.[24] Representative David Obey (D-WI) had already been on record a month earlier (February 6) calling for an explicit Arab recognition of Israel and a "recognition of the right and necessity of the Palestinian people to have their own homeland on a major portion of the land that constitutes the West Bank and Gaza..."[25] The day after President Bush gave his speech to Congress, Congressman David Bonior (D-MI) introduced House Concurrent Resolution 93 calling for the creation of a Palestinian homeland, to be achieved through a negotiated settlement between Israel and its neighbors, including the Palestinians."[26]

No one, however, was ready to lift the ban on the PLO. In fact the ongoing campaign of PLO delegitimization was stepped up with yet new congressional requirements from the administration. After Representative Nita Lowey (D-NY) introduced a provision to the State Department Authorization Bill in May 1991, which required the State Department to report every 180 days to Congress on the "progress which the Arab states have made towards recognizing Israel," Congressman Mel Levine (D-CA) attempted to add another provision to the bill prohibiting U.S.-PLO contacts, unless the PLO amended its national covenant to reflect recognition of "Israel's right to exist."[27] The final draft, however, requested the State Department to report every 120 days on a variety of issues including whether the PLO "threatens through violence or other intimidation Palestinians in the West Bank and Gaza" who favor bringing the uprising (*Intifada*) to an end.

Following the White House signing of the Oslo Accord on September 13, 1993, it became clear that the ban on the PLO made very limited sense, now that the chairman of the PLO himself appeared at the White House and had several meetings with the congressional leadership. Moreover, with the signing of Oslo, Arafat had effectively transformed the very nature and character of the PLO. Having renounced violence for the umpteenth time, recognized Israel's right to exist, and agreed to negotiate a limited autonomy for Palestinians in the West Bank and

Gaza, Arafat had, in effect, removed the objectionable features of the PLO and made it less unacceptable to Israel and to its U.S. congressional supporters. No longer standing for national restitution based on UN resolutions, and no longer claiming the right of national resistance to achieve redress, the threatening features of the PLO which had caused the ban in the first place were effectively relinquished. Accordingly, the peace accords made the PLO an agent of the Israeli occupation authorities, having agreed to police the semi-autonomous enclaves on Israel's behalf. Meanwhile, Rabin's government made it clear that failure to do so to Israel's satisfaction would deny the Palestinians further extension of the so-called self-governance in the rest of the West Bank and would deny election and development funds pledged by international donors.

And yet, the pro-Israel congressional activists had seen to it that the sweeping concessions by Yasir Arafat, which have diminished the PLO, reducing it to the status of an executor for Israel, were worthy of a mere temporary waiver of the anti-PLO legislation. This was incorporated into the Middle East Peace Facilitation Act in October 1993, which was adopted hurriedly by voice vote after almost no debate.[28] Accordingly, an enfeebled PLO was allowed to re-open an office and collect money from U.S.-funded NGOs (non-governmental organizations). But the list of requirements was at least as humiliating as the pre-Oslo encumbrances. The PLO, which was not recognized by the U.S. as the legitimate representative of the Palestinian people, was required to adhere to its commitments to recognize Israel, to renounce and refrain from terrorism, to "control" all PLO factions and abide by the Declaration of Principles. In return, U.S. legislators agreed to waive the ban for six months, until January 1, 1994, and later extended it until July 1, 1994, in order to have more time for scrutiny and reassessment. The waiver itself was made contingent on the fact that it must serve the "national interest," a requirement designed to give Congress leverage, since the onus of demonstrating that fell on the president.

Meanwhile a Senate Peace Accord Monitoring Group (PAM) was formed in June 1994 to monitor PLO compliance with the DOP and the Cairo and Paris Agreements of May 1994. The membership of this body makes a Who's Who list in the Zionists congressional establishment. Senators Arlen Specter (R-PA), and Richard Shelby (D-AL) plus thirteen others, including Jesse Helms (R-NC), Paul Simon (D-IL), Larry Pressler (R-SD), Connie Mack (R-FL), Frank Lautenberg (D-NJ), Joseph Lieberman (D-CT), David Durenberger (R-MN), Alfonse D'Amato (R-NY), Daniel Inouye (D-HI), Richard Bryan (D-NV), and Harry Reid (D-NV). A similar panel was established in the House under the leadership of Representatives Elliot Engel (D-NY) and James Saxton (R-NJ).

It should be noted that some of these congressional watchdogs for Israel have recently acquired additional political prominence as a result of the Republican party's victory in the 1994 mid-term election. In January 1995, Senator Jesse Helms became chair of the Senate Foreign Relations Committee, and Senator D'Amato became chair of the Banking, Housing and Urban Affairs Committee. Representative Benjamin Gilman of New York, an ardent Zionist, replaced Lee Hamilton of Indiana as chair of the House Foreign Affairs Committee, renamed International Relations Committee, as noted in the previous chapter.

Both groups went to work almost immediately keeping up the pressure on the already crippled PLO, demanding more concessions. Senators Mack and Lieberman, the authors of the PLO Commitments Compliance Act, wrote Secretary of State Warren Christopher on June 9, 1994 denouncing the State Department report which, as required by law, gave Congress an overview of PLO activity since January 1994.[29] They said that "the report does not clearly describe standards for adherence." The report was also faulted because of the distinction it made between Arafat's condemnation of terrorist acts he can control and those beyond his control. The letter argued that such a distinction could condone "a 'division of labor' between the PLO and rejectionist groups—in which the PLO negotiates while acquiescing in terrorism and the rejectionists terrorize while acquiescing in negotiations." The commitment to Rabin by Arafat upon signing the DOP must be kept, they warned.

The House monitors also initiated a denunciatory letter to Warren Christopher, authored by Representatives Engel and Saxton, the leaders of the group, joined by Benjamin Gilman (R-NY) and Howard Berman

(D-CA).[30] According to them, the State Department's report failed to systematically address the PLO's commitments, and to censure Arafat's "inadequate response to terrorism." They argued that even when he condemned acts of terrorism, "the extremely mild language used by the PLO...is in itself an indictment of the PLO's weak condemnation of terrorism." The congressional watchdogs argued that the U.S. was not holding the PLO to a "sufficient standard of compliance," and that Arafat should be made to give "swift and unequivocal responses to all acts of terror."

While the State Department's response to the congressional critics had expectedly upheld its own report as containing a "complete and objective discussion" of terrorism and PLO compliance, it conceded that PLO responsibility "goes beyond issuing statements."[31] But at the same time, it cited the PLO crackdown on Hamas activists as well as Palestinian police cooperation with the Israeli authorities as evidence that the PLO is trying to "contain acts of violence and terrorism." The overzealous nature of the letter by the congressional Zionist activists did not go unnoticed by the State Department. In the latter's response, there was a subtle hint that the letter signers might have tried to "out-Israel" the Israeli government: "We agree with the Israeli assessment that it is unrealistic to hold the PLO responsible for the actions of rejectionist groups, whose sole aim is to derail the peace process."

In fact, the monitors were soon to find themselves at odds with the pro-Israel lobby, AIPAC, the Israeli embassy and President Clinton, all of whom had acted consistently in support of Israel's interest. The monitor group (PAM) had already demonstrated its clout when in mid-July 1994, a House-Senate Conference Committee adopted an anti-PLO amendment to the 1995 foreign aid bill, originally sponsored by Senators Arlen Specter (R-PA) and Richard Shelby (R-AL). The amendment to FY95 Foreign Operations Appropriations Bill, which passed the Senate on August 10, 1994 by a vote of 88-12, over the objections of AIPAC and the lack of support by the Israeli embassy, has placed tangible limits on the president's authority to conduct his Middle East policy.[32] It prohibited the executive branch from giving any amount of the promised $80 million to the Palestinian Authority until the PLO "amends the sections of its covenant calling for the destruction of the State of Israel; changes that Yasir Arafat is obliged to make, according to the Israel-PLO accords."

This amendment altered the initial legislation, which had required Arafat to *submit* the covenant matter to the Palestine National Council, which hadn't convened since the Madrid conference in 1991 and was unlikely to convene, due to widespread opposition by Palestinian leaders and to Arafat's own fear that the council might abrogate his entire project. The amendment was, therefore, seen as having placed Arafat in the impossible position of securing the nullification of the relevant articles in the Palestinian covenant. On the other hand, it was also seen as having eliminated a waiver in the appropriations bill that would have allowed the president a needed flexibility on the issue of PLO compliance. It is not certain whether such flexibility was enhanced by the modification of the language, prior to voting, which states that the Senate "expects" the PLO covenant to be amended.

Meanwhile, the Specter-Shelby amendment was deemed inappropriate by the Appropriations Subcommittee chairs, Rep. David Obey (D-WI) and Senator Patrick Leahy (D-VT). In their view, it was an infringement of the president's authority to conduct foreign policy. It would tie his hands and prevent him from waiving the PLO's compliance with the accords in the name of the "national interest."[33] Because of the amendments, funding for the PLO is now dependent on Congress' view (i.e., that of the pro-Israel Peace Accord Monitoring Group) of PLO compliance which emphasizes progress towards amending the Covenant. By 1995, funding became almost totally at the mercy of Representative Gilman and Senator Mack.

4. Congress and the Rift Within the Pro-Israel Lobby

The shift in the dynamics of the Arab-Israeli conflict inside the U.S. domestic political arena can be illustrated by the fact that Senator Leahy, a staunch advocate of pro-Israel policies, supported Bill Clinton, the most pro-Israel president in history, against the congressional Zionist establishment, which itself seems to be somewhat at odds with the mainstream lobby, AIPAC and with Rabin's government.

However one looks at the passage of the amendment to FY95 foreign aid bill, the episode represents a landmark case in which the right-wing sector of the U.S. pro-Israel lobby decided to assert itself in Congress and to directly compete with the recognized mainstream within that lobby for the attention of Congress. In fact, the outcome of the controversy, surrounding aid to the Palestinian Authority (PA) and the compliance requirements, revealed that Congress responded to the right-wing Zionists and to their in-house instrument, PAM, rather than to the mainstream lobby.

The division within the active American Jewish community as it affects congressional policy is between the mainstream, which supports Rabin's policies and the right-wing, which favors the Likud. While AIPAC made its peace with Rabin and his Labor party upon their victory in June 1992 elections, a good number of the constituent organizations, which make up the Presidents of the Major American Jewish Organizations, continued to support the Likud program.

Labor's conception of an Israeli-Palestinian settlement, supported by the Clinton administration and AIPAC, envisions a peace treaty with Jordan, defining political and military borders between the two states. The Palestinians would be accorded limited autonomy in West Bank enclaves and in Gaza, with overall security and control of the borders in Israeli hands. The Likud conception differs from this functional autonomy scheme only with regard to the size and location of the Palestinian "cantons," but not in the essence. Hence, Labor's historical concern with ethnic purity would lead to the establishment of Palestinian cantons in areas heavily populated by Palestinians, while Likud would be less deterred by geographic and demographic limitations. For them, a certain level of population mixtures would be acceptable, providing the Palestinians are held in a permanent status of legal and political subordination, as in apartheid systems.

AIPAC and its current pro-Labor president, Steve Grossman, who used to chair the Massachusetts Democratic party Committee, have a vested interest in the success of the Oslo process, as do Rabin and Clinton, which explains why all of them support maximum flexibility in granting waivers to the PLO. Such waivers would open the door to U.S. public funds needed to stabilize the situation in Gaza. The PA has become a U.S.-Israeli investment, whose survival is crucial for the success of the "peace process" and Clinton's Mideast policy.

Reacting to the PAM amendment, which was spearheaded by Senators Shelby and Specter, an Israeli Embassy official echoed AIPAC's concerns about the legislative restrictions on the meaning of compliance. The statement welcomed "any steps that would help the Palestinian Authority comply with their commitments, but we need to balance this concern with the need for the Palestinian Authority to get funds."[34]

And yet, AIPAC published a detailed report on PLO compliance in order not to be accused of being soft on the PLO.[35] Quoting extensively from Rabin, Peres, and the Israeli security establishment, the report concludes that Arafat can do more to stop the violence. And while it faults him for not living up to his commitments, it nevertheless cites statistics showing mixed results regarding the level of violence in the PA-controlled zones before and after the peace accords. Although the statistics quoted in the report fail to reveal a clear pattern, some of them, particularly those generated by the IDF chief of staff and the Shin Bet (whose U.S. equivalent is the FBI), show a decline in the number of "violent incidents" since the PA assumed control in Gaza.[36] Regarding the PLO Covenant, AIPAC's special report states that "despite Arafat's repeated commitments to convene the PNC and alter the Covenant...leading members of both Fatah and the PNC have ruled out an early session...no date has been announced as yet."[37] No further demands are made by AIPAC on Arafat to do what seems at the time as impossible. This attitude stands in sharp contrast to that of the right-wing sector of the lobby and the PAM members of the Congress, who made the change of the covenant a pre-condition for releasing funds to the PA, effectively barring a presidential waiver of compliance in the "national interest."

The right-wing Zionists, on the other hand, with the Zionist Organization of America (ZOA) in the lead, are opposed to granting the Palestinians any measure of autonomy and they view that as the ultimate result of the PLO-Israel accords. ZOA chair, Morton Klein, who has emerged as a spokesman for the extreme right-wing, led the effort in Congress, which produced the controversial amendment to the FY95 Appropriations Bill. Not only did the PAM group endorse his position, but PAM was also able to carry the Congress, to the chagrin of the White House and AIPAC. Klein described the Senate passage of the amendment thus:

> [It] is an important step that will insure that U.S. aid is not given to the PLO until the PLO stops its numerous violations of the Israel-PLO peace accords...the PLO must prove that it has sincerely transformed itself from a terrorist group, before it receives hard-earned American tax-payers' dollars.[38]

Klein's role in the passage of the amendment was recognized by a number of senators. In addition, the *Congressional Quarterly* cited "the significant role of the ZOA" in facilitating passage, which is bound to prolong the pariah status of the PLO in the U.S. political arena.[39]

Now that mainstream Zionists have secured sensitive positions throughout the Executive branch, and right-wing Zionists have acquired major influence in congressional deliberations of Middle East policy, all the requirements of fairness and balance seem to have been set aside. In their campaign to keep the PLO discredited, despite the White House lawn handshake, the extra-legislative watchdog continues to use the terrorist label with monotonous regularity. PAM members in the Congress frequently contrast what they describe as PA reticence in the face of terrorism against Israelis with the "firm" and "principled" Israeli response to the Hebron massacre, which they refer to as the "Hebron Killing." In their view, a double standard separates Israeli and Palestinian society with regard to the perception of terrorism and the need to condemn it. Absent from their consciousness is the fact that settler terrorism against innocent Palestinian civilians, as well as state terrorism by the Israeli army and so-called security forces,are not only condoned by the U.S. government, but also financed by tax-payer dollars. The Brooklyn-born army reservist, Baruch Goldstein, who carried out the "Hebron Killings," and many of his compatriots and accomplices, former constituents of the same congressmen and senators leading the PAM campaigns, are even allowed to carry a dual citizenship.

Not only are the killings by these government-armed settlers reprehensible, but their existence in the occupied West Bank is illegal by virtue of the 1949 Geneva Convention, which the U.S. government, as signatory, is required to enforce. In fact, a special burden for enforcement falls on the U.S. government, because some of the funds, which PAM members and other U.S. legislators vote for Israel year after year, eventually find their way to the illegal Jewish settlements, and contribute to settler terrorism, and hence to the retardation of real peace.

PAM's scarcely-hidden agenda, of course, is to deter the already battered diplomatic efforts to achieve a settlement on the basis of the Labor program. By giving Congress the effective power to determine PLO "compliance" within the meaning of U.S. law, they made it impossible for the PLO to ever comply, without risking a Palestinian civil war.

It remains to be seen whether Arafat's first armed assault on the Islamic opposition in Gaza on November 18, 1994 would constitute sufficient compliance. That bloody incident, the likes of which has not been seen since the early days of the *Intifada*, has firmly established Arafat in the minds of most Palestinians as Israel's collaborator and executioner. Having killed at least 17 Palestinians and injured more than 200 during a demonstration in Gaza City, Arafat's police and intelligence agents might have enabled him to argue that he is not soft on Hamas and that he is able and willing to "keep order". Whether that would meet the compliance requirements of the ZOA and the U.S. congressional monitors (PAM) remains an open question. The State Department, however, appeared somewhat satisfied. In a report to Congress dated December 2, 1994, it stated that the attack by Arafat's police "may auger a more determined effort by the PLO to prevent violent challenges to the peace process.."[40]

Notes

1. *Israel And Palestine: A Congressional Report Card, 1989–1990.* Cambridge, Mass.,: The Middle East Justice Network, 1990. p. 7.

2. *Ibid.* p. 3.

3. Cheryl Rubenberg, *The Palestine Liberation Organization: Its Institutional Infrastructure,* Belmont, Mass., Institute for Arab Studies, 1983.

4. United Nations, *Life of the Palestinians Under Israeli Occupation,* New

York, UN Department of Public Information, 1992; also, Naseer Aruri (ed.) *Occupation: Israel Over Palestine* (2nd edition), Belmont, Mass., AAUG Press, 1989, pp. 413-428; also, "Health and Medical Care in the Occupied Territories," Washington, Center for Policy and Analysis on Palestine. 1991.

5. Letter to the Honorable Edouard Brunner from Rep. Barney Frank, et al., July 21, 1989.

6. *Israel And Palestine: A Congressional Report Card. op. cit.* p. 3.

7. *Ibid.*

8. *Ibid.*, p. 2. For a discussion of the PACs role, see Richard Curtiss, *Stealth PACs: How Israel's American Lobby Took Control of U.S. Middle East Policy,* Washington, D.C., The American Educational Trust, 1990.

9. All figures for 1994 are from *The Washington Report on Middle East Affairs,* September/October, 1994, pp. 30–34.

10. *Ibid.* p. 30; see also *Breaking the Siege,* newsletter of the Middle East Justice Network, Vol 6, No. 5, December 1994-January 1995, p.7.

11. See for example, Jack Shaheen, *The T.V. Arab,* Bowling Green, Ohio, Bowling Green State University Press, 1984.

12. *New York Times,* November 27, 1988.

13. *Yediot Aharonot,* Feb. 24, 1989.

14. Senate Resolution 97, 101st Congress, 1st Session, April 7, 1989.

15. Quoted in *Israel and Palestine, op. cit.,* p. 3.

16. House Resolution 3005, 101st Congress, 1st Session, July 25, 1989.

17. *Israel and Palestine.* op.cit.; see Baker's Testimony before the House Foreign Affairs Committee, June 13, 1990 in *Journal of Palestine Studies,* Vol. XX, No. 1, Autumn, 1990, pp. 184-186.

18. See transcript of President Bush's news conference on the suspension of the dialogue in Huntsville, Alabama, June 20, 1990 in *Ibid,* pp.186-190.

19. Letter to the Honorable James A. Baker from Senator Connie Mack, et al., September 21, 1989.

20. Naseer Aruri, *Occupation Israel Over Palestine,* op. cit., pp. 491-563; see also Sarah Graham-Brown, *Education, Repression, Liberation: Palestinians,* U.K., World University Service, 1984.

21. "Dear Colleague," letter signed by Howard Nielson, May 17, 1989.

22. "Congress and the Palestinians," Issue Briefs by the National Association of Arab-Americans, Washington, D.C., October 1989.

23. *Ibid.*

24. Text of the speech in Journal of Palestine Studies, Vol XX, No. 4, Summer 1991, pp. 180-181.

25. Quoted in *Breaking The Siege*, Vol 3, No 1, April-May 1991.

26. *Ibid.*

27. *Breaking The Siege*, Vol. 3, No. 2, June-July 1991, p.7.

28. *Ibid.*, Vol 5, No. 5, December 1993-January 1994, p.6.

29. *Near East Report*, June 20, 1994, p. 11.

30. *Near East Report*, June 20, 1994.

31. *Near East Report*, July 18, 1994, p. 127.

32. *Washington Jewish Week*, August 4, 1994.

33. *Ibid.*

34. *Jewish Bulletin* (San Francisco) July 15, 1994, quoted in Jeffrey Blankfort, "Fight Over Palestinian Funding Proves Congress More Interested in Pleasing Right Wing Zionists Than AIPAC or Israel." *Middle East Labor Bulletin*, Vol. 5, No.1, Fall, 1994, p. 17.

35. Problems In the PLO's compliance With Its Commitments, Special AIPAC Report," *Near East Report*, Vol. XXXVIII, No. 39, September 26, 1994, pp. 172-174.

36. *Ibid.*, p. 173.

37. *Ibid.*, p. 174.

38. *Jewish Press*, August 5, 1994, quoted in Blankfort, *op. cit.*

39. *Ibid.* p. 18; also Sidney Blumenthal, "The Western Front", *The New Yorker*, June 5, 1995, pp. 36-42.

40. Quoted in the *New York Times*, December 3, 1994.

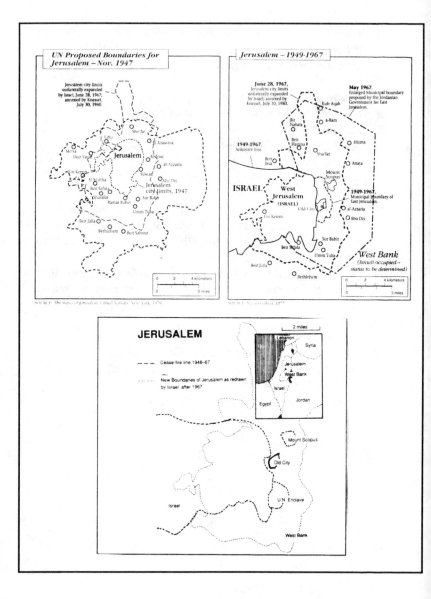

13

Jerusalem and a Changing American Policy

The Annexation of Jerusalem

Defying UN resolutions on Jerusalem and the entire Palestine question, the Israeli Knesset adopted three legislative acts on June 27 and 28, 1967, extending Israeli law to the occupied eastern sector of the city and enlarging the municipal boundaries of "united" Jerusalem.[1] On July 4, 1967, the UN General Assembly adopted Resolution 2253, calling upon Israel to "rescind all measures already taken [and] to desist forthwith from taking any action which would alter the status of Jerusalem."[2] The Security Council also adopted Resolution 252 in 1968 declaring the measures taken by Israel to change the status of Jerusalem as invalid. As far as the United Nations was concerned, the legal status of Jerusalem was the one governed by General Assembly Resolution 181-II of November 29, 1947, which called for the partition of Palestine into a Jewish state and an Arab state, and for the establishment of the City of Jerusalem "as a *corpus separatum* under a special international regime [which] shall be administered by the United Nations."[3] This resolution continues to constitute international legality with regard to the city, and no subsequent resolution was ever adopted altering that status. In fact, the international status of Jerusalem was reconfirmed in General Assembly Resolution 194-III of December 11, 1948. And yet Israel had committed unilateral acts which illegally altered that status. Prior to the extension of Israeli law to the occupied Arab sector, the Knesset had proclaimed the city as Israel's capital on January 23, 1950, and made the annexation official on July 30, 1980. In doing so, Israel was ignoring Security Council Resolution 242 of 1967, which called on Israel to withdraw to the lines of June 4, 1967.

The Israeli argument, however, has been based on the denial of the existence of the Palestinian people and the assertion that no other state can produce a legal claim to Palestine equal to that of Israel.[4] Israeli jurists pressed the argument that the Jordanian occupation of the city in 1948 was an act of aggression, hence illegal; and that by accepting the "illegal" act, the Palestinians relinquished their right to establish a Palestinian state under UN General Assembly Resolution 181-II. Moreover, they maintain that Jordan "again" committed aggression in June 1967 and lost Jerusalem, which had been accorded a special status under resolution 181-II. That resolution, therefore, was "overtaken by events."[5] This polemical thesis is at the core of the continuing colonization of the occupied territories, including Jerusalem, because Israel does not view them as occupied. It was the basis for the Israeli measures which altered the status of Jerusalem, and which themselves were the prelude to the de facto annexation of the West Bank. On December 17, 1967, for example, Israel dropped the term "West Bank" from official usage and adopted the biblical name "Judea and Samaria." To reconfirm that change, Israel introduced another measure on February 19, 1968, according to which the occupied territory was no longer referred to as "enemy territory."[6] These measures exemplify Israel's ability and willingness to manipulate the law in pursuit of strategic political objectives. They also reflect its tenacity in defying the world community and international public opinion. Gradually but persistently, Israel was able, over a period of quarter of a century, to sway the U.S. position towards its own.

Jerusalem in the U.S. Political Arena

Ever since Israel annexed Jerusalem and enlarged its boundaries, nineteen days after its occupation, the status of the occupied territories, including Jerusalem, became a matter of major controversy. It gains attention at least once every four years, when the matter is elevated to a U.S. campaign issue and inevitably picked up by presidential aspirants. Massachusetts Governor Michael Dukakis and President Bill Clinton were the most recent in a line of succeeding politicians to do Israel's bidding on Jerusalem. But although the Clinton administration has effectively acquiesced on the Israeli issue, it has not yet formally recognized Israel's annexation of East Jerusalem, nor has it recognized West Jerusalem as Israel's capital. That, however, seems to be a matter of time.

The issue is also activated occasionally by UN resolutions criticizing Israeli measures, as happened in 1980, when the Carter administration voted in the Security Council to condemn Israeli settlements in the occupied territories, "including Jerusalem." Having provoked an uproar in the midst of the presidential primary campaign, the U.S. vote, which was cast on a Friday, was disavowed by Carter on the following Monday. That, however, seems to be a matter of time.

An important controversy over the status of Jerusalem took place in the American political arena on March 3, 1990, when President George Bush was questioned about a statement made by Secretary of State James Baker in congressional testimony two days earlier. Baker had said that he would seek assurances that $400 million, requested by Israel for housing new immigrants, would not be used in the occupied territories. Actually Baker was testifying about foreign aid in general before the House Appropriations Subcommittee on Foreign Operations, in which he also enraged Israel and its domestic supporters by suggesting an across-the-board reduction of aid in order to help new U.S. clients in Nicaragua and Panama and to bolster the new anticommunist regimes in eastern Europe.[7] The impact of that suggestion would have fallen heaviest on Israel, being the top recipient of U.S. aid, and together with the implied threat to reopen the Jerusalem file, Baker's statement was bound to mobilize U.S.-Israeli supporters against the administration. In fact, when President Bush was asked during a news conference in Palm Springs, California whether he would tie U.S. aid for the re-settlement of Soviet Jews to Israel's willingness to refrain from housing them in West Bank settlements, he went out of his way to assert that Jerusalem would also be included in the ban:

My position is that the foreign policy of the United States says we do not believe there should be new settlements in the West Bank or in *East Jerusalem.* And I will conduct that policy as if it's firm, which it is, and I will be shaped in whatever decisions we make to see whether people can comply with that policy. And that's our *strongly held view,* and we think it's constructive to peace—the peace process, too—if Israel will follow that view. And so there is division in Israel on this question, incidentally. Parties are divided on it. But this is the position of the United States and I'm not going to change that position.[8] [Emphasis added]

Not unexpectedly, the added emphasis by the president, absent throughout the Reagan era, was assaulted by the major American Zionist organizations, the Israeli government, and their supporters in Congess. The president, however, was simply reiterating U.S. policy and reaffirming the U.S. obligation under the Fourth Geneva Convention of 1949, in his capacity as chief diplomat and chief executive. As chief executive, he has a constitutional responsibility to "take care that the laws be faithfully executed." Moreover, his solemn pledge to "protect and defend the Constitution," includes the Geneva Conventions, among other treaties, encompassed in the "supreme law of the land" (Article VI of the U.S. Constitution). Why, then, should he be attacked so vigorously by so many constitutionally minded politicians when he was simply reaffirming U.S. policy and legal commitments?

The answer lies in the fact that the United States has maintained two asymmetric positions on Jerusalem sheltered in ambiguity. There is a *presumed policy* and a *symbolic position*. When the latter is resurrected, even temporarily, it sets off a controversy and reopens a whole new series of clarifications, retractions, and confirmations, casting even thicker clouds over the two positions and creating additional confusion.

President Bush was rebuked for having questioned his predecessor's presumed policy, which was to push the U.S. symbolic position to the sidelines while giving unqualified support to Israel's policy that Jerusalem must never again be divided. President Reagan's policy was also shrouded in the cliché that the city's "final status should be determined through negotiations," and as long as U.S.-sponsored negotiations in the Middle East remained sterile, that policy effectively paralleled the status quo, i.e. Israel's annexation. Bush's statement on March 3, however, threatened to further the ambiguity of the Reagan period, and was consequently attacked because of its potential to create an unacceptable balance between the presumed policy and the symbolic position. President Bush was apparently guilty of attempting to deviate from an unwritten U.S.-Israeli agreement to violate international law, hence his critics, including a former judge,

Senate Majority Leader George Mitchell (D-ME), utilized strictly polit-ical arguments, paying no attention to legal or moral principles.

The Symbolic Position

The United States tacitly agreed with the majority of the world by abstaining in the vote on U.S. General Assembly Resolution 2253 of July 4, 1967, calling on Israel to rescind the annexation and enlarge-ment of Jerusalem's boundaries in violation of Resolution 181. The United States again abstained on UN General Assembly Resolution 2254 of July 14, 1967, which "deplores Israel's failure to implement General Assembly Resolution 2253," and "reiterates its call to Israel...to rescind all measures...which would alter the status of Jerusalem." The U.S. implied association with that broad consensus was strengthened when Security Council Resolution 242 of November 22, 1967, calling for Israeli withdrawal to the boundaries of June 4, 1967, became a cor-nerstone of U.S. Middle East policy.

U.S. association with the international consensus on this issue, how-ever, has undergone serious transformation during the past two decades, and came to a dead halt when President Reagan ventured into the area of jurisprudence with the original, albeit dimwitted, opinion that Israeli settlements were not illegal. Meanwhile, Israel managed to keep the question of settlements in the enlarged boundaries of Jerusalem, i.e., on Arab land confiscated since June 1967, outside the general discourse on settlements, whose total population stands at 310,000. Thus the Jewish settlers in that area were not included in the contrived statistics on settlers, which stand now at 140,000, up from 112,000 when Rabin was elected in 1992 and double the number in 1990, when Shamir could easily claim that less than 1 percent of the new immigrants were settled in "occupied territories," when in fact 11 percent have settled in occupied Jerusalem. For the first time ever, the Jewish population of East Jerusalem exceeds that of the Arab popula-tion. It now stands at 160,000 with the near-term outlook favoring rapid Jewish population growth. It is interesting to note that the Jewish population in East Jerusalem in June 1967 stood at zero.

As U .S. adherence to the withdrawal clause of UN Resolution 242 changed its focus from the letter to the spirit of the resolution, and as the Israeli-U.S. special relationship was institutionalized and eventually transformed into a strategic alliance, the issue of Jerusalem became largely dormant. The American association with international legality was reduced to a symbolic level, and was occasionally upheld during UN rituals, which have almost no substantive effect on the situation.

As U.S. ambassador to the United Nations in 1971, George Bush had a chance to participate in the formalities on Jerusalem. On September 25, 1971, he reaffirmed Ambassador Charles Yost's 1969 statement that Jerusalem is "occupied territory and thereby subject to the provisions of international law governing the rights and obligations of an occupying power."[9] He also decried Israel's failure to acknowledge its obligations as contrary to the "letter and spirit" of the Fourth Geneva Convention and cautioned against adverse effect on the "eventual disposition of the occupied section of Jerusalem." Although the Bush statement was strong and forthright, it nevertheless contributed to the process leading toward a presumed U.S. policy:

> But an Israeli occupation policy made up of unilaterally determined practices cannot help promote a just and lasting peace any more than that cause was served by the status quo in Jerusalem prior to June 1967, which I want to make clear, we did not like and we do not advocate reestablishing.[10]

The Presumed Policy

Then Ambassador Bush's statement made it clear that the United States was dissatisfied with the division of Jerusalem and preferred unification. But while U.S. policymakers continued to reject Israeli sovereignty over the city and to hold that its final status must be negotiated, they looked the other way while Israel took physical and legal steps which left nothing to negotiate about. When Israel dissolved the East Jerusalem Municipal Council on June 29, 1967, expelled the Arab Mayor, Rouhi Al-Khatib, expropriated Arab land surrounding Jerusalem, demolished Arab homes, and built an expansive network of suburbs in accordance with the Master Plan for Greater Jerusalem, the United States limited its response to occasional statements upholding the symbolic position. It did the same when Israel employed the euphemism "controlled territories" to avoid the internationally recognized obligations of an occupying power. It paid no attention when Prime Minister Levi Eshkol declared Jerusalem, "by the grace of the unfolding of Jewish history," to be the "whole and sovereign capital" of Israel.[11] Nor did the United States threaten to reassess its economic, military, or diplomatic underwriting of Israel when Israel moved ministerial and other government offices to East Jerusalem, placing the United States in the position of aiding and abetting serious violations of international law. Moreover, the 1969 and 1974 Israeli-sponsored elections in the city demonstrated the separateness between the two parts of the city when no Arab candidates and less than 10 percent of the eligible Arab voters took part; and yet the United States clung to a façade of unity as the logical alternative to division.

Two decades which witnessed a decisive and determined Israeli effort to make Jerusalem "an emphatically Jewish city" and an "eternal capital" with U.S. acquiescence convinced most Israelis and their U.S. supporters that Israel could rely on U.S. support for keeping Jerusalem. Since the Camp David accords, which introduced the concept of autonomy, that assumption was extended to the West Bank and the Gaza Strip as well. Any lingering doubts about that probability were dispelled by eight years of uncritical support under Reagan and Shultz.

By contrast, the March 1990 statements by Baker and Bush unleashed tremors which seemed to disrupt the harmonious atmosphere that prevailed under Reagan. These statements called in the symbolic position as a means of pressure to resuscitate a peace process facing a death sentence by its original author—Yitzhak Shamir. No one was under any illusion that Bush's statement entailed the possibility of a change in the U.S. Jerusalem policy. What was at issue was whether the presumed policy would be allowed to continue with no inhibitions or encumbrances, and that no precedents would be allowed to modify it, even when U.S. national interests might dictate such modifications. In short, President Bush's comment was seen as a possible interruption of ten years of U.S. acquiescence in Israeli plans for Jerusalem.

The Challenge and the Outcome

The statement by President Bush triggered the inevitable battle in the American public opinion arena. The lineup of forces pitted Shamir's caretaker government, the U.S. Zionist lobby, and the U.S. Congress on one side, against the president of the United States.

Israel's ambassador to the United States, Moshe Arad, leveled severe criticism at George Bush in a Washington speech to the United Jewish Appeal on March 13, 1990, saying that Bush's statement harmed the peace process, at least in the short run, because of the political crisis it triggered in Israel.[12] Another embassy official, Oded Aran, expressed anxiety about the future of U.S.-Israeli strategic cooperation, nurtured carefully during eight years of Reagan's presidency. He said that there was a lurking threat to the Arrow missile project, a joint U.S.-Israeli enterprise.[13] Shamir's defiance of Bush was expressed in a statement to American-Jewish fund raisers on March 4, 1990 in which he said "there are no settlements in Jerusalem…it is part of Israel and it will never be divided again."[14] It was also dramatized in the April 2, 1990 decision to begin the construction of four settlements on confiscated Arab land north of Jerusalem.

Congress and the Jerusalem Controversy

Mr. Bush was the target of some powerful salvos delivered by Senate majority leader Mitchell. "Heavy-handed blunder" was the way Senator Mitchell referred to Bush's comment. Mitchell accused Bush of undermining the "peace process" through "insensitivity or conscious provocation", of having contributed to the fall of the Shamir government, and of "casting doubt upon America's intentions and role in promoting peace in the Middle East."[15] The Arab-American senator, who was often favored with Jewish political-action committee (PAC) money, added:

There was simply no reason to suddenly thrust into the forefront of debate the issue of Jewish Israelis' rights to live in East Jerusalem…certainly the status of East Jerusalem must be decided as part of a negotiated, comprehensive peace. But the president's comments served no purpose but to impede progress toward establishing the very process needed to resolve this issue[16]

At the same time the campaign against Bush was sweeping the U.S. Senate in the aftermath of the majority leader's harsh rebuke. Senator Daniel Patrick Moynihan (D-NY) who has often sponsored pro-Israel resolutions with Senator Jesse Helms, dutifully pushed Concurrent

Resolution 106 through the Senate, securing approval by voice vote on March 22, 1990. A similar resolution declaring Jerusalem as Israel's capital was also adopted by the House on April 24th.[17]

Giving full credence to the Israeli position on Jerusalem, which has been at variance with the accepted view throughout the international community, the resolution begins thus: "whereas the State of Israel has declared Jerusalem to be its capital," and disregarding any need for accuracy, it proceeds:

whereas from 1948 to 1967, Jerusalem was a divided city and Israeli citizens of all faiths were not permitted access to holy sites in the area controlled by Jordan; whereas since 1967 Jerusalem has been a united city administered by Israel and persons of all religious faiths have been guaranteed full access to holy sites within the city...

The congressional view of Jerusalem, which paralleled the official Israeli position, and was at variance with the U.S. government position, was made clear in the fifth "whereas":

whereas ambiguous statements by the government of the United States concerning the right of Jews to live in all parts of Jerusalem raise concern in Israel that Jerusalem might one day be redivided and access to religious sites in Jerusalem denied to Israeli citizens.

The Senate and the House then, resolved that the Congress:

1) "acknowledges that Jerusalem is and should remain the capital of the State of Israel"
2) "strongly believes that Jerusalem must remain an undivided city..."

An interesting rebuttal of the congressional endeavor was mounted by then Senate Minority Leader Bob Dole, who had signed the concurrent resolution, but took the Senate floor on April 19, 1990 to announce; "I made a mistake.... I bear a personal responsibility here.... I should have said more loudly: 'Wait a second, let's look at

JERUSALEM
OCCUPIED AND EXPANDED 1967 – 1991

Giv'at Ze'ev

Jerusalem Airport

Mukhmás

Jaba'

Ateros

Ar Rãm

Biddũ

Newe Ya'eqov

Hizmã

Pisgat Ze'ev

Tall al Fũl

Bayt Iksã

Ramot Allon

Shu'fãt

Shu'fãt (UNWRA Camp)

'Anãtã

Giv'at HaMivtar

Giv'at Shapira

Ramat Eshkol

Mount Scopus

Jerusalem

Old City

Ma'ale Adummim

Bet HaKerem

New City

Al 'Ayzarĩyah

Qiryat Ha Yovel

Abũ Dĩs

Meqor Hayyim

East Talpiot

Bayt Safãfã

Jus Bãhir

Khirbat ash Shaykh Sa'd

Gilo

Har Gilo

Bayt Jãlã

Bethlehem

0   1   2 km
0   1   2 mi

The designations employed and the presentation of
material on this map do not imply the expression of any
opinion whatsoever on the part of the Secretariat of the
United Nations concerning the legal status of any country,
territory, city or area or of its authorities, or concerning the
delimitation of its frontiers or boundaries.

——————— Jerusalem municipal boundary, 28 June 1967
– – – – – East Jerusalem municipal boundary, May 1967
– – – – – – Armistice Demarcation Line, 1949

MAP NO. 3640   UNITED NATIONS
JUNE 1991

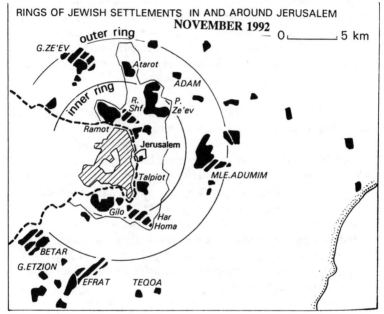

RINGS OF JEWISH SETTLEMENTS IN AND AROUND JERUSALEM
NOVEMBER 1992

0 ⌞_____⌟ 5 km

outer ring

G.ZE'EV

Atarot

ADAM

inner ring

R. Shf

P. Ze'ev

Ramot

Jerusalem

Talpiot

MLE.ADUMIM

Gilo

Har Homa

BETAR

G.ETZION

EFRAT   TEQOA

Source: *News From Within*

this'. I certainly shouldn't have signed on this resolution."[18] Having just returned from a trip that took him to Jerusalem, among other places in the Middle East, where he was questioned repeatedly about Resolution 106, Dole set aside the usual restraints which politicians observe when speaking on the Middle East. He said on the Senate floor:

Senate Concurrent Resolution 106 deals with one of the most sensitive and emotional issues in the Middle East…(it) declares Jerusalem the capital of Israel—the position of the Israeli government; a position 180 degrees contrary to the views of the Arab states and the Palestinians. Most important, the resolution declares on an issue that our government-and many outside observers-see as better left to negotiations among the parties involved, rather than decided by unilateral action.[19]

He considered it wrong for the Senate to plunge into a sensitive issue, and without debate, and for more than half the sponsors to sign on during the first 24 hours while the other forty members join in on the second day. He reflected that he was among the hasty and careless signers and expressed regret and perhaps contempt for such ad hoc methods of decision-making: "So we're all wrong. The process is wrong. And the results can be very damaging."

He was publicly criticized by his Republican colleague Newt Gingrich, an ardent supporter of Israel, at a specially convened press conference. He particularly resented Gingrich's labeling of him as "anti-Israel." In a toughly-worded letter to the future speaker of the House, the future Senate Majority leader wrote:

Unfortunately if you disagree with a single policy or practice of the Israeli government, or criticize anyone who lobbies on behalf of Israel, you should be characterized as…"anti-Israel." That is bunk, and I am surprised that you have joined in the narrow but shrill chorus of the people who take that tack.[20]

When Dole was asked on April 22 on television to comment on Gingrich's attack against him at a public press conference, he said,"Ah, Newt was trying to make a few brownie points with AIPAC." Ironically, as the Republican presidential frontrunner, Bob Dole delivered a speech

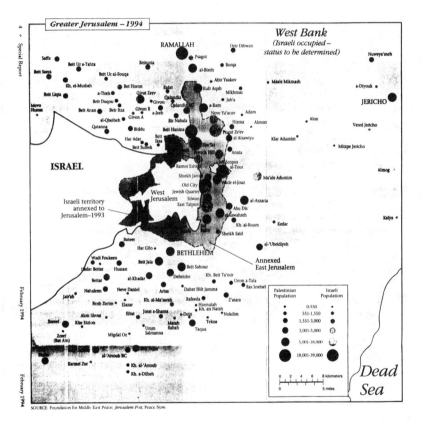

Greater Jerusalem – 1994

RAMALLAH

West Bank
(Israeli occupied –
status to be determined)

JERICHO

ISRAEL

Israeli territory
annexed to
Jerusalem–1993

West
Jerusalem

Old City
Jewish Quarter

East Talpiot

BETHLEHEM

Annexed
East Jerusalem

Dead
Sea

Palestinian Population	Israeli Population
0–550	
551–1,550	
1,551–3,000	
3,001–5,000	
5,001–18,000	
18,001–39,000	

0   2   4   6   8 kilometers
0   5 miles

SOURCE: Foundation for Middle East Peace; *Jerusalem Post*, Peace Now.

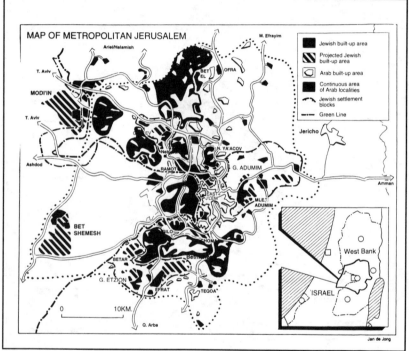

MAP OF METROPOLITAN JERUSALEM

Legend:
- Jewish built-up area
- Projected Jewish built-up area
- Arab built-up area
- Continuous area of Arab localities
- Jewish settlement blocks
- Green Line

M. Efrayim

T. Aviv

Ariel/Halamish

MODI'IN

BET EL

OFRA

Jericho

T. Aviv

Ashdod

N. YA'ACOV

G. ADUMIM

RAMOT

Amman

EAST J'LEM

MLE. ADUMIM

BET SHEMESH

GILO

HOMA

Beit...

BETAR

G. ETZION

EFRAT

TEQOA

Q. Arba

0   10KM.

West Bank

ISRAEL

Jan de Jong

Source: *The Challenge*

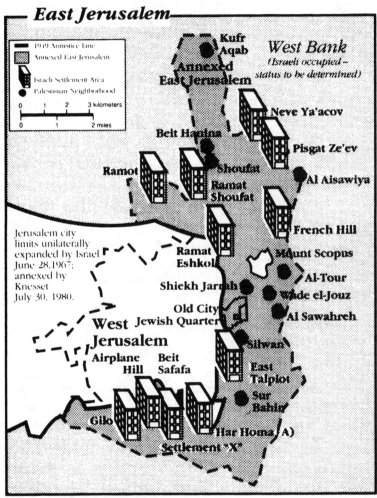

East Jerusalem

Legend:
- 1949 Armistice Line
- Annexed East Jerusalem
- Israeli Settlement Area
- Palestinian Neighborhood

0 1 2 3 kilometers

0 1 2 miles

West Bank
(Israeli occupied –
status to be determined)

Kufr Aqab

Annexed East Jerusalem

Neve Ya'acov

Belt Hanina

Pisgat Ze'ev

Ramot

Shoufat

Al Aisawiya

Ramat Shoufat

French Hill

Jerusalem city
limits unilaterally
expanded by Israel
June 28, 1967;
annexed by
Knesset
July 30, 1980.

Ramat Eshkol

Mount Scopus

Al-Tour

Shiekh Jarrah

Wade el-Jouz

Old City

West Jerusalem

Jewish Quarter

Al Sawahreh

Silwan

Airplane Hill

Beit Safafa

East Talpiot

Sur Bahir

Gilo

Har Homa (A)

Settlement "X"

SOURCE: Foundation for Middle East Peace.

before AIPAC's Policy Conference on May 8, 1995 in which he himself tried to collect bigger brownie points by announcing a bill that would force a move of the U.S. embassy from Tel Aviv to Jerusalem against the wishes of the Clinton Administration and even the Rabin government.

Meanwhile, the The House action on the 1990 resolution was initiated by Edward Feighan (D-OH), Dan Burton (R-IN), and Newt Gingrich (R-GA), who called a special order session attended by 47 members. That led to a full session, which endorsed House Resolution 290 by a roll call vote of 378 against 34 and 6 abstentions. It was identical to Senate Resolution 106. It should be pointed out that the House resolution was voted on with the House rules suspended, which meant that debate was severely limited and no amendments were allowed. Such procedure is normally used when the resolutions in question are "non-controversial." Obviously, Resolution 290 was very controversial. It should also be pointed out that these "sense of the Congress" resolutions are not binding on the administration and do not reflect official and longstanding U.S. policy. They are known in congressional parlance as "throwaway" resolutions because their signers know that they have no legal standing and yet will help endear them to special interests. They have been utilized, however, by the pro-Israel lobby repeatedly in their campaigns to convey "public" sentiments in support of their policy agenda, and to pressure the executive branch.

The consequent denial of self-determination for the Palestinian people, which this resolution implied, was in sharp contrast to the Senate action on Lithuanian self-determination. Also, most of its signers from both the House and the Senate had supported the Security Council resolutions, which called Iraq's occupation illegal and called for their implementation. But double standards on various domestic and foreign issues are more the rule than the exception in Congress. Israel is apparently an exception when issues pertaining to the application of international law are raised.

Media Assault

Joining in the 1990 campaign against the Bush administration were the major Jewish-American organizations and the *New York Times*, as well as the *Washington Post*. William Safire's diatribe against Bush was venomous. His blatant distortion of historical facts and his inclination toward inventing reality were expressed in such a way that left no distinction between responsible journalism and hollow propaganda:

> Mr. Bush, by extending his anathema on "settlements" to a portion of Israel's capital, is the first to raise the prospect of a divided Jerusalem. Mr. Bush pretends that his bombshell, which brought down the Likud government, is no change in U.S. policy; that legalistic half-truth fools nobody.[21]

His hyperbole went to the extent of equating international law on Jerusalem with the potential for genocide against Jews:

> Come the first pogrom, which God forbid, who in the Bush White House will accept responsibility for failing to facilitate the new exodus while there was little time? Who among supporters of Israel will step forward on some future Passover and admit they were so caught up with the "peace process" that they refused to confront the real possibility of a death process?[22]

Safire's colleague, A.M. Rosenthal, echoed the Israeli position as well:

> There have been no Jewish "settlements" in Jerusalem, as Mayor Teddy Kollek noted. The very use of the word "settlement" to describe Jews moving into Jewish neighborhoods in Jerusalem is insulting.[23]

The *Washington Post's* news stories on the controversy, though more subtle than Safire's prose, sounded more like editorials than news reporting.[24]

Stripped to its essentials, the criticism by the anti-Bush coalition rested on two spurious arguments: first, that the president's comment undermined the "peace process," when in fact it was Shamir who failed to meet the Labor party's deadline on the Baker Plan; and second, the implicit notion that the Reagan-Shultz policy was almost tantamount to customary law or practice, and thus ought not be challenged.

Bush Caves In

Although the president rose to the occasion by insisting that he was "reiterating U.S. policy" and by delivering an unqualified "no" to the question of whether he regretted raising the issue, he apparently found it necessary to seek a peaceful conclusion to the controversy. Initially, Bush insisted that his remark was consistent with the U.S. position of the past twenty-two years.

State Department spokesperson, Margaret Tutwiler was instructed to say that, and to confirm that the United States defined the occupied territories as including all the land seized by Israel in 1967.[25] But in less than two weeks from the start of the controversy, Bush began to equivocate and "clarify," under pressure. He dispatched a letter to the Israeli mayor of Jerusalem, Teddy Kollek, saying "there is no intention on our part to focus now on the final status of Jerusalem."[26] That letter won him praise from the director of the Anti-Defamation League of B'nai B'rith, who said: "The president put this issue on the front burner through his statement in California, and now with this letter, he is putting it on the back burner."[27]

The president's fence-mending also included an earlier assurance which he communicated to Seymour Reich, the president of the Conference of Presidents of American Jewish Organizations, on March 6, 1990, that "U.S. policy toward Jerusalem is unchanged."[28] Moreover, White House Chief of Staff, John Sununu told representatives of the Wiesenthal Center, which is concerned with study of the Holocaust, that the administration's policy on the city is unchanged and that the United States does not oppose Jews living in predominantly Arab East Jerusalem. Implying that the president may have been misunderstood, Sununu added: "Statements on other issues, which unfortunately may have been mixed together, do not impact on the (Jerusalem issue)."[29]

The controversy of March 1990 over U.S. policy on Jerusalem failed to clarify the matter; in fact, U.S. policy became clouded in more ambiguity. George Bush had attempted to demystify it by redefining the presumed policy, but he ended up in taking cover under the umbrella of the symbolic position.

Israel's friends on Capitol Hill, who tried to send a strong message with their Concurrent Resolution 106, proceeded with another resolution two years later (May 26, 1992) calling upon the president to congratulate Israel on the 25th anniversary of the "reunification" of Jerusalem. Concurrent Resolutions S-316 and H-113 made the claim, again, that the Israeli occupation authorities have guaranteed full access for Palestinian Muslims and Christians to Jerusalem, ignoring the fact that Palestinians from all over the occupied territories were barred from entering the city during the 25th anniversary festivals. Incidentally, a year later Jerusalem was closed to all Palestinian men under age 40, except workers carrying special passes. The age limit was raised to 50 and later eliminated altogether, making it a punishable offense for any Palestinian from the West Bank and Gaza to enter Jerusalem without a permit. This arbitrary closure remains in effect until the present time, and yet the broad support in the U.S. Congress for freedom of movement and for religious freedom continues to be applied selectively.

The Jerusalem Question During Clinton's Presidency

1. Greater Jerusalem In Formation

By the time Bill Clinton assumed the presidency, "Greater Jerusalem" covered nearly one-fourth of the entire West Bank. An Israeli committee consisting of representatives of the Jerusalem municipality and the ministries of housing and interior had set up a special commission of planners to prepare a master plan for "Metropolitan Jerusalem" by 1993. The area now includes about 40 settlements in addition to the annexed eastern sector of the city. These settlements extend in all directions, reaching Ramallah in the north, a position half way between Hebron and Bethlehem (Gush Etzion) in the south, Ma'ale Adumim settlement in the east, whose municipal boundary was expanded in 1993 all the way to Jericho. These settlements annex to Jerusalem, and therefore to Israel, the area from Ramallah to Jericho to Bethlehem.[30]

The commission has been working on plans for transportation, commerce, housing, industry, health, education, water and sewage. A guiding principle of its work is that "Metropolitan Jerusalem" will be a "single district for its entire population", and regardless of any political agreements, "the free movement of people, goods, services and capital will be assured." It is significant that the commission's mandate extends over a sizable area of the West Bank, over which Israel has no statutory authority. The current trends in planning support the view that the deferral of Jerusalem to a "final status" issue, in the negotiations between Israel and the PLO, is an exercise in futility. Nothing in the ongoing work by Israel's planners would suggest that the comprehensive nature and complementary aspects of these plans would be jeopardized by political agreements. Naturally, Israel is not planning a meticulously constructed metropolis with an expensive and sophisticated infrastructure, only to hand a share of it to the Palestinians after final status talks a few years from now. The fate of the city had, in fact, been sealed since it was occupied in June 1967.

Both of Jerusalem's mayors, the Laborite Teddy Kollek, who served for 28 years until 1993, and the current Likudist mayor, Ehud Olmert, are on record with statements that the status of Jerusalem is not negotiable. Teddy Kollek was reported to have told President Clinton that Jewish claims in Jerusalem were unique: "In another few years we in Jerusalem will celebrate 3000 years since the construction of the city by King David, whereas the Palestinian claim is less than one generation old."[31]

In April 1995, Olmert unveiled a plan to commemorate 3000 years of "Jewish sovereignty" over the city, which involves a 15-month long campaign of celebrations and festivals scheduled to begin in September 1995.

This non-negotiable stand on Jerusalem has been supported by every Israeli prime minister since 1967. Ignoring the fact that Jerusalem was classified as a final issue item by the DOP, to be resolved in 1996, Rabin declared the following before the Knesset on September 2, 1993:

This government, like all of its predecessors, believes there is no disagreement in this House concerning Jerusalem as the eternal capital of Israel. United Jerusalem will not be open to negotiation. It has been and will forever be the capital of the Jewish people, under Israeli sovereignty, a focus of dreams and longings of every Jew.

Housing minister, Benjamin Ben Eliazer announced on the BBC on October 20, 1993 that thousands of new units would be built in East Jerusalem. On the next day the Jerusalem City Council approved a plan to build a housing project on the Mount of Olives in East Jerusalem. And just a few days earlier (October 18th) Deputy Defense Minister Mordechai Gur announced that the settlement city of Ma'alé Adumim (population 18,000), whose boundaries had been expanded by 12,000 acres eastward to Jericho, was included in "Greater Jerusalem." The municipality of Ma'alé Adumim awaits approval for a new master plan that would accommodate 50,000 residents on top of the 50,000 targeted in the present plan.[32] Housing Minister Ben Eliazer announced in February 1995 that the special parliamentary committee on "Greater Jerusalem" has approved 500 housing units for Ma'alé Adumim in 1995 and 500 more in 1996.

Israel's policy now is to consolidate settlements in East Jerusalem and all around the city in order to give Jerusalem a unique character distinguishing it from the West Bank. Jerusalem then would become Jewish physically, ethnically, and politically. The closure of the city to Palestinians from the West Bank and Gaza, ongoing since March 1993, was intended to reinforce that plan and to hasten the foreclosure on the future of the city. The Security Council resolutions, which declared the annexation of East Jerusalem null and void, which have, in turn, prevented international recognition of Jerusalem as the capital of Israel, would become, in effect, hollow.

This has been the strategy behind the pattern of grouping the ever expanding settlements around Jerusalem into blocs. The Ma'alé Adumim bloc, approved in November 1993, comprises seven settlements and cities, which according to the mayor of Ma'alé Adumim, Benny Kashriel, would create a band of housing for 70,000 Israelis between the East Jerusalem settlement of Pisgat Ze'ev and the Jericho enclave, created for the Palestinians under the DOP.[33] The Gush Etzion bloc is another one in the south and Giv'at Ze'ev is another bloc, which extends Jerusalem strategically in a northwest direction. Gush Etzion has approval for plans targeting 50,000 inhabitants before the end of the century while Giv'at Ze'ev no less that 30,000.[34] In February 1995, some 800 units were approved for Giv'at Ze'ev.

Another current project is the development of the Abu-Ghoneim region, which is located at the northern border of the Arab town of Beit Sahour, south of Jerusalem. This region also includes a hill east of Abu-Ghoneim (Abu-Alsokhour) and a plain to the east (Khirbat al-Mazmouriyah). Most of this area, which constitutes approximately 2000 donums, belongs to families in the Arab town of Beit Sahour and the village of Um-Tuba. It was part of the Bethlehem district, but after the 1967 occupation, Israel included all of it in the extended borders of Jerusalem. The current plans for Abu-Ghoneim call for the building of a settlement with all the required infrastructure on expropriated land for approximately 35,000 Jewish settlers.

The completion of this project would finalize the encirclement of the original city with Jewish settlements on *all* sides, and would alter the demographic balance decidedly in Israel's favor in East Jerusalem. Not only would it be a final step in Judaizing East Jerusalem, but it also represents an advanced stage in the Judaization of Bethlehem. Bethlehem would become as vulnerable to the Etzion bloc of settlements as Hebron has been to Kiryat Araba, from which the Brooklyn settler Goldstein and his accomplices launched the Hebron massacre in February 1994.

The fact that the Abu-Ghoneim colonization is taking place since the signing of the Cairo Agreement on May 4, 1994 is rather ominous. It does not bode well for the political future of those Palestinians who look to the PLO agreements with Israel as the means to end occupation, and halt colonization. Worse still, under the Cairo agreement the zoning authority remains in Israeli hands. Unlike Jewish settlements and neighborhoods in the West Bank, Palestinian population centers are prevented from expanding beyond the areas allotted to them, even though those areas are Palestinian-owned. Such discriminatory zoning was retained under the provisions of the Cairo agreement.[35]

The Abu-Ghoneim area represents the only path for solving a chronic shortage of housing for the residents of Beit Sahour and Um-Tuba. Their requests to build on their own land in the area have all been rejected by the Jerusalem municipality and the Israeli government, despite the fact that the average number of residents in each house in Um-Tuba is twelve. Palestinian residents throughout East Jerusalem suffer from severe housing shortages, and at the same time the expropriation of their privately-owned lands continues unabated.

While Arafat consented to deferrring the issue of Jerusalem for the final stage, Israeli bulldozers and cranes have been put to work on the most ambitious project to complete a three-ringed encirclement of Palestinian communites in East Jerusalem. There is the expanding outer ring of Ma'alé Adumim, Gush Etzion, and Giv'at Ze'ev; the intermediate ring of

Ramat Shufat, Sheikh Jarrah and Jabal al-Mukabber and Wad al-Jouze; and the inner ring surrounding the old city, which covers Silwan, Ras al Amoud and the Mount of Olives. The plan aims to reduce the 450,000 Palestinians of the West Bank part of "Metropolitan Jerusalem" to a scattered minority in separate enclaves in and around the Israeli de facto Capital. The new infrastructure of highways extending about 250 kilometers by-passes them and renders them totally peripheral.

The reaction of the Clinton administration and the U.S. Congress to these illegal and unilateral measures, which have effectively foreclosed the Oslo option of "final status," has been one of unusual toleration if not of outright complicity.

The Shift in U.S. Policy

Since 1967, U.S. policy has officially been that East Jerusalem is part of the occupied territories. That policy, however, which was watered down in 1990, under intense pressure from the Israeli government, its Washington lobby as well as from pro-Israel legislators, all of whom intimidated President Bush, is undergoing a serious change under the Clinton administration.

The first visible sign of a shifting U.S. policy on Jerusalem appeared in the State Department's Declaration of Principles of June 30, 1993 (not to be confused with the Oslo DOP). That paper, it will be recalled, embodied the Clinton administration's ideas of how to resolve the impasse in the "peace process" after twenty-two months of futile negotiations in Washington. For the first time, the United States hinted broadly that it considered the occupied territories as "disputed," a term which bears close proximity to the Israeli position. By that time, the controversy over the $10 billion loan guarantees to Israel was over. The Bush administration had reached an accord, which did not obligate Israel to halt settlement activity. U.S. officials were no longer scrutinizing expenditure on settlement activity in and around Jerusalem. After the "historic handshake" on the White House lawn on September 13, 1993 between Arafat and Rabin, all discussion of settlement building in East Jerusalem between the U.S. and Israel has, in fact, has come to a dead halt. Israeli Housing Minister, Benjamin Ben Eliazer admitted, after meeting with top officials from the Clinton administration in Washington in November 1993, that the subject had never even come up in their talks: "They didn't ask and I didn't tell them," he said, according to AIPAC's newsletter *Near East Report*.[36]

The Clinton administration has embraced Israel's position on Jerusalem to the extent that it no longer has the issue of settlement construction on its agenda. Assistant Secretary for State of Near Eastern and South Asian Affairs, Robert Pelletreau, who coined that term, enunciated a visible shift in U.S. policy not only towards Jerusalem but also towards settlements in general. According to Geoffrey Aronson, a well-informed settlement expert, the U.S. is "no longer maintaining its historical policy of opposing unilateral actions—such as Israeli settlements—that are aimed at determining the final status of Jerusalem. Indeed, Pelletreau refused to characterize settlement per se as a unilateral action prejudicial to Jerusalem's final status."[37] In addition, the U.S. began in March 1993 to overlook the expansion of settlements, mainly taking place around Jerusalem under Rabin, due to "natural growth," yet another euphemism used by the Clinton administration to effect its changed policies.

Bill Clinton was the first president who actually moved towards translating campaign rhetoric on Jerusalem into policy. He told American Jewish leaders on March 13, 1994 that he opposed any reference to Jerusalem as occupied territory and that he would adhere to his campaign promise to support the Israeli view of Jerusalem as the "eternal capital."[38] Vice-President Al Gore, who developed close ties to the Likud party and to Christian Zionists in the United States when he was a member of the U.S. Senate, told AIPAC's annual policy conference on the same day: "I want to assure you at this critical moment, that the President and I have not forgotten the meaning of Jerusalem."[39]

The March 1994 session of the UN Security Council in the wake of the Hebron massacre was considered as the litmus test for Clinton and Gore with regard to Jerusalem. The original draft, which condemned the massacre, seemed acceptable to all members of the Council and, incidentally, to the Rabin government and to the Clinton administration. As a sign of changing times, Rabin had reportedly demanded that AIPAC and the Conference of Presidents of Major Jewish Organizations "neither protest the inclusion of Jerusalem in [the resolution] nor try to mobilize support in Congress for an American veto of the resolution."[40]

Apparently, Rabin and Clinton accepted the original draft as the price for resuming peace talks in the wake of the massacre and the declared PLO suspension of its participation in the talks. The "peace process" was too much of a good deal for them to pass up, and another condemnatory UN resolution would simply be added to a long list of ineffectual UN documents, thanks to an impenetrable U.S. diplomatic shield. Nevertheless, Rabin was unable to control the American Jewish lobby, while Clinton was unable to control Congress. Despite Rabin's reported urgings, AIPAC's annual conference adopted a position, contrary even to that of its own President Steven Grossman, in favor of condemning the UN resolution. There was considerable lobbying on Capitol Hill by Jewish organizations and Congress was inclined to press for a veto of the resolution. So intense was the lobbying, in fact, that Secretary of State Warren Christopher, who was on a visit to Japan during the Council session, had received a telephone call from Lester Pollack, Chairman of the Council of Presidents of Major Jewish-Americans Organizations requesting assurances that Jerusalem would not appear in the resolution. According to Pollack, Christopher "made it abundantly clear that any effort to prejudge the status of Jerusalem would be met with opposition from the U.S. government."[41] Meanwhile, Congress, in defiance of Clinton and Rabin, called on President Clinton to veto the resolution. The Senate passed a resolution on March 17, 1994 by voice vote and attached it to an unrelated banking bill. It urged the administration to veto any UN resolution that "states or implies that Jerusalem is 'occupied' territory."[42]

Letters were also sent by 81 senators and 29 representatives urging a veto. The senators asked the president to oppose "biased and counterproductive language" in the UN resolution. It stated:

Clearly, the United States understands that Jerusalem is a 'final status' issue to be negotiated between the parties. The United States must not be party to attempts to prejudice this issue through United Nations Security Council resolutions.

The House letter to Clinton of July 25, 1994 left little doubt where the signers stood on the issue: "Jerusalem is the indivisible capital of

Israel, and must remain united under sole Israeli sovereignty."

Both House and Senate moved to prohibit any new offices or official meetings in Jerusalem to deal with the Palestinian Authority, which was created by the "Gaza-Jericho First" accord on May 4, 1994. Their objective is to prevent any Palestinian symbols of sovereignty in Jerusalem and to render any Palestinian claims illegitimate. To that end they asked the Clinton administration not to open offices in Jerusalem to manage aid to the Palestinian Authority in Gaza and Jericho.

It is rather significant that the House signatories of the letter cited recent Israeli legislation on Jerusalem as a basis for U.S. policy, thereby ignoring not only international law, but also U.S. policies of a long standing:

> We note that the government of Yitzhak Rabin has approved new legislation that will prohibit both the PLO and the Palestinian Authority from maintaining offices and conducting business in Jerusalem. In light of these developments, we are very concerned about actions by the U.S. government that could give any credibility to Palestinian claims on Jerusalem.... Jerusalem is the capital of only one country, Israel, and we urge you to implement a policy that does not in any way support a Palestinian claim to the city.

The pro-Israel congressional establishment was able to secure sponsorships for the House letter from John Lewis, a ranking member of the Black caucus, and from Newt Gingrich, who later became the new Speaker of the House. The two other sponsors were Bill Saxton and Charles Schumer, who are considered regular supporters of Israeli positions.

The House letter did not leave room for the subtleties, nor did it invoke the new diplomatic gimmickry about prejudging a "final status" issue, which became the hallmark of the Clinton administration. It simply parroted the Israeli position; and Congress, this time, actually "out-Israeled" the Israeli government.[43]

Perhaps it is a sign of the times when a number of U.S. politicians seem to be intent on making desperate attempts to retain their pro-Israel credentials before voters, when the Israeli government itself is negotiating with the PLO.

Even before these letters were sent, domestic pressure had proven its worth. The Executive branch, which normally defends its foreign policy turf, was forced to bow to pressure from the Jewish community and from Congress. When the vote on the controversial resolution finally came before the Security Council, U.S. Ambassador Madeleine Albright insisted that the resolution be voted on paragraph-by-paragraph, a rather unprecedented procedure. She abstained from voting on two Jerusalem paragraphs, and threatened to veto future UN resolutions that had similar language. Reaffirming the new policy, enunciated in the State Department's Declaration of Principles of June 30, 1993, she said:

> We simply do not support the description of territories occupied by Israel in the 1967 war as 'occupied Palestinian territory.' In the view of my government, this language could be taken to indicate sovereignty—a matter which both Israel and the PLO have agreed must be decided in negotiations on the final status of the territories....[44]

To demonstrate this shift in U.S. policy on Jerusalem, which is not acknowledged officially, Albright said that she would have vetoed the entire resolution had the reference to Jerusalem as occupied territory appeared in the operative paragraph, which the U.S. ostensibly supports:

> The United States supports the operative paragraph of the resolution.... However, we sought a paragraph-by-paragraph vote...because we wanted to record our objections to language introduced there. Had this language appeared in the operative paragraph...let me be clear—we would have exercised our veto. In fact, we are today voting against a resolution in the Commission on the Status of Women precisely because it implies that Jerusalem is occupied Palestinian territory.[45]

In fact, Albright made good on her promise to use the veto on May 17, 1995, when all other fourteen members of the Security Council supported a draft resolution describing the Israeli intent to seize 140 acres of Arab land in the villages of Beit Hanina and Beit Safafa as merely "unhelpful." It was the 30th veto by the U.S., but this time it was on behalf of illegal land seizure in the vicinity of Jerusalem.

According to Donald Neff, sources told him that the veto was used at the insistence of Albright when the consensus in the State Department was to abstain, given the mild language of the resolution and the absence of a condemnation.[46] Albright is said to have ambitions for the position of Secretary of State, and apparently thinks that AIPAC is a principal avenue.

Earlier, Albright had taken an important step toward changing U.S. policy when she sent a letter to all member states of the UN General Assembly in August 1994 suggesting that the assembly session, scheduled to open in September, drop from its Middle East resolutions language dealing with matters still to be negotiated. That would include resolutions on Jerusalem and all other issues classified by the Oslo process as "final-status" issues. Her letter states:

> We…believe that resolution language referring to 'final status' issues should be dropped, since these issues are now under negotiations by the parties themselves.[47]

Should Albright prevail on the Jerusalem question and all other final status issues, a new global consensus based on the supremacy of the Oslo and Cairo agreements as the effective framework of an Arab-Israeli settlement would supplant the UN resolutions which constituted international legality for the past 46 years. Jerusalem would be a principal casualty as U.S. policy becomes, in effect, a substitute for international law.

Further efforts by Congress to bolster Israeli plans for Jerusalem, including the elimination of any Arab political presence—manifest or implied—in the city, were also undertaken in August 1994. In addition to the amendments which were tacked onto the FY95 Foreign Operations Appropriations bill, which jeopardized PLO funding, a further amendment was added by the conservative Senator Helms (R-NC), who later assumed the chairmanship of the Senate Foreign Relations Committee and the liberal Senator Daniel Moynihan (D-NY). It prohibits U.S. officials from holding meetings in Jerusalem with any member of the Palestinian Authority. It also prohibits the establishment of any U.S. offices for the purpose of conducting business with the

Palestinians, on the grounds that such offices could give credence to the Palestinian claims of sovereignty over the eastern part of Jerusalem. In late July 1994, after a congressional outcry and Israeli government pressure, the Clinton administration withdrew plans to open an Agency for International Development branch office in East Jerusalem which would oversee the disbursement of funds to the Palestinian Authority.

Perhaps the baldest action so far by Congressional members are two pending bills introduced in May 1995 in both houses, by Senate Majority Leader Bob Dole and Speaker of the House Newt Gingrich. These would require the U.S. to begin actual construction in 1996 for an embassy building and to move the embassy from Tel Aviv by May 31, 1999. It is ironic that the land on which the embassy would be build is actually the property of the Islamic Endowment's Administration (WAQF). The action by Dole and Gingrich, which was preceded by a letter bearing the signatures of 93 senators out of 100 urging Secretary of State Christopher to move the embassy by May 1999, is considered unwelcome by both Clinton and Rabin, but only for tactical reasons. It would have an adverse effect on their investment in the "peace process," thus placing Clinton in the untenable position of having to oppose the bill, and thereby lose votes to Bob Dole.

Various members of Congress had earlier expressed outrage at Arafat's call in South Africa for a "Jihad" to liberate Jerusalem. Senator DeConcini placed the following restrictions on President Clinton:

[He should make it] very clear that the U.S. is not part of a peace accord, a peace process, or a statement of principles that talks about the liberation of Jerusalem. That is not part of the agreement. It is my understanding that under the accords the status of Jerusalem would be discussed, but it is not part of the agreement that there would be any pullout by the Israelis.[48]

The Clinton administration, which needed no prodding on the question of Jerusalem, went a step further in September 1994 by applying financial leverage against the Palestinian Authority (PA), headed by Yasir Arafat, in order to gain concessions for Israel on the status of Jerusalem. On September 13, 1994, Arafat was compelled to drop his insistence that international donor assistance be allocated for

Palestinian institutions in East Jerusalem, which Israel regards as a section of its capital and in which the Palestinian Authority has no jurisdiction. The agreement, which was reached by Arafat and Shimon Peres, after serious pressure from the U.S., the EU and Japan, stipulates that neither Israel nor the PLO "shall bring before the donor community those political issues that are of disagreement between them. They will deal with such issues between themselves, based on the [Oslo] Declaration of Principles and subsequent agreements."[49]

Having agreed to Israel's demand that Jerusalem is out of bounds even for symbolic Palestinian development, the PA was rewarded with funds to support its expanding bureaucracy for the next six months and pay the police force, which relieved Israel of upholding "law and order" in Gaza, as was tragically illustrated on November 18, 1994 when the first Gaza massacre was committed by Arafat's police.

By early 1995, the annexation of East Jerusalem by Israel and the incorporation of more than one-fifth of the West Bank into the metropolitan Jerusalem area seemed to be nearly complete. Meanwhile the deferral of the Jerusalem question, under the Oslo accords, to a final status issue, has enabled Israel to use the three-year transitional period to seal the fate of the city. Building new settlements around the city on land occupied since 1967 and expanding existing settlements have proceeded without interruption during the past two years since Clinton assumed the presidency. Washington no longer places real conditions on its loan guarantees, nor does it feel obliged to remind Israel that the settlements are an obstacle to peace, not to say anything about being illegal. The use of the term "illegal" as ascribed to settlements had vanished with the end of the Carter administration. With Reagan and Bush in power, the illegal status had given way to a new formula; an "obstacle to peace." Now under Clinton, settlements are considered, at best, as a "complicating factor" in Israeli-PLO negotiations, but neither illegal nor an obstacle to peace. The statement of Madeleine Albright at the UN on March 18, 1994, her letter to members of the General Assembly in August on the status of Jerusalem and her May 17 1994 veto constitute an unambiguous challenge to the principle of inadmissibility of conquest by force, which the U.S. frequently invokes, as a tenet of a brave new world under its own leadership. By repeating the phrase that "our policy on Jerusalem has not changed," Secretary of State Warren Christopher and UN Ambassador Madeleine Albright are simply negating the historical facts. The former U.S. position was articulated by the U.S. ambassador to the UN, Charles Yost as early as 1969, when he told the Security Council that the Arab sector which Israel seized in June 1967 was "like other areas occupied by Israel, in occupied territory." And as late as 1991, the U.S. voted for Resolution 694 which referred to "all the Palestinian territories occupied by Israel since 1967, including Jerusalem."

Moreover, the new code phrases of the Clinton administration that "final status" issues such as Jerusalem must not be "preempted" and that the final outcome of negotiations must not be "prejudiced" are rather disingenuous. What is being prejudiced, *in fact* is Israel's annexation of East Jerusalem, which *should* be prejudiced and preempted, because it is illegal and has been declared as such by a majority of the nations in the world, including the United States. That annexation would surely make an equitable and a durable peace impossible.

Notes

1. Ibrahim Dakkak, "The Transformation of Jerusalem: Juridical Status and Physical Change," Naseer Aruri (ed.), *Occupation: Israel Over Palestine* (2nd Ed.), Belmont, Mass.: AAUG Press, 1989,. pp. 139–171.

2. *The Status of Jerusalem,* (prepared for, and under the guidance of the Committee on The Exercise of the Inalienable Rights of the Palestinian People), New York; United Nations, 1979,. pp. 17-18.

3. The Status of Jerusalem, New York; United Nations, 1979.

4. The late Prime Minister Golda Meir, who was born in Russia and grew up in the United States, summed up this position thus: "There is no such thing as a Palestinian...it was not as though there was a Palestinian people in Palestine considering itself as a Palestinian people and we came and threw them out and took their country away from them. They did not exist." *London Sunday Times,* June 15, 1969.

5. "Testimony of Yehuda Zvi Blum" *Hearings Before the Subcommittee on Immigration and Naturalization of the Committee on the Judiciary,* U.S. Senate, 95th Congress, October 17 and 18, 1977. (Washington:

Government Printing Office, 1978) pp. 25–26; 35. See also "Judea, Samaria and Gaza-The Israeli Record," statements by Ambassador Yehuda Z. Blum, Permanent Representative of Israel to the United Nations in the Security Council, 13, March 19, 1979. Jerusalem: Ministry of Foreign Affairs. (n.d.). A number of scholars argued that the Israeli thesis is a rationalization of unilateral acts undertaken illegally and not a bona fide legal judgment. See, for example, Seth Tillman, "The West Bank Hearings," *Journal of Palestine Studies*(Winter 1979), pp. 21, 27; see also "Testimony of W.T. Mallison" in *Hearings Before the Subcommittee on Immigration and Naturalization.* op. cit., pp. 46–56; Henry Cattan, "The Status of Jerusalem," *Journal of Palestine Studies* (Spring 1981); Kathleen Kenyon, *Digging Up Jerusalem* (London: Ernest Benn, 1974); M.A. Amiry, *Jerusalem: Arab Origin and Heritage* (London: Longmann, 1978); W. T. and S. Mallison, *The Palestine Problem in International Law and World Order* (London: Longman, 1986).

6. Raja Shehadeh, *The West Bank and the Rule of Law* New York, International Commission of Jurists and Law in the Service of Man, 1980.

7. Adam Pertman, "Baker Cautions Israel," *Boston Globe,* March 2, 1990. Senator Bob Dole wrote an article in the *New York Times* (January 21, 1990) proposing that 5% of the monies allocated to the top recipients of U.S aid (Israel, Egypt, Turkey, The Philippines, Pakistan) be reallocated to eastern and central Europe. On May 1, 1990, Dole rose in opposition on the Senate floor to loan guarantees for Israel and cited the generous pattern of U.S aid since the early 1970s. He filled twenty pages of the *Congressional Record* with studies by the respected Congressional Research Service detailing congressional generosity toward Israel over the years and other material critical of aid to Israel. See Donald Neff, "The U.S. and Israel: Tilting at a Windmill", *Middle East International,* May 11, 1990, p.9.

8. From "Excerpts of President Bush's Remarks at News Conference At End of Talks [with Japan's Prime Minister]," *New York Times,* March 4, 1990.

9. *New York Times,* September 26, 1971.

10. *Ibid.*

11. *Israel Government Year Book, 1968–1969* (Jerusalem: Central Office of Information, Prime Minister's Office, S739), p. 9.

12 . Tom Kenworthy, "Mitchell Upbraids Bush About East Jerusalem,

Washington Post, March 6, 1990.

13. Jerusalem Press Service, Washington D.C., March 6, 1990.

14. *Ibid.*

15. Tom Kenworthy, *op. cit.*

16. *Ibid.*

17. Text in *Congressional Record,* April 24, 1990. See also Tom Kenworthy, "House Supports Jerusalem As Israeli Capital," *Washington Post,* April 25, 1990: also Major Garret "House Supports Jerusalem As Israeli Capital," *Washington Post,* April 25, 1990.

18. Quoted in Donald Neff, "The Formidable Bob Dole Faces Up to Israel," *Middle East International,* April 27, 1990, p.3.

19. *Ibid.*

20. *Ibid.,*p.4

21. William Safire, "Bush Versus Israel," *New York Times,* March 26, 1990.

22. *Ibid.*

23. A.M. Rosenthel, "The President's Bomb," *New York Times,* March 8, 1990.

24. See David Hoffman, "Bush: I Don't Regret Comment on East Jerusalem," *Washington Post,* March 14, 1990, in which he writes: "It was rare for a president publicly to criticize the settlements in East Jerusalem as equivalent to those in the occupied territories of the West Bank and Gaza Strip."

25. Jackson Dieh, *op. cit.*

26. David Hoffman and Al Kamen, "Bush's remark Under-Cut Peace Plan," *Washington Post,* March 15, 1990.

27. *Ibid.*

28. John Goshko, "Bush's Remarks on East Jerusalem Clarified," *Washington Post,* March 6, 1990.

29. *Ibid.*

30. John Tyler, "Finishing Jerusalem," *Challenge* (Jerusalem), No. 28, November–December 1994, pp. 15–16.

31. "Plans Gaining Momentum for Metropolitan Jerusalem," *Report on Israeli Settlements In the Occupied Territories,* Vol. 3, No. 2, March 1993. Washington, D.C., Foundation For Middle East Peace.

32. Jan de Jong, "The Secret Map of Non-Negotiable Jerusalem," *Challenge,* No 28, November–December 1994, p.12.

33. *Jerusalem Post,* November 11, 1993.

34. Jan de Jong, *op. cit.,* p. 12.

35. Raja Shehadeh, "A Legal Analysis of the Gaza-Jericho Agreement," *Journal of Palestine Studies,* Vol. XXIII, No. 4, Summer 1994, pp. 20–21.

36. *Near East Report,* November 15, 1993.

37. Geoffrey Aronson, "U.S. Policy Shifts on Settlements," Report on Israeli Settlement In the Occupied Territories, Vol. 4, No. 6, November 1994, p.6.

38 *Mideast Mirror,* March 14, 1994.

39 *The Jewish Advocate,* March 18–24, 1994.

40. Leon Hadar, "Muddling Through In The New World Disorder—And In The Middle East," *Journal of Palestine Studies,* Vol. XXIII, No. 4, Summer 1994, p. 68.

41. Donald Neff, "AIPAC Puts on the Pressure", *Middle East International,* No. 471, March 18, 1994, pp. 7–8.

42. Donald Neff, "Embracing Israel's Claims at the UN," *Middle East International,* No. 472, April 1, 1994, p.4.

43. Leon Hadar, *op. cit.*

44. Excerpts from the text of Albright's speech are reprinted in *Journal of Palestine Studies,* Vol. XXIII, No. 4, Summer 1994, pp. 151-152.

45. *Ibid.*

46. Donald Neff, "The 30th Veto to Shield Israel", *Middle East International,* No. 501, (May 26, 1995), pp. 5-6.

47. Excerpts from Albright's letter dated August 8, 1994 in Journal of Palestine Studies, Vol XXIV, No. 2 (Winter 1995), pp. 152-153.

48. *Congressional Record,* May 23, 1994.

49. *Jerusalem Post,* September 14, 1994, p. 1.

Conclusion

The Peace Process as a Negotiating Strategy

The Essence and the Derivatives: Reversing the Order

The Madrid process has already yielded important benefits to Israel—full peace with Jordan and a serious embarkation on the road to peace with Syria. The separate-tracks approach, devised by Israel and sold to the Arabs by James Baker III, has enabled Israel to accomplish a broad strategic goal; a separate peace with the Arab states not contingent on the necessity of meeting Israeli obligations to the Palestinian people as spelled out in various UN resolutions. Thus, the withdrawal clause of Security Council Resolution 242 was an issue between Israel and Jordan regarding a little known patch of desert in southern Jordan, and an issue between Israel and Syria regarding the Golan Heights, but not in the West Bank and Gaza, and certainly not in Jerusalem, which Israel does not consider as occupied.

The second diplomatic instrument of Madrid, i.e., negotiations in stages, also conceived by Israel and brokered by Baker, has enabled Israel to accomplish another strategic goal; deferral of the Palestine question, while normalizing relations with the Arab world and reorganizing its occupation of Palestinian lands, with Yasir Arafat's full complicity and active cooperation. Moreover, the Palestinian Authority has emerged as the instrument to help effect that reorganization and simultaneously to preempt and marginalize the PLO as the anchor of Palestinian national rights.

Rarely are nations able to achieve so much in negotiations while making negligible concessions in return. Israeli diplomats and businessmen shuttle freely between Arab capitals, all the way from Qatar in the east to Casablanca in the west. The Arab boycott of Israel is effectively non-existent. The concept of Arab defense has been rendered a subversive phenomenon by the Israel-Jordan peace treaty. Israel is planning its own NAFTA throughout the Arab world, and the list goes on.

Clearly, this growing normalization has sidelined the Palestinian track. Arafat's apologists blame the Gulf War and the end of the Cold War for the Palestinian travail, but rarely, if at all, do they accept responsibility for their own mistakes or acknowledge having been fooled into a no-win strategy. Nor is there any awareness by Arafat or his top echelons that they do not have a negotiating strategy, while Israel's diplomatic resources and legal talents have been fully mobilized since Madrid.

Global and regional considerations aside, Arafat cannot escape responsibility for having exchanged the Madrid framework, in which autonomy was deemed as the beginning of a transitional phase, for the Oslo framework, which effectively makes autonomy the end of the road, at best. Nor could he be exempted from the responsibility for having released Syria and Jordan from their obligations towards the Palestine question, despite the two tracks. For despite the obvious short-comings of the Madrid framework, it still contained some safe-guards against Palestinian isolation from the Arab parties. Baker's eight trips to the Middle East, prior to Madrid, testify to the controlling nature of the Palestinian dimension of the Arab-Israeli conflict and its central role in the diplomatic process.

Having opted for the Oslo venue instead of Washington, Arafat was able to negotiate without a proxy. But while he, together with his organization, ceased to be a pariah, he managed to place the entire Palestine question under probation. And together with the bureaucrats of his organization, he was tempted by the prospect of international donations and a place to call home. Having sensed Arafat's economic and psychological needs, the Israelis offered him what they largely conceived as a "good riddance." It was a good deal; he assumed their burden and paid a price too.

The diplomatic instruments of Madrid, which Arafat failed to employ, have been utilized by Israel to lure the Palestinians into a blind alley, put them on hold, while at the same time using them as the green light for entry into Amman and Damascus. The penetration of Amman and the approach towards Damascus are being achieved with virtually no cost to Israel, since the Palestinians are stuck in Gaza trying to qualify as guardians for the occupation, leaving the nexus of the Arab-Israeli conflict to the "final stage". While placing the nexus on hold, Israel is strategically positioned, for the first time, to address the derivatives; the Jordanian and Syrian issues, which can be reduced to technical items, such as borders to be adjusted, water to be redistributed, security to be arranged and armies to be reconfigured and redeployed.

This is not to say that Israel's conflict with the Palestinians is not about border security and water. It is about all these issues; but above all, it is about a right to exist, which the Palestinians had non-reciprocally conceded to Israel. Israel's non-recognition of the Palestinians as a sovereign people is the single most important obstacle to a genuine peace. Having acquiesced in that denial, the Palestinians have enabled Israel to give the derivatives of the Arab-Israeli conflict precedence over the essence of the conflict. Israel continues to orchestrate Middle East diplomacy in such a way as to subordinate the main issues to the derivative issues and reap tremendous benefits in the process.

It is in this context that Israel's negotiating strategy becomes clear: the Gaza-Jericho First formula is the bait, which facilitates the entire diplomatic flow in the region. Ironically, for Israel, it opened the gateway to the Arab world, but it simultaneously closed to the Palestiniasns the doors to the West Bank. Instead of being the saviour of Arafat's career, it served as his trap. Unlike Sadat, who concluded a single agreement with Israel to be implemented in stages, Arafat had concluded an agreement to reach agreement, which would be negotiated in stages. His path to the West Bank will, therefore, be arduous, and the road to Jerusalem is likely to be closed. It is the logical result of Israel's strategy and Arafat's ad hoc or non-strategy. Dreaming about final status talks while paying little attention to the interim phase has taken a heavy toll on the Palestinians. Gaza has become their purgatory while heaven in the West Bank is a long way off. And for the diaspora Palestinians there is neither purgatory nor the awaited heaven; only hell. This has been mandated by negotiations in stages, on separate tracks, in which Israel's legal and diplomatic skills were deployed against Arafat's instant diplomats, who must struggle through the language, ponder the nuances, and contend with what they surely perceive as inscrutable and excessive legalism.

Redeployment Reconsidered

Israel has succeeded thus far in setting the agenda for the negotiations. By determining the framework and the scope of the "peace process", Israel was able to keep the course of diplomacy consistent with its national goals and acceptable to its various constituencies, including important segments of the right-wing opposition and the expansionist settler movement. Thus, while the Gaza-Jericho agreement enjoys a broad consensus in the Israeli body politic, a replication of it in the West Bank would be out of the question, in both the short and medium ranges, given the expected opposition by the 310,000 Jewish settlers in the West Bank and "greater Jerusalem", and by their numerous supporters inside Israel. Knesset member Hashem Mahameed was quoted as saying that settlement activity has come to "enjoy a consensus within Israel, even among the Israeli left."[1]

Rabin's government is deeply aware of the fact that the redeployment of the Israeli Army to the fifteen Gaza Strip settlements was much more feasible, in political and security terms, than a redeployment in the West Bank. And yet, according to a May 1994 report of the Gaza Center For Rights and Law, an estimated 4000 to 4500 Israeli soldiers are assigned to fifty-four settlements, camps, and checkpoints. Given that, one wonders how many soldiers and how many years would be required to assure the security of Israeli installations in the West Bank. The demographic and geographic character of the 140 Jewish settlements in the West Bank would make it nearly impossible for any Israeli government to extend limited self-rule from Gaza to the West Bank. As long as the Zionist ideology of acquiring the land without the people prevails, a negotiated settlement based on the right of the two peoples to dignity and self-determination will continue to be elusive. Thus the Gaza-Jericho agreement was part of Israel's negotiating strategy calculated to put the onus on Arafat to prove his ability to govern

Gaza before he is allowed to govern the West Bank, while Israel is released from the pressure of finding a solution to its continuing occupation of the West Bank and Jerusalem. As long as Hamas and Islamic Jihad persist in launching attacks against Israeli soldiers and civilians, Arafat's obligation to Israeli security under the Cairo agreement will continue to dominate the diplomatic agenda and overshadow the issue of extending self-rule to the West Bank.

Palestinian obligations for Israeli security under the Cairo agreement are now being reinterpreted to include the security of the settlements. Thus, by December 1994, Rabin's government made it clear to the Palestinian negotiators that the redeployment clause in the Cairo agreement is an obstacle to the continuation of their talks. As Likud and the settler movement threaten to make the "settlements security" a campaign issue in 1996, Rabin and his Meretz allies, who previously endorsed a two-state solution, now favor amending the Oslo accords so that Palestinian elections in the West Bank would not have to be preceded by Israeli redeployment. The relevant provision of the DOP is Article XIII, which states:

> 1. After the entry into force of this Declaration of Principles and no later than the eve of elections for the Council, a redeployment of the Israeli military forces in the West Bank and Gaza Strip will take place...
> 2. In redeploying its military forces, Israel will be guided by the principle that its military forces should be redeployed outside populated areas.

Emphasizing Israel's "rethinking" of the Oslo terms, Minister Yossi Sarid of Meretz told the *Jerusalem Post* (November 15, 1994) that the Palestinians "...have no choice. If they do not understand now, they will eventually understand." Meanwhile, U.S. Secretary of State Warren Christopher dutifully added: "No one expects Israel to redeploy outside the territories during the second stage of the interim agreement, unless the PLO assures security in the area under its control." The onus has been placed on the Palestinians by the "honest broker," who seems to modify his own rules to suit the exigencies of not only U.S. domestic politics but also of Israeli domestic politics. Palestinian domestic considerations, on the other hand, are not an issue for Christopher, since the only real opposition to Arafat's policies is coming from the religious bloc, which is being dismissed as a law and order issue rather than political opposition. With the Gaza-Jericho project under way, the effective dynamics of Palestinian politics have become almost exclusively external. Arafat's legitimacy is now derived from Israel and the United States.

Thus, the presently-declared position of Israel and of the peace sponsor marks yet a new and ominous departure from the rules, which used to govern the Palestine question. The framework for a solution had descended from the UN resolutions to the Madrid assurances, to Oslo and Cairo with their two-tracks and two-stages, and now to the point when the concept of two-stages is itself rendered superfluous. Israel's security and Palestinian rights were the concomitant principles of Madrid. Now settlement security is a condition for the pursuit of the "peace process." Thus the settlements, which the U.S. had considered illegal under Carter, which then became an "obstacle to peace," under Bush and Baker, reduced to a "complicating factor" in the negotiations during the initial period of Clinton's presidency, are now being elevated to a security issue, the assurance of which is a prerequisite for the extension of the peace talks. Given that, how can the Palestinians argue with any credibility, during the so-called final status talks, that these settlements exist illegally on occupied land and must, therefore, be dismantled? Having accepted the paramountcy of their security now, could they reasonably expect their destruction in 1996? Israeli strategy has succeeded in altering the diplomatic framework from international legality, manifested in UN resolutions, to colonial settler legality, anchored in settlement security, and, therefore, permanence. In the words of the late Yehoshofat Harkabi, the former Israeli Chief of Military Intelligence, settlements have become "an instrument to prevent the establishment of a sovereign Palestinian authority west of the Jordan River."[2]

The goal of keeping the West Bank on the diplomatic "back burner" was enhanced by the Israeli-Jordanian peace treaty of October 1994. The hasty peace with King Hussein was timed for easing pressure on Rabin to do "too much" at once. Israeli and world public opinion would have to digest the peace and wait for Arafat to fulfill his obligations under the Oslo and Cairo agreements, which have already been expanded. That, and the increased attacks by Islamic militants on Israelis, constitute a ready-made excuse for Rabin.

A "No Win" Situation for Arafat

The Israeli-supplied framework of the "peace process," as well as Israel's negotiating strategy, have placed Arafat in a "no win" situation. His deal with Israel is predicated on an impossible equation. There can be no serious discussion of Israeli redeployment or extension of limited self-rule to the West Bank until Arafat decides to utilize the "strong police force, called for in the Oslo accords, to suppress all forms of Palestinian resistance to the occupation. But while such a decision was made a condition for further diplomatic progress, it by no means constitutes a guarantee of success. And yet, while Arafat might appear to Israel as more qualified when pursuing that course, he would be condemned by his fellow Palestinians as a puppet and a quisling. That had already happened, in fact, when the police force of an increasingly isolated Arafat fired on Hamas demonstrators on November 18, 1994, after Friday prayers in Gaza. Ten days before the incident, in words that can be seen as prophetic, Arafat's chief negotiator, Nabil Sha'ath, expressed the Palestinian dilemma when he told the Israeli newspaper *Yediot Aharonot* on November 8:

I would suggest not making Arafat look like an Israeli agent, like an "Uncle Tom" serving his masters...the effect on us is devastating. I am in despair. Rabin does not even try to hide how much he despises us. If there wouldn't be a miracle the agreement between us will collapse. [3]

Had Nabil Sha'ath understood the essence of Israel's negotiating strategy, he would have spared himself the indignity of supplication. Indeed, miracles do not happen in negotiations. Israel's embarkation on that road was a strategic decision. Yet the agreement is structurally difficult, if not impossible, to implement because it relates to the nature of the Israeli state, which precludes genuine coexistence with the Palestinian people on equal basis. Thus, when the Rabin government diverted the negotiations venue from Washington to Oslo, it was making a strategic shift away from the hardly concealed stalling tactics of its Likud predecessors, while creating its own gridlock that had the appearance of diplomatic progress. In a subtle contrast to the Likud, Rabin opted for an agreement with a built-in conflict over meaning and objectives. It is because of that conflict and the diametrically opposed outcomes desired that the impasse continues. Indeed, one could say that the impasse born of this conflict is responsible for the worsening of the situation in the occupied territories, where Palestinian frustration at being thwarted at every step is turned inward threatening a civil conflict.

Segmentation of the Palestine question by issues, regions and even negotiation stages have thus far constituted the biggest roadblock which continue to sustain the impasse. Had the issues of settlements, Jerusalem, and sovereignty not been deferred in accordance with a two-phased strategy, the question of settlement security would not have become a barrier for redeployment. Initial Palestinian self-governance would not have been probationary; Palestinian legitimacy would not have been held in abeyance awaiting elections, which are being hampered by the lack of Israeli redeployment, which itself is being blocked by security concerns for West Bank settlements. Could such a self-defeating process be meant for implementation?

There is an urgent need now for collapsing the two phases in order to prevent the imminent diplomatic collapse which Sha'ath has cautioned about. Placing all issues on the table is the only sure way towards breaking the present impasse and resolving the dilemma in which Arafat has placed himself and the rest of the Palestinian people. That option, however, will require a major referendum which will ultimately affect the nature of the Israeli state and determine its readiness to reach a territorial compromise with the Palestinians. Only through such a compromise will the Palestinians be able to obtain a meaningful autonomy as a transitional measure toward independence. That, however, is not a predicate of the "peace process" as now conceived by the Rabin government. Nor is there a possibility in the foreseeable future that any other Israeli coalition could put forth a viable alternative that would better meet the minimum expectations of the Palestinian people. Meanwhile, Rabin, who was favored by 52 percent support against

42 percent for Likud's Benjamin Netanyahu in November 1994, was in no position to challenge the maxims of the greater Eretz Yisrael idea, supported openly by the settler movement and Likud but less publicly supported by labor.[4] In early 1995, most public opinion polls gave Rabin little chance of leading his party to the 1996 elections, let alone winning the elections for Labor against Likud.[5]

The Role of Zionism and the Nature of the State

Any forward movement beyond the "Gaza-Jericho First" formula would require a genuine debate of Zionist history in which the difficult questions, submerged since 1948, would be raised. The ongoing debate of Zionist historiography is limited to Israeli intellectuals and has no bearing on the active political arena. Professor Ehud Sprinzak, for example, writes in his book, *The Ascendance of Israel's Radical Right,* that a major civil conflict cannot be ruled out in Israel in the event of a territorial compromise.[6] The writer Aharon Megged says that the debate among Israeli intellectuals raises the question of whether Zionism is "...a movement of national plundering or a movement of a persecuted people acting according to a humane ethic, seeking compromise and peace."[7] The historian Benny Morris, author of *The Birth of the Palestinian Refugee Problem, 1947-1949*, wrote in *Haaretz* (June 24,1994) that " the Zionist Ethos claims that we came to this land not to exploit the natives and expel them, and not to occupy them by force. Instead, we came here to 'build and be built,' i.e., to create an independent life alongside another nation."[8] Another intellectual, historian Ilan Pappe (author of T*he Making of the Arab-Israeli Conflict 1947-1951*) wrote in the same issue of *Haaretz* (June 24,1994) that "there is a need to dissolve the sharp contradiction between a Zionist and Jewish state and human rights and democracy. A democratic pluralistic Israel as a part of the Mediterranean is also Israel with many historical narratives. Such an Israel has a chance at a common future."[9]

Only when and if a similar critique of Zionist history enters the general Israeli discourse, would the present "peace process" be likely to assume substantive dimensions. Otherwise it will continue to be a strategy in itself; peace as the continuation of war through other means. Israeli strategists are candidly speaking of the "peace process" as "part of a military strategy". The *Boston Globe* reporter Ethan Bronner quoted an Israeli general as saying, "That is how Israel will turn Clausewitz on his head." Through the peace process, "Israel is making diplomacy into war by other means." The process is designed to enable Israeli strategists to focus on the high-tech war for the twenty-first century, building long-range missiles, and anti-missile missiles, and developing enormous fire power, laser-guided projectiles, and night vision equipment, while leaving the role of repressor to Yasir Arafat. It is a cost-effective strategy based on the notion of the "small smart army."

In light of Israel's skills at utilizing legal concepts and diplomatic means for accomplishing strategic goals, movement beyond the Gaza-Jericho affair will continue to be hampered by Israel's strategic priorities. Palestinian basic needs, on the other hand, are relegated as tertiary and are manipulated through the incremental process of negotiations in phases. "Early empowerment" and the entire concept of splitting the negotiations into interim and final status stages is/are based on the flawed assumption that the real barriers to conflict resolution in the Israeli-Palestinian case are psychological. Palestinians must therefore demonstrate their willingness and ability to live in peace with the Israelis in order to enjoy the rights conferred upon them by international law and the dictates of the Universal Declaration of Human Rights. Early empowerment can be meaningful only if it is the result of a political decision to establish true self-governance in the West Bank, instead of being considered as the necessary first step towards that self-governance. How can the Palestinians in the West Bank be "empowered" in the field of taxation regulations, when they have neither legislative nor judicial authority nor even police powers? How can their institutions tax a population lacking representation? Representation requires national elections, which cannot be held until the occupation army withdraws or redeploys. Yet how can the army redeploy while there are numerous settlers spread over the West Bank to protect? How can the Palestinians assume responsibility for health conditions when they have no control over the sewage disposal of the settlements, and when such sewage contaminates their springs and streams? How can the Palestinians manage education when the Army subordinates normal educational activities to the security of settlers, closing schools at will or requiring students to start classes at 7:00 A.M., before the settlers begin their early commuting to work? How can the Palestinians manage tourism under "early empowerment" when the Palestinian "Minister of Tourism" Elias Friej had to submit an application in October 1994 to make the fifteen minute journey from Bethlehem to Jerusalem for the purpose of attending a trade and tourism conference?

These and other questions illustrate the folly of early empowerment, which is merely a device to finesse Israel's reluctance to move beyond the Gaza-Jericho deal. Unwilling to comprehend this reality and the strategic imperative behind it, headlines such as that appearing on the front page of the *New York Times* (November 9,1994) "Israel Will Speed up Talks for Palestinian Self-Rule," can be very misleading. Quoting Rabin in the *Times* story, correspondent Clyde Haberman writes: "The discussion will be comprehensive—all the issues that need to be solved to move to the next stage." Not only are the structural problems facing the next stage being ignored, but also the blame for lack of progress is placed on "terrorism" and/or attributed to the lack of funding from western donors. At least this is what Rabin has claimed according to a story by John Battersby in the *Christian Science Monitor* (November 10,1994) under the headline, "Lifeboat Politics: Israel and PLO Battle Extremes." The *Washington Post's* Jim Hoagland expressed unwarranted optimism about the prospects for peace in an editorial paying tribute to Rabin and Peres under the title "Two Who Earned A Noble Prize," October 27,1994:

> In achieving peace with Jordan, Syria and the Palestinians, Israel will give up more than land. Rabin and Peres also give up part of the future. They give up a legal limbo that holds open the option of redrawing Israel's boundaries from time to time by military conquest. They accept the limits and existence of a normal state, with its own special characteristics, in the international community.[10]

In fact, if what Hoagland has concluded is true with regard to Israel's approach to the Palestine question, then the principal obstacles and impediments to peace no longer exist. That assumption, however, would hold only if the nature of the Israeli State has been reevaluated in order to accommodate real coexistence with the Palestinian people. According to Hoagland, such reevaluation has already taken place with regard to Israel's relations with Syria: "The debate is essentially an ideological one about the nature of Israel, not Assad's character or negotiating strategy."[11] If that indeed is what the latest Israeli Nobel laureates have done with regard to Syria, the same presumed reevaluation has not been extended to Israel's attitude towards Palestine.

When and if that happens, gimmicks such as "early empowerment" and "secondary legislation" would not be necessary to maintain the gridlock while keeping the facade of negotiations alive. Early empowerment would be replaced by real empowerment sustained by representative institutions deriving their legitimacy from the will of the people. There would be no need to camouflage the occupation with a token legislative council assigned administrative tasks. Only a genuine national legislature, like the Israeli Knesset, could truly empower the Palestinian people and signal the end of the military occupation.

That prospect, however, will have to await the crucial yet unlikely debate about Zionist history and the nature of the Israeli state. If the Zionists ethos claim is correct about coming to Palestine "to build and be built", not to "exploit the natives and expel them, and not to occupy them by force", then Israel would have to make hard choices between peace and the settlements, between peace and a permanent exile for the refugees, between peace and Jerusalem as the eternal capital, between peace and Israel as a perpetual Western colonial project.

The latest chapter of the "peace process," ongoing without real success for nearly three decades, is less about peace and more about bureaucratic procedures designed to countenance and reconfirm the existing situation while creating the pretense of a diplomatic breakthrough. The illusion of peace produced by the agreements is far more dangerous than the untenable status quo. The forces behind that illusion have distorted the essence of the conflict and paralyzed the efforts toward a real solution. Consequently, they have prolonged the occupation and obstructed the opportunity for a peace with justice—the only peace which can promise an enduring coexistence between Arab and Jew, the only peace capable of transforming the political landscape of the Middle East from a perpetual battleground to a terrain of progress and prosperity.

Notes

1. *Palestine Report* (Jerusalem: Jerusalem Media and Communication Center), Vol. 8, No. 2, February 13, 1995, p. 9.
2. *Ha'aretz*, September 1, 1994.
3. *New York Times*, November 9, 1994.
4. Public opinion poll in the *Jewish Advocate*, November 18, 1994.
5. article by Israel Shahak "Downtown In Rabin's Popularity Has Several Causes," *The Washington Report on Middle East Affairs*. Vol. XIII, No. 6, (March 1995), p. 11.
6. "Revising History: Unveiling Zionism", *Issues: Perspectives on Middle East and World Affairs*, Vol 3, No. 2, (October 1994), Paris, p. 16. See also Ethan Bronner, "Rewriting Zionism," *The Boston Globe Magazine*, November 27, 1994, pp. 22–47
7. *Haaretz* (Weekend Supplement), June 10, 1994. Quoted in *Ibid*.
8. *Ibid*.
9. *Ibid*, p. 15.
10. *Washington Post*, October 27, 1994.
11. *Ibid*.

Index

A

Abbas, Mahmoud, 239, 241
Abu Al-Abbas, 296
Abdul-Shafi, Dr. Haider, 125
Abed, George, 158
Abourezk, James, 261
Abrams, Elliot, 118
Abu Dhabi, 34
Afghanistan, 117, 174
Agency for International Development, 339
AIPAC. *See* American-Israel Public Affairs
    Committee
Airborne Warning And Control System. *See*
    AWACS
Albright, Madeleine, 226, 337-338, 340-341
Allen, Richard, 118
Allon, Yigal, 113
al-Amaliya al-Wataniya, 239
ambiguity, 314
Amend the Covenant, 142
America; Americans. *See* United States
American-Arab   Anti-Discrimination
    Committee, 264
American-Israel Public Affairs Committee
    (AIPAC), 129, 142, 197-198, 199, 251, 254,
    259, 261, 276, 281, 289, 304, 326, 334, 335
American Jewish Committee, 129, 148n51
American Jewish community, 101, 133, 134,
    251, 260-262, 264-266, 268-269, 272, 274,
    304, 334, 337
    and Carter administration, 254, 259
    and Johnson administration, 253
    and United States policy, 127-129
American Jewish Congress, 128
Americans for Peace Now, 197, 199, 200
Amitay, Morris, 199
Amman, 79, 166, 243, 347
Amnesty International, 162
Angola, 33, 117
Anti-Defamation League, 96, 328
apartheid, 12, 213, 228, 266
Arab Democratic party, 154
Arabian peace imperative, 113
Arabian Sea, 49
Arab-Israeli conflict, 11, 19, 37, 45, 46, 53, 54,
    71, 112, 172, 303, 347
    bilateral dimension of, 111
    and demography, 204-205

and Oslo accords, 191
and public opinion polls, 124-125
resolution of, 151
settlement of, 180
three dimensions of, 120
as United States national interest, 170, 176,
    193
and United States policy, 98
Arabists, 198
Arab League, 38, 164, 171, 257
Arab Liberation Front, 296
Arab nationalism, 35, 63, 105
Arab socialism, 44
Arab solution, 164
Arab states, 36, 171-172
Arad, Moshe, 318
Arafat, Yasir, 9-11, 17, 23, 27, 73, 105, 135, 140,
    195, 345-348
    in cartoon, 164
    and Diaspora millionaires, 242-243
    Force 17 of, 294
    and Israel right to exist, 172, 225, 285, 299
    and Jerusalem, 332
    negotiations and, 218-219
    and Oslo accords, 191, 193,219, 299-300
    and Palestine Liberation Organization
    (PLO), 307
    and Palestinian Authority, 339-340
    on peace in Palestine, 121
    and peace process, 351-353
    as President of Palestine, 223-224
    and recognition issue, 145, 225
    and Resolution 799, 208
    and terrorism, 301-302
    usefulness of, 237-242
    mentioned, 166, 200, 201, 297, 350
Arafat-Peres agreement (1994), 235
Aran, Oded, 318
Arens, Moshe, 12, 55
Arms Control Act, 55
Arms Export Control Act, 95
Aronson, Geoffrey, 334
Ashrawi, Hanan, 125, 126, 196
al-Assad, Hafez, 179, 180, 210, 276, 356
Aswan Dam, 41
Authorization No. 97, 204
autonomy, 130, 187, 233, 317, 346, 352
AWACS, 49, 50, 88, 90, 91, 92, 129, 250, 259, 290

B

Baghdad Pact, 38, 41, 67, 176
Baker, James III, 22, 24, 25, 71, 74, 102, 140-145, 152, 288-289, 345-346
  and bilateral talks, 172
  diplomacy of, 183
  five points of, 143, 162, 174
  and Jerusalem, 313, 317
  and letter of assurances, 195
  opportunity for, 175-176
  and Palestine Liberation Organization (PLO), 144
  shuttles of (1991), 178
  mentioned, 89, 198, 201, 214, 273, 274, 296
Baker Plan, 169, 220, 327
Baker proposal, 173
Balawi, Hakam, 210
Ball, George, 48-49, 84n9
Bandung conference, 38
Bard, Mitchell Geoffrey, 254
Bar-Yosef, Avinoam, 197
Basuk, Motti, 12-13
Battersby, John, 355
Begin, Menachem, 22, 78, 92, 97, 112, 114-115, 229
  mentioned, 250, 260
Begin Plan (1977), 115
Beilin, Yossi, 16, 199
Beirut, 97, 117
Beit Lid, 9, 12
Beit Safafa, 337
Beit Sahour, 331, 332
Ben-Gurion, David, 39
Ben-Nun, Rabbi Yoel, 13
Berbera, Somalia, 52
Berman, Howard, 128, 301
Bernea, Nahum, 15
Bethlehem, 329, 332
Beit Hanina, 337
Big Four talks, 45, 75
bilateral negotiations, 73, 175, 180
Biltmore Program, 249, 251
Black September, 23
B'nai B'rith International, 270
Bonior, David, 299
Bookbinder, S. Hyman, 129
Boschwitz, Rudy, 128, 288, 290
boycotts, 257, 282n13
Brezhnev, Leonid, 120
Brezhnev Plan, 78-79, 121
Bronner, Ethan, 354

Brookings Report, 77
Brown, Jerry, 280
Bryan, Richard, 301
Bryoade, Henry, 252
Brzezinski, Zbigniew, 36, 49, 115, 259
B'Tselem. *See* Israeli Information Center on Human Rights
Buchanan, Pat, 279-280
Buckley, James, 106n8
Burton, Dan, 326
Bush, Barbara, 273
Bush, George, 26, 33, 35, 49, 61, 62-63, 64, 65, 66, 68, 69, 89, 100, 105
  address to Congress (1991), 298-299
  administration of, 140-145
  and Arab-Israeli settlement, 170
  and Baker, 140-145, 194, 208, 275-276
  campaign of, 267-268, 274-275
  and Gulf War, 154
  and Jerusalem, 313, 317-318, 326-329
  at Kennebunkport, 105, 273
  and Madrid agreement, 185
  and Palestine Liberation Organization (PLO), 295
  and Palestinian Liberation Organization (PLO), 163
  strategic relationship and, 101
  three NOs of, 165, 327
  mentioned, 88, 89, 176, 198, 207, 214, 271, 277, 314, 333
Bush administration, 171
  and Palestinian Liberation Organization (PLO), 177
  Reagan-Shultz legacy to, 139-140
Bush administration accord, 333
Byrd, Robert, 281

C

Cairo Agreement, 229, 332, 348
Cairo Agreements, 95, 99, 105, 143, 212-214, 217-225, 224, 226, 233, 238, 338
  and statehood, 223-225
Camp David accords, 24, 25, 26, 27, 48, 56, 74, 77-78, 111-115, 130, 218, 254, 259, 261, 317
Carter, Jimmy, 22, 25, 51, 76, 77-78, 95
  and American Jewish community, 254-259
  and Camp David, 111-115
  initiatives of, 74
  and Jerusalem, 313
  quoted, 168n38
  and security, 50

mentioned, 250, 253, 276, 350
Carter Doctrine, 31, 48-50, 55, 61, 90
Chafee, John, 291, 298
Chamoun, Camille, 42
Charny, Benjamin, 272
Cheney, Dick, 102
Children's Defense Fund, 200
Chou En-Lai, 38
Christopher, Warren, 11, 13, 205, 301, 335, 339, 341, 348
    and Declaration of Principles, 191, 208
    quoted, 206
    mentioned, 89, 211
Citizen's Party, 262
Civil Admininstration, 153
Civil Administration, 213
Clinton, Bill, 12, 13, 14, 17, 21, 22, 23, 27, 69, 195
    and Arab-Israeli conflict, 226
    campaign of, 275-278
    and Jerusalem, 312
    and Jerusalem question, 329-341
    Middle East policy of, 200, 205-209, 302, 305
    Middle East tour of, 105
    and Oslo Agreement, 191, 214
    and Syria, 210
    and Zionists, 196-199
    mentioned, 88, 89, 253, 304, 350
Clinton, Hillary, 200, 276
Cohler, Larry, 268
Cold War, 31, 41, 50, 57, 61, 89, 99-103, 105, 116, 117, 253, 262, 272, 346
communism, 32, 35, 42, 57, 273
    containment of, 62
    and Ronald Reagan, 50
comprehensive peace, 89, 97
Comprehensive Plan, 13
comprehensive security, 54, 57, 89, 96, 97
comprehensive settlement, 73, 77, 130
containment, 36, 37, 66, 67
Country Report on Human Rights Practices (1987), 195
Cronkite, Walter, 51
curfews, 155-156, 159-160

D

Dahran base, 42
Damascus, 347
Damascus Communiqué, 166
D'Amato, Alfonse, 301
Darawsheh, Abd al-Wahab, 154

Davar, 12
Dayan, Moshe, 75, 78, 114
    and Carter working paper, 114
Declaration of Principles (DOP), 9, 12, 14, 15-16, 208-213, 219, 299-300
    of Oslo, 217-219, 226, 230-231, 349
    of State Department, 333, 337
    See also Cairo Agreements; Oslo Agreement
de Gaulle, Charles, 75
Demjanjuk, John, 268
Democratic Front for the Liberation of Palestine, 239
Democratic party, 250, 253, 257, 262, 264-266
Desert Caucus PAC, 289
Desert Storm, 66-67, 177, 273
    See also Gulf War
Deutsch, Peter, 291
Dhofar, Oman, 48
Diego Garcia base, 49
Djerejian, Edward, 274
Dole, Robert, 295, 319, 322, 339
DOP. *See* Declaration of Principles
Douglas, Chuck, 295
Dukakis, Kitty, 272
Dukakis, Michael, 267-272, 277, 278, 312
Dulles, John Foster, 22, 38, 39, 41, 42, 251-252
Durenberger, David, 301

E

Eagleburger, Lawrence, 207
early empowerment, 214, 225, 227-230, 235, 354-356
East Jerusalem Municipal Council, 316
Eban, Abba, 41, 83n2, 252
EC. *See* European Community
economic aid to Israel, 253
economic cooperation, 224
economic impact of Gulf War, 153-158
Edelman, Marion Wright, 200
Edelman, Peter, 200
Egypt, 10, 24, 25, 38-39
    and Arab nationalism, 41
    and Britain treaty, 39
    as enemy, 43
    and Gulf War, 67
    and Israel, 74
    and military, 39, 49
    as regional influential, 48
    sale of arms to, 257, 258-259
    stability and, 46
Egyptian-Israeli agreement, 53, 111

Eisenhower, Dwight, 39, 40
   mentioned, 251, 253
Eisenhower Doctrine, 31, 41-43
Eitan, Rafael, 153
Eizenstat, Stuart, 197, 198
Eliazer, Benjamin Ben, 330, 331, 333
Ellenoff, Theodore, 148n51
Emerson, Steven, 14-15
Engel, Elliot, 301
Eran, Oded, 123
Eretz Israel, 112, 114, 353
Eshkol, Levi, 44, 317
Ethiopia, 68, 117
EU. *See* European Union
European Community (EC), 34, 73
European Union (EU), 73, 170
exchange of land for peace, 194, 209, 299
Ezrahi, Yaron, 137-138

F

Fahd Plan, 54, 78-79
Fanoun, Salah Abdullah, 158-159
FAO. *See* Food and Agricultural Organization
Al-Faris, Tahseen, 153
Farrakhan, Louis, 264-265
Fascell, Dante, 291
Fateh, 239, 241-242
Federation of Cooperatives for Agricultural Marketing, 153
Feighan, Edward, 291, 295, 326
Ferraro, Geraldine, 260
Fez conference, 166
Fez Plan, 54
FIDA, 239
fighter planes, 47, 68, 89, 94, 98, 104, 134, 259
Food and Agricultural Organization (FAO), 287
Ford, Gerald, 22, 77, 84n9, 255, 256-259
   commitment to Saudi Arabia and Egypt, 257
   mentioned, 250
Foreign Affairs Committee. *See* International Relations Committee
France, 39, 75, 83n4
Frank, Barney, 128, 287-288
Friej, Elias, 355
Fuch-Rabinovich family, 272
Fur, Mordechai, 330

G

Gaza, 9, 10, 15, 20, 26, 195, 217, 220-221, 307, 336
   Israeli army in, 38, 217
   massacre in, 340
   self-rule in, 236
   settlements in, 223
   unemployment in, 236-237
   withdrawal from, 211
   See also West Bank and Gaza
Gaza Center For Rights and Law, 348
Gaza Center for Rights and Law, 245
Gaza-Jericho First, 217-218, 225, 226, 336, 347, 350, 353, 355
   See also Cairo agreements
GCC. *See* Gulf Cooperation Council
Gejdenson, Samuel, 291
Geneva Conference, 33, 72, 76, 78, 113-114, 255
Geneva Convention, 27, 195, 207, 211, 222, 287, 298, 307, 314, 316
Germany, 66-67
Ghoneim, Abu-Maher, 241
Abu-Ghoneim, 331, 332
Giddi Pass, 255
Gilman, Benjamin, 281, 291, 301, 303
Gingrich, Newt, 281, 291, 322, 326, 336, 339
Giv'at Ze'ev, 331, 332
Golan Heights, 26, 76, 145, 255, 280, 345
   annexation of, 54, 94, 97, 98
Goldstein, Baruch, 221, 306, 332
Gorbachev, Mikhail, 26, 120
Gore, Al, 241, 276, 334
Government Accounting Office (GAO), 100
Grassley, Charles, 294, 295
Greenberg, Maxwell, 96
Grenada, 118
Gromyko, Andrei, 81
Grossman, Steven, 304, 335
Gulf Cooperation Council (GCC), 158, 162, 164
Gulf Crisis, 152
Gulf War, 35, 61, 99, 105, 145, 193, 346
   and balance of power, 184
   consequences of, 191
   impact of, 151-166
   Palestinian rights, 175
Gur, Mordechai, 211
Gush Etzion, 331, 332

H

Haberman, Clyde, 355
Habib, Philip, 106n13, 131
Hague Convention, 195
Haifa, port of, 102, 104

Haig, Alexander, 51, 53, 54, 57, 67, 89, 90, 91, 94, 118, 267
Haleileh, Samir, 157
Haloul, West Bank, 159
Hamas, 191, 230, 241, 244, 302, 307, 348
Hamilton, Lee, 281, 301
Al-Haq, 245
Al-Haram Al Sharif massacre, 152
Harkabi, Yehoshofat, 350
Harkin, Tom, 280
Hart, Gary, 260
al-Hasan, Hani, 239
Hatfield, Mark, 291, 298
Hebron, 159, 329
    massacre in, 221-222, 235, 306, 332, 334
    See also joint Hebron committee
Helms, Jesse, 280, 281, 294, 295, 301, 318, 338
Hersh, Seymour, 75
Hertzberg, Arthur, 129
Higher Court for State Security, 244-245
historic handshake, 9, 191-192, 209, 220, 230, 333
    See also Camp David
Hoagland, Jim, 355-356
Hormuz, Strait of, 52, 55
Howe, Irving, 129
Hudson Valley PAC, 289
human rights, 65, 203-204
Human Rights Watch, 211
Humphrey, Hubert, 253
Hussein, King, 10, 23, 27, 41-42, 45, 55-56, 79-80, 81, 131, 350
Hussein, Saddam, 24, 26, 35, 57, 63, 64, 68-69, 152
    in cartoon, 164

I

IDF, 211
imperialist penetration, 46
independent Palestinian state
    and Shultz Plan, 132
Indyk, Martin, 197-199, 200-201, 277
Inouye, Daniel, 301
International Court of Justice, 279
International Day of Solidarity with the Palestinian People, 264
international law, 206-208, 233, 251, 314, 316, 317, 326, 336
international peace conferences, 71ff, 83n1, 201, 250
International Relations Committee, 53, 112, 301

International Security and Development Cooperation Act (1985), 293
Intifada, 97-98, 121, 124-125, 130, 131, 134, 136, 137, 140, 141, 142, 152, 225, 279, 294, 299
    achievements of, 173
    and exports, 153-154
    and Gulf War, 160-161, 173
    leaders of, 164-165
Iran, 10, 34, 117
    captives of, 51
    and Contras, 119
    and international terrorism, 118
    Islamic Republic of, 24, 63
    Islamic revolution in, 48
    as regional influential, 48
Iran, Shah of. See Shah of Iran
Iran-Iraq War, 24, 35, 61, 64, 69, 174
Iraq, 24, 34, 38
    destruction of, 24, 49, 169, 193
    military coup in, 41
    occupation of, 326
    and Palestine, 163
    United States aid and, 64
    uprisings in, 43
Iraq nuclear reactor
    Israeli raid on, 54, 55, 89, 97, 268
Islam, 10, 36, 63, 195, 238-239
Islamic Endowment's Administration (WAQF), 339
Islamic fundamentalism, 10, 98, 104, 117, 202
Islamic Jihad, 241, 348
Israel, 40, 46, 48, 68, 73, 172
    autonomy plan for Palestine of, 174
    economics and, 85-88
    expansionism of, 95
    expulsion policy of, 202-208
    fighter jets and, 253
    hegemony and, 101-102, 280
    intelligence of, 92
    interventionism and, 253
    and Intifada, 122
    and invasion of Lebanon, 25
    military aid to, 97-98, 102
    military bases in, 50
    military technology of, 45, 118, 176
    and Nixon Doctrine, 43-48
    occupation issue and, 20, 52, 74, 195, 209
    and Palestinian Liberation Organization (PLO), 9, 303, 332, 340

Reagan expectations of, 92
and recognition issue, 210, 299
regional role of, 103-105
and rejectionism, 144, 180
reserved powers of, 212
and right to exist, 136, 172, 194, 225, 264, 285, 299, 347
right-wing of, 151-153, 173, 183
sale of arms to, 259
and security, 45, 90, 100, 102, 113, 130, 184, 205, 225-226, 255, 274
settlement policy of, 130, 179
and Six Day War, 43-44
strategic goals of, 345
as unique strategic asset, 118
and United States, 52, 72, 77, 116, 170, 255, 313
West Bank of. *See* West Bank
Zionism and, 120
Israel Aircraft Industries, 104
Israeli Economic Ministry, 157
Israeli-Egyptian Peace treaty (1979), 224
Israeli Information Center on Human Rights (B'Tselem), 160, 203
Israeli-Jordanian peace treaty, 350
Israeli Physicians for Human Rights, 159
Israeli Plan, 184
Israeli-Syrian settlement, 280
Israeli-United States Mutual Defense Assistance Agreement (1952), 94
Israel Shipyards, 104

J

Jabal Al-Mukabber, 333
Jackson, Henry, 252
Jackson, Jesse, 262-265, 266, 270, 271
Japan, 66-67, 170
Jarring, Gunnar, 75, 142
Jericho, 9, 220-221, 236, 329, 331, 336
Jericho Area, 217, 219, 243
    withdrawal from, 211
Jericho-Gaza option, 231
Jerusalem, 100, 125, *320, 321, 323, 324, 325*
    annexation of, 311-312
    discussion of, 208
    division of, 181
    Israeli conquest of, 236
    Israeli foreign ministry in, 251
    Israeli settlement of, 334
    move of American Embassy to, 260-261, 326
    Notre Dame Hotel in, 151

as occupied territory, 194, 337
and Palestinian Liberation Organization (PLO), 164
and Palestinians, 329
settlement and, 278
and United States, 312-315, 318-326
Jerusalem, Metropolitan, 329-333
A Jewish Peace Action Committee, 129
Jewish Defense League, 264
Jewish Leadership Council, 275-276
Jewish peace faction, 199-200
Jewish Peace Fellowship, 129
Jewish Peace Lobby, 197
JHC. *See* joint Hebron committee
JLF. *See* Jordanian Logistics Force
Johnson
    mentioned, 253
Johnson, Lyndon B., 20, 21, 89
Johnson administration, 255
Johnson Doctrine (1965), 31
joint Hebron committee (JHC), 222
Jordan, 23, 27, 144-145, 251, 345
    and attack on Palestinians, 45
    and Eisenhower Doctrine, 41
    and exports, 153
    and Gulf War, 158
    and international conference, 179
    laws of, 212
    negotiating problem of, 56
    and Palestine Liberation Organization (PLO), 113
    Palestinians, 166
    Palestinians in, 164
    and peace treaty with Israel, 224
    political order of, 43
    sale of arms to, 261
    security problem of, 56
    and Shultz Plan, 132
Jordanian Logistics Force (JLF), 55
Jordanian sovereignty, 79
Jordanian strike force, 54
Jordan option, 117, 131
J-PAC. *See* Jewish Peace Action Committee
Judea and Sumeria, 312

K

Kaddoumi, Farouk, 239, 241
al-Karameh, battle of, 45
Kashriel, Benny, 331
Kassebaum, Nancy, 291, 298
Kasten, Robert, 100, 286, 288

Kennan, George, 36
Kennedy, Edward, 254
Kennedy, Joe, 261
Kennedy, John F., 21, 31
Kenya, 49-50
Kerrey, Bob, 280
Khalaf, Salah, 294
Khalidi, Walid, 163
Khalifa House, 35
Al-Khatib, Rouhi, 316
Khirbat al-Mazmouriyah, 331
Kilometer 101, 76
Kim, Hanna, 13
Kirkpatrick, Jeanne, 118
Kiryat Araba, 332
Kissinger, Henry, 32, 33, 45, 48, 75, 76, 112, 285
    and 1974, 172
    and detente, 51
    diplomacy of, 46, 255-256
    Memorandum of, 47
    Memorandum of Agreement of, 292-293
    and Nixon resignation, 254
    and Palestine Liberation Organization
        (PLO), 135, 266
    quoted, 147n12
    and Soviet Union, 51, 120
    mentioned, 122
Klein, Morton, 305, 306
Knesset, 105, 114, 117, 151-152, 203, 311, 330, 348, 356
Koch, Edward, 270
Kollek, Teddy, 328, 330
Kostmayer, Peter, 291
Kristol, Irving, 118, 265
Kuwait, 26, 34
    and George Bush, 184
    invasion of, 62-63, 64, 103, 135, 151
    Palestinians in, 158, 161-162

L

Labor party (Israel), 202, 304, 327, 330, 353
    territorial autonomy and, 131-132
Lance Pershing missile, 47
Lantos, Tom, 128, 286, 287, 291
Lautenberg, Frank, 288, 290, 296, 301
Leahy, Patrick, 100, 286, 288, 303
Lebanon, 10, 23-24, 118
    and Arafat, 196
    bombardment of, 89, 191, 202
    civil war in, 41
    expulsion of Palestinians to, 191, 199, 202,

203-205
    Israeli invasion of, 54, 55, 78, 94, 95, 268, 287
    political order of, 43
    and United States, 119
Lebanon War, 172
Leiberman, Joseph, 301
letter of assurances, 180-181, 209
Levin, Carl, 128, 290, 297
Levine, Mel, 295, 296, 299
Lewis, Anthony, 163
Lewis, John, 336
Lewis, Samuel, 199
Libya, 118, 119
Lieberman, Joseph, 281, 290, 297
Likud, 122, 131-132, 143, 144, 202, 254, 273, 281, 304, 330, 334, 348, 352, 353
The Lobby. See American-Israel Public Affairs
    Committee
Lowey, Nita, 291, 299
Lydda, 204

M

Ma'alé Adumim, 329, 330-331, 332
Mack, Connie, 281, 292, 297, 301, 303
Madrid Conference, 24-26, 72, 79, 95, 174, 183, 193, 200-201, 209, 233-234, 303, 345-346
    and Arab-Israeli conflict, 194
Magen, David, 157
Mahameed, Hashem, 348
Master Plan for Greater Jerusalem, 316
McClure, James, 291
McConnel, Mitch, 281
McFarlane, Robert, 118
McGovern, George, 253, 257, 262-265
Meese, Edwin, 106n13
Megged, Aharon, 353
Meir, Golda, 274, 341n4
Memorandum of Agreement, 98
Memorandum of Understanding (MOU), 93, 267
Mendelbaum, Michael, 197, 198, 199
Meretz, 13, 205, 349
Metzenbaum, Howard, 290
Middle East
    as Cold War arena, 98
    congressional sub-committee on, 43
    Diaspora of, 174, 177, 181, 242-243, 287, 347
    military balance in, 258-259
    negotiations in, 314
    recolonization of, 61, 176, 186n13
    United States strategy in, 53

Middle East Command, 38, 39
Middle East Defense Organization, 38
Middle East Peace Facilitation Act (1993), 300
Middle East Watch, 161, 168n29
Military Order 1086, 204
Mitchell, George, 295, 315, 318
Mitla Pass, 255
Mogadishu, Somalia, 52
Molodet party, 152
Mondale, Walter, 260-261, 264-265
Morris, Benny, 353
Mossad, 245
MOU. See Memorandum of Understanding
Mount of Olives, 330, 333
Movement for Reforms and Democracy, 238-239
Moyers, Bill, 164
Moynihan, Daniel Patrick, 318, 338
Mubarak, Hosni, 10, 79-80, 131, 141, 144
    ten-point plan of, 143, 162, 173
Murphy, Richard, 137, 138, 139
Mutual Recognition statement, 191

N

Najah University, 154
Nasser, Jamal Abdul, 25, 38, 39, 69, 89, 169
Nasserism, 44, 98
National Charter, 136
National Security Council, 277
NATO. See North Atlantic Treaty Organization
Neff, Donald, 98, 338
Neria, Jacques, 16
Netanyahu, Benjamin, 184, 353
New Jewish Agenda, 129
New World Order, 61, 62, 67-69, 99, 104-105, 170, 193, 214
New York Council on Foreign Relations, 137
NGO. See Non-Governmental Organizations
Nielson, Howard, 297-298
Nixon, Richard M., 22, 32, 44, 45, 75, 90, 250, 253, 254, 258, 274
Nixon Doctrine, 43-48, 61, 67
Nixon-Kissinger Doctrine, 31, 44
Non-Governmental Organizations (NGO), 154, 300
North Atlantic Treaty Organization (NATO), 14, 36
Novick, Ivan, 96
NSC, 198

O

Obey, David, 299, 303
occupied territories, 188-189, 222
    Agricultural Relief Committees of, 153
    disputed, 333
    elections in, 288
    as enemy territory, 312
    final status of, 217
    Israeli closure of, 165, 191, 202
    regions of, 160
    settlement of, 273, 315-316
    See also Gaza; Jericho; West Bank
October 1973 War, 71, 75-76, 82, 116
Office of Special Investigations, 268
oil, 34, 45, 170
Old Jerusalem, 255
Olmert, Ehud, 330
Oman, 34, 48
    El Messira base and Se'ed airfield of, 52
    military bases in, 50
Omnibus Counter-Terrorism Act (1995), 17n4
Operation "Bright Star," 50
Oslo Agreement, 10, 16-17, 23, 95, 99, 191, 193, 209, 217-219, 225, 233ff, 299, 338, 346, 348, 351
    and Arafat, 196
    interpretation of, 218 237
    opposition to, 238
    results from, 243
    See also Declaration of Principles (DOP)

P

PA. See Palestinian Authority
Pahlevi, Muhammad Reza Shah. See Shah of Iran
Pakistan, 38, 52
Palestine
    and agriculture, 153-155
    elections in, 15-16
    guerilla movement of, 45
    partition of, 311
    peace initiative of, 140
    self-government of, 194
    Soviet Jews in, 68
    two political cultures of, 243-244
    two states in, 72
Palestine-Israeli conflict, 82, 132, 209
Palestine Liberation Organization (PLO), 14, 20, 82, 112, 285-290, 299-300
    and Camp David, 144
    Central Council of, 238

concessions and, 172
and concessions to Israel, 46-47
Declaration of Independence of, 145, 166,
172, 286
dialog with, 134-136
diplomatic focus of, 162
and Geneva Conference, 76
and Geneva conference, 114-115
and international terrorism, 118
and *Intifada*, 145
irrelevance of, 196
and Israel, 140
Israeli recognition of, 224
leadership of, 244
and negotiations, 172
and public opinion polls, 124
as representatives of Palestine people, 237
as representing Palestinians in Madrid, 175
and Resolution 242, 47
and Shultz Plan, 132
transformation of, 234
and United States policy, 120, 292-297
mentioned, 260
Palestine National Council (PMC), 121
Palestine National Council (PNC), 73, 238,
243, 286
Palestine National covenant, 281
Palestine question, 46, 52, 54, 57, 71, 177, 236,
345-346, 352
and domestic environment, 122-129
and global environment, 120-121
Israel as cause of, 255
marginalization of, 111, 116
and Zionism, 266
Palestinian Economic Coordinating and
Planning Committee, 155
Palestinian-Arab-Israeli conflict, 71
Palestinian Arab state, 72
Palestinian Authority (PA), 17, 217, 218, 221,
223, 225-226, 244, 302, 304, 305, 336, 345
and early empowerment, 227-230
governance of, 234-237
Palestinian autonomous area, *187*
Palestinian Council, 212, 218
Palestinian initiative, 149n75
Palestinian *Intifada*, 10
Palestinian-Israeli settlement, 89
Palestinian National Council, 80, 303
Palestinian national movement, 10, 23, 37, 45,
72-73, 98, 105, 172
and special relationship, 117

Palestinian rights, 25, 72, 114, 130, 195, 209,
218, 227
marginalization of, 47, 112, 165
Palestinians
autonomy and, 305
autonomy of, 254, 299
deportation of, 89
empowerment of, 280
expulsion of, 191, 199, 202, 203-205
and Gulf War, 151-166, 162-166
marginalization of, 145
self-government of, 181, 183-184
Palestinian self-government, 11, 77, 174, 201,
209, 213
Palestinian sovereignty
in West Bank and Gaza, 47
Palestinian state, 19, 27, 144, 276
opposition to, 95, 276, 278, 288
and Shultz, 133
Palestinian territories
occupation of, 111
Palestinian terrorism, 117
Palestinian uprising. *See Intifada*
PAM. *See* Peace Accord Monitoring Group
Pappe, Ilan, 353
Paris agreement, 33
Paris economic accord, 224
Peace Accord Monitoring Group (PAM), 300,
302-307
peace camps, 9, 11, 152
Peace Now, 13, 294
peace process, 9, 15, 16, 21, 26, 71, 74, 81-82,
98, 112, 116, 117, 145, 169, 200, 206, 214,
242, 273, 318, 327, 333, 335, 348, 350, 353,
356
and Arafat, 202
division of, 220
ground rules of, 223
and Soviets, 134
suspension of, 162
and West Bank and Gaza, 122
Pelletreau, Robert, 294, 334
People's Party, 239
Percy, Charles, 290
Peres, Shimon, 16, 104, 105, 131-133
quoted, 218
mentioned, 268, 305
Persian Gulf War. *See* Gulf War
petroleum. *See* oil
Pickering, Thomas, 207
Pipes, Richard, 118

Pisgat Ze'ev, 331
PLO. *See* Palestine Liberation Organization (PLO)
PLO Commitments Compliance Act, 292-293, 301
PNC. *See* Palestine National Council
Podhoretz, Norman, 118, 265
Pollack, Lester, 335
Popper, Amy, 296
Presidents of Major Jewish Organizations, Council of, 96, 252, 304, 328, 334
Pressler, Larry, 301

Q

Qabus House, 35
Qibya, 40
Quayle, Dan, 271
Qurei, Ahmad, 239

R

Rabat Conference, 20, 166, 171
Rabbinical Council of America, 274
Rabin, Yitzhak, 9-10, 13, 16, 23, 75, 80, 104, 105, 141, 219
    and expulsion, 202-205
    and Gaza, 195, 348-349
    and *Intifada,* 294
    and Jerusalem, 315, 330
    and Kennebunkport visit, 273-275
    and Oslo Agreement, 191
    and Palestinian Liberation Organization (PLO), 335
    policy of, 127
    quoted, 203, 206, 210, 211, 220-221, 355
    and West Bank, 300
    mentioned, 88, 241, 281, 304, 334, 350, 352
Rahman, Sheikh Abdul, 10
Rainbow Coalition, 263
Ramallah, 329
Ramat Shufat, 333
Ramleh, 204
Rapid Deployment Force (RDF), 49, 50
Ras al Amoud, 333
Ras Banas, 52
RDF. *See* Rapid Deployment Force
Reagan, Ronald, 22, 25, 42, 50-57, 52, 54, 55, 89-90, 94, 95, 132, 314
    and arms sales, 259-260
    campaign of, 260-261
    and communism, 119
    and comprehensive security, 96
    and interventionism, 119
    and Jerusalem, 315, 317
    legacy of, 66
    and Memorandum of Agreement, 98
    and Palestine Liberation Organization (PLO), 112, 285, 293
    and Palestine question, 99, 116-119
    policies of, 51, 146n14
    and Shamir, 134
    and Soviet Union, 51
    and special relationship, 92
    and terrorism, 119, 172
    mentioned, 88, 199, 207, 250, 268
Reagan Codicil, 31, 50, 55, 135
Reagan Doctrine, 61, 118
Reagan Plan, 25, 26, 54-55, 56, 74, 78-79, 80, 117, 130, 134, 146n15, 173
Reagan-Shultz policy, 327
Redman, Charles, 122
regional influentials, 36, 48-50
Reich, Seymour, 328
Reid, Harry, 301
Republican party, 250, 253, 255, 272, 280, 301
Resolution 93, 299
Resolution 106, 319, 322, 326, 328
Resolution 124, 298
Resolution 138, 296
Resolution 181, 315
Resolution 242, 20, 45, 47, 72, 75, 80, 111-112, 134, 139, 143, 151, 174, 175, 179, 193, 210, 279, 315-316, 345
Resolution 252, 311
Resolution 290, 326
Resolution 338, 71, 72, 76, 80, 151, 174, 175, 210, 279
Resolution 681, 195, 222
Resolution 694, 341
Resolution 726, 207
Resolution 799, 207-208
Resolution 904, 222
Rhodes Formula, 75
Rishon Le Zion, 152, 296
Rogers, William, 19, 74
Rogers Plan, 45, 75, 134
Rosenthal, A.M., 327
Rosovsky, Henry, 129
Ross, Dennis, 199
Rusk, Dean, 84n9

S

Sabah family, 35, 67, 161

Sadat, Anwar, 48, 76, 77-78, 96, 113-115
Safire, William, 118, 268, 326-327
Said, Edward, 237
Salem, Mamduh, 84n8
Sarid, Yossi, 13, 205, 348
Saud, King, 42
Saud House, 35
Saudi Arabia, 34, 41, 44, 88, 90, 91, 92
    air force of, 52
    and AWACS, 52, 129, 290
    and Palestinian Liberation Organization
        (PLO), 164
    and Reagan Doctrine, 61
    as regional influential, 48
    sale of arms to, 257, 258-260
Saunders, Harold, 112-113
Saxton, Bill, 336
Saxton, James, 296, 297, 301
Scheur, James, 128
Schifter, Richard, 122, 199
Sciolino, Elaine, 205
Scranton, William, 84n9
security
    American perception of, 138
    and border control, 219-220
    Israeli perception of, 138
    and two-stage concept, 220-225
    See also Israel: and security
Segal, Eli, 200
Sha'ath, Nabil, 196, 351, 352
Shafi, Haider Abdul, 195, 196, 233
Shahal, Moshe, 16
Shah of Iran, 36, 48, 90, 92, 96
Shaker, Zayd Ibn, 56
Shamir, Yitzhak, 22, 25, 89, 98, 100, 101, 104,
    128, 131, 132-133, 141, 145, 273-274
    and Baker Plan, 169, 327
    election plans of, 143, 152
    and Jerusalem, 315, 317-318
    and Palestine Liberation Organization
        (PLO), 143
    quoted, 183
    and rejectionism, 144
    and settlement building, 180
    versus Shultz, 133-134
    and Twenty Point Program, 141, 142
    and West Bank and Gaza, 173
    mentioned, 250, 260
Shamir Plan, 173, 289
    Basic Premises of, 165
Shaniu, 93

Sharon, Ariel, 93, 94, 97, 267
Sheikh Jarrah, 333
Sheinbaum, Stanley, 200
Shelby, Richard, 301, 302, 303, 305
Shiite Iranian threat, 24
Shin Bet, 245
Shindler, Rabbi Alexander, 128
Abu-Shukr, Dr. Abd al-Fattah, 154, 157
Shultz, George, 74, 79, 80, 81, 98, 118, 122, 123,
    128, 135
    and Arafat, 140
    in Israel (1988), 131-132
    and Jerusalem, 317
    and Middle East, 138
    and Palestine Liberation Organization
        (PLO), 293
    quoted, 138-139
Shultz Plan, 25, 26, 97, 98, 120, 129-134,
    147n17, 148n53, 173, 220
Shumer, Charles, 336
Silwan, 333
Simon, Paul, 290, 301
Sinai Accord, 47, 48, 77, 84n8, 112, 255
Sinai Peninsula, 53, 76, 111, 134, 219, 254
Singer, Joel, 213
Sitta, Fawaz Abu, 157
Six Day War, 43
Smith, Christopher, 286
Smith, Lawrence, 286, 291, 296
Sneh, Ephraim, 16
Somalia, 49, 52
Sourani, Raji, 245
sovereignty, 47, 79, 130, 131, 194, 208, 210, 211,
    225-226, 316
Soviet Jews, 100, 152, 278, 313
Soviet Union, 32, 33, 41, 263
    as arbiter of peace, 120-121
    Cold War and, 96
    collapse of, 62, 169, 191, 193
    expansion of, 49, 53, 117-118
    and Gulf War, 68
    and Israel, 81, 174
    and Middle East, 114, 143
    threat of, 54, 57, 102, 269
special relationship, 42, 54, 57, 63, 97, 206, 267,
    316
    and anti-terrorism, 116-119
    and Palestine Liberation Organization
        (PLO), 135
    and Palestinian nationalism, 117
    and Reagan, 89-92

and strategic alliance, 85-105
Specter, Arlen, 301, 302, 303, 305
Spiegel, Steven, 197, 198
Sprinzak, Ehud, 353
Squadron, Howard, 96
Star Wars. *See* Strategic Defense Initiative
State Security Court. *See* Higher Court for
   State Security
Stockholm Document, 73
Strasbourg, 121
strategic alliance, 81-83, 97, 316
strategic asset, 102
strategic consensus, 54, 55, 56
Strategic Defense Initiative (Star Wars), 93
strategic relationship, 94, 98, 105
Sudan, 10, 52
Suez Canal, 75, 250
Suez War, 39-41, 40, 252
suicide attacks, 9, 11, 15, 236
Sununu, John, 270, 328
Syria, 26, 41, 43, 266, 345, 356
   and Geneva Conference, 76
   and Gulf War, 67
   and international conference, 179
   and Israel, 46-47
   and Lebanon, 23
   and terrorism, 118
Szep (cartoonist), 164

T

Taba, 218, 235
Taft, Robert, 250
Tel Aviv, 251, 260-261, 326, 339
Temporary International Presence in Hebron
   (TIPH), 222
terrorism, 14, 17, 94, 104, 196, 202, 285, 288,
   294, 299-300, 301-302, 306-307
Thani House, 35
Thatcher, Margaret, 150n75
Tikkun, 129
TIPH. *See* Temporary International Presence in
   Hebron
Tivnan, Edward, 251
Torricelli, Robert, 291
Truman, Harry S, 21, 37-38, 42, 251
   quoted, 261
Truman Doctrine, 37-39
Truman Doctrine (1948), 31, 61
Tsongas, Paul, 280
Tulkarem region, 155
Tunis, 136, 144, 172

Tunisia, 52
Turkey, 38, 52, 68
Tutwiler, Margaret, 328
Twinam, Joseph W., 91, 106n8

U

Um-Tuba, 332
UN. *See* United Nations
Union of American Hebrew Congregations,
   128
Union of Palestinian Medical Relief
   Committees (UPMRC), 159-160
United Arab Emirates, 64
United Arab Republic, 43
   See also Egypt; Syria
United Jewish Appeal, 318
United Nations (UN), 27, 40, 72-73, 204-205,
   278, 300
   contempt for, 118
   General Assembly of, 42, 285, 338
   General Assembly Resolutions of, 73, 74,
      151, 184, 186n14, 226, 274, 311-312, 315
   and international conference, 180-181
   at peace conference, 174
   Security Council of, 24, 123, 205, 334, 337
   Security Council Resolutions of, 226, 250,
      296, 326, 331, 335
   strengthening of, 74-75
   See also individual Resolutions
United States, 9, 19, 34, 172
   custodianship of the Middle East of, 130
   foreign policy of, 62
   global strategy, Israeli role in, 146-147n16
   and hegemony in Middle East, 20-21
   interventionist policies of, 35
   Jerusalem policy of, 317
   and Middle East, 34, 46
   Middle East policy of, 22-23, 31-33, 85, 135,
      176, 249, 306, 333-341
   military actions by, 65
   military of, 49, 52, 61
   nationalism of, 111
   policy of, 95, 106n5, 164, 258
   presumed policy of, 315, 316-317
   and rejectionism, 165
   security policy of, 102
   strategic alliance and, 133
   as superpower, 82
   symbolic position of, 314, 315-316
   unilateralism of, 111

United States Anti-Apartheid Act (1986), 119

United States hegemony, 62, 170, 252
  in Middle East, 132, 176, 191, 193, 214

United States-Israeli Memorandum of Agreement, 47, 207, 314

United States-Israeli relations, 19, 22, 40, 85, 136-140, 249, 252
  See also special relationship

United States Navy, 104

United States-U.S.S.R. Joint Statement on Middle East (1977), 114

Universal Declaration of Human Rights, 278, 354

UPMRC. See Union of Palestinian Medical Relief Committees

U.S.S.R.. See Soviet Union

V

Vance, Cyrus, 49, 84n9, 113-114

Venice Declaration, 73

Vorspan, Albert, 128-129

W

Wad al-Jouze, 333

Wadi Araba, 21

Wagner, Robert, 251

Walzer, Michael, 129

WAQF. See Islamic Endowment's Administration

War of 1967, 82, 252

Washington Institute for Near East Policy, 141, 198, 277
  and Palestine Liberation Organization (PLO), 201

Washington PAC, 289

Waxman, Henry, 128

Weinberger, Caspar, 52, 93

West Bank, 9, 11, 13, 15, 20, 26, 40
  and agriculture, 155
  annexation of, 312
  and early empowerment, 228-229
  Israeli colonization of, 100
  and Jerusalem, 330-331
  new settlements in, 56
  and Palestine Liberation Organization (PLO), 218
  Preparatory Transfer of Powers And Responsibilities in, 225
  See also early empowerment
  self-government of, 354
  settlement of, 313, 348

withdrawal from, 211
  See also Israel

West Bank and Gaza, 76, 97, 111, 299-300, 317, 345
  Administrative Council for, 115
  autonomy in, 304
  destruction of Palestinian institutions in, 95
  as disputed territories, 191, 218
  as disputed territory, 208, 233
  elections in, 273
  and Geneva conference, 113-115
  and Palestine Liberation Organization (PLO), 145
  Palestinians in, 135, 164
  as single territorial unit, 192
  and sovereignty issue, 131

Whitehead, John, 123

WHO. See World Health Organization

Wiesenthal Center, 328

Will, George, 118

Wilson, Charles, 291

Wilson, David, 112

Wilson, Pete, 297

Winkler, Judith, 157

World Affairs Council, 49

World Health Organization (WHO), 286

World Tourism Association (WTA), 287

World Trade Center, 10

WTA. See World Tourism Association

Y

Yemen, 43

Yost, Charles, 341

Young, Andrew, 265-266

Z

Ze'evi, Rehavam, 152

Zionism, 14, 143, 175, 196-199, 201-202, 250, 251, 263, 265, 270, 276, 300, 302, 303-304, 313, 318, 334, 348, 353, 356

Zionist Organization of America, 96, 305-306

Zohar, Gadi, 228

Zuckerman, Mortimer, 14